Agile Software Development

Scrivener Publishing
100 Cummings Center, Suite 541J
Beverly, MA 01915-6106

Publishers at Scrivener
Martin Scrivener (martin@scrivenerpublishing.com)
Phillip Carmical (pcarmical@scrivenerpublishing.com)

Agile Software Development

Trends, Challenges and Applications

Edited by

Susheela Hooda
Vandana Mohindru Sood
Yashwant Singh
Sandeep Dalal

and

Manu Sood

Scrivener
Publishing

WILEY

Wiley Global Headquarters

111 River Street, Hoboken, NJ 07030, USA

For details of our global editorial offices, customer services, and more information about Wiley products visit us at www.wiley.com.

Library of Congress Cataloging-in-Publication Data

ISBN 978-1199639-5

Cover image: Pixabay.Com
Cover design by Russell Richardson

Set in size of 11pt and Minion Pro by Manila Typesetting Company, Makati, Philippines

Printed in the USA

10 9 8 7 6 5 4 3 2 1

Contents

Preface   xv

1 Agile Software Development in the Digital World – Trends and Challenges   **1**
Kapil Mehta and Vandana Mohindru Sood
1.1 Introduction   2
     1.1.1 Organization of Chapter   4
1.2 Related Work   4
     1.2.1 Teamwork Development   4
     1.2.2 Project-Based Learning (PJBL)   5
     1.2.3 Planning the Agile Software Development Methodologies   6
1.3 Agile Architecture Trends in the Digital World   9
     1.3.1 Agile Implementation at Scale   11
1.4 Challenges Faced in the Digital World Through Agile Software Development   12
     1.4.1 Challenges for Small to Mid-Scale and Large-Scale Agile Projects   13
     1.4.2 Reported Challenges – Cause and Potential Solutions   15
1.5 Generic Guidelines to Improve the Agile Transformation in Digital World   18
1.6 Conclusion and Future Perspective   18
     References   19

2 Agile Framework Adaptation Issues in Various Sectors   **23**
Anita Sardana and Vidhu Kiran Sharma
2.1 Introduction   24
     2.1.1 Human-Human Linkages   25
2.2 Agile Followers   27
2.3 Proposed Work   29
2.4 Resolution Matrix   32

	2.5 Conclusion and Future Work	34
	References	34
3	**Vulnerability Assessment Tools for IoT: An Agile Approach**	**39**
	Pooja Anand and Yashwant Singh	
	3.1 Introduction	39
	3.2 Agile Methodology: SCRUM	42
	3.3 Scrum Agile Benefits for IoT	43
	3.4 Critical Factors for Implementing Agile Methodology	46
	3.5 Conclusion	47
	References	48
4	**Interoperable Agile IoT**	**51**
	Bharti Rana and Yashwant Singh	
	4.1 Introduction	52
	4.2 Agile Software Development	53
	4.2.1 Scrum Methodology	54
	4.2.2 Extreme Programming (XP)	55
	4.2.3 Adaptive Software Development (ASD)	56
	4.2.4 Dynamic Software Development Method (DSDM)	57
	4.2.5 Feature Driven Development (FDD)	58
	4.2.6 Kanban Method	59
	4.3 Internet of Things (IoT)	59
	4.4 Agile–IoT Project for Interoperability	60
	4.5 Agile–IoT Project for Smart Domains	62
	4.6 INTER-IoT Framework for Interoperability	64
	4.6.1 Interoperability Aspects	65
	4.7 Conclusion	67
	References	67
5	**Functional and Non-Functional Requirements in Agile Software Development**	**71**
	S. Saroja and S. Haseena	
	5.1 Introduction	72
	5.2 Agile Requirements Gathering	73
	5.3 Types of Requirements	74
	5.4 Functional Requirement Gathering	77
	5.5 Non-Functional Requirement Gathering	79
	5.6 Testing Functional and Non-Functional Requirements	82
	5.7 Conclusion and Future Scope	82
	References	83

6   Minimizing Cost, Effort, and Implementation Complexity
for Adopting Security Requirements in an Agile Development
Process for Cyber-Physical Systems   87
Zakir Ahmad Sheikh and Yashwant Singh
6.1   Introduction   88
6.2   Literature Review   91
6.3   Proposed Methodology   94
6.4   Conclusion   97
      References   97

7   A Systematic Literature Review on Test Case Prioritization
Techniques   101
Ajmer Singh, Anita Singhrova, Rajesh Bhatia
and Dhavleesh Rattan
7.1   The Motivation for Systematic Review   102
      7.1.1   Existing Literature Reviews on Test Case
              Prioritization   102
      7.1.2   Resources Used for SLR   103
      7.1.3   Search Criteria   103
      7.1.4   Research Questions   104
7.2   Results   106
      7.2.1   What is the Current Status of Test Case
              Prioritization?   106
      7.2.2   How Various Test Case Prioritization Techniques
              are Classified? And What are Those Classifications? 107
              7.2.2.1   Code Coverage-Based   109
              7.2.2.2   Requirements-Based   112
              7.2.2.3   Model-Based Prioritization   113
              7.2.2.4   Time and Cost-Aware Prioritization   114
              7.2.2.5   History-Based Prioritization   114
              7.2.2.6   Risk Factor-Based Prioritization   115
              7.2.2.7   Fault Localization-Based   115
              7.2.2.8   Soft Computing Techniques-Based   116
              7.2.2.9   Web-Based   121
              7.2.2.10   Object Oriented Testing-Based   122
              7.2.2.11   Similarity-Based   122
              7.2.2.12   Combinatorial Interaction Testing-Based 123
              7.2.2.13   Machine Learning-Based   124
              7.2.2.14   Adaptive Random Testing (ART)-Based   124
              7.2.2.15   Prioritization for Continuous Integration
                         (CI) and Software Product Lines (SPL)   125

		7.2.2.16 Hybrid Approaches	125
		7.2.2.17 Comparative Studies	125
		7.2.2.18 Surveys and Reviews	126

7.3 What Subject Systems Have Been Used to Evaluate
Test Case Prioritization Techniques? What is the Type
of Programming Platform for Subject Systems?   126

    7.3.1 What is Research Status in Model-Based Test Case
Prioritization?   128

    7.3.2 What Evaluation Criterion Has Been Used
to Evaluate Model-Based Prioritization
and How are The Results Reported?   128

    7.3.3 How Model-Based Test Case Prioritization Has
Evolved Over the Years? Which Studies Have
Discussed the Benefits of Model-Based Test Case
Prioritization in Object-Oriented Systems?   132

    7.3.4 What Subject Systems Are Used to Evaluate
the Model-Based Test Case Prioritization?   133

    7.3.5 What is the Research Status of Test Case
Prioritization for Object-Oriented Testing?   133

    7.3.6 What Specific Parameters of Object-Oriented Testing
Have Been Highlighted by Various Studies?   134

    7.3.7 What Studies Exist Based on Multi-Objective
Algorithms for Test Case Prioritization in Object-
Oriented Testing?   135

    7.3.8 Whether Comparative Analysis of Multi-Objective
Algorithms for Test Case Prioritization in Object-
Oriented Testing Has Been Performed? And What
are The Results?   135

7.4 Research Gaps   136

References   136

8 A Systematic Review of the Tools and Techniques
in Distributed Agile Software Development   161

Dipti Jadhav, Jyoti Kundale, Sumedha Bhagwat and Jyoti Joshi

8.1 Introduction   162

    8.1.1 Why Agile?   162

    8.1.2 Distributed Agile Software Development (DASD)   162

    8.1.3 Challenges of DASD   163

        8.1.3.1 Documentation   163

        8.1.3.2 Pair Programming   163

        8.1.3.3 Different Working Hours   163

		8.1.3.4	Training on Agile Practices	163
		8.1.3.5	Distribution of Work	163
8.2	Literature Review			164
8.3	Techniques for DASD			164
	8.3.1	Effective Communication		165
	8.3.2	Face Visits or Contact Visits		165
	8.3.3	Team Distribution		165
	8.3.4	Distribution of Work		165
	8.3.5	Documentation		165
8.4	Tools for DASD			166
	8.4.1	Monday.com		166
		8.4.1.1	Features	167
		8.4.1.2	Pricing	167
	8.4.2	nTask		167
		8.4.2.1	Features	168
		8.4.2.2	Pricing	168
	8.4.3	Jira		168
		8.4.3.1	Pricing	169
		8.4.3.2	Version Control	169
		8.4.3.3	Key Features	170
	8.4.4	ActiveCollab		170
		8.4.4.1	Pricing	170
		8.4.4.2	Features	171
	8.4.5	Pivotal Tracker		171
		8.4.5.1	Features	171
		8.4.5.2	Pricing	172
	8.4.6	Clarizen		172
		8.4.6.1	Software Features	173
	8.4.7	Axosoft		173
		8.4.7.1	Software Features	173
		8.4.7.2	Pricing	173
	8.4.8	MeisterTask		174
		8.4.8.1	Software Features	174
		8.4.8.2	Pricing	174
	8.4.9	GitLab		174
		8.4.9.1	Features	175
		8.4.9.2	Pricing	176
	8.4.10	Productboard		176
		8.4.10.1	Features	176
	8.4.11	ZohoSprints		178
		8.4.11.1	Features	178

	8.4.11.2	Pricing	179
8.4.12	Taskworld		180
	8.4.12.1	Features	180
	8.4.12.2	Pricing	180
8.4.13	CoSchedule		180
	8.4.13.1	Features	180
	8.4.13.2	Pricing	181
8.4.14	Nostromo		181
	8.4.14.1	Features	181
	8.4.14.2	Pricing	182
8.4.15	Todo.vu		182
	8.4.15.1	Features	183
	8.4.15.2	Pricing	183
8.4.16	VersionOne		183
	8.4.16.1	Pricing	184
	8.4.16.2	Features	184
8.4.17	ProofHub		184
	8.4.17.1	Features	184
	8.4.17.2	Pricing	185

8.5 Conclusion 185
References 185

9 Distributed Agile Software Development (DASD) Process 187
Samli, Monisha Gupta, Abhishek Sharma, Susheela Hooda and Jaswinder Singh Bhatia

9.1 Introduction 188
9.2 Distributed Software Development 189
  9.2.1 Factors Influencing Agile Distributed Software Development 190
9.3 Distributed Agile Software Development Team 192
  9.3.1 Distributed Agile Development/Teams 194
    9.3.1.1 Some Common Practices for Agile Teams are Specified as Below 195
9.4 Scrum in Global Software Development (GSD) 196
  9.4.1 Aim and Objectives of Scrum Practices in GSD 198
  9.4.2 Background 198
  9.4.3 Scrum Practices in GSD 199
9.5 Tools and Techniques for Agile Distributed Development 199
9.6 Conclusion 201
References 202

10 Task Allocation in Agile-Based Distributed Project
    Development Environment   205
    Madan Singh, Naresh Chauhan and Rashmi Popli
    10.1 Introduction   206
          10.1.1 Traditional Software Development   206
          10.1.2 Agile Software Development (ASD)   207
          10.1.3 Distributed Software Development   211
          10.1.4 Motivation and Goal   213
    10.2 Task Allocation   214
          10.2.1 Traditional Task Allocation Methods   214
          10.2.2 Need of Machine Learning in Task Allocation   214
    10.3 Machine Learning-Based Task Allocation Model   215
    10.4 Conclusion   216
          References   217

11 Software Quality Management by Agile Testing   221
    Sharanpreet Kaur, Susheela Hooda and Harsimrat Deo
    11.1 Introduction   222
    11.2 A Brief Introduction to JMeter   222
    11.3 Review of Literature   223
    11.4 Performance Testing Using JMeter   225
    11.5 Proposed Work   225
    11.6 Results and Discussions   227
    11.7 Conclusion   231
          References   232

12 A Deep Drive into Software Development Agile
    Methodologies for Software Quality Assurance   235
    Mitali Chugh and Neeraj Chugh
    12.1 Introduction   236
    12.2 Background Work   237
          12.2.1 Factors of Quality Assurance in Agility   239
    12.3 Understanding Agile Software Methodologies   240
          12.3.1 Need for Agile Software Methodology Framework 241
    12.4 Agile Methodology Evaluation Framework   241
          12.4.1 Extreme Programming (XP)   241
          12.4.2 Scrum   243
          12.4.3 Lean Development   243
          12.4.4 Crystal Methodology   246
          12.4.5 Kanban Methodology   247
          12.4.6 Feature Driven Development (FDD) Methodology   247

		12.4.7	Dynamic System Development Method (DSDM)	250
	12.5	Agile Software Development – Issues and Challenges		252
	12.6	Conclusion		252
		References		253

13 Factors and Techniques for Software Quality Assurance in Agile Software Development   **257**

Gagandeep Kaur, Inderpreet Kaur, Shilpi Harnal and Swati Malik

	13.1	Introduction		258
		13.1.1	Values of the Agile Manifesto	259
		13.1.2	The Twelve Agile Manifesto Principles	260
		13.1.3	Agile for Software Quality Assurance	261
	13.2	Literature Review		262
	13.3	Agile Factors in Quality Assurance		263
		13.3.1	Success Factors	263
		13.3.2	Failure Factors	263
	13.4	Quality Assurance Techniques		263
	13.5	Challenges and Limitations of Agile Technology		268
	13.6	Conclusion and Future Scope		269
		References		270

14 Classification of Risk Factors in Distributed Agile Software Development Based on User Story   **273**

Esha Khanna, Rashmi Popli and Naresh Chauhan

	14.1	Introduction		274
	14.2	Software Risk Management		274
		14.2.1	Risk Assessment	275
	14.3	Literature Review		278
		14.3.1	Review	278
		14.3.2	Risk Factors in Distributed Agile Software Development	279
		14.3.3	Current Challenges	284
	14.4	User Story-Based Classification of Risk Factors in Distributed Agile Software Development		285
		14.4.1	User Stories	285
		14.4.2	Classification of Risk Factors on the Basis of User Story	285
	14.5	Future Scope		286
	14.6	Conclusion		287
		References		287

**15 Software Effort Estimation with Machine Learning –
A Systematic Literature Review**   **291**
Ritu and Pankaj Bhambri
15.1   Introduction   292
15.2   Method   292
    15.2.1   Questionnaires for Research   293
    15.2.2   Search Process   293
    15.2.3   Criteria for Inclusion and Removal   294
    15.2.4   Data Gathering   295
    15.2.5   Analyzing Data   295
15.3   Result   296
    15.3.1   Findings   296
15.4   Discussion   300
    15.4.1   What Kinds of Research are Being Conducted?   301
    15.4.2   Who is the Research Leader in SLR?   301
    15.4.3   The Study's Limitations   304
15.5   Conclusion   304
15.6   Future Scope   305
    References   305

16 Improving the Quality of Open Source Software   **309**
Sharanpreet Kaur and Satwinder Singh
16.1   Introduction   310
16.2   Literature Review   311
16.3   Research Issues   313
16.4   Research Method and Data Collection   314
16.5   Results and Discussion   317
16.6   Conclusion and Future Scope   320
    References   321

**17 Artificial Intelligence Enables Agile Software Development
Life Cycle**   **325**
Sima Das, Ajay Kumar Balmiki and Nimay Chandra Giri
17.1   Introduction   326
17.2   Literature Survey   327
17.3   Proposed Work   328
    17.3.1   Advantages and Limitations of Agile Software
        Development   331
17.4   Conclusion   340
    References   341

18 Machine Learning in ASD: An Intensive Study of Automated Disease Prediction System   **345**
Saindhab Chattaraj, Taniya Chakraborty, Chandan Koner and Subir Gupta

18.1   Introduction   346
18.2   Overview of ML   347
     18.2.1   Types of Machine Learning   348
         18.2.1.1   Supervised Machine Learning   348
         18.2.1.2   Unsupervised Machine Learning   349
         18.2.1.3   Reinforcement ML   350
     18.2.2   Popular ML Algorithm   350
         18.2.2.1   Artificial Neural Network (ANN)   350
         18.2.2.2   K-Means Clustering Algorithm   351
         18.2.2.3   Hierarchical Clustering   351
         18.2.2.4   Linear Regression in Machine Learning   351
         18.2.2.5   Support Vector Machine (SVM)   352
         18.2.2.6   Decision Tree   352
         18.2.2.7   Random Forests   352
         18.2.2.8   Agile Software Development (ASD)   353
18.3   Case Study   355
     18.3.1   Methodology   355
     18.3.2   Result Analysis   357
18.4   Conclusion   358
     References   360

Index   **363**

Preface

Agile Software Development (ASD) has become a popular technology because its methods apply to any programming paradigm. It is important in the software development process because it emphasizes incremental delivery, team collaboration, continuous planning, and learning over delivering everything at once near the end. Before finalizing anything, Agile goes through several iterations based on feedback. As a result, the process becomes more dynamic because everyone is working toward a common goal. Agile has gained popularity as a result of its use of various frameworks, methods, and techniques to improve software quality. Scrum is a major agile framework that has been widely adopted by the software development community.

Metaheuristic techniques have been used in the agile software development process to improve software quality and reliability. These techniques not only improve quality and reliability but also test cases, resulting in cost-effective and time-effective software. However, many significant research challenges must be addressed to put such ASD capabilities into practice. With the use of diverse techniques, guiding principles, artificial intelligence, soft computing, and machine learning, this book seeks to study theoretical and technological research findings on all facets of ASD. Also, it sheds light on the latest trends, challenges, and applications in the area of ASD.

This book will benefit the software development community by providing conceptual and technological solutions to problems that commonly arise when developing software. Furthermore, the 18 chapters herein were written by eminent experts in the fields of software testing, quality, and reliability in ASD. Following is a summary of the information presented in each chapter of the book.

– Chapter 1 provides a theoretical foundation for ASD and discovers problems and challenges that small, medium and large agile projects face when it comes to requirement engineering, and structuring probable proposals for improving the overall RE process. The goal of this chapter is also to discover the challenges of putting Agile into reality in the digital era.

– Chapter 2 sheds light on issues concerning the adaption of the Agile framework in various sectors. The issues found in various sectors could be resolved by addressing a need matrix, which will list a need of a particular sector, and a resolution matrix, which will list all proposed solutions for all listed needs in the need matrix. Also, different use cases are presented for more clarity on the resolution part in different sectors.

– Chapter 3 discusses the agile methods adopted to develop software projects dealing with growing vulnerabilities and threat implications. This adoption is necessary because agile methods are iterative in nature and facilitate service/product delivery in smaller batches, allowing developers to add security activities to software development via agile methodologies. Moreover, the reiterative aspect of this approach encourages the expansion of software that can very well come up with growing threat variants and vulnerabilities.

– Chapter 4 focuses on the importance of agile methodology in IoT. It highlights the functionalities of the AGILE-IoT project funded by the European Union and five pilot projects such as pollution monitoring, retail service, port-area monitoring, quantified self-application, and cattle monitoring. This chapter also discusses the interoperability of the AGILE-IoT project.

– Chapter 5 discusses the concepts of software requirements and their types (functional and non-functional requirements). It presents the various ways of gathering functional and non-functional requirements and testing them in the context of ASD.

– Chapter 6 presents the ASD framework and methodology and discusses the time and cost relation during software development. This study proposes a secure ASD methodology that includes three stages, namely aggressive training, prototype development stage, and actual development stage and maintenance.

– Chapter 7 caters to a systematic literature review on test case prioritization using agile methodology. The study concludes that the field of prioritization has been explored considerably and many prioritization techniques have evolved. However, there are still possibilities for improvements, especially in implementation and analysis. The study also highlights the current status of prioritization and provides a comparative analysis with similar works.

– Chapter 8 aims to provide deeper insights into the most current agile planning tools used by distributed agile professionals. The agile tools studied and compared are both open-source as well as proprietary tools. This chapter discusses the benefits of distributed ASD and the various distributed agile planning tools that are available to resolve these concerns.

– Chapter 9 sheds light on the concept of distributed ASD, its benefits, and the challenges which are faced by an agile software team during the software development process. It also discusses the various tools and techniques which are being currently used for agile development. Scrum is also discussed in detail in this chapter.

– Chapter 10 introduces an unsupervised learning-based model for assisting in project development activities such as task allocation and backlog prioritization. It also discusses how machine learning-based mechanisms can be applied at their lowest level to every activity of project management so that the processes of software project management become more useful, and may also help in faster, hassle-free delivery of the finished product.

– Chapter 11 sheds light on the usage of the JMeter software tool in ASD. The authors also suggest that JMeter may be an extremely useful tool for evaluating how to modify your web application server setup to decrease bottlenecks and boost performance.

– Chapter 12 analyzes software development agile methodologies from the viewpoint of software quality assurance and presents a technique to understand similarities in diverse agile processes. It also covers the various issues and controversies in ASD that are the grey areas of agile methodology related to innovative thinking, the cost of projects developed using agile methodologies, etc.

– Chapter 13 provides a detailed introduction to ASD, addresses its importance in the information technology sector, and presents a comprehensive overview of the factors and techniques followed by challenges and limitations of agile technology.

– Chapter 14 discusses the importance of software risk management in distributed agile software development (DASD) and also reviews the existing literature and presents risk factors associated with DASD. It further presents the current challenges in the existing literature and proposes a novel user story-based DASD risk classification technique, in addition to discussing the scope of improvement in DASD risk management that will help both practitioners and researchers.

– Chapter 15 assesses the present state of research trends and patterns of software effort estimation with machine learning techniques. It also evaluates the effect of numerous factors, such as cost and effort, concerning the accuracy of the various models related to effort estimation.

- Chapter 16 aims to develop a metrics-based code smells prediction model based on deep learning neural network technique. The research methodology proposed in this chapter is based upon the field of deep learning, which is an integrated field of machine learning associated with algorithms aroused by the arrangement and similarity of the brain, called artificial neural networks.
- Chapter 17 presents a plan and fosters a specialist framework to help the product designer in the total programming advancement life cycle with various space experts like telecom, banking, coordination, medical services, satellite, and a lot more information procurement. This chapter also contains the study of artificial intelligence, along with a brief discussion of its pros and cons.
- Chapter 18 introduces a module that was developed with the help of machine learning, which is very helpful in an emergency when a patient requires an immediate decision. Here, Agile software is designed to be very effective in detecting a particular disease more efficiently. In this specific system, preventing errors and malfunctions has been proven to be 95% effective in the medical field.

In closing, we would like to express our gratitude to our co-authors for their invaluable contributions, without which this book could not have been written. Also, our sincere thanks go to the reviewers for the timely manner in which they provided their insightful remarks. Last but not least, we give thanks to God for providing us with the wisdom and strength to complete this work effectively despite the challenging times.

We anticipate that the high-caliber research presented in this book will be useful to science, technology, and mankind.

Dr. Vandana Mohindru Sood
Assistant Professor, Department of Computer Science and Engineering,
Chitkara University, Rajpura, Punjab, India
Dr. Ravindara Bhatt
Assistant Professor in the Department of Computer Science and Engineering,
Chitkara University, Rajpura, Punjab, India
Dr. Yashwant Singh
Associate Professor & Head, Department of Computer Science &
Information Technology, Central University of Jammu, J & K, India

Dr. Manu Sood
Professor, Department of Computer Science, Himachal Pradesh University,
Shimla, Himachal Pradesh, India
Dr. Sandeep Dalal
Assistant Professor, Department of Computer Science and Applications,
Maharshi Dayanand University, Rohtak, Haryana, India
January 2023

Agile Software Development in the Digital World – Trends and Challenges

Kapil Mehta[1] and Vandana Mohindru Sood[2*]

[1]Department of Computer Science & Engineering, Chandigarh Group of Colleges,
Mohali, Punjab, India
[2]Chitkara University Institute of Engineering and Technology, Chitkara University,
Punjab, India

Abstract

Traditional businesses face fast-changing client needs, increased marketplace changing aspects, and the constant appearance of new technological progressions in an increasingly digital world. Faced with the demands of a digital world, businesses are attempting to embrace agile methodologies on a bigger level to satisfy these demands. Researchers were compelled to design new techniques and methodologies to fulfill marketing needs as company requirements grew rapidly. Traditional-driven development approaches, which emphasize requesting and detailing requirements that take extra time in comparison to changing dynamics of the market, have been superseded by Agile methodology. On the other side, there is a need for a development process where customers can interact and collaborate in teams. Instead of the benefits of agile development and new tools introduction, various challenges are required to be discussed. In the agile software development process, various techniques have been used for improving software quality and reliability. The goal of such techniques is to improve test cases, which leads to cost-effective and time-effective software. Particularly, various theoretical perspectives have been provided by researchers on agile software development which contribute rich insights. This work provides a theoretical foundation for ASD. Agile has given an adequate solution to varying requirements of customers in the marketplace; it is built on iterative enhancement, with each line representing its minimal size and independent Software Development Life Cycle (SDLC). Essentially, using agile in the right way necessitates a thorough comprehension of

---

*Corresponding author: vandanamohindru@gmail.com

Susheela Hooda, Vandana Mohindru Sood, Yashwant Singh, Sandeep Dalal and Manu Sood (eds.)
Agile Software Development: Trends, Challenges and Applications, (1–22) © 2023 Scrivener
Publishing LLC

the technique. Despite their benefits, which included a fresh strategy, the ability to adapt to changes fast, new tools, coordination, and cooperation concepts, several obstacles arose, necessitating their resolution. The goal of this article is to discover challenges of putting Agile into reality in digital era. Challenges necessitate answers for agile and its techniques towards progress, therefore novel trends and expansion technologies will now be mirrored in Agile.

Keywords: Agile software development, agile research, software development life cycle, agile methodology, software quality, reliability

1.1   Introduction

In today's world, the growth of information and technology continues to gain strength and speed as it embarks on an expedition of digital transformation, posing a significant challenge in terms of how to develop individuals with digital and IT capabilities. The 21st-century skills encompass 16 aspects [1–3], which include required traits of communication as well as interpersonal skills, according to the World Economic Forum Survey [4] analyzing the demand for workforce and technological approaches in large scale organizations worldwide. In the digital age, technology becomes a multiplier [5]. The distinction between the development as well as production environments is increasingly blurred as a result of modern practices, technology, and tools, resulting in a combined ecosystem. In the digital age, agile architecture scales to grouped ecosystems, which can be influenced by novel techniques and approaches.

Agile is a scalable technique that gains a lot of traction in the software development world due to its major rate of success and impressive output. Agile software development (ASD) outpaces old-style development methodologies and procedures for a variety of details, including varying customer needs, business requirements, and flexibility. "Requirement engineering" (RE) is critical in software development since the overall effectiveness of the product is dependent on the requirements accuracy acquired during engineering phase [6]. As a result, when the nature of the demand changes, acquiring, analyzing, comprehending, and managing needs is not an easy task [7]. During the progress from start to end, the active character of needs and consideration of project conclusion becomes vital. Hence, change consideration is an important aspect that is employed in a big proportion of projects after maintenance.

As demonstrated in Figure 1.1, the agile methodology enables continuous development and testing throughout the project's development of

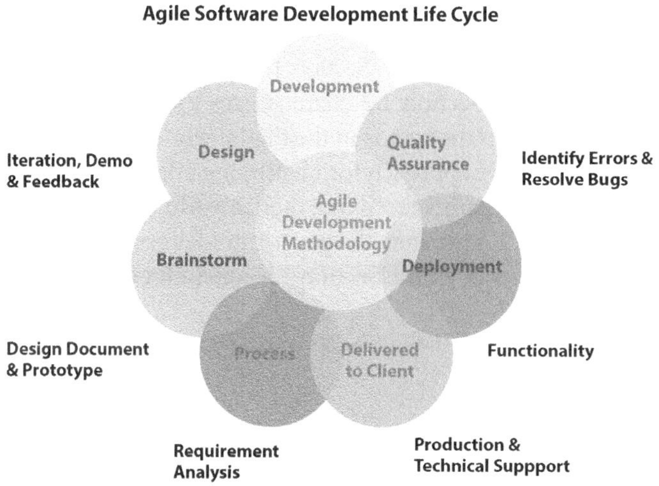

Agile Software Development Life Cycle

Development

Iteration, Demo
& Feedback

Design

Quality
Assurance

Identify Errors &
Resolve Bugs

Agile
Development
Methodology

Brainstorm

Deployment

Design Document
& Prototype

Process

Delivered
to Client

Functionality

Requirement
Analysis

Production &
Technical Suppport

Figure 1.1 Agile software development life cycle.

software life cycle which combines iterative aspect and levelled process concepts (SDLC). The focus of swiftly delivering a workable software solution is on process adaptability and customer satisfaction. The project is divided into incremental builds of small size by using the Agile SDLC. The customer may decide whether the outcome of agile SDLC meeting the expectations or not. The difficulty is that there are no fixed requirements to predict resources and cost of development as one of its flaws.

This article provides a thorough analysis as well as relevant inferences and references. The goal of this article is to discover problems and challenges that small-, mid- and large agile projects face when it comes to requirement engineering, and to structure probable proposals for improving the overall literature RE process. We can evaluate and analyze the background that will be analyzed and evaluated to make a recommendation for future work. The post intends to address the aforementioned issues using recently published publications in the several ages using agile development, having the goal on the requirement engineering process, as well as finding challenges related to agile engineering activities/practices.

The digital world offers new issues that necessitate a creative approach to identifying effective solutions while keeping the larger ecosystem in mind. In this regard, current agile architecture trends and practices in the digital world must be thoroughly examined. No study systematically studies trends and techniques of agile in the digital era, based on available facts and statistics.

1.1.1   Organization of Chapter

This chapter is organized as follow: Section 1.1 introduces the concept of Agile Software Development. Section 1.2 characterizes the literature background. Section 1.3 elaborates on the trends in the digital world that offers new issues that necessitate a creative approach for identifying effective solutions Section 1.4 emphasizes the challenges faced in a digital world through agile software development. Section 1.5 presents the generic guidelines to improve the agile transformation in a digital world. Section 1.6 concludes the chapter.

1.2   Related Work

In studies on the large-scale application of agile methodologies, the concept of "agile" [8] and how large-scale agile development may be conceived are frequently explored [9]. Extensive application of agile methods includes a) agile methods use in large enterprises, b) agile methods use in extensive projects or teams, c) agile methods use in multiple teams, and d) the use of agile techniques and philosophies in extensive firms as a whole. Agile Software Development is a concept that examines and synthesizes the intangible framework for a learning process to improve team capabilities through project-based learning. Agile also examines suitability of a learning management approach for computer graduates, which encourages collaboration through project-based learning. The following phases are central to the literature.

1.2.1   Teamwork Development

Teamwork development is a flexible, lively, and periodic strategy involving team members' behaviors working together for achieving a mutual goal. Working in Teams is vital for successful performance, because it governs how tasks and goals are achieved in a group setting [10].

Israt Fatema and Kazi Sakib [11] recommended the use of critical inquiry in their observations "Factors Influencing Productivity of Agile Software Development Teamwork: A Qualitative System Dynamics Approach." In an Agile software development approach, workgroup productivity impacts overall project performance. As a result, investigating the productivity of team members was of interest. Because agile teams are self-managed, they should be educated to evaluate and achieve productivity aspects frequently. Only if all of the variables are managed and monitored at the same time will productivity development programs be effective.

1.2.2   Project-Based Learning (PJBL)

Project-based learning is an education style that exposes students to real-world scenarios such as study, investigation, research, demonstration, production, and development for them to generate a major piece of work that they can apply in the real world [12]. The following are the characteristics of PJBL:

(i)   Interdisciplinary – PJBL is a program that focuses on involving students in real-world situations. Because practical difficulties are hardly resolved using data or abilities from a solitary topic area, this is an interdisciplinary approach.

(ii)   Rigorousity – Not simply memory or identification, but the submission of skills required in PJBL. PJBL is more complicated than rote learning, which is focused on a single fact. Students applying a range of theoretical knowledge in novel circumstances can ensure that. Scholars follow a process that begins with inquiry when working on a project. The inquiry leads to more in-depth learning, not only in terms of academic subject but also in terms of applying that content in real-world circumstances [13].

(iii)   Student Centric Approach – The teacher's role in PJBL evolves from material delivery to facilitation and project management. Students work autonomously in the PJBL process than they would in a regular classroom, with the trainer only stepping in to help when necessary. Students are motivated to take their self-decision about the completion of a task and practice their comprehension.

(iv)   Agile Scrum Software Development – In the early 1990s, to manage development on complicated projects, Scrum is a process framework. Scrum isn't a strategy, method, or set of principles. Somewhat, it is an agenda that may be used to implement multiple procedures and techniques. Scrum highlights the comparative effectiveness of managing product and work management systems, allowing for continuous improvement of the product, team, and operating environment [14]. The Scrum framework is made up of Scrum Teams, as well as responsibilities, events, objects, and rules. People must improve their ability to live by these five qualities to implement Scrum effectively: Courage, Commitment, Focus, Openness, and Respect. Individuals make a personal commitment to the Scrum Team's objectives.

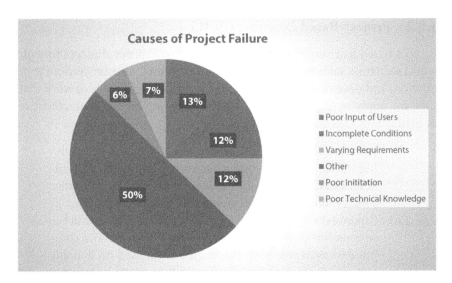

Figure 1.2 The causes of project failure.

Traditional and linear development techniques have significant disadvantages as compared to agile software development. It is adequate to obtain components for deliberation that affects the process of development [15] but examine for a moment whether all of the factors affecting the system must be obtained. The response would be "no" empirically. An adaptive method should be utilized to deal with change, uncertainty, and unknown elements.

Many sources, obstacles, and unsuccessful factors of software research were highlighted in Standish Group International CHAOS Survey. According to studies, project development problems increase by 37% from the demand phase, as shown in Figure 1.1 [16, 17]. The issues and keys of condition traceability in ASD have been discussed, as well as various ARE (agile requirement engineering) principles. The popular software projects do not succeed, according to [18], because of the worst requirements administration and frequent obstacles that lead to project failure as shown in Figure 1.2.

1.2.3 Planning the Agile Software Development Methodologies

In light of the digital economy's issues and industry-academic collaboration, this segment evaluates the prevalent agile software development approaches for identifying distinctiveness and added value. We'll look at the following frameworks: Agile development methodologies include Extreme

Table 1.1 Agile methodology frameworks for software development.

Parameter	Scrum	FDD	XP	Kanban	Crystal
Size of Team	Member size 3-9	Not Fixed	Maximum Twelve	Not Fixed	Variable Team Structure
Responsibility	Fixed Responsibilities contains: Scrum Master Product Author	Several may involve: Class Holder Feature Team Coder	Required: Customer Coder Variable: Tester Monitor	Project Leader Team Associate	Variable Roles: Executive Tester Team Associate Coordinative
Length of Iteration	Static and supreme Ore Month	Characteristics based Variable 2–10 days	Changed One to Two weeks	Constant movement	From week to four months
Release Announcement	Sprint End	Feature building	Constant Integration	Constant Delivery	Release strategy
Large adaptation of Project	Scaling Scrum for managing teams	Flowing the project topographies into lesser groups	Not Feasible	Appealing similar Method	Crystal transparent, yellow, orange, red and maroon

(Continued)

Table 1.1 Agile methodology frameworks for software development. (*Continued*)

Parameter	Scrum	FDD	XP	Kanban	Crystal
Planning of Iteration	Per sprint per size	Per feature per size	Release announcement Iteration planning	For each variant	Every step
Collaborative Interaction	Scrum functions Cross-functional team Self-managing Team	Communicate on documenting	Pair Coding	Optional Kanban meeting Customer Importance	Requires documenting Fast communication

Programming (XP), Crystal methodology, Feature Driven Development (FDD), Kanban method, and Scrum. After a short-term overview of the most prominent agile methodologies for software development, Table 1.1 above summarizes each of these frameworks, containing team scope, responsibilities, iteration (sprint) length, issue, status of release, large project adaptability, and value-driven development, and iteration planning.

In 1996, Extreme Programming (XP) was introduced [19]. Customer satisfaction is prioritized in this method, which is ensured by ongoing feedback. This strategy allows the software development team for responding changes in the program requirements as described by client [20]. It entails partnership between the customer and a development team of small size. The growth team consists of 2–10 people who work on software small components like an issue to for addressing a novel useful necessity.

The crystal technique is a light methodology with minimal documentation, organization, and writing requirements. It makes the procedure adaptable generically and flexibly. Conditioning on the project setting and team size, the adaption recommends different crystal approaches, including clear yellow shining, orange and red crystal [21]. Every methodology necessitates its own set of practices, procedures, and policies. The emphasis in this strategy is on human interactions, with process adaption based on what works best for the team, building on the finest practices in software engineering.

The Kanban approach [22] provides a visual SDLC workflow management framework. The three primary practices of Kanban are visualization of work in process limitation, and enhancement of workflow. Limiting work in the process means all pending tasks are completed before moving on to the next stage of the process.

In business, the most utilized framework of agile is Scrum. It is worth noting that it's the framework of agile listed in the area of the world's most famous job search sites [23]. This popularity stems to improve the process of software development, as well as the rapidity with which it is delivered and the quality of the program.

1.3   Agile Architecture Trends in the Digital World

The digital world offers new issues that necessitate a creative approach to identifying effective solutions while keeping the larger ecosystem in mind. In a digital world, current agile architecture trends and practices should be thoroughly evaluated. There has never been a systematic research studies trends and practices of agile architecture based on data availability. Several technological innovations are emerging that are having a substantial impact on agile architecture and design [24]:

(i)   Integration – new technologies and services must be able to link and integrate with existing technologies and services.

(ii)   Micro-services – Such services are on the rise, with a slew of little add-ons, apps, and other specialized and specialized technologies and services enhancing user functionality, technology customization, and flexibility. Microservices are an important part of the evolutionary and revolutionary development chain for technologies, software, infrastructure, and consumers.

(iii) Digital Behaviors and Routines – Users will no longer need to shift systems and technologies since digital architecture and technology are becoming increasingly invisible and incorporated into their daily work. Many technologies are now speech or behavior activated, and they learn from the users' behavior and routines, resulting in increased productivity through automation.

(iv)   Agile Adaptation – Adaptation and anticipating user requirements are at odds. While many agile software and technology development cycles are adaptable, they also require a high level of creativity, invention, and foresight into future technologies, architecture, and software.

(v)   Speed – The increase in the speed with which technologies adapt and respond to user requirements and demands has been an important trend in technology-based evolution and revolution. As a result, many modern technologies and software are intrinsically flexible to user preferences to some extent and have some level of learning capability built-in, which accelerates their progress.

(vi)   Continuous monitoring – Many modern technologies and applications are 'linked to the base,' allowing designers to collect real-time data about usage, issues, and, to a degree, demands. Furthermore, the capacity of designers to update technology or software on-the-fly and discreetly to the user is becoming increasingly popular. It has been discovered that this improves technological adaptability and learning.

The Systematic Literature Review (SLR) approach and the Kitchenham criteria [25] were used to experiment on the agile architecture trends and practices in the digital era. SLR is a technique for conducting secondary research based on the findings of primary research. The SLR procedure was used to specify the following: research topic, searching procedure, addition/prohibition criteria, quality valuation, information-gathering technique, and analytic method. The purpose is to find answers to the below mentioned research-based questions (RQ):

RQ1-What are the recent trends in Agile architecture, given the rise of multiple software engineering methodologies such as Continuous, Lean, and Evolutionary?

RQ2-In a modern digital context, what are the best approaches for building and executing Agile architecture?

1.3.1   Agile Implementation at Scale

A greatly expanded project is defined by a company objective or by complete measures like the count of developers participating, the size of the budget, the complexity, or the count of developing expanded teams [25]. Agile adoption is quickly replacing traditional approaches, and the positive performance and possible achievement rate of agile adoption in small grouped projects piqued curiosity of teams of software development and the agile adoption by industry in large projects. The authors illustrate how the environment aids and supports distributed agile frameworks in [26].

The large-scale adoption of software project coding may provide management of project issues. Despite challenges, the implementation of agile at a broad stage is fast expanding [27, 28].

According to the analysis by Jørgensen [29], the results of many software projects have been reviewed, and they show that the implementation rate of agile methodology is high in various ranges of projects. The results of Projects as compared to agile application rate are shown in Figure 1.3.

On the other hand, adopting agile at scale has significant limits in some circumstances, for example, SCRUM is best suited for short projects with less team size, and used on larger projects which slows down expansion. Abrar *et al.* [30] identified 21 promoters for large-scale agile implementation. Furthermore, they were analyzed and classified, for example, into

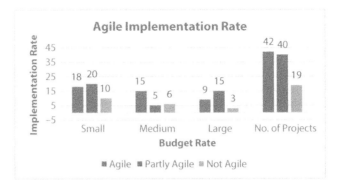

Figure 1.3 The agile implementation rate over projects.

essential factors, using predetermined criteria. Studies, questionnaires, and an experiential investigation of the availability and assistance of agile software development experts validate the identified motivators. The challenges for the SCRUM technique in a distributed context were identified by Khalid *et al.* [31].

1.4   Challenges Faced in the Digital World Through Agile Software Development

Apart from the specific field of large-scale agile transformations, various challenges are a recurring issue in agile techniques study. Examples include exploring agile method adaption and building on development related to process customer, developer, and organization-related difficulties for a better understanding of organizations' motives to modify agile techniques [32]. Furthermore, earlier studies discuss the difficulties of applying agile techniques in enterprises SD departments, addressing concerns like selecting an effective agile method and the problem of a lack of developer competence [33]. Current empirical investigations, however, provide useful information on this subject. This article provides a thorough analysis as well as relevant decisions and suggestions. The goal of the study is to discover problems and challenges that small-, mid- and large agile projects face when it comes to requirement engineering, which designs various suggestions for improving the agile process based on literature. Table 1.2 lists the public challenges encountered in agile projects at the time of the requirement engineering phase, as well as their actions.

Table 1.2 Summary of agile requirement engineering challenges and actions.

Requirement engineering (phase)	Agile activities	Challenges	Effect
Elicitation	Questionnaire and Interview	Problematic scoping, mistake	requirement analysis is affected by the ill-defined requirements.
Elicitation	Brainstorming	Group Brainstorming	Ambiguity
Elicitation	Prototyping	Safety, Scalability, and Strength	Maintenance issues
Investigation	Prioritization	Idea Conflicts	Uncertainty
Documenting	User feedback	Absence of customers	Misleading code
Documenting	Product Accumulation	Reduced documentation	Knowledge Loss
Authentication	Client stories	Unavailability of proper prototyping issues	Reduced Quality
Managing	Change control	Tool selection	Time Consumption
Managing	Traceability of Requirements	Ineffective requirement management	Non-traceability

1.4.1   Challenges for Small to Mid-Scale and Large-Scale Agile Projects

Although agile implementation addresses the shortcomings of the serial paradigm, it nevertheless has limitations [34]. The problems of Requirements Engineering are incompatible interfacing, non-functional requirement neglect, lack of clarity, and Requirements Engineering activities. Agile techniques reduced a solid framework for sufficient citation and documenting user requirements, and because requirements are variable, labor must be redone. De Lucia and Qusef offered few rules for their long term because a lack of good documentation could cause problems for the team. These criteria include assigning certain employees to write minimal documentation, modeling with computer tools, and developing reverse engineering procedures [35]. The challenges analyzed by the authors are presented in the Table 1.3:

Table 1.3 Summary of challenges for small to mid-scale and large-scale agile projects.

Requirement engineering (phase)	Challenges
Elicitation Requirements	Clarity issues, requirement prioritizing, and tricky scoping
Management Requirements	Prioritization, Absence of variable management, and adequate managing tools
Documentation Requirements	Absence of enough documentation, non-availability of customer representative
Validation Requirements	Non-availability of approaches or tools

Software businesses are concentrating on adopting agile approaches in disseminated environments known as distributed software development, due to rapid development rates and lower development costs [36]. The research focuses on identifying desired challenges and prioritization in an agile development context in a dispersed setting. To discover these problems, a literature review was undertaken, and they were then classified into four divisions: team, process, current technology, and management.

Agile methodologies are becoming increasingly popular in the software business due to their multiple advantages. If a predictable process model is employed in complicated projects of software development like supply chain management with unbalanced and variable requirements, implementation becomes complex [37]. Understanding and managing high-level needs are essential in large development initiatives. As a result, understanding and handling high-level needs are critical, as this is widely known that issues in requirements have an impact on quality.

1.4.2   Reported Challenges – Cause and Potential Solutions

The following are the issues with the software, according to Lee *et al.* [38]: (a) Due to scheduling slippage, it is seldom delivered on time, resulting in cancellation; (b) ineffective software that is unable to tackle the correct problem because the software requirement is incompatible with the need; (c) When employees depart or their interests shift, they become burnt out; and (d) modest adjustments take a lot of time and effort. Issues we discovered in the literature are listed below:

(i)   Less Direct Client/Stakeholder communication – The issue of requirement trackless is caused by less direct communication [39]. It can happen for a variety of reasons, including a lack of time, a distance element, a lack of client councils, and so on. Client engagement and presence have a direct impact on requirement change and validation from a business standpoint. Requirements are prioritized when users aren't engaged in the process of decision-making process.

Solution – Direct conversation, questionnaires, and meetings should be performed to address this issue. When acquiring requirements from clients, avoid collecting long-term requirements and conducting lengthy formal interviews.

(ii)   Reduced Documentation Focus – Shortage of sufficient reports can generate challenges for the development team as well as the issue with requirement tracking. Minimal documentation throughout the requirement gathering process leads to challenges such as a lack of staff assistance and no support for reverse engineering procedures [40].

Solution – Do some documentation, and pay more attention and care to the criteria, as it will help to trail, manage, and check them. As a result, the agile process and RE activities must be standardized.

(iii)   Missing Ambiguity and Conflicting Requirements – The inconsistency of user stories and the multiple levels of abstraction generate issues. As a result, unclear criteria have a significant impact on quality and schedule. More rework in the future version due to a missing interface between requirements [41].

Solution – To accommodate the missing, confusing, and contradictory needs, more formal methods for requirement formulation are required. To integrate evolving requirements, use more explicit techniques to specify requirements. RE-COMBINE is a model used to formally express needs and is more adaptable to change.

(iv) Prototyping Issues – We can pick design thinking based on empathizing, defining, ideating, prototyping, and testing over traditional approaches. The usage of prototyping and agile development creates a misunderstanding regarding development speed among stakeholders. Too much coding in early prototyping generates concerns like excellence issues caused by the practice of code reusability in prototypes, and investors may be unwilling to adopt more scalable and resilient development cycles [42].

Solution – Prototyping should not include a lot of implementations. It is preferable for using paper prototyping rather than wizard prototyping, which saves time and eliminates user confusion by displaying a wizard prototype that you implemented quickly. In this scenario, paper prototyping will aid in a variety of ways, including acting as a design test before coding, being readily adjustable, and eliminating the specific technology variables.

(v) Tacit Knowledge – Tacit knowledge is what one knows but can't say; it's what we've learned from personal experience and can be difficult to describe at times. Because this data is not specified in the requirement, transferring business information to the development team is difficult.

Solution – Tactic information is commonly reduced via direct conversation, observation, surveys, and interviews. The three aspects of domain experts, the conversion process, and the audience will assist in overcoming the tacit knowledge issue. Allowing practice for information distribution of both positive and negative experiences, will benefit team members and allow them to get from, as knowledge allocation is a significant achievement concern in the phase of development.

(vi) Changing Requirements – The produced product in a prior iteration may cause interface compatibility concerns due to changing client needs [43]. The agile project gets costly as requirements change, resulting in increasing project and maintenance costs. System failure is caused by a failure to manage to change needs.

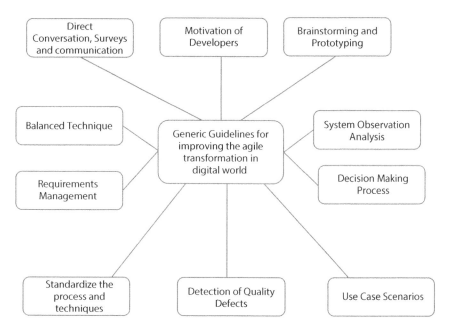

Figure 1.4 Generic guidelines for improving agile transformation in the digital world.

Solution – ARCM-RM (agile requirement change management readiness model) was proposed consisting of primary modules: maturity, factor and valuation level. The prototype encourages worldwide software development for ARCMRM measurement and improvement.

(vii) Requirement Prioritization – Because investors are not participating in the process of decision-making and customers are not always available for daily meetings, prioritizing requirements in an agile approach after each step is difficult owing to the lack of technique.

Solution – In agile development, a methodology for prioritizing requirements builds a framework consisting of identification, verification, estimation, and prioritizing. The methodology offered will also assist in dealing with change at any phase of the software development.

(viii) Negligence of non-functional requirements – There is no approach for obtaining and evaluating non-functional requirements (NFRs), agile techniques, extreme programming, and SCRUM are famous because of yielding high-quality functional requirements. The excellence of the developed product is assessed after each iteration.

Solution – NORMATIC, a java-based simulation tool for non-functional requirement modeling in the process of agile development, is proposed. To implement the NFRs in agile projects, a planning and visualization approach is proposed [44–46]. By conducting experimentation on master's students from the SED (software engineering department), we were able to examine the process of NFR elicitation and acquire encouraging results.

1.5   Generic Guidelines to Improve the Agile Transformation in Digital World

Many academics have provided a variety of guidelines and approaches, including agile implementation processes, agile principles, guidelines, and conventions for corporate distributed plans, among alternatives. The Figure 1.4 depicts some broad suggestions for improving the requirement engineering process, which will aid in incorporating agile development issues.

Requirement elicitation, clarification, analysis, prioritization, documentation, and decision are all major issues connected with agile Requirements Engineering activities. It has been claimed that the agile software development approach also mixes and ensures software security. The authors suggested a strategy for developing acceptably safe software that provides security assurance and claims to partially mitigate associated hazards. These discoveries represent obstacles to agile development success.

1.6   Conclusion and Future Perspective

It has been remarked that the Agile implementation as a Scrum framework module is apt, as evidenced by the Strongly Agree grade, as an effect of their evaluation of the Learning Process Design in a digital world. This chapter emphasizes that Agile Software Development is adaptable, which allows students to maximize their learning capacity. Students are more forceful when they are motivated and stimulated to think systematically at every step. It encourages students to share their expertise while also strengthening relationships and friendships. The challenges and recommendations from the study may be utilized to improve the abilities and competencies of development organizations during agile software development.

Researchers interested in this field may find our findings useful as a starting point. It's ideal for researchers who want to get involved in this subject, which necessitates realistic discoveries and studies employing several agile approaches including crystal and extreme programming. Conflicts and difficulties that occur after the procedure are non-stated. As a result, the study indicates that the agile domain is still in its early stages and that establishing standards and standardizing the process is key to achieving better results. There is a requirement for rules and uniformity in our industry.

References

1. Kanbul, S. and Uzunboylu, H., Importance of coding education and robotic applications for achieving 21st-century skills in North Cyprus. *Int. J. Emerg. Technol. Learn.*, 12, 1, 130–131, 2017. https://www.onlinejournals.org/index.php/i-jet/article/view/6097/4264. https://doi.org/10.3991/ijet.v12i01.6097.
2. Cavus, N. and Uzunboylu, H., Improving critical thinking skills in mobile learning. *Procedia Soc. Behav. Sci.*, 1, 1, 434–438, 2009. https://doi.org/10.1016/j.sbspro.2009.01.078.
3. Resnick, M., Kafai, Y., Maloney, J., Rusk, N., Burd, L., Silverman, B., *A Networked, Media-Rich Programming Environment to Enhance Technological Fluency at After School Centers in Economically-Disadvantaged Communities*, Proposal to National Science Foundation, Cambridge, United States, 2003.
4. World Economic Forum, *New Vision for Education: Fostering Social and Emotional Learning Tthrough Technology*, pp. 4–5, 2016, retrieved from http://bit.ly/2NWzer3.
5. WEF & Accenture, *Digital Transformation Initiative*, 2017, Retrieved March 12, 2018 from: https://www.accenture.com/t20170116T084450__w__/us-en/_acnmedia/Accenture/Conversion-Assets/WEF/PDF/Accenture-DTI-executivesummary.pdf.
6. Ochodek, M. and Kopczynska, S., Perceived importance agile requirements engineering practices-a survey. *J. Syst. Softw.*, 143, 29–43, 2018.
7. Sebega, Y. and Mnkandla, E., Exploring issues in agile requirements engineering in the South African software industry. *Electron. J. Inf. Syst. Dev. Ctries*, 81, 1, 1–18, 2017.
8. Rolland, K. *et al.*, Problematizing agile in the large: Alternative assumptions for large-scale agile development. *39th International Conference on Information Systems*, Association for Information Systems (AIS), 2016.
9. Sharma, M. and Gupta, A.K., An algorithm for target detection, identification, tracking and estimation of motion for passive homing missile autopilot guidance, in: *Mobile Radio Communications and 5G Networks*, pp. 57–71, Springer, Singapore, 2021.

10. Sales, E., Shuffler, M., Thayer, A., Bedwell, W., Lazzara, E., Understanding and improving teamwork in organizations: A scientifically based practical guide. *Hum. Resour. Manage.*, 54, 4, 599–622, 2015.

11. Fatema, I. and Sakib, K., Factors influencing productivity of agile software development teamwork: A qualitative system dynamics approach. *24th Asia-Pacific Software Engineering Conference*, Nanjing, China, December 4–8, 2017, pp. 737–742, 2017, https://doi.org/10.1109/apsec.2017.95.

12. Bansal, A., Mehta, K., Arora, S., Face recognition using PCA and LDA algorithm. *2012 Second International Conference on Advanced Computing & Communication Technologies*, IEEE, 2012.

13. Mehta, K. and Kumar, Y., Implementation of efficient clock synchronization using elastic timer technique in IoT. *Adv. Math. Sci. J.*, 9, 6, 4025–4030, 2020.

14. Garg, R., Garg, M., Chadha, A., Mehta, K., Brain gate technology-an analysis. *Int. J. Adv. Sci. Technol.*, 28, 19, 890–93, Dec. 2019. http://sersc.org/journals/index.php/IJAST/article/view/2676.

15. Szalvay, V., *An Iintroduction to Agile Software Development*, vol. 3, Danube Technologies, Bellevue, WA, 2004.

16. Arora, T. and Dhir, R., Geometric feature-based classification of segmented human chromosomes. *Int. J. Image Graph.*, 20, 01, 2050006, 2020.

17. Hussain, A., Mkpojiogu, E.O., Kamal, F.M., The role of requirements in the success or failure of software projects. *Int. Rev. Manage. Mark.*, 6, S7, 306–311, 2016.

18. Kumar, S.A. and Kumar, T.A., Study the impact of requirements management characteristics in global software development projects: An ontology-based approach. *Int. J. Softw. Eng. Appl.*, 2, 4, 107, 2011.

19. Fojtik, R., Extreme programming in the development of specific software. *Procedia Comput. Sci.*, 3, 1464–1468, 2011. [CrossRef.]

20. Wells, D., *Extreme Programming*, 2009, Extremeprogramming.org., [Online], Extremeprogramming, US. Available online: http://www.extremeprogramming.org/(accessed on 20 November 2020).

21. Jones, C., *Software Methodologies: A Quantitative Guide*, Auerbach Publications, Boca Raton, FL, USA, 2017.

22. Zayat, W. and Senvar, O., Framework study for agile software development via scrum and Kanban. *Int. J. Innov. Technol. Manag.*, 17, 04, 2030002, 2020.

23. García-Barriocanal, E., Sicilia, M.A., Sánchez-Alonso, S., Cuadrado, J.J., Agile methods as problem-based learning designs: Setting and assessment, in: *Proceedings of the Sixth International Conference on Technological Ecosystems for Enhancing Multiculturality (TEEM'18)*, Salamanca, Spain, October 24–26, 2018, Association for Computing Machinery, New York, NY, USA, pp. 339–346, 2018. [CrossRef.]

24. Dragičević, Z. and Bošnjak, S., Agile architecture in the digital era: Trends and practices. *Strategic Manage.*, 24, 2, 12–33, 2019.

25. Conboy, K. and Carroll, N., Implementing large-scale agile frameworks: Challenges and recommendations. *IEEE Softw.*, 36, 2, 44–50, 2019.

26. Lous, P., Tell, P., Michelsen, C.B., Dittrich, Y., Kuhrmann, M., Ebdrup, A., Virtual by design: How a work environment can support agile distributed software development, in: *Proceedings of the 2018 IEEE/ACM 13th International Conference on Global Software Engineering (ICGSE)*, IEEE, Gothenburg, Sweden, pp. 97–106, May 2018.

27. Moe, N.B. and Dingsøyr, T., Emerging research themes and updated research agenda for large-scale agile development: A summary of the 5th international workshop at XP2017, in: *Proceedings of the XP2017 Scientific Workshops*, Cologne, Germany, pp. 1–4, May 2017.

28. Fuchs, C. and Hess, T., Becoming agile in the digital transformation: The process of a large-scale agile transformation, in: *Proceedings of the 39th International Conference on Information Systems (ICIS 2018)*, San Francisco, USA, December 2018.

29. Jørgensen, M., Do agile methods work for large software projects?, in: *Proceedings of the International Conference on Agile Software Development*, Springer, Montreal, QC, Canada, pp. 179–190, May 2018.

30. Abrar, M.F., Khan, M.S., Ali, S. *et al.*, Motivators for largescale agile adoption from a management perspective: A systematic literature review. *IEEE Access*, 7, 22660–22674, 2019.

31. Khalid, A., Butt, S.A., Jamal, T., Gochhait, S., Agile scrum issues at large-scale distributed projects. *Int. J. Softw. Innov.*, 8, 2, 85–94, 2020.

32. Rai, V. *et al.*, Automated biometric personal identification-techniques and applications. *2020 4th International Conference on Intelligent Computing and Control Systems (ICICCS)*, IEEE, 2020.

33. Mehta, K. *et al.*, Enhancement of smart agriculture using internet of things. *ECS Trans.*, 107, 1, 7047, 2022.

34. Rasheed, A., Zafar, B., Shehryar, T., Aslam, N. A., Sajid, M., Ali, N., ... & Khalid, S., Requirement engineering challenges in agile software development. *Math. Probl. Eng.*, 2021, 1–18, 2021.

35. Heck, P. and Zaidman, A., A systematic literature review on quality criteria for agile requirements specifications. *Softw. Qual. J.*, 26, 1, 127–160, 2018.

36. Mehta, K., Kumar, Y., Aayushi, A., Enhancing time synchronization for home automation systems. *ECS Trans.*, 107, 1, 6197, 2022.

37. Pereira, J.C. and de FSM Russo, R., Design thinking integrated in agile software development: A systematic literature review. *Procedia. Comput. Sci.*, 138, 775–782, 2018.

38. Bedi, T.S., Kumar, S., Kumar, R., Corrosion performance of hydroxyapaite and hydroxyapaite/titania bond coating for biomedical applications. *Mater. Res. Express*, 7, 1, 015402, 2019.

39. Alam, S., Shah, S.A.A., Bhatti, S.N., Jadi, A.M., Impact and challenges of requirement engineering in agile methodologies: A systematic review. *Int. J. Adv. Comput. Sci. Appl.*, 8, 411–420, 2017.

40. Kirikova, M., *Continuous Requirements Engineering in Sociotechnical Systems: Challenges and Solutions*, DBLP, Taipei, Taiwan, 2022.

41. Mateen, A., Abbas, K., Akbar, M.A., Robust approaches, techniques and tools for requirement engineering in agile development. *2017 IEEE International Conference on Power, Control, Signals and Instrumentation Engineering (ICPCSI)*, IEEE, 2017.

42. Rai, V. *et al.*, Cloud computing in healthcare industries: Opportunities and challenges, in: *Recent Innovations in Computing. Lecture Notes in Electrical Engineering*, vol. 855, P.K. Singh, Y. Singh, J.K. Chhabra, Z. Illés, C. Verma, (Eds.), Springer, Singapore, 2022, https://doi.org/10.1007/978-981-16-8892-8_53.

43. Akbar, M.A. *et al.*, Success factors influencing requirements change management process in global software development. *J. Comput. Lang.*, 51, 112–130, 2019.

44. Farid, W.M. and Mitropoulos, F.J., Visualization and scheduling of non-functional requirements for agile processes, in: *Proceedings of the 2013 IEEE Southeastcon*, IEEE, Jacksonville, FL, USA, pp. 1–8, April 2013.

45. Mohindru, V., Sharma, A., Mathur, A., Gupta, A.K., Brain segmentation using deep neural networks. *Int. J. Sens. Wirel. Commun.*, 11, 1, 81–88, 2021.

46. Mohindru, V., Vashishth, S., Bathija, D., Internet of Things (IoT) for healthcare systems: A comprehensive survey, in: *Recent Innovations in Computing. Lecture Notes in Electrical Engineering*, vol. 832, P.K. Singh, Y. Singh, M.H. Kolekar, A.K. Kar, P.J.S. Gonçalves, (Eds.), Springer, Singapore, 2022, https://doi.org/10.1007/978-981-16-8248-3_18.

Agile Framework Adaptation Issues in Various Sectors

Anita Sardana[1]* and Vidhu Kiran Sharma[2]

[1]AIT-CSE, Chandigarh University, Punjab, India
[2]Chitkara University Institute of Engineering and Technology, Chitkara University, Punjab, India

Abstract

Agile software development (ASD) is a grown environment for achieving goals such as customer satisfaction, an error free application etc. by incorporating best practices such as test driven/design development (TDD), pair programming (PP), refactoring, daily meeting, small product vision, workflow practice, retrospective, demos, simplicity, open work culture, small iteration, small user story, or small team. Traditionally, software development life cycle (SDLC) such as waterfall model, prototyping model, iterative model, spiral model etc. are in trend. No doubt this agile way of working has brought various questions among users of agile working environment. In this chapter, various issues will be addressed which are creating hurdles for newbie's while doing a switch from traditional model to an agile model. A basic issue while switching is an adaptation issue as team needs to work in a tightly coupled environment. Human-Human linkages are of different kinds for different kind of people. These linkages play a significant role when pair programming practice is used. In PP practice, one person behaves like a driver and other person behave like a reviewer for the driver. An adapting practice of agile is little bit cumbersome but not impossible. Agile outcomes are so positive that everyone wants to be an agile follower. Demand is more but sectors who are actually implementing this agile culture are very less. Specifically, in this chapter, issues of various sectors would be resolved by addressing a need matrix which will list a need of a particular sector and a resolution matrix which will list all proposed solution for all listed needs in the need matrix. Also, different use cases will be presented so as to have more clarity on resolution part in different sectors. Various

---

*Corresponding author: anita.sardana@chitkara.edu.in

Susheela Hooda, Vandana Mohindru Sood, Yashwant Singh, Sandeep Dalal and Manu Sood (eds.)
Agile Software Development: Trends, Challenges and Applications, (23–38) © 2023 Scrivener Publishing LLC

sectors pertaining to agile adaptability are education, research, counselling, and software development office.

Keywords: Agile, Test Driven Development (TDD), Pair Programming (PP), refactoring, Scrum, Extreme Programming (XP)

2.1   Introduction

ASD [1–3] is catering the need of the time that is due to COVID 19 [3, 4] situation, teams are working remotely and team members are distributed [3–5] at different locations. A global survey on agile is intelligently described in [6]. There might be so many challenges [7] while working in an agile environment and moving from traditional approach to agile environment [8, 9] but working in remote is not just tough rather need good management skill so that quality [10] and productivity [11] can be increased. The management [12] of agile practices in COVID time can also be implemented using various artificial intelligence (AI) [13, 14] techniques and Internet of things (IOT) [14, 15, 48, 50] techniques. Accordingly, effort [16] can be estimated for various practices. In this scenario, a strong decision support system [17] (DSS) is required that can cater to the needs of remote working matrices like human-human linkages. These human-human linkages are explained in [18] using egocentric network. Anybody can visualize ASD outcomes in software sector. Many software companies are using this framework since years. This framework landed in the year 2001. This framework has many methodologies like SCRUM [19–22], XP [19, 23, 24], and FDD etc. In this, TDD [25–27] is the best practice in which test cases are designed first before doing coding. This unique feature of agile differentiates it from other SDLC models. After that, many changes were done in the existing methodologies based on the failure encountered by various people in one or more scenarios. These scenarios are based on various client projects, requirements, needs, market growth. These days, many software development companies are trying to adapt this agile framework with its best practices [28] and many are leaders of this framework. This change may be troublesome for newbie's as for beginners there are many things to adapt with different mindset. An agile testing life cycle [29] different from a traditional SDLC model is utilized in achieving good quality product. There are different agile testing techniques like test case prioritization (TCP) [30–33, 50], regression test selection [34] etc. The foremost requirement is that newbie must be of positive nature. Once decision is taken then, in mid it might be tough to leave. With positivity changes occurrence may be smooth. This ever famous framework is attracting many new players with its outcome. Since its inception, many worked so hard to achieve the outcome. Its methodologies like feature driven development (FDD), extreme programming (XP) and SCRUM, etc. are some of the famous ones because of their unique features. In all these, PP [35–38, 47] is an important feature while implementing agile culture. It is common one and toughest to implement as this is based on human-human linkages. Meaning of these linkages is that agile is based on small teams who work in close environment with each other. These small teams are the tightly coupled environment for execution of the results. Small numbers of people are in the small teams and accordingly, PP is implemented. In small teams, couples work in parallel with each other. This couple has one tester and one programmer for achieving good quality of work in software industry. Good quality is an outcome of testing [39]. If linkage is not perfect then connection would break and accordingly, work quality would suffer. In the small teams, firstly these couples/pair are formed, and then work is distributed. There are various ways in which couples may be formed. Some of the examples of forming pair are experience among team members, nature of team members, previous reports on relationship from various teams/leaders, new trials, likings of team members etc. Linkages may also be functional by considering aspect oriented programming (AOP) [40–43] concepts. AOP is implemented using machine learning [49] concepts including fuzzy logic [44], fuzzy clustering [44, 45], genetic algorithm [46] etc. The abovementioned ways are common one which is in practice in software sectors. There might be other ways of building human-human linkages for good outcome. Our chapter covers this aspect in detail and agile in various sectors is also taken covered by mentioning its need and resolution matrix for resolving need. Section 2.1 in this chapter is about introduction of the agile, its methodologies, and new implementation possibilities. Section 2.2 talks about various sectors that are or may be followers of agile. Section 2.3 discusses about implementation scenarios for various sectors. Section 2.4 provides a new mapping of the solutions with the implementation possibilities. Section 2.5 is about conclusion and future work in this direction.

2.1.1   Human-Human Linkages

Human-Human Linkages are of many types based on the requirements. These can be of mainly following types such as

- Weak,
- Partially weak,
- Partially strong, and
- Strong

Weak linkages are with least transparency, meaning that these Human-Human linkages cannot sustain for a long time. While working in agile environment, agile trainers focus on conversion from weak human-human linkages to strong type of linkages. This conversion takes time but if converted successfully may produce fruitful results. On the other side, strong linkages are based upon transparency. Daily Scrum meetings of 15 minutes promote transparency among meetings. During these meetings, everything that needs to be done on daily basis is discussed in brief among team members. Further, strong human-human linkages are formed for achieving good quality work. Gradually, performance starts upgrading when linkages will shift from weak to strong linkages among team members of small team.

Further, partially weak and partially strong types lie between weak and strong type linkages. In Agile, partially strong can sustain for some time but ultimately need is to shift to strong linkages for betterment of the quality work. Software development is a term with sustainability. Any developed application can sustain the high risks only when it has gone through various phases of regression analysis with coordination, communication and collaboration of team members. This approach is 3 C approach of Agile which is successful only when strong type of human-human linkages are working in the development company. Bonding among team members may of different levels such as novice, experienced, domain level, interest level etc. Based on these levels different pairs exist such as

- Novice-Novice pair: fresher-fresher
- Experienced-Experienced
- Novice-Experienced
- Domain-Domain: IOT-IOT
- Interest-Interest: Sports-Sports

These pairs work in strong relationship for easy going development life. Meaning that success of any project is largely dependent of successful working of pair workers. Identification of these pairs is implemented as soon as team structure is announced before starting any iteration in Scrum methodology of Agile. During this identification phase of pairs, decision is based on either Scrum master or self centric approach is implemented. This self centric approach stands on the pillar of mutual interest and trust. Mutually pairs are formed and work progresses towards next phase for early delivery. Mostly, the self centric approach is better than leadership created pairs. This sounds little bit awkward but this is the reality. Considering leadership created pairs, creation time is more and process execution is slow. These kinds of pairs flourished under the umbrella of leadership so pressure is always felt among the pairs and fear factor roles down in between which may affect the performance of the individuals. This is not always the case. Still, some of the implementers believe in the self centric approach of pair creation. Considering COVID timelines, online mode is in discussion which is turning the picture altogether for sustainability of agile teams with quality deliverables. Online mode of pair building is a cumbersome process so as to meet the outcomes of the company, leader, Scrum master and team. In this, even recruitments are online so there is no point of self centric creation of pairs. Through video calling only every-thing is possible including recruitments to on boarding, project allocation, team structuring, pair creation, trust building and many more tasks. Here, trust building is little bit tough and if built then tough to survive. If we talk about normal scenario, gradually people adapt to work. In agile, adaptabil-ity is the basic expectation from every team member. With adaptability, 3 C like collaboration, coordination and communication can be implemented.

2.2 Agile Followers

In agile, everybody is aware that software industry is using agile with full pace. That's why many companies are able to satisfy their client needs to such an extent that nobody is in trouble. In market, there are various other sectors who also want to follow agile working environment. Things are not very tough as a few are already following. A list of agile to be followers is an education industry, research industry, aerospace training, Military train-ing, and consultancy etc. if we talk about these sectors, these are already developed one but agile can make life easier for various stakeholders of these sectors, although every sector is based on human–human linkages like family relationship. Although there is no escape on the other hand in other kind of relationships like education sector aerospace there is a need for resolution for getting rid of weak relationship maintenance. Before that identification of weak relationship is must. A detailed description about these sectors is given below.

1. Education sector - in this sector, various stakeholders are university, students, faculty or industry. To achieve various program outcomes of this sector is already in its full pace still there is always a chance of improvement to cater to the needs of the industry. In this sector, human-human linkages are important based on relationship of student with faculty, faculty with parent, university with industry, and mentor with mentee. Above mentioned roles work as per the relationship with each other. If linkage is food, productivity and efficiency of each stake holder will increase. Agile in education sector is also small team working where all stakeholders participate in direct linkage with each other. Accordingly a strong bond can be established for proper growth of each sector.

2. Research sector - this sector has one special bond that is guide and scholar. Other bond also exists which is scholar and industry. Like, education sector, this sector can also adapt to PP practice of agile. Adaptation is tough but can be achieved using some of the best practices. Human-human linkages play a significant role in this sector. If bonding is of diminishing type then outcome of the research will not be proper. To cater to this need, a relationship linkage is presented.

3. Aerospace sector - this sector is high risk sector in which pilots are given training as per direct relationship and indirect relationship. In direct mode, trainers provide theoretical concepts of aero vehicle landing and taking off. On the other side, in indirect mode, pilot is trained based on flying simulator. In direct bond, human-human linkages play a significant role. Like PP, these linkages help in generating trained pilots for flying aerospace vehicles.

4. Military sector - this sector, is also another high risk sector in which wrong human-human linkages may have an adverse affect on the generation of good quality staff. So, these linkages play significant role if PP practice is to be adapted to adopt agile way of working. There might be so many challenges in adapting to new way of agile working but if linkages are tightly coupled and strong then journey becomes easier.

5. Consultancy sector - this sector relates to providing consultancy in banking area, trading area, technical projects, and personal relationship concerns. Like other sectors, if agile is to be implemented in this area, then need is to create client relationship first and then provide the consultancy of the specific sector. Like other sectors, need is to bring human-human linkages in better way. In this manner, pair working model can be created.

All above mentioned sectors are based on Human-human linkages. For implementation of agile in all these areas need is to understand these linkages in detail. First step is to identify types of linkages that could be possible in that sector. Next step is to build a healthy environment for smooth working of existing projects with agile introduction. These linkages can be formed by a hybrid approach of working. The hybrid approach is based on existing way of linkages. The existing way of Linkages can be of type:

- Similar nature of employees
- Similar hobbies of employees
- Similar gender [11] of employees
- Similar experience of employees
- Similar history of employees
- Similar traits of employees
- Different performance of employees (for guiding purpose)
- Different locality of employees

Based on the above types, a hybrid version of any of the above way of linkages can be considered. The so formed blended approach will help the employees in building strong bonds with each other and accordingly work performance will enhance and productivity of each sector will increase.

2.3   Proposed Work

Table 2.1 shows a need matrix that has been prepared for various sectors which will show the need of every type of work that may be done in various sectors. Work categories may be many in various sectors, but for the sake of implementation or understanding scope of this chapter only major task and their stakeholders are discussed here.

Table 2.1 Need matrix.

Education sector	Types of linkages	Need
	Teacher-Student	1. Transparent 360 degree feedback among stakeholders
	Mentor-Mentee	2. Analysis of the feedback
	Student-Industry	3. Demonstrations for improvement
	Management-Leaders	4. Performance of Students
	College-Industry	5. Performance of Faculty
		6. Employee engagement methods
		7. Employee satisfaction matrices
		8. Number of appreciations earned by teacher and student
		9. Number of Conferences/ Workshops attended by Teachers
		10. Number of events organized by the Teacher
		11. No of co curricular activities attended by the student
Research sector	**Types of linkages**	**Need**
	Guide-Scholar	1. Academic performance of scholar and research publications of Guide
	Industry-Scholar	2. Personal relationship among scholars
	Institute-Industry	3. Previous bonding of research institute with industry
	Scholar-Scholar	4. National Ranking criteria of the research institute
		5. Number of patents filed by the research institute
		6. Number of patents granted
		7. Number of products launched in market
		8. Number of grants received from Government
		9. Number of Litigations going on
		10. Number of Licensing projects handled

(*Continued*)

Table 2.1 Need matrix. (*Continued*)

Aerospace sector	Types of linkages	Need
	Pilot-Trainer	1. Training feedback of Pilot from trainers
	Pilot-Airhostess	2. Passenger feedback analysis
	Airhostess-Airhostess	3. Past Accidental records of Trainers
	Pilot-Traffic Controller team	4. Past performances of technical and maintenance team
		5. Past analysis of successes and failures
		6. Past records of International training and certifications by the aerospace experts
		7. Feedback implementations hurdles
		8. Aerospace staff work life balance statistics
		9. Aerospace staff health records data
		10. Number of funding and amount of funding received
Military sector	**Types of linkages**	**Need**
	Leaders-Subordinates	1. Analysis of the existing training styles
	Subordinates-Subordinates	2. Offline to online mode of training
	Trainers- Subordinates	3. Feedback implementation Strategies
	Purchase Team-Subordinates	4. Psychological state of subordinates
	External Trainers-Internal Trainers	5. Work life balance of subordinates
		6. Emotional state of subordinates
		7. Reason of Performance degradation if any
		8. Family history of Subordinates
		9. Family appreciations in the Military
		10. Military Tools training resources

(*Continued*)

Table 2.1 Need matrix. (*Continued*)

Consultancy sector	Types of linkages	Need
	Consultant-Customer	1. Analysis of the market standards
	Customer-Customer	2. Analysis of the survey study
	Consultant-Service Provider	3. Feedback evaluation of different service providers and customers
	Service Provider-Service Provider	4. Implementation of customer relationship management software
		5. Relationship sustainability measures
		6. Customers retention measures
		7. Customer handling criteria
		8. Customer satisfaction survey

2.4   Resolution Matrix

To cater to the need of various sectors, we are proposing various models that may be incorporated in distributed COVID-19 environments so that sectors can work intelligently for the purpose of attaining same productivity and quality which was the target in the non-COVID environment. The remote working culture with no offline interaction brings so many challenges. One of the challenges is in SCRUM which has small meetings as the major practice but this cannot be done in online mode with same efficiency parameters. Also, implementation of PP seems to be little bit cumbersome. Here, we have to be at the managerial role for all. We mean if every team member is his/her own manager then things might be somewhat less complex. The management of human-human linkages can be taken care of by the individual team members by taking care of all the points discussed in the previous sector in reference to the specific sector. In online mode, bonding among human-human pair may not be so strong but efforts need to be put so that human-human linkages can exist strongly and can sustain for many projects under the agile umbrella. If every team member will be responsible for his/her own goals with every other team member of the human-human linkages then outcomes may be fruitful and quality would be as per the standards. Quality measurement metrics may be defined as per the sector previous policies or as per the standard adopted by the competitors in the market in the same domain. Various techniques for an efficient working of human-human linkages may arrive from the AI or IOT Field. Some of the proposed resolutions for these human-human linkages are:

Human-human linkages will work in an efficient manner if technology will have some control over the problems faced in any sector. One of the proposed AI techniques is to intelligently embed software to check the quality of the product to be delivered to the client. For example, Alexa voice assistant type devices can play this role in COVID-19 type environment. If we talk about education sector, this type of device can be customized as per the need of the sector. Accordingly, for handling human-human linkages, customized voice assistant can store individual data as per the similarity index of the individuals, viz teacher/faculty and Student. This similarity index represents a way of bonding among individuals. The individual data may comprise knowledge of the teacher in terms of life or any other course in which student is interested or his/her interest. On the other hand, student data may comprise history of student data including his/her past performance in academics or sports or any other activity. For example, in this voice assistant 4 teacher and 45 student data is stored or feeded. This assistant might get back with the companion matrix for teacher and student so that human-human linkages are of strong type. The companion matrix will intelligently categorize teacher and student based on various factors including interest/similarity index. The matrix would be stored on the cloud and anyone interested would be able to access the information by giving the voice command to the assistant at any time anywhere. In COVID-19, really this is a much awaited requirement. In that scenario, cost might be high as customized version will cater to need of various sectors as per the requirement. To handle such a situation, an alternative way is to take help of Microsoft excel to identify the similarity index of the interest among different stakeholders to build strong human-human linkages. The Excel might handle all these similarities as per the need of the specific sector.

Additionally, there might be IOT implementation for various kinds of sectors. For example, in IOT, everybody is connected in one or another manner by one or more devices. In this scenario, every device is connected via network. This connection is used in implementation of human-human linkages in various sectors. Specifically, in training of pilots, every device of pilot can act as a source of information. For example, trainee watch, mobile phone, tablet, laptop, headband, ear phones, are interacting with each other. These devices are used to verify the speech of the trainee and accordingly training information is provided to the trainee as per his need. For example, an advanced version of pilot training is provided to the pilot by collecting the information from various sources and segregating that information as per the proficiency level of the trainee like fighter plane training guidelines, special occasion training. During training wireless way of communication plays a significant role.

Similarly, in consultancy sector, information regarding market scenario of banking domain is gathered from various sources using authenticated sources. After amalgamation and segregation of information, relevant information is shared with the client using wireless services like Bluetooth, Zigbee etc.

2.5   Conclusion and Future Work

In this chapter, we have discussed various ways of defining human-human linkages that can be used in the many upcoming agile sectors like education, military, consultancy, aerospace, research etc. During this COVID-19 sector, there is a need for adopting best SDLC model of software industry to other prevailing sectors. The Agile model makes use of methodologies like SCRUM, XP, PP, TDD, refactoring etc. Each of these methodologies has various pros and cons. Any sector may utilize various methodologies. In this chapter, we have focused our efforts in the PP methodologies which are very common. PP is based on different kinds of human-human linkages. We have discussed various ways of forming these kinds of linkages by considering various factors which are prevalent needs of those sectors. Finally, IOT and AI are discussed to cater to the needs of the various sectors in brief.

In future, IOT techniques and AI techniques may be implemented using some languages so that execution of the human-human linkages can be done in an automatic manner. In this chapter, linkages are created based on need but if automatic version is released then time and effort will decreased and accordingly efficiency will decrease.

References

1. Janssen, M. and Van Der Voort, H., Agile and adaptive governance in crisis response: Lessons from the COVID-19 pandemic. *Int. J. Inf. Manage.*, 55, 102180, 2020.
2. Bushuyev, S., Bushuiev, D., Bushuieva, V., Project management during infodemic of the COVID-19 pandemic. *Innovative Technol. Sci. Solutions Industries*, 2, 12, 13–21, 2020.

3. Domanskyi, V. *et al.*, A hybrid method for managing agile team in a distributed environment. *2021 11th IEEE International Conference on Intelligent Data Acquisition and Advanced Computing Systems: Technology and Applications (IDAACS)*, vol. 1, IEEE, 2021.
4. Nundlall, C. and Nagowah, S.D., Task allocation and coordination in distributed agile software development: A systematic review. *Int. J. Inf. Technol.*, Springer, 13, 1, 321–330, 2021.
5. Anita, and Chauhan, N., A framework for quality improvement in distributed agile environment. *IEEE International Conference on Research And Development Prospects On Engineering And Technology*, E. G. S. Pillay Engineering College, Tamil Nadu, India, March 2013.
6. Anita, and Chauhan, N., State of the art search-Agile Software development in global market. *Int. J. Adv. Sci. Eng. Technol.* Institute Res. & Journals, 2, 2, 55–59, April 2014. http://www.iraj.in/journal/IJASEAT/volume.php?volume_id=46.
7. Conboy, K. and Carroll, N., Implementing large-scale agile frameworks: Challenges and recommendations. *IEEE Softw.*, 36, 2, 44–50, 2019.
8. Popli, R., Anita, Chauhan, N., A mapping model for transforming traditional software development methods to agile methodology. *Int. J. Softw. Eng. Appl.*, 4, 4, 53–64, July 2013. http://airccse.org/journal/ijsea/papers/4413ijsea05.pdf.
9. Popli, R., Anita, Chauhan, N., Mapping of traditional software development methods to agile methodology. *The Third International Conference on Computer Science and Information Technology (CCSIT-2013)*, Bangalore, India, February 18-20, 2013, http://airccj.org/CSCP/vol3/csit3612.pdf.
10. Neelu, L. and Kavitha, D., Estimation of software quality parameters for hybrid agile process model. *SN Appl. Sci.*, 3, 3, 1–11, 2021.
11. Nandakumar, V. and Qorri, A., *Improving Team Performance Working on Global Software Development Projects Using Agile Methods. A Case Study of Team Performance in GSD, Sweden*, Chalmers tekniska högskola/ Institutionen för teknikens ekonomi och organisation, Chalmers Open Digital Repository (ODR), Sweden, 2021.
12. Matta, M. and Marchesi, M., Understanding approval rating of agile project management tools using Twitter, in: *2015 10th International Joint Conference on Software Technologies (ICSOFT)*, vol. 1, IEEE, 2015.
13. Tipping, B., Agile systems engineering in building complex AI systems, in: *Engineering Artificially Intelligent Systems: A Systems Engineering Approach to Realizing Synergistic Capabilities*, vol. 13000, p. 192, 2021.
14. Chhabra, R., Verma, S., Krishna, C.R., *A Survey on Driver Behavior Detection Techniques for Intelligent Transportation Systems*, https://ieeexplore.ieee.org/document/7943120.
15. Dhingra, V. and Arora, A., Pervasive computing: Paradigm for new era computing, in: *2008 First International Conference on Emerging Trends in Engineering and Technology*, https://ieeexplore.ieee.org/document/4579923.

16. Tanveer, B., Guzmán, L., Engel, U.M., Effort estimation in agile software development: Case study and improvement framework. *J. Softw. Evol. Process*, 29, 11, e1862, 2017.

17. Man, T., *et al.*, A decision support system for DM algorithm selection based on module extraction. *Procedia Comput. Sci.*, 186, 529–537, 2021.

18. Anita, and Chauhan, N., Agile learning model: Self centric learning. *2014 IEEE International Conference on MOOC, Innovation and Technology in Education (MITE)*, Patiala, pp. 377–381, 2014, https://ieeexplore.ieee.org/document/7020307/references#references.

19. Merzouk, S. *et al.*, The proposition of process flow model for Scrum and extreme programming. *Proceedings of the 4th International Conference on Networking, Information Systems & Security*, 2021.

20. Anwer, F. *et al.*, Comparative analysis of two popular agile process models: Extreme programming and scrum. *Int. J. Comput. Sci. Telecommunications*, 8, 2, 1–7, 2017.

21. Azanha, A. *et al.*, Agile project management with scrum: A case study of a Brazilian pharmaceutical company IT project. *Int. J. Manage. Proj. Bus.*, 10, 1, 121–142, 2017.

22. Morampudi, N.S. and Raj, G., Evaluating strengths and weaknesses of agile Scrum framework using knowledge management. *Int. J. Comput. Appl.*, 65, 23, 1–6, 2013.

23. Lozada-Martinez, E. *et al.*, SCRUM and extreme programming agile model approach for virtual training environment design. *2019 IEEE Fourth Ecuador Technical Chapters Meeting (ETCM)*, IEEE, 2019.

24. Asri, S.A. *et al.*, Web based information system for job training activities using personal extreme programming (PXP). *J. Phys. Conf. Ser.* IOP Publishing, 953, 1, 2018.

25. Baldassarre, M.T. *et al.*, Studying test-driven development and its retainment over a six-month time span. *J. Syst. Softw.*, 176, 110937, 2021.

26. Munir, H., Moayyed, M., Petersen, K., Considering rigor and relevance when evaluating test driven development: A systematic review. *Inf. Softw. Technol.*, 56, 4, 375–394, 2014.

27. Bissi, W., Neto, A.G.S.S., Emer, M.C.F.P., The effects of test driven development on internal quality, external quality and productivity: A systematic review. *Inf. Softw. Technol.*, 74, 45–54, 2016.

28. Sandsto, R. and Reme-Ness., C., Agile practices and impacts on project success. *J. Eng. Proj. Prod. Manage.* Elsevier, 11, 3, 255, 2021.

29. Anita, and Chauhan, N., A simplest agile life cycle in an agile environment. *CSI Sponsored 7th International Conference on Software Engineering CONSEG-2013, Humanizing Software Engineering*, Pune, India, Nov 15th-17th, 2013, http://www.conseg.in/pune2013/proceedings.html.

30. Anita, and Chauhan, N., A linguistic approach for test case priortization in an agile environment. *13th Annual International Software Testing Conference*,

Crossing The Chasm, From Assurance To Confirmation, Bangalore, India, Dec. 4th-5th, 2013.

31. Anita, and Chauhan, N., A risk based story prioritization technique in an agile environment. *Int. J. Adv. Found. Res. Comput.*, 1, 7, 16–25, July–2014. http://www.ijafrc.org/issue7.html.

32. Anita, and Chauhan, N., A pattern based approach to prioritize test cases for user stories in an agile environment. *Int. J. Adv. Found. Res. Comput.*, 1, 5, 185–194, July–2014. http://www.ijafrc.org/issue5.html.

33. Anita, and Chauhan, N., An extended test case prioritization technique using script and linguistic parameters in a distributed agile environment, in: *Towards Extensible and Adaptable Methods in Computing*, S. Chakraverty, A. Goel, S. Misra, (Eds.), Springer, Singapore, 2018, https://doi.org/10.1007/978-981-13-2348-5_2.

34. Arora, A. and Chauhan, N., A regression test selection technique by optimizing user stories in an agile environment, in: *2014 IEEE International Advance Computing Conference (IACC)*, Gurgaon, pp. 1454–1458, 2014, https://ieeexplore.ieee.org/document/6779540.

35. Wei, X. *et al.*, The effectiveness of partial pair programming on elementary school students' computational thinking skills and self-efficacy. *Comput. Educ.*, 160, 104023, 2021.

36. Satratzemi, M. *et al.*, A two-year evaluation of distributed pair programming assignments by undergraduate students, in: *Research on E-Learning and ICT in Education: Technological, Pedagogical and Instructional Perspectives*, pp. 35–57, 2021.

37. Bigman, M. *et al.*, PearProgram: A more fruitful approach to pair programming, in: *Proceedings of the 52nd ACM Technical Symposium on Computer Science Education*, 2021.

38. Kuttal, S.K. *et al.*, Trade-offs for substituting a human with an agent in a pair programming context: The good, the bad, and the ugly, in: *Proceedings of the 2021 CHI Conference on Human Factors in Computing Systems*, 2021.

39. Anita, and Chauhan, N., Testing in an agile environment: A project. *International Conference on Next Generation Communication and Computing Systems (ICNGC2S-10)*, Chandigarh, India, December 25-26, 2010.

40. Dalal, S., Hooda, S., Solanki, K., Comparative analysis of various testing techniques used for aspect-oriented software system. *Indones. J. Electr. Eng. Comput. Sci.*, 12, 1, 51–60, 2018.

41. Jyoti, and Hooda, S., A systematic review and comparative study of existing testing techniques for aspect-oriented software systems. *Int. Res. J. Eng. Technol.*, 4, 05, 879–888, 2017.

42. Hooda, S., Dalal, S., Solanki, K., A systematic review of model-based testing in aspect-oriented software systems, in: *2016 3rd International Conference on Computing for Sustainable Global Development (INDIACom)*, IEEE, pp. 2944–2949, 2016.

43. Jyoti, and Hooda, S., Optimizing software testing using fuzzy logic in aspect oriented programming. *Int. Res. J. Eng. Technol.*, 4, 04, 3172–3175, 2017.

44. Dalal, S. and Hooda, S., A novel technique for testing an aspect oriented software system using genetic and fuzzy clustering algorithm, in: *2017 International Conference on Computer and Applications (ICCA)*, IEEE, pp. 90–96, 2017.

45. Dalal, S. and Hooda, S., *Test Suite Minimization using Fuzzy Clustering for Aspect-Oriented Software System Using Genetic and Fuzzy Clustering Algorithm.*

46. Dalal, S. and Hooda, S., A novel approach for testing an aspect oriented software system using prioritized-genetic algorithm (P-GA). *Int. J. Appl. Eng. Res.*, 12, 21, 11252–11260, 2017.

47. Akalin, A. *et al.*, Exploring the impact of gender bias on pair programming. *Proceedings of the 17th ACM Conference on International Computing Education Research*, 2021.

48. Kiran, V., Rani, S., Singh, P., Towards a light weight routing security in IoT using non-cooperative game models and dempster–shaffer theory. *Wirel. Pers. Commun.*, 110, 1729–1749, 2020.

49. Kaur, P., Sharma, A., Chahal, J.K., Sharma, T., Sharma, V.K., *Analysis on Credit Card Fraud Detection and Prevention using Data Mining and Machine Learning Techniques*, pp. 1–4, 2021.

50. Kiran, V., Rani, S., Singh, P., Trust based defence system for DDoS attack detection in RPL over IoT. *IJCSNS*, 18, 12, 239–245, Dec. 2018.

Vulnerability Assessment Tools for IoT: An Agile Approach

Pooja Anand* and Yashwant Singh

Department of Computer Science and Information Technology, Central University of Jammu, Jammu and Kashmir, India

Abstract

Smart services being more high-handed than ever before increased the security contemplations which faded with growing divergence in threat variants and IoT devices. To adapt with increasing IoT vulnerabilities and thus, multiplying cyber threats, security professionals need to actively work with software developers to develop more secure smart systems. Thus, to ensure long time secure systems, agile methods must be adopted to develop software projects dealing with growing vulnerabilities and threat implications. This adoption is necessary because agile methods are iterative in nature and facilitate service/product delivery in smaller batches allowing developers to add security activities pertaining software development via agile methodologies. Moreover, the reiterative aspect of this approach encourages the expansion of software that can very well cope up with growing threat variants and vulnerabilities. Thus, frequent inspections and patching in IoT firmware's/software's reduces cybersecurity risks and vulnerabilities. Motivated by the facts, this work centers around the detection of growing threat variants and vulnerabilities by applying the efficacy of agile techniques.

Keywords: IoT, vulnerabilities, tools, agile, software, applications

3.1 Introduction

Internet of Things (IoT) has brought the connectivity and communication among the day today things by linking major services like transportation,

*Corresponding author: poojaanand892@gmail.com

Susheela Hooda, Vandana Mohindru Sood, Yashwant Singh, Sandeep Dalal and Manu Sood (eds.) *Agile Software Development: Trends, Challenges and Applications*, (39–50) © 2023 Scrivener Publishing LLC

irrigation, power grids, homes, and so on with the Internet. In general, an IoT ecosystem, consists of sensors with actuators that interact with surroundings, collect information, and transfer the same to the distant users for optimum real-time operations [1], for example, controlling home appliances from anywhere at any point of time. Others include smart farming, where smart drones capture images of fields and other related information collected by on-field sensors, to further find the crop health and thus, can isolate the disease-prone zone. Moreover, with learning-based models, one can predict the crop-yield, fertilizers needed, and changing water-nutrients requirements [2]. Even natural resources are now managed efficiently by connecting the isolated environment [3]. Smart sensors also aid in predicting environmental disasters and then alerting the analysts via corresponding warning systems. Thus, in a few years only, these smart services have become an integral part of our lives. However, with such dependence we have given the contol over our lives to infant technology especially in terms of security [4].

The way smart devices are getting multiplied every day, IoT is making a lead in derivative markets. The CISCO report reveal that every second 127 smart devices are brought on the internet/web [5]. The numbers validate this, as it is seen that there is expected hike in sales of IoT devices from $ 892 billion to $ 4 trillion (2018-25). Such a big number with inherent vulnerabilities vintages a fertile land for the adversaries, validated by the threat report Unit 42, given by Palo Alto Network. In the given report, it is found that 98% IoT data traffic is in unencrypted form and around 83% medical imaging devices use outdated versions of operating systems. Security cameras tops the list with 33% security issues, then IP-based printers with 24% [6]. The statistics also stipulate that along with growing number of IoT devices, their concerning attacks are also growing in the same proportion, causing a three-fold hike in IoT attack traffic [7]. Subsequently, smart devices are now the most vulnerable doorway to get entry into any home network or an organization, as their manufacturers pass them to the markets with easy to play vulnerabilities like open ports and default passwords [8]. Numbers stipulate that Telnet and UPnP are the most exploited ports that has caused the botnet attacks by creating an army of these connected devices [9]. In addition, neglecting security aspects while developing and launching smart projects has been proven to be life-threatening [10]. It could be realized, from the first death in the self-driving car of Tesla which on getting compromised could not detect the 18-wheel truck on the highway or the malfunctioning of implanted devices in the human body by adversaries. Even by compromised on-field sensors, drones, and irrigation systems in smart farms the crop yield could be declined affecting the economy of countries [11].

Nowadays, flexile software and management have become the de facto standard in response to the growing needs of users and micro-management. With this, agile practices have been widely adopted in the IT industry so as to meet the ever-changing requirements of user, system, or product. However, the applicability of such methodologies is not only restricted to the area of information technology, as agile schemes emerged as a viable solution in accounting, state planning, construction, retail, etc. [12]. As per the statistical reports, the major application areas working on agile practices are IT with 61%, followed by marketing with 10%, retail with 8%. Figure 3.1 depicts how the agile practices can be implemented for development of IoT projects [13]. In such areas, the methodologies are being devised on the principles of the agile strategy [14]. The agile methodology works upon the philosophy that requirements evolve with time and thus, could not be gathered completely at the beginning. Also, it assures that all key stakeholders like users, developers, testing team members, sponsors, field experts, maintenance team, interfacing organizations, etc., should be involved in all the activities of the project from the day one. The other principal is requirements could be amended/updated even in the later stages of software development. The third principal assures the frequent delivery of

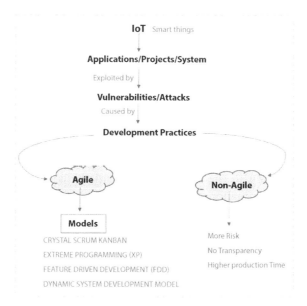

Figure 3.1 IoT with agile practices.

working software, within timespan of few weeks or months, preferably the shorter time span. Unlike other models, in an agile project, coding starts before even knowing all the requirements. The benefits of agile methodology for developing IoT solutions will lead to sustainable IoT in terms of both security and reusability [15].

3.2   Agile Methodology: SCRUM

SCRUM approach being the most popular agile practice due to its simple process has also formed its place in IoT realm. This approach is commonly used for the development of IoT applications [16]. In contrast to other agile practices, this approach also covers the management issues which could be applied to any domain. The SCRUM approach was developed by Beedle and Schwaber specifically for project management [17]. The beauty of this process lies in the fact that it overcomes the faults of almost all the traditional software development methods like waterfall model. Talking about Scrum, it works in different phases called as a sprint that has a backlog associated with it listing different user requirements. This shows it has the flexibility to add new requirements at later stages of development even. It follows the incremental approach for the development. The main features include the requirements are considered as packets, with multiple sprints, which approximately takes 30 days to complete a new sprint, involving several work units working parallelly, continues documentation and different variants of product testing during development, and every iteration with timebound of 24 hours. Then, there are demos, which are not ready products, but lent to the customer for feedback with deadlines [18].

Inspection, adaptation, and transparency are seen as the three pillars of Scrum. There are different events, roles and artifacts building the Scrum. The foremost i.e., events generally include sprint planning meetings, scrum reviews/feedbacks, daily stand-up scrum meetings, and sprint retrospectives. The main artifacts include product backlog, building sprint backlog, listing items chosen to the specific sprint and the corresponding increments, showing summation of the product backlog items of that respective sprint. The different phases of scrum include outline planning, development and the closure of the project. The outline planning is the first phase, in which we determine the general objectives to be achieved. The development phase being the second phase consists of the sprint cycle chain, with the surplus value being complimenting the system, showing the outcome for every sprint cycle. Then the final phase, i.e., the closure phase includes whereabouts of the closing of the project. These include whether we have achieved goals and requirements, matching the contract, working team and product owner, and the most important i.e., if the desired product is ready to be released.

Thus, scrum follows an incremental and reiterative process, where the growth is shown with a series of sprints produced by projects. On delivery, only prioritized features are given to the end user at the end of each sprint. The requirements are gathered by making use of product backlog, showing the idea of the product being detailed to team. In the next stage, we select the user requirements and then create sprint backlogs. It also includes agendas like daily stand-up meetings for product backlog improvement between scrum team. The main focus of the meeting is to discuss the strategies needed to enrich the development process and further elucidate the zeros and ones for the last sprint. Lastly, the solutions are devised to handle vulnerabilities in successive sprints [19].

3.3   Scrum Agile Benefits for IoT

The seamless communication is provided between people and things, owing to smart services enabled with IoT boon in 1999 and thereafter expanded threat landscape for adversaries. Thus, this grossed the attention of security experts and the research community towards dominion of securing IoT. Alongside IoT services being getting stabilized, agile methodology has been adopted widely for software development [20]. Figure 3.2 shows the benefits of applying SCRUM agile approach for developing IoT projects and vulnerability assessment tools. These benefits are discussed as under [21].

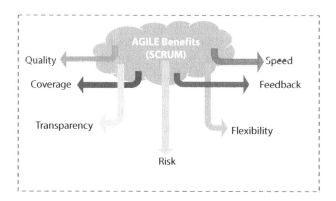

Figure 3.2 Agile benefits for IoT.

i. Quality: AM ensures quality in the versions of the product being delivered, irrespective of short time span taken for development. As the agile project undergoes successive and iterative development cycle, testing is the part of each sprint. This process can be considered as a recurring way to test the product as it matures. It undergoes different types of testing even after specific functionality is delivered. It starts with the confirmation testing, to ensure desired functionality is being delivered. Then, we have the regression testing to make sure that all old functions are performed well when new functionalities are added. Moreover, in the iterative testing, the quality assurance team take more time to execute exploratory testing on different versions before. Thus, we have a better-quality product as the complete agile process has the superior testing coverage aimed at multiple scenarios. Additionally, it provides higher visibility towards the quality and design defects in the product, and provides early addressal too in the SDLC [22].

ii. Coverage: Coverage is another relatable benefit of AM. In waterfall, exploratory testing is performed only once during the overall testing phase. But it's seen that in AM, exploratory testing is done numerous times as a part of individual sprints. Thus, a more reliable pattern is used to find both design and implementation flaws. In general, it's found that more flaws are part of the first four sprints [23].

iii. Transparency: AM ensures transparency in the entire process of providing different sprints. On the completion of a sprint, there is an exceptional session called demo, to show the ongoing deliverables to end users. As an IoT project, it's expected to have changes throughout the development phase, so the throughout active participation by product owner and stakeholders plays a vital role. This provides transparency as the client is in regular touch with all progress and the emerging risk factors with the development phase itself [24].

iv. Risk: Talking about risk, it must be identified early, so that we can respond well in time. This benefit is provided by the flexible Agile approach. It is realized from IoT projects, that the first sprint does not entirely deliver the code. This gives the space to rethink about the factors like the team capacity, modules assigned during the following sprint. Moreover, we can easily move undelivered items to the following sprints in the retrospective/grooming sessions. Grooming sessions can also be called as refinement sessions and are held during the sprint so that one can change the assigning capacity of the employed items. One can also adopt the better practices in technology for IoT as they are constantly evolving. This reduces the risk of technical solutions getting outdated, which is the major concern for IoT projects. Thus, handling such risks reduce the overall chance of project failure [25, 26].

v. Flexibility: The capacity to identify and handle such risk factors provides another main benefit, i.e., flexibility itself. To have 100% clarity about all the parameters of the project and with no flexibility to adapt changes will make the product more valuable. There must be the provisions to adapt new features/functionalities as we develop it with all the documentation of the changes included in different sprints. If the client demands different functionalities, then those should be implemented without intensely impacting the project overall. All these concerns have been resolved in Agile Scrum, as the changes are often expected. In AM proper backlogs are maintained as the product evolves [27, 28].

vi. Speed: The speed of the product when it is launched in the market for the first time is another important benefit of this methodology. It becomes more important when it comes to IoT projects, as they are evolving from constant innovation environments like smart cities, smart agriculture, e-health, smart homes, etc. This brings a little leeway for competitive intelligence while delivering an IoT product/application. As it is seen that one to launch their product first in the market becomes the market leader in that specific domain. Agile practice supports the early and regular releases which could be a decisive factor for the product's market success. Thus, the timing plays a crucial role and becomes more important for the IoT applications [29, 30].

vii. Feedback: Another important benefit of agile practice is the constant feedback. In this approach, the client gets involved from the launch of very first sprint in the development process. The client can communicate all his concerns like customer satisfaction, business value, etc. throughout the development process. The latest trends/technologies and additional needs can be incorporate after presenting the first deliverable copy. Even the structure of whole project can be refactored. Thus, agile practice is beneficial to both the client and the development team [31, 32].

3.4   Critical Factors for Implementing Agile Methodology

For implementing the agile practices in applications developed for IoT, some of the critical factors need to be addressed [33, 34], as depicted in Figure 3.3. They are as follows.

    i.   The Project Team: The project team is considered under both the categories tangible and intangible. This factor includes the size of a team, objectives of the project, and responsibilities of team members.

   ii.   The Psychological and Cultural Aspects: The psychological and cultural factors are intangible factors which are associated with the workforce of the project, like, charisma, motivation, and others. It includes proposed subcategories like teamwork, discipline, relations among team members, and the relationship they share with the working

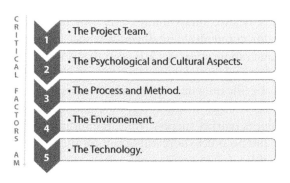

Figure 3.3 Critical factors for implementing Agile practices.

environment, profile of team-members, their attitude and individual characteristics.

iii. The Process and Method: The factors revolving around the process and method are paired up with tools, technology, and techniques that influence Scrum implementations. It includes proposed subcategories like tools, techniques, events, training, role in the team and team work.

iv. The Environment: It include factors associated with the environment of the undertaken project and the hired project team. For example, the project location in the organizational structure, customer-owner relationships, and influence of organization on the project. The following five subcategories are part of this: the conflict among business processes, synchronization among different teams, and connections with the customer, the people's influence outside the project team and external dependencies.

v. The Technology: It include factors associated with the technology and related tools used by the project team. For example, the required technical skills, waiting time for deliverables, and the average time required for implementing tasks by the project team. The following two subcategories are part of this: the consistency of team work and the opted technology required for producing functionalities [35].

3.5   Conclusion

Seeing benefits and critical factors for implementing the agile practices, many of the agile benefits can be mapped to IoT applications and project. The rigidity of other software delivery products like waterfall or V-model fails to deal with different basic requirements of such projects. Even though we are informed from very beginning when applying these methodologies, there is no room further for any change in future technology/improvement. Moreover, the client gets involved in the software development life cycle only at later stages. The difference comes in deliverables of the project as it gets splitted in different phases, with its own defined exit criterion. Bottom line, making use agile practices for IoT applications will determine these practices to be even much more flexible. As the ever changing and evolving IoT realm provides an environment for innovation. Additionally, the delivery procedure itself can be refined to make future enhancements.

The constant application of this method forms a fine-tuning process which can further improvise the delivery approach. Thus, it's feasible to apply agile practices for developing smart applications, leading towards sustainable IoT.

References

1. Rana, B., Singh, Y., Singh, P.K., A systematic survey on internet of things: Energy efficiency and interoperability perspective. *Trans. Emerg. Telecommun. Technol.*, 32, 8, e4166, 1–41, October 2020.
2. Anand, P., Singh, Y., Selwal, A., Singh, P.K., Felseghi, R.A., Raboaca, M.S., IoVT: Internet of vulnerable things? Threat architecture, attack surfaces, and vulnerabilities in internet of things and its applications towards smart grids. *Energies*, 13, 18, 1–23, 2020.
3. The Living Library, *Smart Cities–International Case Studies*, The Living Library, US, 2016, https://thelivinglib.org/smart-cities-international-case-studies/ (accessed Jan. 04, 2020).
4. Borges Amaro, L. J., Percilio Azevedo, B. W., Lopes de Mendonca, F. L., Giozza, W. F., Albuquerque, R. D. O., García Villalba, L. J., Methodological framework to collect, process, analyze and visualize cyber threat intelligence data. *Appl. Sci.*, 12, 3, 1205, 2022.
5. Comprehensive guide to IoT statistics you need to know. https://www. csoonline.com/article/2942596/127-devices-added-to-the-internet-each-second-but-congress-is-clueless-about-iot.html (accessed Jan. 21, 2021).
6. Networks, P.A., *Unit 42 IoT Threat Report*, Palo Alto Networks, North America, 2020.
7. *Cyberattacks On IOT Devices Surge 300% in 2019, 'Measured In Billions'*, Forbes, UK, 2019, https://www.forbes.com/sites/zakdoffman/2019/09/14/dangerous-cyberattacks-on-iot-devices-up-300-in-2019-now-rampant-report-claims/?sh=ccedf1589263 (accessed Jan. 21, 2021).
8. Anand, P., Singh, Y., Selwal, A., *Internet of Things (IoT): Vulnerabilities and Remediation Strategies*, pp. 1–9.
9. Anand, P., Singh, Y., Selwal, A., Singh, P. K., Ghafoor, K. Z., IVQFIoT: An intelligent vulnerability quantification framework for scoring internet of things vulnerabilities. *Expert Syst.*, 39, 5, e12829, 2022.
10. European Union Agency for Cybersecurity, *ENISA Good Practices for the Security of Smart Cars*, European Union Agency for Cybersecurity, Greece, November 2019.
11. Malhotra, P., Singh, Y., Anand, P., Bangotra, D.K., Singh, P.K., Hong, W.C., Internet of things: Evolution, concerns and security challenges. *Sensors*, 21, 5, 1–35, 2021.

12. Abrahamsson, A.P., Salo, O., Ronkainen, J., *Agile Software Development Methods: Review and Analysis*, VTT Technical Research Centre of Finland, 2002.

13. Faid, A., Sadik, M., Sabir, E., An agile AI and IoT-augmented smart farming: A cost-effective cognitive weather station. *Agriculture*, 12, 1, 35, 2021.

14. Ahmed, S., Leary, T., Wydler, G., Schultz, E., Applying agile beyond information technology and software. *Acquisition Research Symposium*, 12, 1, 35. 2021.

15. Anand, P., Singh, Y., Selwal, A., Alazab, M., Tanwar, S., Kumar, N., IoT vulnerability assessment for sustainable computing: Threats, current solutions, and open challenges. *IEEE Access*, 8, 1–1, 2020.

16. Tashtoush, Y.M. *et al.*, Agile approaches for cybersecurity systems, IoT and intelligent transportation. *IEEE Access*, 10, 1360–1375, 2022.

17. Schwaber, K., Scrum development process. In *Business object design and implementation*, pp. 117–134, Springer, London, 1997.

18. Pope, G.M., *Systemic Theoretic Process Analysis (STPA) Used for Cyber Security and Agile Software Development*, 2021.

19. Raval, D., Undavia, J., Patel, A., Agile framework based IoT application for fire detection. *Inf. Technol. Ind.*, 9, 2, 162–167, 2021.

20. Dowling, S., Schukat, M., Barrett, E., New framework for adaptive and agile honeypots. *ETRI J.*, 42, 6, 965–975, 2020.

21. Fireteanu, V., *Agile Methodology Advantages When Delivering Internet of Things Projects*.

22. Bertoli, A., Cervo, A., Rosati, C.A., Fantuzzi, C., Smart node networks orchestration: A new e2e approach for analysis and design for agile 4.0 implementation. *Sensors*, 21, 5, 1–25, 2021.

23. Puzis, R., Zilberman, P., Elovici, Y., *ATHAFI: Agile Threat Hunting And Forensic Investigation*, Arxiv, Cornell University, NY, 2020, [Online]. Available: http://arxiv.org/abs/2003.03663.

24. Hadar, E. and Hassanzadeh, A., Big data analytics on cyber attack graphs for prioritizing agile security requirements. *Proc. IEEE Int. Conf. Requir. Eng.*, September 2019, pp. 330–339, 2019.

25. Tarhan, A. and Yilmaz, S.G., Systematic analyses and comparison of development performance and product quality of incremental process and agile process. *Inf. Softw. Technol.*, 56, 5, 477–494, 2014.

26. Mohindru, V. and Singla, S., A review of anomaly detection techniques using computer vision, in: *The International Conference on Recent Innovations in Computing*, Springer, Singapore, pp. 669–677, March 2020.

27. Ariza, H. M., Silva, L. F. W., Contreras, L. A. L., Descriptive analysis of the agile methodology extreme programming (XP) for its implementation in software development. *Int. J. Eng. Res. Technol.*, 14, 10, 999–1004, 2021.

28. Mohindru, V., Vashishth, S., Bathija, D., Internet of Things (IoT) for healthcare systems: A comprehensive survey, in: *Recent Innovations in Computing. Lecture Notes in Electrical Engineering*, vol. 832, P.K. Singh, Y. Singh, M.H.

Kolekar, A.K. Kar, P.J.S. Gonçalves (Eds.), Springer, Singapore, 2022, https://doi.org/10.1007/978-981-16-8248-3_18.

29. Hoda, R., Salleh, N., Grundy, J., The rise and evolution of agile software development. *IEEE Softw.*, 35, 5, 58–63, 2018.

30. Rai, V. *et al.*, Cloud computing in healthcare industries: Opportunities and challenges, in: *Recent Innovations in Computing. Lecture Notes in Electrical Engineering*, P.K. Singh, Y. Singh, J.K. Chhabra, Z. Illés, C. Verma (Eds.), vol. 855, Springer, Singapore, 2022, https://doi.org/10.1007/978-981-16-8892-8_53.

31. Montanari, D., Bremer, J., Gendotti, A., Geynisman, M., Hentschel, S., Loew, T., ... Wu, S. Development of membrane cryostats for large liquid argon neutrino detectors. In *IOP Conference Series: Materials Science and Engineering*, vol. 101, no. 1, p. 012049, IOP Publishing, 2015, November.

32. Mohindru, V., Sharma, A., Mathur, A., Gupta, A.K., Brain segmentation using deep neural networks. *Int. J. Sens. Wirel. Commun. Control*, 11, 1, 81–88, 2021.

33. Jusoh, Y.Y. *et al.*, *Adoption of Agile Software Methodology among the SMEs Developing an IoT Applications*, 2019.

34. Duc, A.N., Jabangwe, R., Paul, P., Abrahamsson, P., Security challenges in IoT development: A software engineering perspective. *ACM Int. Conf. Proceeding Ser*, vol. Part F129907, 2017.

35. Mohindru, V., Bhatt, R., Singh, Y., Reauthentication scheme for mobile wireless sensor networks. *Sustain. Comput. Inform. Syst.*, 23, 158–166, 2019.

Interoperable Agile IoT

Bharti Rana* and Yashwant Singh

Department of Computer Science & Information Technology, Central University of Jammu, Jammu, India

Abstract

As IoT represents an omnipotent interconnection of smart objects, accomplishing compatibility among them poses a challenge for efficient and reliable communication. IoT is a blend of multiple technologies, protocols, devices, and standards. Also, the data generated from smart objects differ in their data formats and ontologies. IoT is a dynamic network requiring changes now and then. For this, agile methodologies are the best match for the IoT ecosystem ruling over the globe. Keeping in view the dynamic requirements of the pervasive network, we comprehend the agile methodologies for incremental and rapid production of products with feedback and update mechanisms. The study emphasizes on the importance of agile methodology in IoT. We highlight the functionalities of the AGILE-IoT project funded by the European Union. The five pilots set by the AGILE-IoT to actualize the agility in Smart domains by introducing a common gateway are taken into account. To achieve interoperability among the IoT components, several frameworks come into the limelight like BIG-IoT, VICINITY, BIotiope, and INTER-IoT. In our study, we have considered the INTER-IoT framework as it supports semantic, syntactic, functional, device, middleware, and network-level interoperability.

Keywords: Agile, Internet of Things, internet of everything, interoperability, heterogeneity, INTER-IoT, framework

**Corresponding author*: rana9bharti@gmail.com

Susheela Hooda, Vandana Mohindru Sood, Yashwant Singh, Sandeep Dalal and Manu Sood (eds.) *Agile Software Development: Trends, Challenges and Applications*, (51–70) © 2023 Scrivener Publishing LLC

4.1   Introduction

The term Internet of Things (IoT) is a combination of the Internet and Things. The Internet is the global interconnection of laptops, mobile phones, tablets, and computers governed by a set of communication protocols. The internet enables sending and receiving of information, connection with cloud platforms and analytics systems. On the other hand, Thing depicts any physical object, action, situation, or idea. In totality, the Internet of Things is an all-encompassing network of things i.e. alarm clocks, smart wearables, home accessories acting like living entities by computing, sensing, and actuating via embedded devices that interact remotely through the internet.

IoT is an umbrella of multiple heterogeneous communication technologies, data analytic techniques, incompatible devices, diverse frameworks, architectures, platforms, and applications [1]. The diverse applications vary from Geographic to Business and Technological to Spatial. IoT frameworks include seven-layer, five layers, and three-layer as discussed in state-of-the-art studies. The communication technologies include cellular, Low Power Wide Area Network Technologies (LPWAN), and intelligent techniques like deep learning machine learning, and artificial intelligence technologies [2]. The wide inclusion of everything instigates the heterogeneity issue in IoT ecosystems because IoT lacks standardized protocols and architectures. Moreover, the devices are manufactured by different vendors lacking standard specifications, support for protocols, and the same data formats.

Taking into account the heterogeneity in IoT, the Agile approach is of great significance due to the breakdown of a process into small parts called sprints. The sprint model aims to achieve quantifiable progress and fast evaluation thereby helping organizations to produce output in a short time where IoT implementation takes a long time [3]. The agile approach gives positive feedback to team members for investigation and adaptation of new technologies and quick decision-making [4]. Also, most IoT infrastructures are static and are unable to adapt to real-time operations. Therefore, working with an agile approach leverages more flexibility to complete the product lifecycle. The agile approach focuses on short and faster development cycles for fostering efficiency, early update, and maintenance of the existing products. Agile assists cooperation and collaboration among teams to update the technological skills regularly for short product deliverables [5]. The agile approach in IoT bridges the gap to mitigate the heterogeneity issues by performing data and protocol translation, introducing a common gateway approach, use of common APIs in every sprint. The agile approach is a potential solution to accomplish syntactic, semantic, technical, and platform interoperability in IoT.

The rest of the chapter is organized as follows: Section 4.2 discusses the agile software development process versus traditional software development followed by existing agile methodologies. Section 4.3 overviews the concept of IoT and IoE with the significance of the agile approach. Section 4.4 and 4.5 imparts knowledge about the initiatives set by the AGILE-IoT project funded by European Union for interoperability. The INTER-IoT framework for achieving several kinds of interoperability in IoT is detailed in Section 4.6. At last, the study is concluded in Section 4.7.

4.2   Agile Software Development

Agile is a small iterative methodology of software development in which the software is distributed with rapid and littler changes. The agile approach breaks the larger project into small chunks called iterations. Agile methodology is based on a continuous feedback mechanism after the completion of an iteration. The feedback facilitates inculcating more changes in the iterations and releasing the product in increments. Agile methodology aspires to release the product with incremental functionality via self-organizing teams. Thus, assists repeated customer response and correction in development as desired. Agile is committed to strict feedback cycles and continuous improvement. Agile overwhelms the difficulties tackled by the traditional "waterfall" approaches for delivering large products over long periods, during which customer necessities often change [6]. The long delivery cycle is divided into shorter phases, called sprints to ensure that smaller pieces of the product get into the market. This allows clients to give timely feedback so that the final product meets the client's needs. The agile and the traditional methodology is demonstrated in Figures 4.1 and 4.2.

Agile is a canopy term for several approaches and practices. The agile methodologies include Adaptive Software Development (ASD), Scrum, Feature Driven Development (FDD), Extreme Programming (XP),

Figure 4.1 Traditional method.

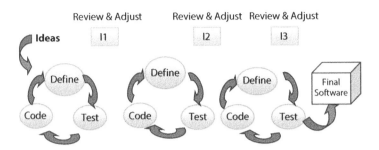

Figure 4.2 Agile functionality [6].

Dynamic Software Development Method (DSDM), and Kanban as discussed subsequently.

4.2.1 Scrum Methodology

Scrum Methodology segregates the work among 7-9 people including the Product Owner and Scrum master as demonstrated in Figure 4.3. The different phases of the work are known as sprints. The agile team comprises 2 to 6 developers, one technical lead, one scrum master, one tester, and one product owner [7]. The Scrum Master and Product owner come under Team Interface and the remaining members come under Technical Interface.

The Scrum Master [8] is the head of the team that guides other team associates to adopt agile practices. The scrum master is responsible for the close teamwork between all the roles and functions. This eliminates the occurrence of blocks and safeguards the team from any disruption to monitor the progress and processes of the company. The product owner breaks down the overall product functionality into small structures. The Product

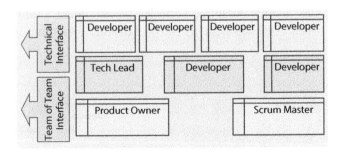

Figure 4.3 Division of team members in Scrum process [7].

Figure 4.4 Scrum process [8].

Owner deals with the product from a business perspective to define the requirements and prioritize values. The Product Owner [9] is responsible for fixing the release date and contents. Also, the product owner manages the iteration planning and holds planning meetings to consider the vital requirement first by team. This satiates the requirements of the customers that fit the definition of acceptance criteria. The regular sprint review and sprint retrospective meetings enhances the coordination among teams to bring review opportunities for the planned and progressive development and faster recovery of errors.

In the scrum process, the requirements of the users are planned. The scope and number of hours are decided by the team to do the planned task. The user requirement defines the requirements of the user in terms of functionalities. A rough estimation based on relative scale points is provided to the user during Software release forecasting. The requirement is fragmented into tasks during iteration forecasting. The User requirement is about the needs of users implemented by tasks [9]. User tasks are time-based, normally between 2 to 12 hours as illustrated in Figure 4.4. The Task on other hand is about how functionality is implemented and evaluated by employing an acceptance test. The agile team decides the completion of the task based on the entire number of tasks completed and the success rate of the acceptance test. Then, the requirement is admitted by the product owner and the product is delivered to the users.

4.2.2 Extreme Programming (XP)

Extreme Programming (XP): XP is also known as Paired Programming first proposed by Kent Beck in the 90s. The extreme agile approach is illustrated in Figure 4.5. The XP agile method aims to improve interpersonal relationships for successful software development. XP method is based on

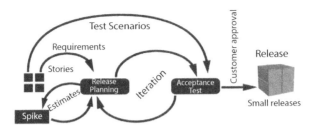

Figure 4.5 XP methodology.

team effort, and regular hands-on training of developers to foster a cordial work environment. In XP agile method, developers work in groups where one develops the programs and the other observes the program in every Sprint. During this process, developers shift their roles often. This helps in the constant monitoring of code review and feedback [10]. The code review and feedback helps to enhance the quality of code and developer skills. Extreme Programming (XP) is based on the smooth interaction between the developers and clients for regular feedback. This eases the process of implementing solutions and the acceptance of challenges with time [8]. XP works with environments including technical risks in projects whose requirements were changing frequently.

4.2.3 Adaptive Software Development (ASD)

Adaptive Software Development (ASD) was developed by Jim Highsmith and Sam Bayer in the early 1990s. ASD follows continuous adaptation i.e. adapt to change and never fight. ASD is a dynamic development process that focuses on Speculation, Collaboration, and learning. ASD commits to offering continuous learning and regular collaboration among customers and developers because of changing business requirements.

ASD is an iterative life cycle that is non-linear where cycles can be iterated and updated paralleling in presence of other executing cycles. This is in contrast with the static lifecycle that includes plan, design, and Build.

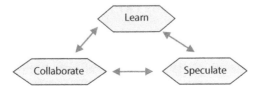

Figure 4.6 ASD methodology [8].

ASD works on the same philosophy as RAD that focuses on high quality and rapid development speed. The main characteristics of ASD are depicted in Figure 4.6 that is discussed subsequently.

1. Speculate: Speculation is the initial phase. This phase sets the objectives and goals regarding the project. The goals and objectives are finalized after a deep understanding of the limitations of the project.
2. Collaborate: This phase dealt with the coordination and communication among different teams to communicate the skills acquired by one team to the members of other teams. Through this, teams upgrade their technical skills continuously. This reduces the overhead to re-learn the skills of other team members from scratch.
3. Learn: The Learn phase includes the sequence of collaboration cycles. The collaboration cycles record the optimistic and pessimistic outcomes that have been learned. The learning stage is vital for the project's efficacy.

4.2.4   Dynamic Software Development Method (DSDM)

DSDM approach was developed by a consortium of experts and vendors for software development in the 1994 year. The software projects with the DSDM approach are associated with strict budgets and schedules. The software development using DSDM is an incremental and iterative process illustrated in Figure 4.7. DSDM assists in the early design and

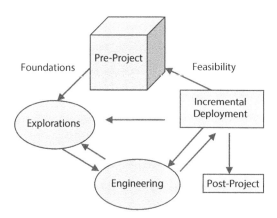

Figure 4.7 DSDM methodology.

provides a roadmap of the product deliverables by executing the incremental and iterative solution. The feedback and adaptation mechanisms are carried out throughout the process to check whether the expected benefits are being met or not. The DSDM Agile approach [7] directs organizations and project teams to alter their ways to improve their technical skills to add more value to the final product design in a short time to be released in a market.

4.2.5   Feature Driven Development (FDD)

Feature Driven Development (FDD) methodology is meant for large teams to work in collaboration as opposed to other methodologies like Scrum that could work with fewer people even. FDD methodology is given by Jeff De Luca and Peter Coad in 1997. FDD emphasizes on short cycles to produce product deliverables in a short period of approx. 2 weeks [8].

Larger Teams working with projects pose a challenge because all teams are not equally skilled, talented, and disciplined. FDD holds particular events and activities to span the communication gap while working on projects. FDD is a five-step process as shown in Figure 4.8 in which the first three are sequentially executed and the last two are iterative [11]. This agile methodology follows a series of steps that are similar to each other. FFD provides solutions to manage the teams and coding programs for the development of the complex software.

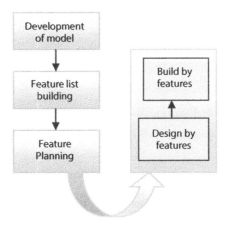

Figure 4.8 Five-stage process of feature-driven development.

4.2.6   Kanban Method

The Kanban method is given by David Anderson to mitigate the challenges of existing agile methods such as Scrum. The agile method becomes the prey of several challenges while trying to mitigate the bottlenecks of traditional waterfall methods. The 3–4-week sprint cycles become too stretched for the organizations that making it difficult to inculcate changes in the structure of the organizations that laid stress on them. Due to this, organizations are not able to fulfill the commitments of quality & scope in sprint [13]. Therefore, actualizing these methods becomes troublesome for organizations.

Kanban is characterized by the most efficient and effective production system. The Kanban method is based on the principle of "Just in Time" production of processes defined by Toyota. The cards are used to determine the material requirements in the production chain. The Kanban Method is an evolutionary method [8] that is nondisruptive for improvement and assists teams to deliver in time buckets of 2-3 weeks, get feedback faster and reduce the lead time to deliver value to the customer [12]. Kanban visualizes both the process (the workflow) and the actual work passing through that process. The motive of the Kanban method is to find blockages in the running process and its fixation cost-effectively visually.

4.3   Internet of Things (IoT)

IoT and Internet of Everything (IoE) are the buzzwords nowadays often used interchangeably. As per the Cisco definition, IoE includes interconnection among data, processes, people, and things. The IoE is an augmented term of IoT to extend the capability to include everything as connected entities. Internet of Everything is bringing enormous opportunities for organizations, communities, individuals, and communities to extract more value from the interconnection of objects, data, processes, and people. The IoE concept is illustrated in Figure 4.9. IoT refers to the interconnection of physical things only [14]. IoT is a transition of mono technology but the IoE is a transition of multiple technologies including IoT. As per Cisco's prediction, 99.9% of tangible objects that seem to be a part of the IoE are still not connected. The motive of IoE is "connecting the unconnected". These interconnections may be Machine to Machine (M2M), People to People (P2P), and Machine to People (M2P) [15].

As IoT is an umbrella of multifarious technologies, platforms, protocols, and smart devices spread across disparate locations, it becomes complex to

Figure 4.9 Internet of everything [16].

implement the full-fledged technology in a single run. Also, IoT devices are manufactured by vendors at a pace that requires different mechanisms for data translation and protocol translation. Therefore, an agile strategy is the best fit for IoT due to its adaptability and flexibility to change requirements to produce the software and hardware rapidly. The agile process focuses on user testing to get a more refined product to accomplish the goals. Agile requires constant communication to update the services thus breaking the silos between the product team and disciplines.

4.4   Agile–IoT Project for Interoperability

The Internet of Things (IoT) engrosses multiple platforms and standards due to the exponential growth in application domains. The application domains range from Consumer to Home, Transportation, Enterprises, and Industries. Each application domain is unique in the sense that needs particular devices, standards, and communication protocols [17]. Nowadays, people are more in favor of purchasing IoT solutions that target their potential customers. This approach instigates the challenge by the creation of many solution platforms supported by many developmental platforms too known as "Heterogeneity in IoT" [18]. These development platforms are dedicated to specific vendors to promote their toolsets and APIs to gain the market edge over their customers. The term "Internet of Silos" has been

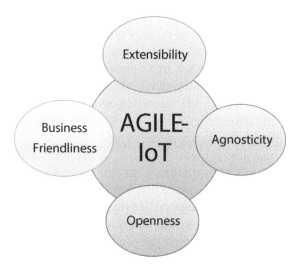

Figure 4.10 Agile-IoT pillars.

originated from the availability of a myriad number of IoT solution platforms. To address the concern, the AGILE - IoT EU [19] funded project
aims to offer an IoT Gateway based on four cornerstones i.e. extensibility,
openness, agnosticity, and business friendliness as shown in Figure 4.10.

   i)   Agnosticity: The software entities of the platform need
to be repetitively reused based on the technical background. In such a case, it is difficult to predict the type
of programming language to be used for the solution.
The programming languages used might be a combination of the languages [20] that have been compiled and
interpreted into intermediate languages (i.e. python, java).
The selection of the platform by a user based on one particular language limits its options for building a solution.
The AGILE-IoT leveraged a microservice-based solution
to support all the programming languages to maintain
the interoperability among languages [21] required by the
platform users for achieving the solution.

  ii)   Openness: Most of the platforms are proprietary in nature
[7]. The vendors make every effort for the wide publicity
of their platforms for acceptance in the market. The ubiq-
uitous network of IoT is growing rapidly where a new

device is produced every day with some unique features [22]. If the user clings on only one platform by one owner he might not avail of the other services and restricted the product to only a small portion of the market on the device level and the cloud level. To mitigate the heterogeneity, the AGILE-IoT intends to offer an open architecture for the connectivity [23] of any device to install the drivers on-demand with any public cloud.

iii) Extensibility: Extensibility could not be skipped with Openness. Acknowledging abrupt changes in IoT day by day poses a challenge to determine the availability of protocols and technologies when the new product built in the platform is released in the market [24]. This demands the APIs that would extend the prevalent architecture to provide support for new devices and cloud service providers. AGILE-IoT puts together a Docker-based architecture integrated with restful API [25] that offers an updated platform that can successfully compete with the IoT world at the same pace.

iv) Business Friendliness: When Business Friendliness is considered, is it important to know where the value is added in the built solution? Is the value is added in the new protocol or in the distinctive solution that has been implemented for customers [26]? In other words, would an organization spend time and resources in maintaining its code continuously as its competitors do? The other option is to mutualize resources among competitors to free space and time that could add value to the solution. AGILE-IoT goes with the latter option to open source the whole platform under the Eclipse Public License to mutualize the resources [4]. This strategy allows code reusability and open collaboration among IoT working groups.

4.5   Agile–IoT Project for Smart Domains

For the validity of the AGILE-IoT project, the Pilot milestone emphasizes on evaluation and testing of the features of the project by implementation in real environments. For the effective assessment of the features of the wide range of deployed IoT applications, five pilots are considered to

Figure 4.11 Pilot project milestone in AGILE-IoT project.

operate with AGILE in real scenarios as discussed subsequently. The five pilots in Agile-IoT are depicted in Figure 4.11.

a) **Pilot A – Quantified Self Application** [7]: Deploying an agile gateway in home automation for data acquisition from sensors and communication among them enables the integration with proprietary devices. Pilot A employing AGILE offers the quantified approach by providing a unique set of features for improved security, computation, and data management on edge and automated data scheduling and device management.

b) **Pilot B – Cattle monitoring using UAVs** [27]: To maintain uninterrupted surveillance in outreached areas, the AGILE gateway is embedded onto a drone for capturing data remotely from sensors deployed in the fields and on animals.

c) **Pilot C – Air Quality & Pollution monitoring** [28]: Pilot C is meant for various monitoring solutions for data processing and publishing on a cloud platform. For this purpose, the industrial version of the AGILE gateway is employed to exhibit the business and technical advantages in industrial applications.

d) **Pilot D – Enhanced Retail Services** [8]: Pilot D is meant for the localization of positions through beacons, sensors, and wireless devices. Employing AGILE provides an improved shopping experience for the customers and assists in the management of the stock.

e) **Pilot E – Port Area Monitoring for Public Safety**: This is intended to investigate the communication technologies used with gas and temperature sensors, humidity, and radioactivity sensors for data transmission in real-time in a cellular network.

4.6   INTER-IoT Framework for Interoperability

INTER-IoT [23] aims to actualize the interoperability among IoT platforms via layered-based solutions. The layered solution enables the interconnectivity between diverse platforms transparently for interoperability at a specific device, middleware, network, application, and semantics layer shown in Figure 4.12. INTER-IoT is an initiative to acquire semantic interoperability for different platforms. This methodology guides and eases

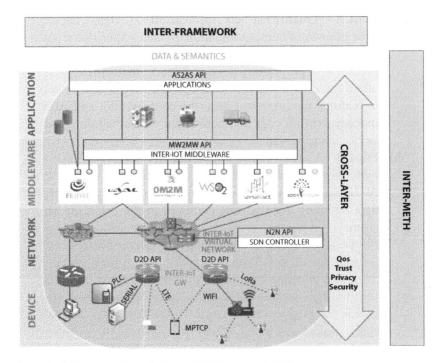

Figure 4.12 Interoperable agile INTER-IoT framework [23].

the implementation for accomplishing interoperability. INTER-IoT is an open framework [29, 30] consisting of a set of tools that can be accessed at each layer via APIs for accomplishing interoperability. INTER-IoT provides virtualization at each layer for assisting rapid working with Docker.

The INTER-IoT solution can be incorporated in any application domain where there is a necessity for collusion among devices. This framework makes it possible to form interoperable devices, services, and ecosystems for quick launch in the market [31]. In the longer run, the capability of smart applications to interact with heterogeneous environments becomes the major enabler for upcoming products and services. The layered architecture has a great potential to facilitate tight integration, extended modularity, adaptability, high performance, flexibility, and reliability for interoperability. The layer-based solution is accomplished via INTER-LAYER and each layer is dedicated to performing some interoperability functionality. Each layer is strongly coupled with other layers to provide an interface. Global interoperability is achieved by interfaces controlled by a meta-framework. The interoperable mechanisms are utilized via APIs. Cross layering enables a deep and complete integration.

4.6.1 Interoperability Aspects

Device-level (D2D): Device-level interoperability enables the involvement of multiple devices and orchestrates interworking among devices with the prevalent ones [32]. The device-level solution offers a modular gateway approach to support a wide variety of protocols and raw forwarding. The device layer comprises the physical part to control network access and the virtual portion handles the gateway functions and services. In case of connection loss, the virtual part handles the command to answer the middleware requests and APIs. The modular method used by a gateway allows the inclusion of additional services for adaptability towards specific use cases thereby enhancing the rapid progress of smart ecosystems.

Network-level (N2N): Network layer in the INTER-IoT framework maintains interoperability from network to network. The network-to-network interoperability assists in the smooth process of routing and support the mobility of smart objects. The network layer permits the offloading and roaming options for interconnectivity among platforms and gateways. The SDN and NFV [33, 34] paradigms are used for achieving interoperability by creating a virtual network along with the support of N2N API. The N2N solution mitigates the object mobility problem and supports the designing and implementation of the fully connected network.

Middleware level (MW2MW): Middleware solution in INTER-IoT is meant for the continuous discovery of resources and orchestrates IoT devices in assorted platforms. Middleware [35, 36] establishes the abstraction layer for interoperability for attaching IoT platforms with it. The modules in the middleware offer services for virtual object representation, and the creation of an abstraction layer to access features and information. The services are accessed by the generalized API. The middleware level interoperability extends the exploitation of smart objects globally in scalable and multiple platforms IoT systems.

Application and Services level (AS2AS): AS2AS allows the integration of heterogeneous services among multiple IoT platforms. This approach deals with the discovery of services, catalog maintenance, and combines services from other platforms [20]. AS2AS makes use of an integrated API in the form of the toolbox for the mapping and translation of existing heterogeneous services with the new services.

Semantics and Data level (DS2DS): DS2DS layer deals with the common translation and interpretation of data among different platforms. The translation is required among different data formats and ontologies making it difficult to communicate information among them [30]. INTER-IoT is the only framework that works on syntactic and semantic interoperability among assorted platforms. It offers the semantic translations of IoT platforms to and from a common central Ontology rather than direct platforms translations. This approach minimizes the number of semantic translations required for universal semantic interoperability. INTER-IoT is free to withstand any ontology and vocabulary. GOIoTP [37, 38] is a modular-based central ontology in INTER-IoT for all devices, services, and platforms available at http://docs.inter-iot.EU/ontology. The syntactic translations enable interoperability among heterogeneous data formats i.e. JSON, XML, etc. INTER-IoT has a potential to offer any number of solutions with a pilot approach and Core Information Model.

Cross-Layer: Cross-layer interoperability takes into account the non-functional requirements like privacy and security, trust, and quality of service metrics. INTER-IoT uses a virtualized version on each layer for easy and quick deployment [23]. Security is ensured in each layer and accessing external API is also secured through encryption, authentication, and security tokens. INTER-IoT realizes the European Data Privacy Law, especially in the case of Healthcare data which is highly sensitive.

In a nutshell, INTER-IoT supports syntactic, semantic, and functional interoperability. INTER-IoT supports cross-platform access and cross-platform domain access via AS2AS ad DS2DS solution. It also supports

Platform Independence, Platform scale Independence, and Platform Platform Interaction via D2D and MW2MW solutions. DS2DS solution offers syntactic and semantic interoperability among diverse data formats and ontologies in any platform. D2D and N2N layer takes into account the functional requirements between smart things to enable continuous connectivity in the network [39, 40].

4.7   Conclusion

IoT represents the gigantic network of tangible things that offers people-centric and industry-centric potential solutions in the current era of information and communication technology. Though the IoT brings several benefits to the forefront, it still faces so many challenges at the ground level. One such challenge is the heterogeneity in IoT. This is because there is no standardized architecture of IoT that follows the same rules and protocols. Therefore, the products manufactured by different vendors have different protocol specifications and data formats. In such a scenario, Agile methodology is of great significance. The study assists the readers with the benefits of merging Agile with IoT to cope with immediate requirements. Incorporating agile with IoT will fulfill the dynamic, abrupt requirements of IoT by using the common APIs for data and protocol translation to accomplish compatibility among platforms and devices.

References

1. Rana, B., Singh, Y., Singh, H., Metaheuristic routing: A taxonomy and energy-efficient framework for internet of things. *IEEE Access*, 9, 155673–155698, 2021.
2. Rana, B. and Singh, Y., Internet of things and UAV: An interoperability perspective, *Unmanned Aerial Vehicles for Internet of Things*, pp. 105–127, 2021.
3. Rana, B. and Yashwant, S., Duty-cycling techniques in IoT: Energy-efficiency perspective, in: *International Conference on Recent Innovations in Computing (ICRIC-2021)*, 2021.
4. Faid, A., Sadik, M. and Sabir, E., An agile AI and IoT-augmented smart farming: A cost-effective cognitive weather station. *Agriculture*, 12, 1, 35, 2022, https://doi.org/10.3390/agriculture12010035.
5. Bhatia, S., Towards the definition of IoT using agile. *J. Emerg. Technol. Innov. Res.*, 6, 11, 325–335, 2019.
6. Jusoh, Y.Y. *et al.*, *Adoption of Agile Software Methodology Among the SMEs Developing an IOT Applications*, 2019.

7. Lobov, A., Martikkala, I., Lanz, M., Ituarte, I.F., Towards the interoperability of IoT platforms platforms: A case study for data collection and data storage. *IFAC Papers Online*, 54, 1, 1138–1143, 2021.

8. Merzouk, S., Cherkaoui, A., Marzak, A., Nawal, S., IoT methodologies: Comparative study. *Procedia Comput. Sci.*, 175, 585–590, 2020.

9. What is agile methodology?-overview of agile software development and agile models. [Online]. Available: https://www.digite.com/agile/agile-methodology/. [Accessed: 14-Feb-2022].

10. Fuchs, C., Hess, T., Hess, T., *Adapting Agile Methods to Develop Solutions for the Industrial Internet of Things*, June 2017.

11. Palmer, S.R. and Felsing, J.M., Feature driven development process, in: *A Practical Guide to Feature-Driven Development,* Pearson Education, p. 271, 2002.

12. What is kanban? An overview of the kanban method. [Online]. Available: https://www.digite.com/kanban/what-is-kanban/. [Accessed: 14-Feb-2022].

13. Agile Alliance, What is BDD (behavior driven development)?. [Online]. Available: https://www.agilealliance.org/glossary/bdd/#q=~(infinite~false~- filters~(postType~(~'page~'post~'aa_book~'aa_event_session~'aa_experi- ence_report~'aa_glossary~'aa_research_paper~'aa_video)~tags~(~'bdd))~- searchTerm~'~sort~false~sortDirection~'asc~page~1). [Accessed: 14-Feb- 2022].

14. Hanes, D., Salgueiro, G., Grossetete, P., Barton, R., Henry, J., *IoT Fundamentals: Networking Technologies, Protocols and Use Cases for the Internet of Things*, vol. 3491, Cisco Press, Tamil Nadu, India, 2017.

15. Snyder, T. and Byrd, G., The internet of everything. *Computer (Long. Beach. Calif)*, 50, 6, 8–9, 2017.

16. Rana, B., A systematic survey on Internet of Things: Energy efficiency and interoperability perspective. *Trans. Emerg. Telecommun. Technol.*, Wiley, 32, 1–41, August 2020.

17. Karunanithy, K. and Velusamy, B., Cluster-tree based energy-efficient data gathering protocol for industrial automation using WSNs and IoT. *J. Ind. Inf. Integr.*, 19, 100156, April 2020.

18. Patel, K., Vyas, S., Pandya, V., IoT: Leading challenges, issues, and explication using latest technologies. *2019 3rd Int. Conf. Electron. Commun. Aerosp. Technol*, pp. 757–762, 2019.

19. Krief, P., Vecchio, M., Menychtas, A., AGILE-IoT: More than just another IoT project. Eclipse Foundation, 2019.

20. Mesmoudi, Y., Lamnaour, M., El Khamlichi, Y., Tahiri, A., Touhafi, A., Braeken, A., A middleware based on service oriented architecture for heterogeneity issues within the internet of things (MSOAH-IoT). *J. King Saud. Univ. Comput. Inf. Sci.*, 32, 1108–1116, 2018.

21. Maddikunta, P.K.R., Gadekallu, T.R., Kaluri, R., Srivastava, G., Parizi, R.M., Khan, M.S., Green communication in IoT networks using a hybrid optimization algorithm. *Comput. Commun.*, 159, 97–107, April 2020.

22. Zhu, X.N., Peko, G., Sundaram, D., Piramuthu, S., Blockchain-based agile supply chain framework with IoT. *Inf. Syst. Front. ACM*, 563–578, February 2021.

23. Arne, *Advancing IoT Platforms Interoperability*, River Publishers, Denmark, Netherlands, 2018.

24. Lee, C., Nkenyereye, L., Sung, N., Song, J., Towards a blockchain-enabled IoT platform using oneM2M standards. *9th Int. Conf. Inf. Commun. Technol. Converg. ICT Converg. Powered by Smart Intell. ICTC 2018*, pp. 97–102, 2018.

25. Blackstock, M. and Lea, R., IoT interoperability: A hub-based approach. *2014 Int. Conf. Internet Things, IoT 2014*, pp. 79–84, 2014.

26. Khaled, A.E., Interoperable communication framework for bridging RESTful and topic-based communication in IoT. *Futur. Gener. Comput. Syst*, 2018.

27. Marchese, M., Moheddine, A., Patrone, F., IoT and UAV integration in 5G hybrid terrestrial-satellite networks. *Sensors*, 19, 1–19, 2019.

28. Kaur, P., Singh, P., Singh, K., Air pollution detection using modified triangular mutation based particle swarm optimization. *Int. J. Eng. Technol.*, 6, 2005–2015, 2019.

29. Inter-IoT | IoT-EPI. [Online]. Available: https://iot-epi.eu/project/inter-iot/. [Accessed: 17-Feb-2022].

30. Mohindru, V., Bhatt, R., Singh, Y., Reauthentication scheme for mobile wireless sensor networks. *Sustain. Comput. Inform. Syst.*, 23, 158–166, 2019.

31. Inter-IoT-Interhare (UPF. [Online]. Available: https://www.upf.edu/web/interhare/inter-iot. [Accessed: 17-Feb-2022].

32. Konduru, V.R. and Bharamagoudra, M.R., *Challenges and Solutions of Interoperability on IoT*, pp. 1–5, 2017.

33. Mohindru, V., Singh, Y., Bhatt, R., Securing wireless sensor networks from node clone attack: A lightweight message authentication algorithm. *Int. J. Inf. Comput. Secur.*, 12, 2-3, 217–233, 2020.

34. Kim, Y., Nam, J., Park, T., Scott-Hayward, S., Shin, S., SODA: A software-defined security framework for IoT environments. *Comput. Netw.*, 163, 13, 2019.

35. Mohindru, V. and Garg, A., Security attacks in internet of things: A review, in: *The International Conference on Recent Innovations in Computing*, Springer, Singapore, pp. 679–693, March 2020.

36. Pramukantoro, E.S., Bakhtiar, F.A., Aji, B., Pratama, R., Middleware for network interoperability in IoT. *Int. Conf. Electr. Eng. Comput. Sci. Informatics*, October 2018, pp. 499–502, 2018.

37. Mohindru, V., Vashishth, S., Bathija, D., Internet of things (IoT) for healthcare systems: A comprehensive survey, in: *Recent Innovations in Computing. Lecture Notes in Electrical Engineering*, vol. 832, P.K. Singh, Y. Singh, M.H. Kolekar, A.K. Kar, P.J.S. Gonçalves, (Eds.), Springer, Singapore, 2022, https://doi.org/10.1007/978-981-16-8248-3_18.

38. *Generic Ontology for IoT Platforms*, Systems Research Institute, Polish Academy of Sciences, March 2018, [Online]. Available: https://inter-iot. github.io/ontology/. [Accessed: 17-Feb-2022].
39. Mohindru, V. and Singh, Y., Node authentication algorithm for securing static wireless sensor networks from node clone attack. *Int. J. Inf. Comput. Secur.*, 10, 2-3, 129–148, 2018.
40. Mohindru, V., Singh, Y., Bhatt, R., Hybrid cryptography algorithm for securing wireless sensor networks from node clone attack. *Recent Adv. Electr. Electron. Eng.*, 13, 2, 251–259, 2020.

Functional and Non-Functional Requirements in Agile Software Development

S. Saroja*[1] and S. Haseena[2]

[1]Department of Computer Applications, NIT Trichy, Tiruchirappalli, Tamil Nadu, India
[2]Department of Information Technology, Mepco Schlenk Engineering College, Sivakasi, Tamil Nadu, India

Abstract

Requirements analysis is an important step in assessing whether a system or software project will succeed. The most prevalent types of requirements are functional and non-functional requirements. The essential characteristics that the system should deliver that the end-user specifically demands are known as functional requirements. Non-functional requirements are the minimum requirements that the system must meet in order to meet the project contract's requirements. The importance of these characteristics, as well as the extent to which they are implemented, varies from project to project. In Agile Software Development (ASD), functional requirements are prioritized, while non-functional requirements are neglected, resulting in worse software quality and higher customer complaints. The stories of non-functional requirements are examined, and acceptance parameters are defined, in order to solve these quality challenges. It is also essential to evaluate the developed system against the desires of the customer to increase customer satisfaction. The proposed chapter lays out the various ways of gathering functional and non-functional requirements and testing them in the context of agile software development.

Keywords: Functional requirements, non-functional requirements, agile, customer, quality

*Corresponding author: activeroja@gmail.com

Susheela Hooda, Vandana Mohindru Sood, Yashwant Singh, Sandeep Dalal and Manu Sood (eds.)
Agile Software Development: Trends, Challenges and Applications, (71–86) © 2023 Scrivener
Publishing LLC

5.1   Introduction

A good user requirement process aids in the development of what the user truly needs [1, 2]. So, we're aware that many users, consumers, or clients don't have a clear understanding of what they want. They are unable to express or foresee what they really mean. As a result, a good user requirement process [3, 4] will assist us in taking what is on their minds and constructing exactly what they were looking for. The second benefit is that it aids in the development of a mutual vision among all product stakeholders. So, whatever the client or user had in view, what they wanted to construct, everyone understands what we're aiming to do [5, 6]. This is accomplished in the Agile approach by two main factors. The first is to encourage interaction, and the second is to be flexible with the changing requirements. As a result, rather than collecting all user wants in one shot, make face-to-face interaction as the primary mode of communication and then enable the process to uncover them. So, in terms of discussion, the agile principles urge that business developers collaborate on the development process, as well as face-to-face interaction amongst team members. As a result, one of the challenges with document-based requirements communication is resolved. The Agile Model aids in the design and release of software in a unified, integrated manner that spans all development phases, artifact kinds, responsibilities, and product lines. Using the appropriate tools contributes to a sophisticated, efficient way of developing software in the agile paradigm. As a result, costs are reduced, productivity is increased, and team engagement is expedited. The agile Software Development Life Cycle appears to be similar to a regular Software Development Life Cycle on the surface, but digging deeper reveals that this is not the case. The responsibilities that people play in the agile Software Development Life Cycle are significantly more robust than on traditional projects since it is extremely collaborative, iterative, and incremental. In the traditional software development world, a business analyst would produce a requirements model, which would then be passed on to an architect, who would create design models, which would then be passed on to a programmer, who would write programs, which would then be passed on to a tester, and so on. In an agile project, developers work cooperatively with constituents to identify their requirements, then pair up and develop and evaluate their solution, which is then delivered to the stakeholder for constant feedback. Agile developers are contextualizing specialists with full life cycle expertise, rather than specialists passing artifacts to one another and thereby injecting errors at every step along the process. Agile developers approach requirements like a sorted stack, extracting only enough work from it for the current iteration (iterations/sprints in Agile are typically 2-4 weeks long, but this can vary according to team and application being developed). The system is demoed to the stakeholders at the end of each iteration to ensure that the work that the team pledged to execute at the start of the iteration was completed.

"Our highest priority is to satisfy the customer through early and continuous delivery of valuable software" is one of the Key Principles followed in Agile Software Development (ASD). As a result, in the case of ASD, Customer satisfaction remains the primary priority. It is important to meet both functional and non-functional requirements given by the client as part of the project's service level agreement in order to obtain customer satisfaction.

5.2   Agile Requirements Gathering

Agile requirement distinguishes collecting from other types of requirements gathering. The gathering, assessment, and approval of precise requirements are emphasized in traditional Waterfall projects. Requirements that have been approved are unlikely to alter. Change requests are frequently expensive and inconvenient. This requirements paradigm is simply not adaptable enough for Agile development. Gathering requirements from consumers and stakeholders is a difficult undertaking that requires more than simply asking them what they want from your system. This is owing to the fact that most of the stakeholders are unaware of all of their requirements and design possibilities. Because they are so focused on the current issue, their technical expertise and vision are limited. Furthermore, there is no one requirement gathering technique that will assist the agile team in eliciting a complete set of needs that will fill all gaps and pass validation [7].

In an Agile methodology, the product owner or the customer begins by producing a huge number of cards with extremely high-level functionality of what they need in front of the entire development team. Then, the team will sort the cards based on the priority of the functionality. The higher the importance of the functionality, then the least rank will be assigned. During the discussion time of each card, "What exactly is it that you require? Okay, I see what you're saying. Let's sketch this out... this is how we'll construct it. This is how it is going to look." As a result, this in-depth discussion of each card establishes a shared understanding between the two parties while also refining the specifics of the functionality they desire.

Then the next important thing is confirmation, which is where the two parties: the client and the company basically write down what they agreed on. So, after the functionality is complete, what criteria (acceptance criteria) will they use to declare it complete? As a result, they are able to comply, as they have a contract (service level agreement) or a mutual understanding that this is exactly what would be built. These are also known as the 3 C's involved in the development of user stories. The card, the conversation, and the confirmation are the 3 C's playing a vital role in the user story's development [8].

5.3   Types of Requirements

There are numerous requirements for software product qualities and quality, as well as information systems. They can, however, be split into only two types: functional and non-functional requirements as given in Figure 5.1. It is indeed essential to make a difference among the two.

Functional requirements specify what must be implemented in a system or product, as well as what actions users must do in response to the development.

Non-functional requirements explain how a system or software product operates, as well as what traits and characteristics it possesses [9].

Functional requirements specify a function that a system or system element must be capable of completing and are documented in a variety of ways. The system's behavior as it pertains to its functionality is described in the functional requirements.

Functional requirements should be written in plain English so that they are easily understood. User Registration, business logic like the search

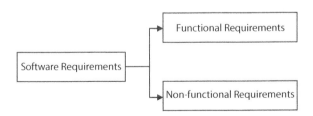

Figure 5.1 Types of requirements.

function, asset tracking, certification requirements, logging, and so on are examples of functional requirements. Functional requirements enable us to check whether the application delivers all of the functionalities expected by the user for improved customer satisfaction. They also facilitate project management by supporting tasks, activities, and user goals.

Functional requirements can be expressed in a variety of modalities. The most popular method is to document them in text form and the document is also called a Software Requirement Specification (SRS) document. Use cases, models, prototypes, user stories, Scenarios, Graphical representations, Mathematical representations, and diagrams are examples of other formats for preparing functional requirements.

Non-functional requirements have a little or zero influence on the functionality of the software. They can be requirements that define the parameters that can be used to determine the performance rather than specific system characteristics. Aesthetics, convenience, availability, privacy, storage, affordability, adaptability, configuration, productivity, legislation or regulatory requirements, and so on are a few examples of non-functional requirements.

The quality of product is influenced by non-functional constraints. The system's overall properties, performance, and capabilities that influence the user's interaction are defined in these criteria. They improve client satisfaction while keeping costs down. Non-functional requirements ensure that the software system complies with all legislation and regulations. Non-functional requirements have an impact on the system's performance rather than its functionality. For a well-performing product, at least some of the non-functional requirements must always be met.

Non-functional requirements aid in the measurement of a system's success, hence they must be quantifiable. Both qualitative and quantitative measures are required. For example, you can need that a system should be ready to support the future extension. That's a qualitative requirement but in order to make it quantitative as well. Within the next two years, there may be a demand for the system to handle a minimum of 20,000 users at the same time.

Focusing on quantitative goals has the advantage of being easily assessed and allowing the company and the client to agree on what success looks like.

Table 5.1 compares the functional requirements with the non-functional requirements.

Table 5.1 Functional versus non-functional requirements.

Functional requirements	Non-functional requirements
The understanding of the system's functions is aided by functional requirements.	They aid in the comprehension of the system's performance.
Functional requirements must be met for the system to be in working condition.	Non-functional requirements, on the other hand, are not required; they are also called optional requirements or add on-s for the system being developed.
They're simple to define.	It is a little bit complex when compared to the functional requirement.
They describe the vital functions of the product.	They describe how a product works instead of what.
It focuses predominantly on the needs of the user.	It focuses on the user's expectations and experience.
It aids in the testing of the software's capabilities.	It aids in the testing of the software's performance rather than the functionality.
The end-user, client, the customer plays a vital role in specifying these specifications.	Software developers, architects, and technical people are the main sources for collecting these criteria.
Functional testing includes API testing, system testing, and integration testing, among other things.	Non-functional testing includes usability, performance, stress, and security, among other things.
Functional requirements include searching a book by author name/title/publisher/year etc. in a library management system.	Non-functional requirements include things like color, look and feel, speed.
These specifications are critical to the system's operation.	These aren't necessarily the most necessary prerequisites, but they're always nice to have.
Completing functional requirements allows the system to function regardless of whether or not non-functional requirements are met.	However, the system will not function with solely non-functional requirements.

5.4   Functional Requirement Gathering

For the purpose of gathering requirements in agile, it is preferable to employ a multi-faceted strategy [10]. The approaches listed below [11–17] can be used to supplement the functional requirements gathering process.

- Conduct Interviews – Interviews with a varied and representative cross-section of the system's stakeholders are required. Interviewees should be asked open-ended questions from which specific data can be extracted. Follow-up inquiries that are useful either delve down for more information or lift up for a larger picture of the situation.
- Circulate Questionnaires or Surveys – It's a useful tool for identifying underlying requirements that stakeholders may not be aware of but that are critical to a successful design. This will be handy for concurrent follow-up with multiple stakeholders.
- Observe Users – Observing end-users as they go about their daily tasks is one of the most effective ways to determine what they truly require. It is possible to observe users passively or actively. Active observation deals with asking questions while watching them. This is the most efficient way to learn about an existing process. The essential takeaways at the end of user observation include keeping track of the actions and activities that occur while observing users and noting the issues those users have with the current strategy.
- Analyze Existing System Documents – Examining the present system's system-level documentation, such as SRS (Software Requirement Specification), Design Documents, Test Plans, Test Reports, and user manuals, will help identify where the business needs are not being addressed. The knowledge gathered from document analysis can aid in the formulation of new questions and the assessment of the requirement set's completeness.
- Workshops – Allow plenty of time for workshops so that participants can hear opposing points of view and explain why they believe what they believe. To obtain a consensus and certify the final requirements, all inconsistencies or conflicts must be resolved. These actions are necessary to ensure

that the produced system serves the demands of all users and stakeholders, not just the most vocal.

- Brainstorming – Conduct brainstorming sessions in which each component of the system gets individual focus. Investigate diverse what-if scenarios and out-of-the-box ideas. The overall goal is to deviate from the conventional norms. Consider novel ways to push the limits of what's possible. Whiteboards, mind mapping software and empathy maps are all useful tools for brainstorming sessions.
  - Role-play – Role-playing helps to ensure that all users' requirements are addressed. Different people perform the roles of various user categories in a role-playing session. Interaction between the various roles aids in the examination of specific system requirements from diverse viewpoints, as well as the generation of new ideas and conversations. Role-playing is, in effect, an additional brainstorming approach. It's a good method to learn how the different components of the system must work together to support the overall process.
- Use Cases and Scenarios – The use cases are the system's unique, individual business goals. They explain the numerous external entities that interact with the system in order to fulfill the corporate objectives. Use cases are comprehensive list of tasks that must be completed during a process. Scenarios, usually referred to as user stories, are similar to use cases in that they define how the system will carry out a process in order to accomplish a business goal. They take the form of a story rather than a list. Use cases and scenarios can be used to test the system's features and functional requirements in a variety of circumstances. They can also assist in identifying potential exclusions and boundary constraints.
- Focus Groups – The goals of the focus group are to make the participants express their demands, assist in the software development process, and provide feedback on your product. External stakeholders are usually involved in the process. Many systems engineers and business analysts are wary of relying on focus groups to acquire requirements. Meetings can be controlled by people who are loud and have certain agendas. These sessions may become ineffective if there are significant differences in needs and features. Focus groups,

on the other hand, can be incredibly beneficial for validating and finalizing requirements.

- Prototyping – End users and other stakeholders frequently lack a clear understanding of what they really desire. They don't have a good understanding of what's doable in the majority of circumstances. However, if you can give them something to try, they will usually be able to tell you what they like and don't like about it. Prototyping is used to solve this problem. Prototyping allows users to explore various ideas for their order to solve the issues. Using today's fast-paced prototyping tools, developers may quickly create a large number of interactive mock-ups for consumers to check out. The procedure is iterative after the initial mock-up has been built. Users can help you quickly discover what will please them using modern prototyping technologies, which make it easier for developers to adjust the prototype on the go. It's thus a simple affair to reverse engineer the criteria that describe the accepted functionality based on that functioning model.

5.5   Non-Functional Requirement Gathering

The main important challenge in agile requirement engineering includes collecting non-functional requirements in addition to changing requirements, and improper communication [18]. It is due to the fact of concentrating more on functional requirements and giving less priority to non-functional requirements [19, 20]. Due to this issue, the developed system possesses inadequate quality [21] and hence leads to poor customer satisfaction [22]. Hence, the following approaches listed below can be used to supplement the requirements gathering process [23–27] in collecting non-functional requirements.

Independent User Story – Non-Functional Requirements are expressly stated in specific technical (user) stories. This implies that the sprint's development and testing are handled in-house. Regression testing is likely to cover this to guarantee that no changes have an impact and that the application as a whole is validated.

Here are several examples:

- As a customer, I want the portal to be available 99.999 percent of the time when I sign in/sign up using the domain name or IP address of the portal so that I can use it to check the status of stock prices all the time.

- As a team head, I want the display panel to be able to fit on huge wall-mounted monitors, workstations, tablets, note-pads, and mobile devices.
- As a marketing lead, I require this website to be available in multiple regional languages in order to attract clients from multiple states and localities.

Each of these stories communicates a constraint and receives the attention it deserves. However, the technical story may be overshadowed by more appealing user-centric features. If this is left until the end of the development phase, the benefits of early detection of the Non Functional Requirement limitation, as well as the benefits of early development, may be negated.

Acceptance criteria – the set of prerequisites for a software product to be accepted by a client, investor, or other participants who may be directly or indirectly benefitted by the developed system. Non Functional Requirements can also be expressed as part of acceptance criteria. The effort spent on solving Non Functional Requirements may not be apparent to stakeholders in circumstances where the constraint is acknowledged as part of the acceptance criteria. A single acceptance criterion, for example, does a lot of the work required at the framework or architectural level. A user story with a few relatively easy features but integrating a check, such as adherence to multiple time zones, may require more effort and time to complete.

As an example, once a user has successfully opened the home page of the portal, the language selection capability should be displayed at the top right corner with auto-focus, and hence the user is allowed to choose the language first prior to the registration process.

Acceptance Criteria for registration page:

- Alphanumeric characters should be accepted in the user nametext box (No special characters are allowed).
- The length of the user name should be between 5 and 15.
- Password should be a mix of uppercase characters, lowercase characters, numbers, and special characters.
- The length of the password should be between 8 and 15.
- To the bottom of the text boxes, there should be a register button.

Within 10 seconds after clicking the register button, the system should respond. (Non-functional Requirement)

Maintain a Checklist – Checklist of required team responsibilities to ensure that only completely finished features are released, not just in terms of usability but also in terms of quality aspects (i.e., Non-functional Requirement). The benefit of including Non-functional Requirement in the checklist is that it keeps Non-functional Requirement visible to and responsive by the entire group as the increments are created. For a quality feature to be specified in the checklist, it must be generally applicable to the application, for example, Portal access in multiple regional languages, Availability of portal for 24 * 7 * 365.

Regression testing – Regression testing is used to identify any unforeseen impacts (such as new or re-opened vulnerabilities) of code updates and alterations made during updated user stories. This procedure is also achieved through the combination of the 'hardened sprint' to guarantee that the application is ready to be used as a whole. It provides a final, but realistic, opportunity to stick Non-functional Requirements to the test. The stage could be a good moment for ethical hacking specialists to arrive on the scene and do independent specialized testing in addition to the basic functional and non-functional checks [28].

To determine which of the three ways is best for gathering non-functional needs, evaluate the ease of use, the time and cost involved, and the requirement's relevance throughout the entire application [29].

It is preferable to include a non-functional requirement in the checklist [30] if it is very straightforward and easy to comprehend, requires very little time and effort, and pertains to all user stories, or is common to the entire application.

It's best to specify a requirement as Acceptance Criteria if it's simple and well understood and incurs less time and money, but it's not common to the entire application and only pertains to certain user stories. Because the Acceptance Criteria play a role of prerequisites of acceptance that must be met before a backlog item is considered acceptable, it must be minimal. It must be something that we can design and test rapidly in order to have quick feedback mechanisms [31].

It may be better to treat highly complex non-functional requirements as a separate item, such as a User Story or a technological accelerator [32, 33]. The team can explore and construct the application iteratively using this technique for non-functional requirements [34, 35].

5.6   Testing Functional and Non-Functional Requirements

TDD is a software development practice in which test cases are built to explicitly specify and evaluate how the code will behave. To put it differently, test cases for each component are first constructed and evaluated, and if the test fails, new code is written to pass the test, leading in simple and fault free code [36, 37].

Developing tests for each individual function of an application is the first phase in the test driven development approach. Developers are asked to write new code only in the case of an automated test fails, according to the TDD methodology. The key to developing a minimal viable product is to test both functional and nonfunctional requirements continuously throughout iterations [38].

TDD has the advantage of allowing the developers to write software in small chunks. It's significantly more efficient than trying to develop code in large chunks. Consider adding some new functional code for a program, compiling it, and testing it. There's a good chance that faults in the new code may cause tests to fail. If we have just created few new lines of code instead of some higher numbers like one thousand LOC, it's far easier to detect and repair those bugs [39, 40]. The corollary is that the faster your compiler and regression test suite are, the more appealing it is to take small moves. Before recompiling and rerunning tests, usually it is suggested to add a few additional lines of functional code, usually less than ten. TDD shortens the programming feedback loop. By following TDD approach, it is easy to achieve high quality in the system development.

5.7   Conclusion and Future Scope

This chapter highlighted the role of the requirement gathering process involved in agile software development. The list of methods applicable for collecting both functional and non-functional requirements is also discussed. Non-functional requirements are receiving increasing attention from the software development community and stakeholders. However, the organization and the development team need a lot of effort to accomplish all the non-functional requirements. Hence, the future interest could be in suggesting effective strategies for achieving all non-functional requirements.

References

1. Lauesen, S., IT project failures, causes and cures. *IEEE Access*, 8, 72059–72067, 2020.
2. Dreesen, T., Diegmann, P., Binzer, B., Rosenkranz, C., Journey towards agility—A retro-and prospective review, in: *Proc. 52nd Hawaii Int. Conf. Syst. Sci*, pp. 6950–6959, 2019.
3. Wagner, S., Méndez Fernández, D., Kalinowski, M., Felderer, M., Agile requirements engineering in practice: Status quo and critical problems. *CLEI Electron. J.*, 21, 1, 15, Apr. 2018.
4. Alsaqaf, W., Daneva, M., Wieringa, R., Quality requirements in large-scale distributed agile projects—A systematic literature review, in: *Proc. Int. Working Conf. Requirement Eng., Found. Softw. Qual.*, pp. 219–234, Springer, Cham, Switzerland, 2017.
5. Charette, R.N., The biggest IT failures of 2018, 2018. Accessed: Jan. 21, 2021. [Online]. Available: https://spectrum.ieee.org/riskfactor/computing/it/it-failures-2018-all-the-old-familiar-faces.
6. Kolf, F. and Kerkmann, C., Lidl software disaster another example of Germany's digital failure, 2018. [Online]. Available: https://www.handelsblatt.com/english/companies/programmed-for-disasterlidl-software-disaster-another-example-of-germanys-digitalfailure/23582902.html.
7. Franch, X., Gómez, C., Jedlitschka, A., López, L., Martínez-Fernández, S., Oriol, M., Partanen, J., Data-driven elicitation, assessment and documentation of quality requirements in agile software development, in: *Proc. Int. Conf. Adv. Inf. Syst. Eng*, pp. 587–602, Springer, Cham, Switzerland, 2018.
8. Boehm, B., Rosenberg, D., Siegel, N., Critical quality factors for rapid, scalable, agile development, in: *Proc. IEEE 19th Int. Conf. Softw. Qual., Rel. Secur. Companion (QRS-C)*, pp. 514–515, Jul. 2019.
9. Kopczyńska, S., Ochodek, M., Nawrocki, J., On importance of nonfunctional requirements in agile software projects—A survey, in: *Integrating Research and Practice in Software Engineering*, pp. 145–158, Springer, Cham, Switzerland, 2020.
10. Saltz, J., Anderson, E., Sutherland, A., Introduction to the minitrack on agile and lean: Organizations, products and development, in: *Proc. 54th Hawaii Int. Conf. Syst. Sci*, pp. 5423–5424, 2021.
11. Alsaqaf, W., Daneva, M., Wieringa, R., Agile quality requirements engineering challenges: First results from a case study, in: *Proc. ACM/IEEE Int. Symp. Empirical Softw. Eng. Meas. (ESEM)*, pp. 454–459, Nov. 2017.
12. Sachdeva, V., Requirements prioritization in agile: Use of planning poker for maximizing return on investment, in: *Information Technology—New Generations*, pp. 403–409, Springer, Cham, Switzerland, 2018.
13. Zamudio, L., Aguilar, J.A., Tripp, C., Misra, S., A requirements engineering techniques review in agile software development methods, in: *Computational Science and Its Applications*, pp. 683–698, Springer, Cham, Switzerland, 2017.

14. Schön, E.-M., Winter, D., Escalona, M.J., Thomaschewski, J., Key challenges in agile requirements engineering, in: *Proc. Int. Conf. Agile Softw. Develop*, pp. 37–51, Springer, Cham, Switzerland, 2017.

15. Heck, P. and Zaidman, A., A systematic literature review on quality criteria for agile requirements specifications. *Softw. Qual. J.*, 26, 1, 127–160, Mar. 2018.

16. Curcio, K., Navarro, T., Malucelli, A., Reinehr, S., Requirements engineering: A systematic mapping study in agile software development. *J. Syst. Softw.*, 139, 32–50, May 2018.

17. Méndez Fernández, D., Wagner, S., Kalinowski, M., Felderer, M., Mafra, P., Vetrò, A., Conte, T., Naming the pain in requirements engineering. *Empir. Softw. Eng.*, 22, 5, 2298–2338, 2017. [Online]. Available: https://www.researchgate.net/profile/Daniel-MendezFernandez.

18. Jurca, G., Hellmann, T.D., Maurer, F., *Agile User-Centered Design*, p. 111, Wiley, Hoboken, NJ, USA, 2018.

19. Jarzębowicz, A. and Poniatowska, K., Towards a lightweight approach for the evaluation of requirements engineering impact on other IT project areas, in: *Integrating Research and Practice in Software Engineering*, pp. 171–186, Springer, Katarzyna, 2020.

20. Weichbroth, P., Delivering usability in IT products: Empirical lessons from the field. *Int. J. Softw. Eng. Knowl. Eng.*, 28, 7, 1027–1045, Jul. 2018.

21. Younas, M., Jawawi, D.N.A., Shah, M.A., Mustafa, A., Awais, M., Ishfaq, M.K., Wakil, K., Elicitation of nonfunctional requirements in agile development using cloud computing environment. *IEEE Access*, 8, 209153–209162, 2020.

22. Dorton, S.L., Maryeski, L.R., Ogren, L., Dykens, I.T., Main, A., A wargame-augmented knowledge elicitation method for the agile development of novel systems. *Systems*, 8, 3, 27, Aug. 2020.

23. Shafiq, M., Zhang, Q., Akbar, M.A., Khan, A.A., Hussain, S., Amin, F.-E., Khan, A., Soofi, A.A., Effect of project management in requirements engineering and requirements change management processes for global software development. *IEEE Access*, 6, 25747–25763, 2018.

24. Alhuseini, M.U. and Olama, M.M., 5G service value chain and network slicing framework using ecosystem modeling, agile delivery, and userstory automation. *IEEE Access*, 7, 110856–110873, 2019.

25. Rigby, D.K., Sutherland, J., Noble, A., Agile at scale. *Harv. Bus. Rev.*, 96, 3, 88–96, 2018.

26. Kišš, F. and Rossi, B., Agile to lean software development transformation: A systematic literature review, in: *Proc. Federated Conf. Comput. Sci. Inf. Syst*, pp. 969–973, Sep. 2018.

27. CollabNet, V., *13th Annual State of Agile Report*, 2019, [Online]. Available: https://stateofagile.com/.

28. Behutiye, W., Karhapää, P., Costal, D., Oivo, M., Franch, X., Non-functional requirements documentation in agile software development: Challenges and solution proposal, in: *Proc. Int. Conf. Product Focused Softw. Process Improvement*, pp. 515–522, Springer, Cham, Switzerland, 2017.

29. López, L., Behutiye, W., Karhapää, P., Ralyté, J., Franch, X., Oivo, M., Agile quality requirements management best practices portfolio: A situational method engineering approach, in: *Int. Conf. Product-Focused Softw. Process Improvement*, pp. 548–555, 2017.

30. Sachdeva, V. and Chung, L., Handling non-functional requirements for big data and IOT projects in scrum, in: *Proc. 7th Int. Conf. Cloud Comput. Data Sci. Eng.*, pp. 216–221, Jan. 2017.

31. Medeiros, J., Vasconcelos, A., Goulão, M., Silva, C., Araäjo, J., An approach based on design practices to specify requirements in agile projects, in: *Proc. Symp. Appl. Comput.*, pp. 1114–1121, Apr. 2017.

32. Younas, M., Jawawi, D.N., Ghani, I., Kazmi, R., Non-functional requirements elicitation guideline for agile methods. *J. Telecommun. Electron. Comput. Eng.*, 9, 3–4, 137–142, Oct. 2017.

33. Ramos, F., Costa, A.A.M., Perkusich, M., Almeida, H., Perkusich, A., A non-functional requirements recommendation system for scrum-based projects, in: *Proc. 30th Int. Conf. Softw. Eng. Knowl. Eng.*, pp. 148–149, Jul. 2018.

34. Ionita, D., van der Velden, C., Ikkink, H.-J.K., Neven, E., Daneva, M., Kuipers, M., Towards risk-driven security requirements management in agile software development, in: *Proc. Int. Conf. Adv. Inf. Syst. Eng.*, pp. 133–144, Springer, Cham, Switzerland, 2019.

35. Mohindru, V. and Garg, A., Security attacks in internet of things: A review, in: *The International Conference on Recent Innovations in Computing*, pp. 679–693, Springer, Singapore, March 2020.

36. Mohindru, V. and Singla, S., A review of anomaly detection techniques using computer vision, in: *The International Conference on Recent Innovations in Computing*, pp. 669–677, Springer, Singapore, March 2020.

37. Mohindru, V., Vashishth, S., Bathija, D., Internet of things (IoT) for health-care systems: A comprehensive survey, in: *Recent Innovations in Computing. Lecture Notes in Electrical Engineering*, P.K. Singh, Y. Singh, M.H. Kolekar, A.K. Kar, P.J.S. Gonçalves (Eds.), vol. 832, Springer, Singapore, 2022, https://doi.org/10.1007/978-981-16-8248-3_18.

38. Rai, V. *et al.*, Cloud computing in healthcare industries: Opportunities and challenges, in: *Recent Innovations in Computing. Lecture Notes in Electrical Engineering*, P.K. Singh, Y. Singh, J.K. Chhabra, Z. Illés, C. Verma (Eds.), vol. 855, Springer, Singapore, 2022, https://doi.org/10.1007/978-981-16-8892-8_53.

39. Mohindru, V., Singh, Y., Bhatt, R., Hybrid cryptography algorithm for securing wireless sensor networks from node clone attack. *Recent Adv. Electr. Electron. Eng.*, 13, 2, 251–259, 2020.

40. Mohindru, V., Singh, Y., Bhatt, R., A review on lightweight node authentication algorithms in wireless sensor networks, in: *2018 Fifth International Conference on Parallel, Distributed and Grid Computing (PDGC)*, pp. 517–521, IEEE, December 2018.

Minimizing Cost, Effort, and Implementation Complexity for Adopting Security Requirements in an Agile Development Process for Cyber-Physical Systems

Zakir Ahmad Sheikh* and Yashwant Singh

Department of Computer Science and Information Technology, Central University of Jammu, Rahya Suchani Bagla, J&K, India

Abstract

There have been development and improvement of numerous software engineering practices but we still need to find and adopt strategies to make the software more secure. Many software engineering practices currently being utilized have been rolled out prior to the development of the World Wide Web and internet and thus lags in ensuring defense against remotely performed and complex cyberattacks. We have techniques to automate the customer functionality requirement process which can be provided explicitly by the customer as well, but something that a customer expects implicitly from the developed system is the security requirements which the developers should be taken into consideration. Agile software development has a provision to adopt changes at the later stages, but the cost and effort of implementation get progressively more exponential in later stages. Moreover, the security requirements might not fix all the bugs in later stages of development. Hence there is a need to use effective strategies at the beginning of the project to define significant functional and security requirements to minimize the efforts, cost, and implementation complexities at the later stages of the agile software development life cycle. There have been improvements in defining the customer functionality requirements but the security defining mechanisms are still immature. This paper thus discusses the existing works that determine the

---

*Corresponding author: zakirah786@gmail.com

Susheela Hooda, Vandana Mohindru Sood, Yashwant Singh, Sandeep Dalal and Manu Sood (eds.)
Agile Software Development: Trends, Challenges and Applications, (87–100) © 2023 Scrivener
Publishing LLC

implicit security requirements in the form of security compliance mechanisms, formal methods of security, security modeling techniques. It discusses techniques namely Fault Tree Analysis (FTA), Failure Modes and Effect Analysis (FMEA), System theoretic process analysis (STPA), Attack Tree Analysis (ATA), and many more. Also, a secure agile development framework is proposed to reduce the costs and efforts throughout the development. The key aspects of our framework rely on aggressive training, prototype development, plan and replan in the prototyping phase, integration of testing in each iteration, and implementation as per security standards.

Keywords: Agile security, cyber-physical systems, security, agile development, security requirements, risk analysis, agile software development, security methods

6.1 Introduction

To enhance software quality Agile was launched in 2001 with four major aims which include a) Interactions over processes b) Comprehensive documentation of software c) Customer collaboration d) Responding to change [1]. Various agile frameworks have been developed till date e.g. Scrum, Extreme Programming (XP), Dynamic Systems Development Method (DSDM), Kanban, to name a few [1, 13, 14]. Scrum and XP are widely used frameworks among all [2, 16]. Figure 6.1 depicts the list of developed agile frameworks or methodologies.

The requirements are identified through a process known as Requirement Engineering (RE). More often, the requirements are documented in natural language which is often prone to misinterpretations, and structural errors [10]. There are mainly two types of requirements i.e. functional and non-functional. The functional requirements are explicitly obtained from the customer/stakeholder, whereas the non-functional requirements are implicitly expected by the customer this also includes the security of the system [9, 11]. Security integration in agile development is a challenging task but is significant to include [12]. The traditional Requirement Engineering (RE) practices fail in the current era of rapidly changing business environments which gave rise to the adoption of agile practices in RE [2]. Agile development has gained widespread adoption in software development, development of various systems, and large projects [3]. Apart from the functional requirements, security as a non-functional requirement that is often neglected needs to be addressed [2, 3]. The widely used software development practices (SDLC models) focus on the development of software and not on its security. The waterfall model is considered

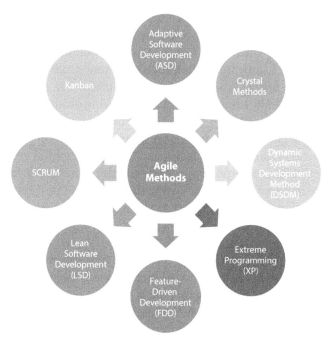

Figure 6.1 Agile development frameworks and methodologies.

to be a heavy-weight and rigid model whereas the agile methods are considered to be flexible and light-weight thus increasing their usage. In agile development, there is a provision to frequent meetings between the development team and between developers and business people, continuous specification changes, and frequent deliveries. A costly overhead is to be expected in a waterfall model when there is a necessity to revisit a previous stage. In the case of agile methods like Scrum, the new arising or evolving requirements can be specified parallelly or after the requirements are implemented. It is mainly achieved by splitting the project into multiple more or less independent stories which are tested independently. It involves cyclic iterations known as sprint which needs to be completed in a specified time [4].

Secure software development is a process that relies on the methods utilized by software design teams while searching and patching bugs with the aim to improve software security. The SDLC models should consider specific security-related tasks at various phases of the development process. These security-related tasks change as per the SDLC model selection, for instance, due to the radical difference between Waterfall and Agile models [4]. The security of software products is ensured by software security engineering through a security capability maturity model or software security development life cycle but the agile development methods and process are in conflict with them [5]. Security costs are commensurated directly with the quality of software. An improved software quality involves better software design, testing, and validation. The quality can be improved by either dealing with the origin of defects or removing product flaws through evaluation and monitoring. The former includes improved training, design reviews, and meetings on quality improvement whereas the latter is achieved through screening, code inspection, and calibration activities [6].

Agile developments provide flexibility to adopt changes at later stages but the cost of adoption increases exponentially. Moreover, the increased complexity in large-scale agile projects is also an issue [7, 8]. The cost and time graph for security patching in software development is shown in Figure 6.2. The figure does not depict the actual stages of any SDLC model but considers the necessary ones so as to conceptualize the cost and time curve. It depicts that the cost of fixing bugs and vulnerabilities rises exponentially at the later stages of its identification [9].

Figure 6.2 depicts the rise in cost at the later stages of software development. So, it is important to minimize errors, bugs, and vulnerabilities, with the inclusion of unambiguous comprehensive documentation, good planning, training, and consideration of security implementation standards. Getting an earlier fix to a bug reduces the cost and effort to fix it.

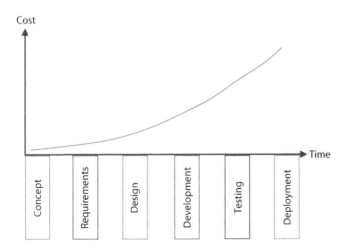

Figure 6.2 Cost and time relation to apply security patches in software development.

6.2   Literature Review

The addressing of security aspects through the agile process is used in diversified ways which include the modification of the agile process itself, the introduction of new artifacts, or introducing security guidelines [15]. The author(s) Villamizar *et al.* [2] and Dingsøyr *et al.* [16] discuss that mostly the security in agile development is considered in the context of Scrum, generic, and XP. The generic is adaptable to any agile method. The agile phases considered for defining security in descending order are specification practices, requirement elicitation, requirement analysis, and requirement validation. Presently, the validation and general quality assurance methods are out of research scope and the main focus is on the conceptual specification, and document & analytical layer [2].

For a large-scale agile context, the author(s) Moy *et al.* [7] proposed a security compliance S^2C-SAFe framework which is an extension to Scaled Agile Framework (SAFe) and relies on the security product development through the integration of IEC 62443-4-1 requirements into SAFe. In the case of SAFe, there is no methodology mentioned for the elicitation of Security Requirements (SR) [17]. The S^2C-SAFe uses a visual modeling language i.e. Business Process Model and Notation (BPMN) to capture essential elements of SAFe and 4-1 namely roles, artifacts, and activities. It is followed by refinement of models and the extension of process framework with security standard model elements. The S^2C-SAFe framework also discusses the conditions to involve roles, generate artifacts, and execute activities. The framework is aligned with the SAFe's Continuous Delivery Pipeline and makes it compliant with Security Requirements (SR), Secure Implementation (SI), and Security Verification and Validation (SVV) [7].

Rygge *et al.* [4] proposed a method Threat Poker to assess the security risks, privacy risks, and cost of patching vulnerabilities in the developed software. The method needs to be exercised by teams and it involves two rounds namely the risk round and solution round. For each threat, the Threat Poker evaluates security and privacy risk and estimates the time and effort requires removing the exploited vulnerability. Kumar *et al.* [6] discuss the benefits of security in agile development than the traditional software development in terms of cost, benefit (effectiveness in terms of bugs), ROI, NPV, and ROA. It also discusses the criteria required to estimate the advantage of using security in terms of software size, bug rate, cost of errors, prerelease component, postrelease component, and post-security component.

Fault Tree Analysis (FTA) is a systematic deductive process to identify faults in system design. It defines undesired events and their immediate causes until the basic causes are identified. A similar relationship is depicted through a logical diagram known as a fault tree. FTA is used to identify the causes of failure, weaknesses in a system, assess design reliability, identify errors, prioritize failure contributors, quantify contributors and failures, etc. [18]. Attack Tree Analysis (ATA) is a risk assessment approach in which the attacks are presented in the form of a graph. To mitigate attacks, a corresponding Attack Countermeasure Tree (ACT) is created to detect and mitigate the attacks [19].

Failure Mode and Effect Analysis (FMEA) is another methodology that is used to define, identify, and eliminate potential errors and problems in a system, process, design, or service prior to its delivery to the customer. It identifies errors, their causes, and effects, evaluates failures, prioritizes failure modes, identifies and suggests actions to reduce or eliminate the effects of potential failures [20].

Systemic Theoretic Process Analysis (STPA) methodology can be used to analyze cyber-attacks and discover mitigations [9]. STPA is originally defined as a hazard analysis methodology based on systems theory rather than reliability theory. It creates a set of scenarios that can lead to hazards and the concept is broader than Fault Tree Analysis (FTA) as it also includes those scenarios where no failures occur but give rise to unintended and unsafe interactions between the components. STPA also gives more guidance to analysts than the traditional FTA with the help of functional control diagrams [21]. The paper [9] explores the usefulness of STPA to explicitly define security requirements during the requirement analysis and gathering or elicitation phase. STPA can be applied in a safety-driven design process during the system engineering and development process [21].

Modeling and evaluation are often used to ensure system requirements including security requirements. It involves two approaches which the first one relies on formal methods such as abstractive methods, and non-abstractive methods and uses strategies namely formalizing methods, functional requirements, and verifying the model constructed. The second approach relies on data-driven analytical approaches such as manual analytical approaches and automated analytical approaches and it assesses the system behavior under attacks [22].

Formal methods and security compliance is used to define and specify systems requirements prior to their development [23]. The paper [24] discusses the requirement-based security mechanisms for cyber-physical systems (CPS). The paper [24] deduces security requirements from the feature model presented and established configurations so as to evaluate the correctness of security requirement specification. Digital twins as a method can be used to create low-cost system twins to assess security specifications. Such approaches can be seen followed by authors in [25–30]. Table 6.1 includes the summarization of existing security methods.

Table 6.1 Existing security methods.

Method	References	Description
Security Guidelines and Artifacts	Daneva *et al.* [15]	It involves defining new security guidelines and their implementation through the inclusion of new artifacts in existing frameworks and architectures.
Scaled Agile Framework (SAFe)	Fernández *et al.* [17]	Inclusion of security aspect considering the scaled agile frameworks and complexity introduced.
S²C-SAFe framework	Moy *et al.* [7]	It is an extension to Scaled Agile Framework (SAFe) and relies on the security product development through the integration of IEC 62443-4-1 requirements into SAFe.
Threat Poker	Rygge *et al.* [4]	Once the software is developed, Threat Poker is used to assess the security risks, privacy risks, and cost of patching vulnerabilities.
Fault Tree Analysis (FTA)	Vesely *et al.* [18]	It is used to assess potential faults in a system and defines undesired events (faults) and their immediate causes until the basic causes are identified. A logical diagram fault tree is created for faults-causes relationship depiction.
Attack Tree Analysis (ATA) and Attack Countermeasure Tree (ACT)	Ten *et al.* [19]	ATA is a risk assessment approach in which the attacks are represented graphically. For mitigation, a corresponding ACT is created to detect and mitigate the attacks.

(Continued)

Table 6.1 Existing security methods. (*Continued*)

Method	References	Description
Failure Mode and Effect Analysis (FMEA)	Wigfield *et al.* [20]	Define, identify, and eliminate potential errors and problems prior to product delivery to the customer.
Systemic Theoretic Process Analysis (STPA)	Pope *et al.* [9], Ishimatsu *et al.* [21]	It utilizes systems theory rather than reliability theory to identify hazards in a system. It can be used to analyze cyber-attacks and discover mitigations. It creates various hazard scenarios and the concept is broader than FTA.
Formal Methods	Contributor *et al.* [23], Varela-Vaca *et al.* [24]	Define security policies prior to product development

6.3   Proposed Methodology

Considering the importance of non-functional requirements in general and security in particular, we propose a generic secure agile development framework. It includes the requirement elicitation through S²C-SAFe framework [7] and IEC 62443-4-1 standard. The IEC 62443-4-1 describes the activities required by the engineers to make products secure [8]. We focus on quality improvement through minimization of flaws and defects, assessments, prototype development, meetings, and aggressive testing. Our proposed methodology is depicted in Figure 6.3.

We focus on quality improvement, and reduction in cost and effort in a generic agile development scenario. As the costs and efforts rise exponentially in fixing bugs and vulnerabilities at the later stages of its identification [9], we focus on their minimization through aggressive training, plan and replan, and low-cost prototype design and development. We include the definition of functional as well as non-function requirements in both prototype development and product development, and ensure the implementation is as per the security standards. The security requirements can be determined through the use of experts' knowledge and mining from the Common Vulnerabilities and Exposures (CVE) repository [31–35]. The development has proceeded with the inclusion of testing at each phase of

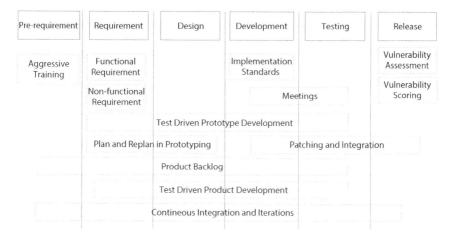

Figure 6.3 Proposed secure agile development methodology.

iteration (also known as sprint) and any bugs identified are placed as product backlog requirements [30]. These backlogs are rectified in the revised in the consequent iterations. Once the product is released it is assessed further to identify any bugs or vulnerabilities and is communicated to the development team for patching. They are also prioritized through the utilization of the vulnerability scoring method. The severe ones are assigned a high priority and rectified earlier than the low severe ones.

The significance of our proposed methodology can be seen through the visualization of the Cost and Effort vs Time graph in Figure 6.4. The comparison is shown with two curves C1 and C2. C1 depicts the normal agile development security patching and C2 depicts our secure agile development. It can be seen that with the inclusion of aggressive training and good planning, the cost and effort can be minimized by reducing the bugs and vulnerabilities. Initially, there is high cost and effort required in our methodology (depicted as line C2) but it gets reduced in consequent phases because of the inclusion of bug avoidance mechanism. The actual development and its preparations are divided into three stages namely the aggressive training stage, development of prototype stage (to assess security and the required security requirement elicitation to develop a secure product or system), and actual software development. The whole process is depicted in Figure 6.5.

Figure 6.5 depicts the proposed methodology stages. It also depicts the time, and cost-effort required for each stage. The methodology begins with the adoption of aggressive training as a pre-requisite to possess the required skills to avoid possible errors and faults in later stages of development.

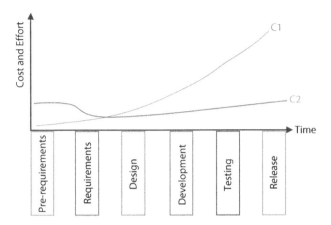

Figure 6.4 Impact of earlier avoidance and minimization through our methodology.

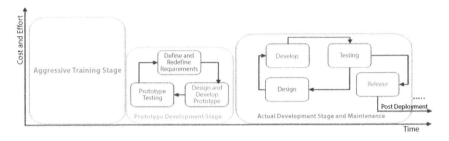

Figure 6.5 Three stages of our proposed methodology.

For sure it requires greater costs, efforts, and time, but we define it as an explicit requirement for avoidance and prevention of errors and faults to reduce their induced costs of patching at later stages of development. Once we possess highly skilled people, we start the prototype development to refine the possible requirement in actual development. This includes both functional and non-functional requirements. The prototype development also involves the testing phase to assess security loopholes. Once we refine all types of requirements in the prototype development stage, we proceed to the actual system development that begins with the design phase. The actual development also performs testing to further filter-out bugs or vulnerabilities and invoke patches in the redesign phase. Once the system is completely developed and assessed for performance (both functional and non-functional), it is released for deployment and all the costs and efforts required hereon are counted as maintenance costs and can be expected to be low through the implementation of the methodology.

6.4   Conclusion

The widely used SDLC practices mainly focus on the functional aspects of the product and neglect the focus on non-functional aspects including security. On the other hand, the clients expect these requirements from the development teams. The requirement reconsideration provision in agile development makes the process significant, but the consideration of security aspects as the later stages increases the cost and effort requirements. Considering these aspects, we thus propose a secure agile development framework relying on aggressive training, prototype development, plan in replan in the prototyping phase, integration of testing in each iteration, and implementation as per security standards. Our methodology follows an avoidance strategy to minimize the bugs and vulnerabilities at the later stages of development. We propose the use of the S^2C-SAFe framework [7] and IEC 62443-4-1 for requirement elicitation and the integration of testing in prototype development. We have compared our methodology with the normal agile development security adoption method and observed a downward shift of cost and effort in our methodology.

References

1. Sacolick, I., What is agile methodology? Modern software development explained, 2020. [Online]. Available: https://www.infoworld.com/article/3237508/what-is-agile-methodology-modern-software-development-explained.html. [Accessed: 10-Jan-2022].
2. Vegendla, A., Duc, A.N., Gao, S., Sindre, G., A systematic mapping study on requirements engineering in software ecosystems. *J. Inf. Technol. Res.*, 11, 1, 49–69, 2018.
3. Tondel, I.A., Jaatun, M. G., Cruzes, D.S., Williams, L., Collaborative security risk estimation in agile software development. *Inf. Comput. Secur.*, 27, 4, 508–535, 2019, https://doi.org/10.1108/ICS-12-2018-0138.
4. Rygge, H. and Jøsang, A., Threat poker: Solving security and privacy threats in agile software development, in: *Lecture Notes in Computer Science (including subseries Lecture Notes in Artificial Intelligence and Lecture Notes in Bioinformatics)*, vol. 11252, pp. 468–483, November 2018.
5. Rindell, K., Ruohonen, J., Holvitie, J., Hyrynsalmi, S., Leppänen, V., Security in agile software development: A practitioner survey. *Inf. Softw. Technol.*, 131, 1–13, 106488, 2021. https://doi.org/10.1016/j.infsof.2020.106488

6. Kumar, S., Kaur, A., Jolly, A., Baz, M., Cheikhrouhou, O., Cost benefit analysis of incorporating security and evaluation of its effects on various phases of agile software development. *Math. Probl. Eng.*, 2021, Article ID 7837153, 1–10, 2021. https://doi.org/10.1155/2021/7837153

7. Moyón, Fabiola, *et al.* How to integrate security compliance requirements with agile software engineering at scale?, in: *International Conference on Product-Focused Software Process Improvement*, pp. 69-87, Springer, Cham, 2020.

8. Dannart, S., Constante, F.M., Beckers, K., An assessment model for continuous security compliance in large scale agile environments: Exploratory paper, in: *Lecture Notes in Computer Science (including subseries Lecture Notes in Artificial Intelligence and Lecture Notes in Bioinformatics)*, vol. 11483, pp. 529–544, May 2019.

9. Pope, G.M., *Systemic Theoretic Process Analysis (STPA) Used for Cyber Security and Agile Software Development*, 2021.

10. Yanambaka Venkata, R., Kamongi, P., Kavi, K., *ICSEA 2020 The Fifteenth International Conference on Software Engineering Advances*, October. 2020.

11. Ionita, D., van der Velden, C., Ikkink, H.J.K., Neven, E., Daneva, M., Kuipers, M., Towards risk-driven security requirements management in agile software development, in: *Lecture. Notes in Business Information Processing*, vol. 350, pp. 133–144, May 2019.

12. Rindell, K., Hyrynsalmi, S., Leppänen, V., Aligning security objectives with agile software development. *ACM Int. Conf. Proceeding Ser*, vol. Part F147763, May, 2018.

13. Kumar, K., Agile software development methodologies and it's applications, 2018. [Online]. Available: https://blog.eduonix.com/software-development/agile-software-development-methodologies/. [Accessed: 11-Jan-2022].

14. Brush, K., Agile software development. [Online]. Available: https://searchsoftwarequality.techtarget.com/definition/agile-software-development. [Accessed: 10-Jan-2022].

15. Daneva, M. and Wang, C., Security requirements engineering in the agile era: How does it work in practice? *Proc.-2018 1st Int. Work. Qual. Requir. Agil. Proj. QuaRAP 2018*, August 2018, pp. 10–13, 2018.

16. Dingsoeyr, T., Falessi, D., Power, K., Agile development at scale: The next frontier. *IEEE Softw.*, 36, 2, 30–38, 2019.

17. Fernández, D.M. and Wagner, S., Naming the pain in requirements engineering: Design of a global family of surveys and first results from Germany. *ACM Int. Conf. Proceeding Ser*, pp. 183–194, April 2013.

18. Vesely, B., *Fault Tree Analysis (FTA): Concepts and Applications*, pp. 1–193, 2002.

19. Ten, C., Liu, C., Govindarasu, M., *Vulnerability Assessment of Cybersecurity for SCADA Systems Using Attack Trees*, 2007.

20. Mohamed B. D., Failure mode and effect analysis, in: *Handbook of maintenance management and engineering*, Springer, vol. 1, pp. 75–90, 2013.

21. Ishimatsu, T., Leveson, N., Thomas, J., Katahira, M., Miyamoto, Y., Nakao, H., Modeling and hazard analysis using STPA. *European. Space Agency, (Special Publication) ESA SP*, vol. 680, 2010.

22. Orojloo, H. and Azgomi, M.A., Modelling and evaluation of the security of cyber-physical systems using stochastic petri nets. *IET Cyber-Phys. Syst. Theory Appl.*, 4, 1, 50–57, 2019.

23. TechTarget, C., Formal methods. [Online]. Available: https://whatis.techtarget.com/definition/formal-methods. TechTarget, 2018. [Accessed: 17-Nov-2021].

24. Varela-Vaca, Á. J., Rosado, D.G., Sánchez, L.E., Gómez-López, M.T., Gasca, R.M., Fernández-Medina, E., CARMEN: A framework for the verification and diagnosis of the specification of security requirements in cyber-physical systems. *Comput. Ind.*, 132, 1–14, 2021.

25. Eckhart, M. and Ekelhart, A., *Security and Quality in Cyber-Physical Systems Engineering*, Springer, 2019.

26. Mohindru, V. and Singh, Y., Node authentication algorithm for securing static wireless sensor networks from node clone attack. *Int. J. Inf. Comput. Secur.*, 10, 2-3, 129–148, 2018.

27. Kritzinger, W., Karner, M., Traar, G., Henjes, J., Sihn, W., Digital twin in manufacturing: A categorical literature review and classification. *IFAC-Papers Online*, 51, 11, 1016–1022, 2018.

28. Mohindru, V., Bhatt, R., Singh, Y., Reauthentication scheme for mobile wireless sensor networks. *Sustain. Comput. Inf. Syst.*, 23, 158–166, 2019.

29. *A Digital Twin-based Privacy Enhancement Mechanism for the Automotive Industry*, 2018.

30. Mohindru, V., Singh, Y., Bhatt, R., A review on lightweight node authentication algorithms in wireless sensor networks, in: *2018 Fifth International Conference on Parallel, Distributed and Grid Computing (PDGC)*, IEEE, pp. 517–521, December 2018.

31. Becue, A. *et al.*, Cyber factory 1-securing the industry 4.0 with cyber-ranges and digital twins. *IEEE Int. Work. Fact. Commun. Syst.-Proceedings, WFCS*, June 2018, vol. pp, pp. 1–4, 2018.

32. Mohindru, V. and Singh, Y., Performance analysis of message authentication algorithms in wireless sensor networks, in: *2017 4th International Conference on Signal Processing, Computing and Control (ISPCC)*, IEEE, pp. 468–472, September 2017.

33. Wang, W., Gupta, A., Niu, N., Mining security requirements from common vulnerabilities and exposures for agile projects. *Proc.-2018 1st Int. Work. Qual. Requir. Agil. Proj. QuaRAP 2018*, pp. 6–9, 2018.

34. Mohindru, V., Vashishth, S., Bathija, D., Internet of things (IoT) for health-care systems: A comprehensive survey, in: *Recent Innovations in Computing. Lecture Notes in Electrical Engineering*, vol. 832, P.K. Singh, Y. Singh, M.H. Kolekar, A.K. Kar, P.J.S. Gonçalves (Eds.), Springer, Singapore, 2022, https://doi.org/10.1007/978-981-16-8248-3_18.

35. Tashtoush, Y.M. *et al.*, Agilea approaches for cybersecurity systems, IoT and intelligent transportation. *IEEE Access*, 10, 1360–1375, 2022.

A Systematic Literature Review on Test Case Prioritization Techniques

Ajmer Singh[1]*, Anita Singhrova[1], Rajesh Bhatia[2] and Dhavleesh Rattan[3]

[1]*Computer Science and Engineering, DCRUST Murthal, Sonipat, India*
[2]*Computer Science and Engineering, PEC, Chandigarh, India*
[3]*Computer Science and Engineering, Punjabi University, Patiala, India*

Abstract

Software Testing consumes very significant amount of time in the life cycle of software. Test case prioritization is a way to provide priorities to test cases, to meet various testing goals. This study reports a systematic literature review of prioritization techniques. The survey adheres to the guidelines of eminent researchers in the field of software engineering. This survey is based on a review of 312 articles selected from leading research journals and proceedings of premier conferences. The survey provides a deep insight into the area of prioritization and highlights 22 different techniques that have been emerged in the past. The study not only throws light on different possible techniques for prioritization but also presents a set of applicable tools and subject systems in this domain. The survey also has a specific focus on prioritization in model-based testing and object-oriented testing since these two paradigms have become popular among the researchers. The study concludes that the field of prioritization has considerably been explored and many prioritization techniques have evolved. But still, there are possibilities of improvements, especially in implementation and analysis. The study also highlights the current status of prioritization and provides comparative analysis with similar works. Results presented in this survey would benefit the researchers to gain knowledge of the field of prioritization in general, and object-oriented prioritization, in particular.

This review follows the guidelines of eminent researchers like Kitchenham *et al.* [1, 2] and Budgen *et al.* [3].

**Corresponding author*: ajmer.saini@gmail.com

Susheela Hooda, Vandana Mohindru Sood, Yashwant Singh, Sandeep Dalal and Manu Sood (eds.)
Agile Software Development: Trends, Challenges and Applications, (101–160) © 2023 Scrivener
Publishing LLC

Keywords: Test case prioritization, software testing, test case prioritization techniques, systematic review

7.1   The Motivation for Systematic Review

It is noticed that the volume of research in the field of prioritization is evolving very rapidly. To know about the latest trends in this field, the need for a systematic literature review is very much justified. The work reported here, not only has tried to highlight the latest trends in the field but has also given different insights into this field. The study presented here has the following objectives:

a) To summarize the existing shreds of evidence concerning prioritization.
b) To identify the different existing approaches to the solve prioritization problem.
c) To acquaint with a set of tools that may be helpful in solving prioritization problem.
d) To enlist various subject systems that researchers have used for evaluation of their research.
e) To identify any research gaps in current research in order to suggest areas for further investigation.

7.1.1   Existing Literature Reviews on Test Case Prioritization

In the review of the literature, it was found that some systematic review studies [4–8] have also been carried out by the researchers. Yoo and Harman [4] were the first to present a systematic study on test case minimization (RTM) and regression test case selection (RTS) and regression test prioritization (RTP). Their study was based on total of 159 articles out of which only 47 articles were related to RTP. And the authors identified 10 different approaches to RTP problem. Catal and Mishra [5] systematically reviewed 120 articles related to prioritization and found 9 different approaches to solve prioritization problem. A study by Singh, Kaur, Suri, and Singhal [6] was based on 65 articles and identified 18 composite approaches to prioritization. Campos *et al.* [8], explored 90 articles related to prioritization and categorized articles into 12 categories. A recent study by Khatibsyarbini *et al.* [7] presented 14 different categories from the review of 80 articles. Further, there also exist some brief review studies [9–13] in the literature. As compared to all the previous studies the study being reported here has the longest time frame i.e. from year 1999 to 2018 and it explores the largest number of articles. Also list of tools and subject systems used in the literature has been presented. As compared to the existing systematic studies this study is a more comprehensive one.

7.1.2 Resources Used for SLR

The study considers the following set of resources (R_1 to R_7) for exploring the related literature:

1. ACM digital library (dl.acm.org)   (R_1)
2. IEEE explore (www.ieeexplore.ieee.org)   (R_2)
3. Science Direct (www.sciencedirect.com)   (R_3)
4. Springer Link (www.springerlink.com)   (R_4)
5. Wiley Science (onlinelibrary.wiley.com)   (R_5)
6. Google Scholar (scholar.google.com)   (R_6)
7. Scientific Literature Digital Library and Search Engine (http://citeseerx.ist.psu.edu/)   (R_7)

7.1.3 Search Criteria

It is very much essential for any systematic literature review to have a fixed time frame. This survey has considered time frame 1999-2018 (both inclusive). The resources listed in subsection 7.1.2 were exhaustively searched for the relevant articles using following search strings were applied to the resources given in the previous subsection.

i. Test case prioritization (S_1)
ii. Prioritizing test cases (S_2)
iii. Test suite prioritization (S_3)
iv. Prioritized test cases (S_4)
v. Prioritizing test suite (S_5)
vi. Prioritized test suite (S_6)
vii. Ordering test cases (S_7)
viii. Giving the order to test cases (S_8)

After selecting the set of resources (R_1 to R_7) and search strings (S_1 to S_8), the search was performed in such a way, that every resource could be searched for every search executing all the strings on all the selected resources, total 56 such sets (N_{11} to N_{87}) string. The String S_i, when applied on resource Rj, produced a set of articles N_{ij}. After the sets were obtained,

N_{11} through N_{87} were further operated on for inclusion/exclusion criteria. After removing the irrelevant articles from N_{11} through N_{86}, their corresponding subsets $F_1, F_2,..F_{56}$ were obtained. To minimize chances that same article might have been included in these sets from more than one resource, union operation was performed manually on these sets. After cross-examination of results, total of 312 articles were finalized.

7.1.4 Research Questions

The main focus points of the study are model-based prioritization, prioritization for object-oriented testing, and model-based techniques for object-oriented testing. To give directions to search and to confine it within the time frame, some research questions were framed.

Table 7.1 below gives various research questions and sub-questions.

Table 7.1 Research questions.

Research questions	Motivation
1 What is the current status of Test Case Prioritization?	To acquaint with the current trend in the field of prioritization.
1.1 How various Test Case Prioritization techniques are classified? And what are those classifications?	It helps in understanding the various prioritization techniques and also presents the possibilities of research in the area.
1.2 What subject systems have been used to evaluate test case prioritization techniques? What is the type of programming platform subject systems?	Subject systems differ in programming platform, complexity, context, application etc. This research question would help the in deciding the subject system for a prioritization technique.
2 What is the research status in Model-Based Test Case Prioritization?	Model-based prioritization has turned out to be a recent trend in this field. This research question looks into the research status of Model-based prioritization.
2.1 What evaluation criteria have been used to evaluate Model-Based Prioritization and how the results are reported?	This research question reports the different evaluation criteria used by model-based prioritization and results of each such study.

(Continued)

Table 7.1 Research questions. (*Continued*)

Research questions	Motivation
2.2 How Model-Based Test Case prioritization has evolved over the years? What are the studies discussing the benefits of model-based test case prioritization in object-oriented systems?	The answer to this question reports the studies pertaining to model-based prioritization in object-oriented testing. Also, the evolution of model-based technique till this time is described.
2.3 What subject systems are used to evaluate the model-based test case prioritization?	It will help to understand the nature of the subject system which can be used for model-based prioritization technique.
3 What is the research status of Test Case Prioritization for object-oriented testing?	The research status of prioritization in the context of object-oriented test is reported.
3.1 What specific parameters of object-oriented testing have been used by various studies?	This question explores that in the context of object-oriented testing whether object-oriented features like inheritance, polymorphism affects prioritization.
3.2 What studies exist based on multi-objective algorithms for Test Case Prioritization in object-oriented testing?	It reports the research(s) done for prioritization in the context of object-oriented testing using multi-objective algorithms.
3.3 Whether a comparative analysis of multi-objective algorithms for test case prioritization in object-oriented testing has been performed? And what are the results?	Comparative analysis of various multi-objective prioritizations in the context of object-oriented testing will help to get tradeoffs of these algorithms.

7.2   Results

The primary focus of this survey is to investigate the related literature to meet the answers to research questions raised in Section 7.1.4. To estimate precise and authentic results, articles from journals of repute and proceedings from related conferences, workshops, and symposiums were considered. Out of a total of 312 articles, 69% of the articles belongs to the conferences, whose proceedings could be traced in our online resources and 31% of articles belong to various research journals of repute. Research questions raised in previous section are addressed here as follows.

7.2.1   What is the Current Status of Test Case Prioritization?

Since its inception, prioritization has been continuously investigated by researchers from different perspectives. prioritization was firstly employed with code coverage information. Gregg Rothermel *et al.* [14] introduced the concept of prioritization in 1999. With the evolutions in testing strategy, development and deployment etc., prioritization also has been broadened its usage. Figure 7.1 shown below provides information about year wise articles published in our survey resources. The trend shows that interest in the field of prioritization is continuously increasing. If we notice the trend in recent years, the last three years have witnessed nearly 35% percent of the articles of total articles published in a 19-year period. That proves prioritization is still an open area of research.

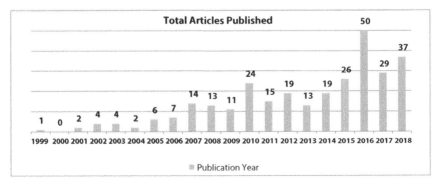

Figure 7.1 Publication trend.

7.2.2 How Various Test Case Prioritization Techniques are Classified? And What are Those Classifications?

After selecting the relevant articles from authentic resources, the articles were thoroughly examined to find out various methods/techniques being used by researchers for prioritization. Table 7.2, given below presents the techniques from the literature.

The knowledge of authors was utilized for this categorization. Also, colleagues, having domain knowledge, were consulted for refinement. The following text in this subsection depicts the different identified categories of the studies related to prioritization.

Table 7.2 Techniques wise distribution of articles.

S. n	Category (with % age share)	Sub category	Citations
1	Code Coverage based (17.2%)	Statement Coverage	[14–22, 25–45]
		Path Coverage	[46–52]
		Code Slicing	[53–58]
		Call graph	[59–67]
		Program Refactoring	[68]
2	Requirements based (6.73%)	NA	[56, 69–89]
3	Model based (8.33 %)	NA	[49, 54, 90–115]
4	Time and cost aware (2.24%)	NA	[116–122]
5	History-based (5.12%)	NA	[123–131]
6	Risk-Based (1.92%)	NA	[139–144]
7	Fault Localization based (5.44%)	NA	[145–161]
8	Soft Computing Techniques based (21.79%)	Ant Colony Optimization	[47, 133, 162–164, 170]

(Continued)

Table 7.2 Techniques wise distribution of articles. (*Continued*)

S. n	Category (with % age share)	Sub category	Citations
		Particle Swarms Optimization (PSO)	[33, 171–173]
		Analytical Hierarchy Process	[174, 175]
		Non-Dominated Sorted Genetic Algorithm (NSGA)	[176–181]
		Pareto Convergence Genetic Algorithm (PCGA)	[182, 183]
		(1+1) EA	[184]
		Genetic Algorithm	[28, 108, 117, 126, 185–193]
		Local beam search	[26, 194–196]
		Simulated Annealing	[197]
		Clustering	[174, 198–206]
		Other search algorithms	[207–210]
		Bayesian network based	[211–213]
		Multi-objective approaches	[214–224]
9	Web based (4.49%)	NA	[225–238]
10	Object Oriented Testing based (5.12%)	NA	[23, 24, 53, 54, 57, 60, 61, 66, 67, 239–245]
11	Similarity based (4.48%)	NA	[202, 246–258]

(*Continued*)

Table 7.2 Techniques wise distribution of articles. (*Continued*)

S. n	Category (with % age share)	Sub category	Citations
12	Combinatorial Interaction Testing based (6.73%)	NA	[259–279]
13	Machine learning based (2.56%)	NA	[280–287]
14	Adaptive Random Testing based (2.56%)	NA	[195, 265, 288–293, 318]
15	Continuous Integration (CI) and Software product lines (2.56%)	NA	[294–301]
16	Hybrid Approaches (1.92%)	NA	[302–307]
17	Comparative studies (1.92%)	NA	[308–313]
18	Survey and review studies (3.3%)	NA	[4–8]

7.2.2.1   Code Coverage-Based

Code coverage based prioritization executes test cases in an order with the objective to maximize the coverage of code by test cases to be executed. Code coverage considers all its subcategories like statement coverage, condition coverage, block coverage, additional statement coverage, function coverage, additional function coverage, additional condition coverage, and various variants of these subcategories. The research work related to these sub-categories is briefly explained in following sub-sections.

a) Statements coverage-based
Rothermel *et al.* [14] presented the idea of test case ordering on the basis of code coverage information and proposed basic techniques for prioritization viz. unordered, random, optimal, branch_total, branch_additional, total Fault Exposing Potential (FEP), FEP_additional, statement_total,

and statement_additional. The authors [15–21] have investigated coverage based techniques for prioritization. Elbaum, Rothermel, and Kanduri [22] proposed an approach for selecting cost-effective prioritization technique and also provided a cost-benefit model for various techniques. Do, Rothermel, and Kinneer [42, 43] used test cases for object oriented software and a tool 'Junit' was used for analysis. Do and Rothermel [25] analyzed the utility of mutants in assessments of different prioritization techniques. Li, Harman, and Hierons [26] experimentally compared the performance of the greedy algorithm, genetic algorithm and optimal algorithm for prioritization. Smith and Kapfhammer [27] extended the work to greedily reduce and prioritize the tests by using both: test cost and the ratio of code coverage to test cost. Test cost considered by them is execution time. Masri and El-Ghali [28] proposed techniques that considered elements such as blocks or statements (*BB*), basic-block edges or branches (*BBE*) and def-use pairs (*DUP*). The study by Khan, Rehman, and Malik [29] analyzed the effectiveness of code coverage based prioritization. Fang, Chen, and Xu [30] prioritized test cases on the basis of logic coverage. As per the study of Daniel *et al.* [31], coverage based techniques with a finer granularity of code performed better than the one with coarse granularity. Dario *et al.* [32], proposed hyper volume based search on program code to solve the prioritization problem. The authors used hyper volume solvers for finding the multi-objective solution to the prioritization problem. Further, authors found Hyper Genetic algorithm to be more effective than multi objective additional greedy algorithm. Khin, YoungSik, and Jong [33] gave the execution and coverage units to Particle Swarm Optimization (PSO) and ordered test cases on the basis of modified parts of the software. A unified system by Hao *et al.* [34] considered total and the additional strategy. Do and Rothermel [35] studied the effectiveness of mutants on various coverage based prioritization techniques. Zengkai and Jianjun [36] considered Testing Importance of Module (TIM) and ordered the test cases on TIM scores. Lou, Hao, and Zhang [37] isolated the statements, that which were different, in two versions of the software and killed mutants in those statements for prioritization. Author in [38] applied the multi-heuristic technique for solving prioritization on the coverage of code. An approach in [39], considered the weights according to statements and methods by the test cases. As per study of [40–42]. [43–45] worked on similar concepts.

b) Path coverage-based

Path testing is a white box testing technique for designing test cases. In path testing, the code is analyzed for different execution paths. Path based prioritization uses different logical paths/sequences in the software to order the test cases. The research work of Sabharwal, Sibal, and Sharma [46] derived Control Flow Graph (CFG) from the given code of SUT. By using the information flow model, nodes in CFG were then assigned weights. Suri and Singhal [47] considered a set of test cases as the connected graph. Kaur, Bansal, and Sibal [48] considered path length, information flow logic and predicate nodes and later prioritized the test cases based upon this complexity. Athira and Samuel [49] evaluated tests as per the most promising nodes covered in the activity diagrams of original and modified programs. Based upon the weighted interactions between the modified diagram and the original diagram, the test cases were prioritized. Kheirkhah and Mohd Daud [50] designed CFG in the context of non-object oriented programming languages by using 'IF' and 'ELSE' metrics. Srivastava *et al.* [51] created different CFGs for original source code and the modified code. Further differences in the nodes in both the CFGs were identified. Rummel, Kapfhammer, and Thall [52] used def-used (du) paths in control flow graphs for prioritization.

c) Slicing-based prioritization

A program slice is a part of the program that behaves independently of the other parts of the program. In the survey, it was found that the researchers have been using program slicing to prioritize the test cases. Ray, Lal Kumawat, and Mohapatra [53] presented a prioritization technique based on forward slicing. Jaroenpiboonkit and Suwannasart [54] derived associations from the function calls in between the classes and applied object oriented slicing to find test order for integration tests in the dependency graphs. The authors in [55, 56] applied the concept of relevant slices for coverage-based prioritization and assigned a higher weight to the test case that had a large number of statements in its relevant slice. Panigrahi and Mall [57, 58] applied forward slicing for object oriented system in extended SDG of the affected model.

d) Call graph-based

A call graph is a directed graph, where nodes represent the methods and an edge between them represents a function call. The studies of [59–61] designed static call graphs from 'Junit' test cases. Authors analyzed the call graph to prioritize test cases with estimated code coverage. The study of [62, 63] found that static call-graph-based technique was better than the other static techniques. A two-layer prioritization model developed by authors in [64], suggested composite rewards to test case based on event and function call. The studies [65, 66] considered dependencies of functions covered for determining the weights of test cases. The [67] proposed a combined fault exposing capability of test cases using the methods called and the coverage of modified code.

e) Refactoring-based
Program refactoring refers to the change in the program code without changing its external behavior. Very less research is reported under this category. Alves *et al.* [68] prioritized test cases as per the type of audit made. As per their approach, firstly the location and type of audits were found from the two versions of SUT. And then, with the help of coverage of affected source code, test cases are assigned priorities.

7.2.2.2   Requirements-Based

Software requirements can be classified as functional, non-functional requirements, user requirements and system requirements [69]. Srikanth [56], introduced the concept of requirement based prioritization and assigned the priorities to test cases as per the significances of requirements covered by them. And extended their work further in [70] to support both regression and new prioritization. Authors in [71] considered business values of the requirements covered for prioritization. Srikanth and Williams [72] applied multi-criteria based approach to economically prioritize the test cases and proposed a scheme called 'PORT' version 1.0. which incorporated parameters like customer assigned priority, requirements complexity, requirements volatility, and fault-proneness. The study [73] extended PORT 1.0' was extended to 'PORT 2.0' to inculcate risk factor associated with each requirement. The study in [74] replicated the research on a similar set of parameters for ordering both the regression and new test cases. Study of [75] considered coverage of functional factors as weights of the test cases. Arafeen and Do [76] investigated the effectiveness of requirements based clustering approach. The studies [77, 78] considered varying costs for the test cases instead of similar costs.

The study of [79] considered system requirements and [80] considered software requirements. SNIPR approach of McZara *et al.* [81] prioritized the requirements based on satisfiability modulo theories and natural language processing. Studies of [82–87] analyzed the impact of changes in requirements on system reliability and presented reliability oriented approach to prioritization. The study in [88] prioritized requirements on the basis of number of faults related to them [89] argued that prioritization of test cases should have been done in early phases of SDLC namely design and requirement analysis.

7.2.2.3   Model-Based Prioritization

In our survey, it was found that there has been significant research in model based prioritization. It was also found that the model based prioritization is gaining popularity among the researchers.

Korel, Tahat, and Harman [90], introduced the use of system models in prioritization. The authors of [90–93] used the used Extended Finite State Machine (EFSM) model concept of system modeling and performed prioritization based on state-based models by recording the changes in the model and as per the changes in the system. In [90], the authors considered modifications in the model and the source code. The work in [91], considered alterations which do not require any changes in original models. The study in [94] presented heuristic methods for model-based prioritization. An experimental comparison in [95], showed that model-based prioritization significantly improved the early fault detection as compared to code based approach. Panigrahi and Mall [96] used Object-oriented System Dependence Graph (EOSDG) for regression testing using slicing on the model to identify the elements that may be affected by a change. Authors in [97, 98] generated system test cases from the extended UML activity models. Finally, they prioritized the generated test cases, based on the coverage of transitions in the activity model. Mohanty, Acharya, and Mohapatra [99] proposed a technique for prioritization in regression testing for Component-Based Software System (CBSS) and used UML state chart diagrams to represent state changes and components. The model so obtained was later converted into a Component Interaction Graph (CIG) to describe the interrelation among components. Prioritization was done by taking into account the total number of state changes and the total number of database access. The authors of [100–102] and [103] proposed a system level test case generation and prioritization technique for object oriented testing. The authors of [54] tried to minimize the number of stubs through prioritization. The authors in [49] used activity diagram and prioritization was done on the basis of the most promising activity paths. In [104], authors used model-based approach to for prioritization in aspect-oriented programming. Authors of [105, 106] used UML activity diagrams to represent the SUT and applied association rules to get frequently affected nodes in the model. The studies like [107–113] have considered the similar concepts related to model based testing. A review of research work on model-based prioritization using ACO has been presented in [114]. A composite approach in [115, 317], presented the test scenarios using UML activity diagrams and then derived Control Flow Graph (CFG) from it.

7.2.2.4   Time and Cost-Aware Prioritization

As per time aware prioritization, the ordering of test cases can be done not only the basis on fault detection capabilities but also on the execution time of test cases involved.

A pair-wise time aware prioritization by Parashar, Kalia, and Bhatia [116], considered non interdependent test cases and also assumed that a test case would reveal the same faults irrespective of its execution order. [117] proposed prioritization technique for time-constrained testing environments. Authors in [118] used knapsack solvers to order test cases using criteria of requirements coverage in lesser time. The study of [119] used integer linear programming and found that the integer linear program could outperform GA in some circumstances. You et al. [120] used statement coverage as prioritization criteria to study the effectiveness of time aware techniques and found that although time aware techniques performed better but the difference was not very significant in most of the cases. A non-homogeneous Poisson process based study [121] established trade off between cost of testing and testing duration. Authors in [122] prioritized test cases for online testing of service centric systems.

7.2.2.5   History-Based Prioritization

History-based technique is the one that performs prioritization on the basis of historical execution data. The following text briefs about the research work utilizing the historical testing data for the purpose of prioritization. The studies in [123, 124] asserted the usefulness of history-based approaches in regression testing. Park, Ryu, and Baik [125] found the historical value of the test cases on the basis of severe faults covered. Huang et al. [126, 127] estimated the current cost and fault severity for cost-cognizant prioritization based on historical data. The test costs, fault severities, and detected faults of each test case were obtained from previous testing and then GA was applied to find an order as per the severity coverage. The study of Carlson, Do, and Denton [128], used historical values together with clustering to prioritize test case for regression testing. Czerwonka et al. [129] developed a tool called 'CRANE' that predicted the failure in the current version of the software based on previous failures. The prediction combined with change analysis was used for prioritization. Study of Yalda Fazlalizadeh et al. [130] analyzed test case performance by measuring execution time and constraints of resources. Their work is further extended in [131] to incorporate fault exposing potential, execution time and other historical data for prioritization.

Authors of [132] used history of modified source code as weights for subsequent testings. The authors of [133], proposed a history-based prioritization for black box testing. Qu *et al.* [134] prioritized test cases based on test case history for initializing the test suite and reordering was done on the basis of runtime information of test cases. Fazlalizadeh *et al.* [135] used previous priority and execution history of regression test case to determine priorities for the next run of testing. In [136, 137] authors applied correlation analysis on failure history in previous regression versions and reordered the test cases in subsequent testing phases. An industrial case study in [138] prioritized the test cases on relative probabilities in running highly impacted components.

7.2.2.6   Risk Factor-Based Prioritization

In risk-based testing, a list of prioritized risks is maintained. The testing would explore each risk. Risk factor may vary according to the users and usage scenario of the software. When dealing with one kind of risk, another may be needed to adjust. In literature, various authors have used the concept of these risk factors while prioritizing the test cases. Stallbaum, Metzger, and Pohl [139] introduced Risk-based Test case Derivation And Prioritization (RiteDAP). In RiteDAP, the models were augmented with risk information and sum of risks covered by test case was used to prioritize test cases. The author also categorized risk-based prioritization into total risk score prioritization and additional risk score prioritization. Huang *et al.* [140] and Kasurinen, Taipale, and Smolander [141], evaluated risk-based prioritization against design based prioritization for their industrial applicability. Their study concluded that the risk-based approach was preferred by the organizations where testing resources were limited and the product design was allowed to adapt or change during the process. Hettiarachchi, Do, and Choi [142] used the fuzzy system on user requirements to estimate risk information. The correlations of requirements with risk were used for prioritization. A risk based prioritization in [143], constructed information flow based direct network from the transmission of information flow among different software components and analyzed it to predict the testing orders. Study of [144] considered the risk reduction capability of test cases for prioritization.

7.2.2.7   Fault Localization-Based

According to Kim and Baik [145], fault localization techniques are based on idea that a parts of a program executed by failed test cases would have a higher probability of containing fault(s). The authors ordered the coverage entities by using two metrics: *coverage* and *suspiciousness.* Sanchez *et al.* [146–148] provided online prioritization technique and ordered tests on the basis of diagnostic information gain. The authors of [147] proposed greedy diagnostic prioritization by ambiguity group reduction. They used Bayesian diagnostic approach for ordering offline test cases. Their work in [148], improved the diagnostic information per test and considered the possibility of false negatives too. Jiang *et al.* [149, 150] empirically found that strategy, coverage granularity, time and cost of prioritization were the key factors affecting the effectiveness of statistical based fault localization. Yoo, Harman, and Clark [151, 152], used information theory for fault localization and generated entropy model to represent locality of fault and found that reduction in Shannon entropy improved the effectiveness fault localization. Later, they ranked the test cases for early localization of the faults. Jones, Harrold, and Stasko [153] used visual mappings to assist in localization of faults and prioritization.

Jiang and Chan [154], empirically evaluated different prioritization techniques suing statistical fault localization methods. The study concluded that branch adequate test suites were less supportive of effective fault localization. The study [155], incorporated runtime feedback system to prioritize the future test cases on the basis of current fault locality. The study in [156] used associations between faults and test case failures reliable evaluation of prioritization techniques. A spectrum based random FLP in [157], presented the features of test cases that might be helpful in localization and presented various methods to quantify these features. A priority based on fault rate and fault severity was proposed by [158]. In the research work of [159], considered suspicion ranks for the statements using coverage information and results of the previous test case. A fault prediction model based on the fault-proneness of software components was built by [160]. An approach that solved prioritization on the basis of coverage of weighted mutants was presented by [161].

7.2.2.8   *Soft Computing Techniques-Based*

In the survey, it was found that researchers have applied many soft-computing methods to prioritization problem. Articles that fall under this category are further sub-divided into the following sub categories.

a) Ant colony optimization (ACO)-based
ACO is a metaheuristic technique for solving hard combinatorial optimization problems. Many researchers have applied ACO in different manners to solve the prioritization problem. The studies of Suri [47, 162–164] used

ACO to prioritize test cases with two optimal objectives: time and coverage. In [58], results showed that more optimal test cases order could be achieved if time constraint was increased. modified ACO (m-ACO) used by Dalal *et al.* [165] was capable of providing more directions for movements of ants and authors claimed that higher coverage of code was achieved by their approach. Noguchi and Washizaki [133] used ACO for prioritization in black box testing and proposed ACO based framework. Gao, Guo, and Zhao [166] considered prioritization as a multi-objective problem and applied ACO to optimize three objectives: number of faults detected, time taken in execution and their severity. A hybrid approach was adopted by the research work in [167]. ACO algorithm optimized both the execution time and fault rate. The study in [168] modeled the testing scenario with the help of Travelling Salesman Problem(TSP). And later applied ACO to TSP to render the optimal paths from it. A coverage based Ant Colony System (CB-ACS) [169] converted the test cases and corresponding statement coverage into a graph. Artificial ants travelling through the graph generated different optimal tours. Performance analysis of ACO with Bee Colony Optimization (BCO) was performed by [164]. Epistasis Based ACO [170] is a multi-objective approach based on epistasis theory.

b) Particle swarms optimization (PSO)-based
This subsection depicts the approaches that have used PSO to solve prioritization problem. Khin, YoungSik, and Jong [33] applied PSO with objectives: branch coverage, functional coverage, total coverage and execution time. Tyagi and Malhotra [171] used fault coverage and execution time as two objectives for optimization and applied PSO to select a minimal set of tests which covers all faults and also with minimum execution time. A Modified PSO algorithm in [172] considered seven prioritization factors at the same time. Rauf and Alsalem [173], estimated the value of test cases using customer value based partitioning (CVBD) and APFD. The values so calculated, were given to PSO to get priorities of test cases.

c) Analytical hierarchy process (AHP)-based
AHP is a pair wise comparison technique for multi-criteria decision making. Some studies have applied AHP to prioritization problem as given: Yoo *et al.* [174] used AHP with clustering techniques to minimize human efforts in prioritization. Klindee and Promotion [175] applied AHP to give ranks to the test cases and considered three different criteria for decision making like test impact, change requirement prioritization, and change requirement types. Authors in [175] proposed an approach to sort the test cases through AHP.

d) Non-dominated sorted genetic algorithm (NSGA)-based
NSGA finds its application to optimize multiple and generally contrary objectives simultaneously. It is observed that many researchers have solved the problem of prioritization through NSGA based approach as given: Epitropakis et al. [176] empirically evaluated the efficiency of Pareto efficient multi-objective prioritization. Their study compared the efficiency NSGA-II and Two Archive Evolutionary Algorithm (TAEA). Further, the study in [177] applied NSGA-II with three objectives namely Average percentage of change coverage, Average percentage of statements covered and Effective execution time for optimization and evaluated their results on Guava project. A multi-criteria optimization in [178], considered hardware damage risk, budget and uncertainty as optimization parameters. Authors applied NSGA-II on the case study of satellite systems. Author in [179] analyzed NSGA-II, strength Pareto evolutionary algorithm 2 (SPEA2), a multi-objective evolutionary algorithm based on decomposition (MOEA/D), Pareto envelope-based selection algorithm II (PESA-II), and NSGA-III. As per their results, NSGA-II outperformed all the other algorithms. The study in [180] aimed to optimize code coverage, requirements coverage, and execution cost through application of NSGA-II. The research work in [181] outlined a resource-aware prioritization for optimizations execution time, their number, total resources and number of faults detected.

e) Pareto convergence genetic algorithm (PCGA)-based
PCGA is based on Pareto ranking. Some studies like Ray and Mohapatra [182] used Pareto Convergence Genetic Algorithm (PCGA) based on Pareto optimality. Also [183] proposed an improved Pareto-optimal colonel selection algorithm to optimize three objectives: cost-cognizant average percentage of fault detected, execution time and most severity of faults detected.

f) (1+1) EA-based
Wang et al. [184] applied search based multi-objective prioritization in software product line engineering (SPLE). They considered various measures like Overall Execution Cost, Prioritized Extent of test cases, Feature Pair wise Coverage and Fault Detection Capability.

g) Genetic algorithm (GA)-based
As per this survey, Walcott et al. [117] introduced the application of the genetic algorithm to a prioritization problem. Authors described a time-aware test suite prioritization technique by applying a genetic algorithm. Authors of [28] proposed effective test case filtering and prioritization techniques and used GA to leverage combinations of simple program elements

of different types. The study Alexander *et al.* [185] described a comprehensive GA that employed a wide variety of mutation, crossover, and selection operators. Huang *et al.* [126] considered the varying costs for test cases and proposed a cost cognizant metric. Authors applied GA on varying costs and fault severities. A information flow model in [186] used GA to prioritization problem. [187] proposed an approach based on Prioritized Genetic Solver (GS) constructed the test suite by considering priorities in the generation phase. A systematic study by Catal [188] showed that GAs performed better than the competing techniques such as hill climbing, coverage-based, history-based, random ordering, greedy algorithm, and fault aware. Yuan *et al.* [189] used the concept of Epistatic-GA to prioritize test cases.

Wang *et al.* [108] used hybrid-GA to order the test cases on the information extracted from the UML diagrams. An approach in [190] utilized FEP and statement coverage information as inputs to GA and found that Average Percentage of Statement Coverage (APSC) of the proposed strategy was improved. Authors in [191–193], investigated the applicability of GA on code coverage information for prioritization.

h) Local beam search (LBS)-based

Beam search is a heuristic search technique that expands the most promising node first in the limited set. LBS based prioritization techniques spread the test cases across the search space as evenly as possible. The LBS also reduces the search space by pruning unpromising search. Jiang and Chan [194, 195] used discrepancy measure to ensure the even distribution of test cases. The study in [194] LBS based prioritization to be more efficient and scalable as compared to coverage based greedy techniques. The authors in [195], compared the efficiency of LBS based techniques with GA based and adaptive random testing (ART) and concluded that LBS based approach gave better APFD than both GA based and ART.

The study of Li, Harman, and Hierons [26] evaluated five different search algorithms. Their results showed that Genetic Algorithms performed better, although Greedy approaches were also considerably effective. Conrad, Roos, and Kapfhammer [196] analyzed efficiency of Search-Based Test Suite Prioritization. Their research concluded that truncation selection consistently outperformed in terms of test suite effectiveness.

i) Simulated annealing-based

Maia *et al.* [197] tested a greedy randomized adaptive search procedure (GRASP) for prioritization. The study shows that coverage performance of reactive - GRASP is better than GA and Simulated Annealing.

j) Clustering-based

It is found in the survey that many researchers have applied different clustering techniques to prioritization problem. Various studies under this category are briefly explained as: Yoo *et al.* [174] proposed clustering based prioritization based on the AHP. Simons and Paraiso [198], used Failure Pursuit Sampling technique to explore the idea that failed test cases may often be clustered together based on their profile Failure pursuit represents the action of selecting the k-nearest neighbors of any failed tests found by auditing the initially clustered test suite. Carlson, Do, and Denton [128] proposed new prioritization techniques that incorporate a clustering approach and utilize code coverage, code complexity and historical data of real faults. Zhao *et al.* [199] applied a Bayesian network and clustering approach to the prioritization [200] clustered the software change records of previous versions then through the application of singular value decomposition determined the test vectors [201] disseminated Kernel based fuzzy c-means clustering on coverage data for segregating relevant and irrelevant test cases [202], considers symbolic execution, Authors in [203] applied dissimilarity clustering on historical data. A multi features based similarity clustering approach is administered by [204–206] applies clustering to requirements and clusters are mapped to test cases.

k) Other searching algorithms

Williams and Kapfhammer [207], presented two types of synthetically generated test suites to comparatively analyze greedy prioritizers and search-based techniques. They used execution time to measure the efficiency of the prioritization techniques and they found that hill climbing performs better and offers more variability. Li *et al.* [208] with the help of simulation studied performance of search based prioritization. As per their investigation, additional greedy algorithm and 2-optimal greedy algorithm perform better than the other three. Smith and Kapfhammer [27] empirically evaluated the use of cost parameter in prioritization. Their work performed a comparative study of various greedy algorithms. Biographical Based Optimization (BBO) and Grey Wolf Optimizer (GWO) are diffused by the study of [209]. A bat inspired optimization algorithm was employed to adapt code maintainability in the study of [210].

l) Bayesian network-based

Following text gives a brief description of studies that have used Bayesian networks for prioritization. The proposed approach of Mirarab and Tahvildari [211, 212], ordered test cases according to their success probability on Bayesian Networks. In [212] authors extended their work done in [211] by introducing a feedback mechanism and a new changed information gathering strategy. Sanchez *et al.* [148] introduced a prioritization approach that maximized the improvement of the diagnostic information per test using Bayesian reasoning. Zhao, Xiaobin, *et al.* [199] applied Bayesian network and clustering approach to the prioritization. An automatic system to execute and prioritize test cases based on Bayesian network was presented by [213]. Authors considered parameters like code coverage, coupling information, execution time and amount of modifications.

m) Based on multi-objective approaches

It should be noted that soft computing tools like GA, PSO and ACO can provide solutions to multi-objective problems too but the articles considered under "Multi-Objective" have specifically emphasized on solving prioritization in multi-perspective ways. Islam *et al.* [214] proposed a tool named Multi-Objective prioritization technique (MOTCP). MOTCP prioritized test cases explicitly considering at the same time structural and functional information. In study [215], the authors solved prioritization for GUI applications. The authors comparatively studied the effectiveness of two prioritization strategies: statement-based and event-based. And they proposed a new multi-objective strategy to combine these two single- objectives together. Wang *et al.* [216] proposed an approach with five objectives: coverage, FEP, Requirement Property Relevance and History. In [217], authors presented a multi-objective prioritization considered faults using both technical and business criticality. Marijan, Dusica [218] proposed multi-perspective prioritization in time-constrained environments. Authors considered business perspective like: performance perspective, and technical perspective. Z. Li *et al.* [219] proposed parallel multi-objective prioritization on graphics processing unit (GPU). Their proposed framework incorporated GPU-based and parallel crossover computation for prioritization problem. A graph search based approach is proposed by [220]. In [221], authors applied aggregated approach based on factors like code, system, test case and tags. Some studies aggregated different code coverage weights into a single objective [222]. "REMAP" [223]: is an approach that considered fault detection capability and test case reliability together for ranking of tests. Prioritization in [224], was done on the basis of function importance, function associations and fault coverage.

7.2.2.9   Web-Based

This category presents articles, where the test case prioritization has been done in context of web testing: Mei *et al.* [225] referred XML elements as WSDL tags. WSDL tag coverage based prioritization on XML code was done by [226]. Authors in [227] proposed multilevel coverage for coverage of X-path, business process and WSDL. Zhai *et al.* [228–234] have used different aspects of web-based testing to prioritize test cases. Further, [235] proposed a recommender system for web services prioritization. Authors in [236] prioritized Android GUI test cases using RankBoost learning. L. Mei, Zhang, *et al.* [237] prioritized test cases on the basis of *service* interactions and changes requirements analysis of web services. The research work of Garg and Datta [238] was based on dependence graph of web services which involved the parallel distribution of test cases on multiple machines for reducing time to detect faults.

7.2.2.10   *Object Oriented Testing-Based*

Testing of object oriented (OO) software is different from the procedural counterpart due to the features like inheritance, polymorphism and data abstraction. The articles classified under this category have solved prioritization in context of object oriented testing. Some studies like [23, 24, 60, 61] have used object oriented test cases generated by Junit tool. Most of these studies considered the class level testing. Further, some studies [53, 54, 57, 239–241] considered inter class dependencies for ordering the test cases. [66, 67] derived associations in classes on the basis of different function calls among these classes and used object oriented slicing on test dependency graph to priorities test cases. Panigrahi and Mall [57] applied forward slicing to construct extended SDG for affected model. Authors provided higher weights to the affected nodes in extended SDG. A similar study Panigrahi and Mall [239] proposed a model-based regression prioritization technique for object-oriented program. Authors of [240] applied concept of depth of inheritance tree DIT to know the most crucial test cases. The studies of [241] applied object oriented modelling concept to sort the system level test cases. Also some authors [242, 243] have applied clustering approach to the data related to object oriented testing. A multi-factored approach considering both code and cost at the same time has been evaluated by [244]. Authors in [245] applied object coupling driven approach to prioritize test cases in object oriented testing.

7.2.2.11   *Similarity-Based*

Some studies have applied the concept of similarity to prioritization as discussed in following. Noor and Hemmati [246] prioritized and Wu *et al.* [247] proposed similarity based prioritization by using ordered sequence of program elements. Al-Hajjaji [248] used the concept of similarity for two different products with similar configurations. The underlying assumption was that two different products with similar configuration might have similar faults. Zhang, Groce, and Alipour [202] used delta-debugging for minimizing and prioritizing test cases. As per study of Ledru *et al.* [249] Manhattan distance was a better choice for measuring string distances. Fang *et al.* [250] used edit distance to differentiate test cases and introduced two algorithms based on farthest-first ordered sequence. Maheswari and JeyaMala [251] calculated Hamming distance between two binary strings. "FAST" technique in [252], extended the usability of similarity based prioritization to big data. Data were reused on similar context [253]. Different measures of similarity were listed in [254]. The study of [255], empirically evaluated the Similarity based prioritization against random techniques. Information retrieval based approach on Textual similarity and frequency of testing inputs was adopted by the studies [256, 257]. Linguistic similarity of new test cases with test cases of the prior version of the software is exploited by [258].

7.2.2.12   *Combinatorial Interaction Testing-Based*

Combinatorial interaction testing (CIT) works on the basis of input values for individual parameters and combines these values to create test cases. The studies that have applied combinatorial approach to prioritization are discussed in following text. Xiao *et al.* [259–262] have applied CIT to prioritization through different insights. In [259] authors examined the effectiveness of CIT across multiple versions of two software subjects. In [260] authors proposed configuration model based on combinations of configuration options. In [259] the authors prioritized CIT test suites for regression testing and ordered the test cases within a test suite without considering configurations. In [260] they modified the strategy and included configurations too. They generated biased covering array and used the interaction benefit of individual factor and value to determine the final configuration order. In [261] authors provided a framework for configuration aware prioritization techniques and developed eight prioritization heuristics, In [263–265] the authors presented an approach for combinatorial interaction testing that was capable of both constraints support and prioritization. Wu, Nie, and Kuo [266] proposed greedy algorithms and graph-based algorithms, to prioritize a given test suite to minimize its total switching cost. Chen *et al.* [267] proposed a hybrid approach for prioritizing interaction test suite. Srikanth, Cohen, and Qu [262] presented a case study to prioritize configurations on the basis of fault history. Also, some studies [268–272] have considered fixed strength prioritization for CIT. In [273–276] authors used Automated

Combinatorial Testing for Software (ACTS) tool to generates the test cases. The tool provided options for don't care values. Authors further refined these values and prioritized the test cases as per new derived values. A dataflow technique for CIT based prioritization was advocated by [277]. The work in [278] generated test cases through statistical user profile approach and applied constraints driven CIT approach for prioritization. Also, results of some studies showed that CIT based approach to prioritization performed better as compared to their counterparts in black box testing [279].

7.2.2.13   Machine Learning-Based

It is found in the survey that machine learning based approaches are also getting applied in prioritization. Some of the studies under this category are as given: A study that used Fuzzy logic based classification model to prioritization was endorsed by [280], A SVM based ranking system for test cases was designed by [281, 282], Authors in [283] applied Navigation Tree Mining [283] to prioritization similarly Logistic regression model was applied by [284, 285] Another study used Classification-tree method [286] prioritization through machine learning approaches. A predictive test prioritization in [287] utilized 10 different machine learning algorithms to predict the optimal prioritization on the basis features extracted for any given project.

7.2.2.14   Adaptive Random Testing (ART)-Based

Many studies have applied ART approach to prioritization. Such as, Jiang et al. [288] and Hao, Zhao, and Zhang [289] proposed ART based prioritization approach which involved the calculation of the fault-detection capability of unselected test cases based. R. Huang et al. [265] proposed ART based prioritization to tackle interaction test suites by using the interaction coverage information. The approach worked in absence of coverage information. Jiang and Chan [195] inspected domains of the regression test suite and randomized the test case distribution evenly through space provided by inputs. A cloud cum software testing based ART approach on the basis of resource allocation criteria was explored by [290]. G-Rank was a generation cum prioritization strategy that worked on the impact of the test case on values of input domain [291]. A performance comparison of dynamic ART and Static ART was performed by [292]. A category portioned distance based approach was adopted by [293, 318].

7.2.2.15   Prioritization for Continuous Integration (CI) and Software Product Lines (SPL)

SPL engineering is a paradigm that formally represents a set of software products that share many common characteristics. A reinforcement learning based approach in [294], considered feedback based reward values for prioritization in CI. The study in [295], advocated prioritization as a continuous process. Combination of history-based and diversity based heuristics are applied by [296] to prioritization in CI environment. Marijan, Gotlieb, and Sen [297, 298] proposed an algorithm called 'ROCKET' that worked on parameters like historical failure data, execution time and domain specific heuristics and prioritized test cases for continuous regression testing. Ensan *et al.* [299] proposed an approach for reducing and prioritizing the test cases in software product line feature model. The authors also introduced a goal-oriented approach to select the most desirable features from the product line. Lachmann, Remo, *et al.* [300, 301] used delta modeling concept for prioritizing the test cases for the SPL. The difference between the product variants was captured as delta. And the incremental delta approach was used to improve integration testing for SPL.

7.2.2.16   Hybrid Approaches

It was found in the survey that some authors have applied a blend of two or more different approaches, for instance, PSO and GA was adopted in [302], Fuzzy Logic and ACO in [303, 304], Statistical model and Markov reward model in [305]. Some studies also applied an approach that required data from Model, Code coverage based and requirement coverage [306]. A hybrid criteria based algorithm devised by [307], considered test cases with less time and high coverage for prioritization.

7.2.2.17   Comparative Studies

There are some studies that have examined the prioritization for comparisons of different techniques like Huang *et al.* [308] comparatively investigated the abstract prioritization from different domains. Comparative analysis of various techniques [309] for different measures like fault rate, number of faults detected, risk detection ability and effectiveness of test case. The study, comparatively evaluated the performance difference of static code coverage with dynamic code coverage for different total prioritization, additional prioritization, search-based prioritization, adaptive random prioritization and integer linear programming (ILP) based prioritization techniques for different test granularity and coverage criteria. Results of the study indicate that dynamic coverage criteria perform better. The study in [310] compared the performance of static prioritization and dynamic prioritization in the context of modern software development paradigm.

Comparative studies to validate the representative of mutants with real faults in prioritization in the context of regression testing were presented by [311, 312]. Their results found that mutants were closely related to real faults as far as performance of prioritization was concerned. Authors in [313] performed a comparison of manual prioritization with automated prioritization.

7.2.2.18   Surveys and Reviews

Section 7.1.2 has described the exiting surveys and reviews in this field. Readers can read that section for more details.

7.3   What Subject Systems Have Been Used to Evaluate Test Case Prioritization Techniques? What is the Type of Programming Platform for Subject Systems?

The subject program is the software or case study that is used for empirically evaluating the findings of researches. It is found that researchers have used many subject programs. The table below shows such subject programs. The survey also found some online repositories that provide many subject programs and testing data for them. SIR [314] is one such online resource. Table 7.3 given below highlights the various subject programs used by researchers.

Table 7.3 Subject programs in literature.

S. n	Subject program(s)	Nature	Studies
1	Siemens programs	P	[3–5, 8, 9, 20, 21, 30, 49, 54, 63, 64, 68, 85, 86, 97, 161, 162, 167]
2	javac, jikes	O	[11]
3	gcc	P	[11]

(Continued)

Table 7.3 Subject programs in literature. (*Continued*)

S. n	Subject program(s)	Nature	Studies
4	bash, emp-server, flex, grep, gzip, make, sed, xearth	P	[12, 42, 77, 99, 113, 116]
5	Ant, XML-security, JMeter, JTopas	O	[13, 61, 67, 130, 155, 181]
6	ATM model, cruise control model, and fuel pump model	P	[16, 48]
7	JUnit test suites.	O	[23, 24, 50, 156]
8	GradeBook application	O	[28]
9	TerpCalc, TerpPaint, TerpSpreadsheet, TerpWord	E	[33]
10	*ant*, *xml-security*, *jmeter*, *nanoxml*, and *Galileo*, *jedend*	O	[34, 41, 51, 98, 106, 110, 125, 139]
11	ATM model, cruise control model, fuel pump model, TCP model, ISDN	P	[36, 142]
12	VIM from SIR	P	[40]
13	Book, Course project manager	E	[44, 85]
14	*Travel Agent* System	W	[86]
15	*Triangle program*	NA	[56]
16	ATM, Library System, Elevator Controller, Vending Machine	O	[72]
17	Microsoft Dynamics	MP	[87]
18	Library Management System (LMS), Trading house Automation System (TAS)	O	[92]

(*Continued*)

Table 7.3 Subject programs in literature. (*Continued*)

S. n	Subject program(s)	Nature	Studies
19	Elite, GSM, CRM, Bash, MET, CZT	MP	[111]
20	Crossword Sage (CS) and OmegaT (OT)	MP	[118]
21	JMock	O	[121]
22	BPEL Repository	MP	[122]
23	Online Bookstore, Moodle	MP	[124, 131]
24	ATM, LMS and Super Market Automation system (SMA)	MP	[147]
25	own programs	NA	[162, 164]

[P = Procedural, O= Object oriented, MP = Multi-platform, E = Event-based, W = web-based, NA = Not applicable].

It is also found that subject programs are to be selected as per the prioritization technique used. Some subjects programs like ATM, LMS and cruise control are used particularly with model based testing. And the programs like Siemens programs are widely used in the context of code coverage based techniques.

7.3.1   What is Research Status in Model-Based Test Case Prioritization?

Model-based testing uses a model that describes the behavior of the system under test [315]. A total of 30 primary studies were found related to Model based prioritization. The survey concluded that nearly 10 percent of the articles belonged to model based prioritization.

7.3.2   What Evaluation Criterion Has Been Used to Evaluate Model-Based Prioritization and How are The Results Reported?

The evaluation criteria used to evaluate model based prioritization has been summarized in Table 7.4.

Table 7.4 Evaluation criteria for prioritization in MBT.

Ref.	Methodology	Objective	Results/conclusions
[90]	Comparison of original and modified system models together with information collected during the execution of the modified model.	Early fault detection in the modified system.	Model-based test prioritization improves the effectiveness of prioritization for selective prioritization.
[94]	High priority tests are prioritized using model dependence analysis.	Early fault detection in the modified system.	Model-based prioritization and Heuristic prioritization, has given the best effectiveness in an empirical study.
[54]	By analysis of strongly connected components and object oriented slicing.	To minimize use of stubs.	Significant reduction in test stubs is achieved.
[139]	Analysis of test models that have been augmented with risk factors.	Early detection of critical faults.	Prioritizing test case scenarios based on augmented test models enable the early detection of critical faults.
[91]	by comparing the transitions from modified code to the unmodified model.	Early detection of faults.	The performance is best when marked transitions have the same opportunity to be executed during software retesting.

(*Continued*)

Table 7.4 Evaluation criteria for prioritization in MBT. (*Continued*)

Ref.	Methodology	Objective	Results/conclusions
[95]	By comparing the transitions from modified code to the unmodified model.	Experimental comparison of model based prioritization with code based prioritization.	Model based prioritization performs better as compared additional statement coverage provided all marked transition are given equal consideration.
[49]	Comparing activity coverage in the original model and modified model.	To Enhance activity coverage	Improvement in activity coverage was noticed.
[239]	By identifying changes in the modified model and use of forward and backward slicing.	To enhance bugs detection percentage (BDP)	It was found that BDP was better for Model based prioritization.
[92]	By mapping of feature model elements with stakeholders' goals.	To reduce the product line test space	The method is able to significantly reduce test space and effectively prioritize the remaining test cases.
[316]	By classifying events using both unsupervised NN based adaptive CL and FCM clustering algorithm.	To provide orders to test cases on	NA
[102]	By ordering tests according to their preference degrees which are based on event classification.	To order test cases as per classifications of events	Application considered is very small and results are dependent on modelling.

Table 7.4 Evaluation criteria for prioritization in MBT. (*Continued*)

Ref.	Methodology	Objective	Results/conclusions
[186]	Difference between original and modified model	Early detection of faults	Early detection of faults is improved.
[99]	On the basis of coverage of state changes occurred within the components	To select test cases in order of maximized state changes	Improved APFD.
[241]	On the basis of scenario coverage criterion	To maximize coverage.	Higher coverage achieved.
[92]	By identifying changes in system model and system implementations	To evaluate the performance of model based prioritization	Improvement in the effectiveness of prioritization using system models.
[109]	By calculating Jaccard distance between the test cases and Manhattan distance between the array of branches of the model	To study the impact of test case profile and model structure on prioritization	Results show that the profile of the failed test case may have a definite influence on the performance prioritization techniques.
[104]	By measuring the modifications made in the model by aspects. Transitions with more modifications were given priorities over others	Early detection of faults	Giving the order to aspect tests accelerated the failure report.

(*Continued*)

Table 7.4 Evaluation criteria for prioritization in MBT. (*Continued*)

Ref.	Methodology	Objective	Results/conclusions
[105]	By finding a frequent pattern of highly affected nodes pattern from historical testing data.	Early detection of affected nodes due to changes made in SUT	APFD value for prioritized test cases was improved
[319]	By converting activity diagrams into a tree and giving rational weights to edges and nodes. Then prioritizing scenario as per weights	To determine the path in the tree that has the highest weight.	The critical scenario can be extracted from the activity diagrams
[108]	By converting the Activity diagram into weighted CFG. Then applying Hybrid GA	To enhance early fault detection	Prioritized test scenario resulted in cost saving and improved efficiency of testing
[100]	By mapping model components with code artifacts and user concerns.	Coverage of traceability links in the code	NA

Table 7.4 highlights the various evaluation criteria with their objective(s) and the results obtained. It is obvious that model based testing (MBT) is generally used in the absence of a code of SUT. MBT also reduces the cost of testing.

7.3.3   How Model-Based Test Case Prioritization Has Evolved Over the Years? Which Studies Have Discussed the Benefits of Model-Based Test Case Prioritization in Object-Oriented Systems?

As per our survey model based prioritization was incepted in the year 2005 and Korel *et al.* [16] were the first to use the concept of system model in prioritization. Since 2005, there has been a continuous interest in model based prioritization. In the beginning, Model based prioritization was applied to procedural or traditional programming scenarios but later on, model based testing found its application in object oriented paradigm and web based applications too. Out of the studies found in the field of model based prioritization, only [54, 239, 241] have considered the object oriented features in prioritization.

7.3.4   What Subject Systems Are Used to Evaluate the Model-Based Test Case Prioritization?

Model based testing involves the creation of some kind of model to capture the behavior of the system under test. Many models have been used by the authors in the implementation of model based prioritization. Table 7.5 enlists subject program(s) used by various model based studies. It can be seen from the results that most of the studies have used activity diagrams to represent the functionalities of SUT. It is also seen that the ATM model has been most of the times in such studies.

7.3.5   What is the Research Status of Test Case Prioritization for Object-Oriented Testing?

It is observed that very little work has been done in the prioritization specific to object oriented testing. As per our survey, nearly 5% of articles are related to object oriented testing. Use of object oriented metrics in prioritization is still not been explored. Also, there exist a lot of fault prediction studies in the context of object oriented testing, but the studies have not been extended for prioritization purpose.

Table 7.5 Subject programs for model based prioritization.

Subject program
ATM model, Cruise Control, Fuel Pump, ISDN, TOKEN PRINT, Airline Reservation, Library Information System, e-shop vendor machine, web-based tourist portal, and marginal strip mower, ISLETA (an online reservation system for a hotel) Labeled Transition System-Based Tool and PDF Split and Merge Hotel Management System.

7.3.6   What Specific Parameters of Object-Oriented Testing Have Been Highlighted by Various Studies?

Table 7.6 depicts the various parameters that the researchers have considered for prioritization in the context of object oriented testing.

Following studies have used object oriented approaches to solve prioritization problem.

The authors in [23, 24] considered two types of test cases: method level and class level. Their study investigated the effect of test case granularity on prioritization. The results suggested that method level tests are more promising than class level. The work related to object oriented testing [54], used class slicing for prioritization. The studies of [60, 320] are also based on method level test cases. These considered the test cases and methods calls relationship associated with test cases. Authors in [53] used influence metric for class and method to estimate the code coverage in the absence of coverage information. The study of [96] used static object relations like inheritance, aggregation, and association to identify the elements that may be affected by a change. Research work of [240] ranked the classes by the number of attributes, number of children (NOC), depth of inheritance (DIT) and method inherited by a class. The study of [57] too considered

Table 7.6 Parameters of object-oriented prioritization.

S. n	Studies #	Parameters
1	[23]	Class level testing, method level testing
2	[24]	Class level, method level
3	[54]	Object-oriented slicing, test ordering for OOP.
4	[320]	Class level test cases
5	[53]	Influence of a class
6	[60]	Method level testing, class level test cases
7	[96]	Inheritance hierarchy, polymorphism,
8	[240]	Inheritance
9	[57]	Inheritance, association
10	[241]	Object points, code reuse.

DIT, NOC, and associations to represent dependencies in the code. Study of [241] used sequence diagrams of object oriented system to generate and prioritize system test cases.

7.3.7 What Studies Exist Based on Multi-Objective Algorithms for Test Case Prioritization in Object-Oriented Testing?

It is found that many authors have used multi-objective optimization algorithms to solve the problem of prioritization. Multi optimization techniques find their applicability in optimizing more than one objective at the same time. Suri and Singhal [89, 206] have applied ACO to prioritize test case for two optimal objectives; time and coverage. Authors collected data for 8 object oriented software. But they did not consider the impact of any specific feature of object oriented testing.

Authors in [182] used PCGA, which works on Pareto optimality. They considered ATM model, Library Management System and Shopping mall automation as subject programs but did not consider any specific object oriented feature. The study in [216] considered five objectives for prioritization problem which consists of code coverage, FEP, History, requirement property relevance, and execution. All the objectives were related to procedural programming. MOTCP tool was proposed by [214] which implemented a multi-objective test prioritization technique based on a three-dimension analysis of test cases: structural, functional and cost. MOTCP applied non dominated Sorting Genetic Algorithm II (NSGA-II) to find the final set of test cases. The study considered object oriented software as subject programs.

7.3.8 Whether Comparative Analysis of Multi-Objective Algorithms for Test Case Prioritization in Object-Oriented Testing Has Been Performed? And What are The Results?

As discussed in the previous section, multi-objective prioritization has not been exercised for the objective oriented paradigm. And the studies concerning multi-objective prioritization so far are using parameters which fall either under procedural programming or other parameters like risk coverage, requirement coverage, cost and time. Since there is no study found which incorporated multi-objective prioritization in object oriented testing so, no such comparative study was found.

7.4   Research Gaps

The outcome of the review has given the following research gaps in this field.

❖ Most of the prioritization techniques, in general, apply greedy approach on coverage criteria like statement coverage, additional statement coverage, and function coverage etc. These types of approach may be efficient for testing of procedural software but, these techniques are not that much efficient for object-oriented software since coverage of statement and function is not very meaningful in this context. Instead of object oriented features such as object oriented coupling, inheritance, and dynamic binding are to be weighted more. So there is the potential of research in this direction and a suitable technique utilizing object oriented features for test case prioritization need to be investigated.

❖ The techniques in the context of object oriented testing are mostly based on model based. And most of the work done depends on analyzing the model structure for the localization of the faults/fault prone components of the software. Manual model based analysis of the large software may become cumbersome. Automatic analysis of fault prone components based object oriented metrics and their implication to prioritization is still an open area.

❖ It is also found object oriented metrics have been used for the fault prediction, maintenance prediction, and quality assessment. But studies have not been performed to investigate the usage of object oriented metrics for the test case prioritization.

References

1. Kitchenham, B. *et al.*, Systematic literature reviews in software engineering-a tertiary study. *Inf. Softw. Technol.* Elsevier B.V., 52, 8, 792–805, 2010.
2. Kitchenham, B., *Procedures for Performing Systematic Reviews*, Keele University, Keele, UK, 33, 1–26, 2004.
3. Budgen, D. and Brereton, P., Performing systematic literature reviews in software engineering, in: *Proceeding of the 28th International Conference on Software Engineering-ICSE '06*, 2006.

4. Yoo, S. and Harman, M., Regression testing minimisation, selection and prioritisation: A survey. *Softw. Test. Verif. Realiab.*, 22, 2, 67–120, 2012.

5. Catal, C. and Mishra, D., Test case prioritization: A systematic mapping study. *Softw. Qual. J.*, 21, 3, 445–478, 2013.

6. Singh, Y., Kaur, A., Suri, B., Singhal, S., Systematic literature review on regression test prioritization techniques. *Informatica (Slovenia)*, 36, 379–408, 2012.

7. Khatibsyarbini, M., Isa, M.A., Jawawi, D.N.A., Tumeng, R., Test case prioritization approaches in regression testing: A systematic literature review. *Inf. Softw. Technol.*, 93, 74–93, 2018.

8. de Souza Campos Junior, H., Araújo, M.A.P., David, J.M.N., Braga, R., Campos, F., Ströele, V., Test case prioritization: A systematic review and mapping of the literature, in: *Proceedings of the 31st Brazilian Symposium on Software Engineering*, pp. 34–43, 2017.

9. Kumar, A. and Singh, K., A literature survey on test case prioritization. *Compusoft*, 3, 5, 793–799, 2014.

10. Kumar, S. and Rajkumar, Test case prioritization techniques for software product line: A survey, in: *2016 International Conference on Computing, Communication and Automation (ICCCA)*, pp. 884–889, 2016.

11. Hao, D., Zhang, L., Mei, H., Test-case prioritization: Achievements and challenges. *Front. Comput. Sci.*, 10, 5, 769–777, Oct. 2016.

12. Mukherjee, R. and Patnaik, K.S., A survey on different approaches for software test case prioritization. *J. King Saud. Univ. Comput. Inf. Sci.*, 33, 9, 1041–1054, 2021.

13. Saraswat, P., Singhal, A., Bansal, A., A review of test case prioritization and optimization techniques, in: *Advances in Intelligent Systems and Computing*, vol. 731, pp. 507–516, 2019.

14. Rothermel, G., Untch, R.H., Chengyun Chu, C., Harrold, M.J., Test case prioritization: An empirical study, in: *Proceedings IEEE International Conference on Software Maintenance-1999 (ICSM'99). Software Maintenance for Business Change (Cat. No.99CB36360)*, pp. 179–188, 1999.

15. Elbaum, S., Malishevsky, A.G., Rothermel, G., Test case prioritization: A family of empirical studies. *IEEE Trans. Softw. Eng.*, 28, 2, 159–182, 2002.

16. Rothermel, G., Untcn, R.H., Chu, C., Harrold, M.J., Prioritizing test cases for regression testing. *IEEE Trans. Softw. Eng.*, 27, 10, 929–948, 2001.

17. Jones, J.A. and Harrold, M.J., Test-suite reduction and prioritization for modified condition/decision coverage, in: *IEEE International Conference on Software Maintenance, ICSM*, vol. 29, pp. 92–103, 2001.

18. Elbaum, S., Rothermel, G., Malishevsky, A., Rothermel, G., Incorporating varying test costs and fault severities into test case prioritization. *Proc.-Int. Conf. Softw. Eng.*, pp. 329–338, 2001.

19. Elbaum, S., Gable, D., Rothermel, G., Understanding and measuring the sources of variation in the prioritization of regression test suites. *Proc. Seventh Int. Softw. Metrics Symp.*, pp. 169–179, 2001.

20. Srivastava, A. and Thiagarajan, J., Effectively prioritizing tests in development environment. *ACM SIGSOFT Softw. Eng. Notes*, 27, 4, 97, 2002.

21. Leon, D. and Podgurski, A., A comparison of coverage-based and distribution-based techniques for filtering and prioritizing test cases, in: *Proceedings - International Symposium on Software Reliability Engineering, ISSRE*, January 2003, pp. 442–453, 2003.

22. Elbaum, S., Rothermel, G., Kanduri, S., Malishevsky, A.G., Selecting a cost-effective test case prioritization technique. *Softw. Qual. J.*, 12, 3, 185–210, 2004.

23. Do, H., Rothermel, G., Kinneer, A., Empirical studies of test case prioritization in a JUnit testing environment, in: *Proceedings-International Symposium on Software Reliability Engineering, ISSRE*, 12, 3, 185–210, 2004.

24. Do, H., Rothermel, G., Kinneer, A., Prioritizing JUnit test cases: An empirical assessment and cost-benefits analysis. *Empir. Softw. Eng.*, 11, 1, 33–70, 2006.

25. Do, H. and Rothermel, G., On the use of mutation faults in empirical assessments of test case prioritization techniques. *IEEE Trans. Softw. Eng.*, 32, 9, 733–752, 2006.

26. Li, Z., Harman, M., Hierons, R.M., Search algorithms for regression test case prioritization. *IEEE Trans. Softw. Eng.*, 33, 4, 225–237, 2007.

27. Smith, A.M. and Kapfhammer, G.M., An empirical study of incorporating cost into test suite reduction and prioritization. *Proc. 2009 ACM Symp. Appl. Comput.-SAC '09*, vol. 1, p. 461, 2009.

28. Masri, W. and El-Ghali, M., Test case filtering and prioritization based on coverage of combinations of program elements, in: *Proceedings of the Seventh International Workshop on Dynamic Analysis*, pp. 29–34, 2009.

29. ur Rehman Khan, S., ur Rehman, I., ur Rehman Malik, S., The impact of test case reduction and prioritization on software testing effectiveness. *2009 Int. Conf. Emerg. Technol*, pp. 416–421, 2009.

30. Fang, C.R., Chen, Z.Y., Xu, B.W., Comparing logic coverage criteria on test case prioritization. *Sci. China Inf. Sci.*, 55, 12, 2826–2840, 2012.

31. Di Nardo, D., Alshahwan, N., Briand, L., Labiche, Y., Coverage-based regression test case selection, minimization and prioritization: A case study on an industrial system. *Softw. Test. Verif. Reliab.*, 25, 4, 371–396, 2015.

32. Di Nucci, D., Panichella, A., Zaidman, A., De Lucia, A., Hypervolume-based search for test case prioritization, in: *Lecture Notes in Computer Science (including subseries Lecture Notes in Artificial Intelligence and Lecture Notes in Bioinformatics)*, 2015.

33. Khin, H.S.H., YoungSik, C., Jong, S.P., Applying particle swarm optimization to prioritizing test cases for embedded real time software retesting, in: *Proceedings-8th IEEE International Conference on Computer and Information Technology Workshops, CIT Workshops 2008*, pp. 527–532, 2008.

34. Hao, D., Zhang, L.L., Zhang, L.L., Rothermel, G., Mei, H., A unified test case prioritization approach. *ACM Trans. Softw. Eng. Methodol.*, 24, 2, 10:1–10:31, 2014.

35. Do, H. and Rothermel, G., *A Controlled Experiment Assessing Test Case Prioritization Techniques via Mutation Faults*, 2005.
36. Zengkai, M. and Jianjun, Z., Test case prioritization based on analysis of program structure, in: *15th Asia-Pacific Software Engineering Conference Test*, pp. 471–478, 2008.
37. Lou, Y., Hao, D., Zhang, L., Mutation-based test-case prioritization in software evolution. *2015 IEEE 26th Int. Symp. Softw. Reliab. Eng. ISSRE 2015*, pp. 46–57, 2016.
38. Nawar, M.N. and Ragheb, M.M., Multi-heuristic based algorithm for test case prioritization, in: *Lecture Notes in Computer Science (including subseries Lecture Notes in Artificial Intelligence and Lecture Notes in Bioinformatics)*, 2014.
39. Alazzam, I. and Nahar, K.M.O., Combined source code approach for test case prioritization, in: *Proceedings of the 2018 International Conference on Information Science and System-ICISS '18*, pp. 12–15, 2018.
40. Banias, O., The drawbacks of statement code coverage test case prioritization related to domain testing, in: *SACI 2016-11th IEEE International Symposium on Applied Computational Intelligence and Informatics, Proceedings*, pp. 221–224, 2016.
41. Eghbali, S. and Tahvildari, L., Test case prioritization using lexicographical ordering. *IEEE Trans. Softw. Eng.*, 42, 12, 1178–1195, Dec. 2016.
42. Hirzel, M., Brachthäuser, J., II, Klaeren, H., Prioritizing regression tests for desktop and web-applications based on the execution frequency of modified code, in: *Proceedings of the 13th International Conference on Principles and Practices of Programming on the Java Platform: Virtual Machines, Languages, and Tools-PPPJ '16*, pp. 1–12, 2016.
43. Ammar, A., Baharom, S., Ghani, A.A.A., DIn, J., Enhanced weighted method for test case prioritization in regression testing using unique priority value, in: *ICISS 2016-2016 International Conference on Information Science and Security*, pp. 1–6, 2017.
44. Miranda, B. and Bertolino, A., Scope-aided test prioritization, selection and minimization for software reuse. *J. Syst. Softw.*, 131, 528–549, Sep. 2017.
45. Chen, J., Bai, Y., Hao, D., Xiong, Y., Zhang, H., Xie, B., Learning to prioritize test programs for compiler testing, in: *Proceedings-2017 IEEE/ACM 39th International Conference on Software Engineering, ICSE 2017*, p. pp, 2017.
46. Sabharwal, S., Sibal, R., Sharma, C., A genetic algorithm based approach for prioritization of test case scenarios in static testing, in: *2011 2nd International Conference on Computer and Communication Technology, ICCCT-2011*, pp. 304–309, 2011.
47. Suri, B. and Singhal, S., Analyzing test case selection & prioritization using ACO. *ACM SIGSOFT Softw. Eng. Notes*, 36, 6, 1, 2011.
48. Kaur, P., Bansal, P., Sibal, R., Prioritization of test scenarios derived from UML activity diagram using path complexity. *Int. Inf. Technol. Conf. CUBE 2012*, p. 355, 2012.

49. Athira, B. and Samuel, P., Web services regression test case prioritization. *2010 Int. Conf. Comput. Inf. Syst. Ind. Manag. Appl.*, pp. 438–443, 2010.

50. Kheirkhah, A. and Mohd Daud, S., Prioritization of unit testing on non-object oriented using a top-down based approach in. *2014 8th Malaysian Software Engineering Conference, MySEC 2014*, pp. 72–77, 2014.

51. Srivastava, P.R., Ray, M., Dermoudy, J., Kang, B.H., Kim, T.H., Test case minimization and prioritization using CMIMX technique, in: *Communications in Computer and Information Science*, vol. 59, pp. 25–33, 2009.

52. Rummel, M.J., Kapfhammer, G.M., Thall, A., Towards the prioritization of regression test suites with data flow information. *Proc. 2005 ACM Symp. Appl. Comput.-SAC '05*, p. 1499, 2005.

53. Ray, M., Lal Kumawat, K., Mohapatra, D.P., Source code prioritization using forward slicing for exposing critical elements in a program. *J. Comput. Sci. Technol.*, 26, 2, 314–327, 2011.

54. Jaroenpiboonkit, J. and Suwannasart, T., Finding a test order using object-oriented slicing technique. *Proc.-Asia-Pacific Softw. Eng. Conf. APSEC*, pp. 49–56, 2007.

55. Jeffrey, D. and Gupta, N., Experiments with test case prioritization using relevant slices. *J. Syst. Software*, 81, 2, 196–221, 2008.

56. Srikanth, H., Williams, L., Osborne, J., System test case prioritization of new and regression test cases, in: *2005 International Symposium on Empirical Software Engineering, ISESE 2005*, pp. 64–73, 2005.

57. Panigrahi, C.R. and Mall, R., A heuristic-based regression test case prioritization approach for object-oriented programs. *Innov. Syst. Softw. Eng.*, 10, 3, 155–163, 2014.

58. Panigrahi, C.R. and Mall, R., An approach to prioritize the regression test cases of object-oriented programs. *CSI Trans. ICT*, 1, 2, 159–173, 2013.

59. Smith, A., Geiger, J., Kapfhammer, G.M., Lou Soffa, M., Test suite reduction and prioritization with call trees. *Proc. Twenty-Second IEEE/ACM Int. Conf. Autom. Softw. Eng.-ASE '07*, p. 539, 2007.

60. Mei, H., Hao, D., Zhang, L., Zhang, L., Zhou, J., Rothermel, G., A static approach to prioritizing junit test cases. *IEEE Trans. Softw. Eng.*, 38, 6, 1258–1275, 2012.

61. Zhang, L.L., Zhou, J., Hao, D., Zhang, L.L., Mei, H., Jtop: Managing JUnit test cases in absence of coverage information, in: *ASE2009-24th IEEE/ACM International Conference on Automated Software Engineering*, pp. 677–679, 2009.

62. Chi, J. *et al.*, Test case prioritization based on method call sequences, in: *2018 IEEE 42nd Annual Computer Software and Applications Conference (COMPSAC)*, pp. 251–256, 2018.

63. Luo, Q., Moran, K., Poshyvanyk, D., *A Large-Scale Empirical Comparison of Static and Dynamic Test Case Prioritization Techniques*, pp. 559–570, ACM Press, New York, New York, USA, 2018.

64. Ren, Y., Yin, B.-B., Wang, B., Test case prioritization for GUI regression testing based on centrality measures. *2018 IEEE 42nd Annual Computer Software and Applications Conference (COMPSAC)*, pp. 454–459, 2018.

65. Indumathi, C.P. and Selvamani, K., Test cases prioritization using open dependency structure algorithm. *Proc. Comput. Sci.*, 48, 250–255, 2015.

66. Haidry, S.E.Z. and Miller, T., Using dependency structures for prioritization of functional test suites. *IEEE Trans. Softw. Eng.*, 39, 2, 258–275, 2013.

67. Fu, W., Yu, H., Fan, G., Ji, X., Pei, X., A regression test case prioritization algorithm based on program changes and method invocation relationship. *Proc.-Asia-Pacific Softw. Eng. Conf. APSEC*, December 2017, pp. 169–178, Dec. 2018.

68. Alves, E.L.G., Machado, P.D.L., Massoni, T., Santos, S.T.C., A refactoring-based approach for test case selection and prioritization. *Int. Work. Autom. Softw. Test*, pp. 93–99, 2013.

69. Sommerville, I., *Software Engineering*, 9/E, Pearson Education India, 2011.

70. Srikanth, H., Banerjee, S., Williams, L., Osborne, J., Towards the prioritization of system test cases. *Softw. Test. Verif. Reliab.*, 24, 4, 320–337, 2014.

71. Mei, L., Zhang, Z., Chan, W.K., Tse, T.H., Test case prioritization for regression testing of service-oriented business applications. *Proc. 18th Int. Conf. World Wide Web-WWW '09*, p. 901, 2009.

72. Srikanth, H. and Williams, L., On the economics of requirements-based test case prioritization. *ACM SIGSOFT Softw. Eng. Notes*, 30, 4, 1, 2005.

73. Srikanth, H., Hettiarachchi, C., Do, H., Requirements based test prioritization using risk factors: An industrial study. *Inf. Softw. Technol.*, 69, 71–83, 2016.

74. Krishnamoorthi, R. and Sahaaya Arul Mary, S.A., Factor oriented requirement coverage based system test case prioritization of new and regression test cases. *Inf. Softw. Technol.*, 51, 4, 799–808, 2009.

75. Mahmood, M.H. and Hosain, M.S., Improving test case prioritization based on practical priority factors, in: *2017 8th IEEE International Conference on Software Engineering and Service Science (ICSESS)*, pp. 899–902, 2017.

76. Arafeen, M.J. and Do, H., Test case prioritization using requirements-based clustering, in: *Proceedings-IEEE 6th International Conference on Software Testing, Verification and Validation, ICST 2013*, pp. 312–321, 2013.

77. Zhang, X., Nie, C., Xu, B., Qu, B., Test case prioritization using requirements-based clustering, in *Proceedings-IEEE 6th International Conference on Software Testing, Verification and Validation, ICST 2013*, pp. 15–24, 2007.

78. Ramasamy, K. and Mary., S.A., Incorporating varying requirement priorities and costs in test case prioritization for new and regression testing, in: *Proceedings of the 2008 International Conference on Computing, Communication and Networking, ICCCN 2008*, 2008.

79. Chittimalli, P.K. and Harrold, M.J., Regression test selection on system requirements, in: *Proceedings of the 1st Conference on India Software Engineering conference-ISEC '08*, 2008.

80. Liu, W., Wu, X., Zhang, W., Xu, Y., The research of the test case prioritiza-tion algorithm for black box testing, in: *Proceedings of the IEEE International Conference on Software Engineering and Service Sciences, ICSESS*, pp. 37–40, 2014.

81. McZara, J., Sarkani, S., Holzer, T., Eveleigh, T., Software requirements prior-itization and selection using linguistic tools and constraint solvers? A con-trolled experiment. *Empir. Softw. Eng.*, 20, 6, 1721–1761, 2015.

82. Kavitha, R., Kavitha, V.R., Suresh Kumar, N., Requirement based test case prioritization. *2010 IEEE International Conference on Communication Control and Computing Technologies, ICCCCT 2010*, pp. 826–829, 2010.

83. Ramanathan, M.K., Koyuturk, M., Grama, A., Jagannathan, S., PHALANX: A graph-theoretic framework for test case prioritization. *Symp. Appl. Comput*, p. 6, 2008.

84. Sapna, P.G. and Hrushikesha, M., Prioritizing use cases to aid ordering of scenarios, in: *EMS 2009-UKSim 3rd European Modelling Symposium on Computer Modelling and Simulation*, pp. 136–141, 2009.

85. Vescan, A., Şerban, C., Chisăliţă-Creţu, C., Dioşan, L., Requirement depen-dencies-based formal approach for test case prioritization in regression test-ing, in: *Proceedings-2017 IEEE 13th International Conference on Intelligent Computer Communication and Processing, ICCP 2017*, pp. 181–188, 2017.

86. Sardana, A. and Chauhan, N., An extended test case prioritization technique using script and linguistic parameters in a distributed agile environment, in: *Towards Extensible and Adaptable Methods in Computing*, pp. 13–26, Springer Singapore, Singapore, 2018.

87. Pandey, A.K. and Goyal, N.K., *Reliability Centric Test Case Prioritization*, pp. 105–115, Springer, India, 2013.

88. Kumar, S., Ranjan, P., Rajesh, R., A concept for test case prioritization based upon the priority information of early phase, in: *Lecture Notes in Electrical Engineering*, vol. 396, pp. 213–223, 2016.

89. Ma, T., Zeng, H., Wang, X., Test case prioritization based on requirement correlations, in: *2016 IEEE/ACIS 17th International Conference on Software Engineering, Artificial Intelligence, Networking and Parallel/Distributed Computing, SNPD 2016*, 2016.

90. Korel, B., Tahat, L.H., Harman, M., Test prioritization using system models, in: *IEEE International Conference on Software Maintenance, ICSM*, 2005.

91. Korel, B., Koutsogiannakis, G., Tahat, L.H., Application of system models in regression test suite prioritization, in: *IEEE International Conference on Software Maintenance, ICSM*, pp. 247–256, 2008.

92. Tahat, L., Korel, B., Harman, M., Ural, H., Regression test suite prioritization using system models. *Softw. Test. Verif. Reliab.*, 22, 7, 481–506, 2012.

93. Tahat, L., Korel, B., Koutsogiannakis, G., Almasri, N., State-based models in regression test suite prioritization. *Softw. Qual. J.*, 25, 3, 703–742, Sep. 2017.

94. Korel, B., Koutsogiannakis, G., Tahat, L.H., Model-based test prioritization heuristic methods and their evaluation. *Proc. 3rd Int. Work. Adv. Model. Test.-A-MOST '07*, pp. 34–43, 2007.

95. Korel, B. and Koutsogiannakis, G., Experimental comparison of code-based and model-based test prioritization, in: *IEEE International Conference on Software Testing, Verification, and Validation Workshops, ICSTW 2009*, pp. 77–84, 2009.

96. Panigrahi, C.R. and Mall, R., Model-based regression test case prioritization. *Commun. Comput. Inf. Sci.*, 54, 6, 380–385, 2010.

97. Gantait, A., Test case generation and prioritization from UML models. *2011 Second Int. Conf. Emerg. Appl. Inf. Technol.*, pp. 345–350, 2011.

98. Panda, N., Acharya, A.A., Bhuyan, P., Mohapatra, D.P., Test case prioritization using UML state chart diagram and end-user priority, in: *Advances in Intelligent Systems and Computing*, vol. 556, pp. 573–580, 2017.

99. Mohanty, S., Acharya, A.A., Mohapatra, D.P., A model based prioritization technique for component based software retesting using UML state chart diagram, in: *ICECT 2011-2011 3rd International Conference on Electronics Computer Technology*, vol. 2, pp. 364–368, 2011.

100. Filho, R.S.S., Budnik, C.J., Hasling, W.M., McKenna, M., Subramanyan, R., Supporting concern-based regression testing and prioritization in a model-driven environment, in: *Proceedings-International Computer Software and Applications Conference*, pp. 323–328, 2010.

101. Belli, F., Eminov, M., Gokce, N., Model-based test prioritizing–a comparative soft-computing approach and case studies, pp. 427–434, Springer, Berlin, Heidelberg, 2009.

102. Belli, F. and Gökçe, N., Test prioritization at different modeling levels, in: *Communications in Computer and Information Science*, vol. 117, pp. 130–140, 2010.

103. Kundu, D., Sarma, M., Samanta, D., Mall, R., System testing for object-oriented systems with test case prioritization. *Softw. Test. Verif. Reliab.*, 19, 4, 297–333, 2009.

104. Xu, D. and Ding, J., Prioritizing state-based aspect tests, in: *ICST 2010-3rd International Conference on Software Testing, Verification and Validation*, pp. 265–274, 2010.

105. Acharya, A.A., Mahali, P., Mohapatra, D.P., Model based test case prioritization using association rule mining. In *Computational Intelligence in Data Mining*, vol. 3, pp. 429–440, Springer, New Delhi, 2015.

106. Mahali, P. and Mohapatra, D.P., Model based test case prioritization using UML behavioural diagrams and association rule mining. *Int. J. Syst. Assur. Eng. Manage.*, 9, 5, 1063–1079, Oct. 2018.

107. Emam, S.S. and Miller, J., Test case prioritization using extended digraphs. *ACM Trans. Softw. Eng. Methodol.*, 25, 1, 1–41, 2015.

108. Wang, X., Jiang, X., Shi, H., Prioritization of test scenarios using hybrid genetic algorithm based on UML activity diagram, in: *Proceedings of the*

IEEE International Conference on Software Engineering and Service Sciences, ICSESS, pp. 854–857, 3, 1, 1–28, 2015.

109. Ouriques, J.F.S., Cartaxo, E.G., Machado, P.D.L., Test case prioritization techniques for model-based testing: A replicated study. *Softw. Qual. J.*, 26, 4, 1451–1482, Dec. 2018.

110. Silva Ouriques, J. F., Cartaxo, E. G., Lima Machado, P. D., Revealing influence of model structure and test case profile on the prioritization of test cases in the context of model-based testing. *J. Softw. Eng. Res. Dev.*, 3, 1, 1–28, 2015.

111. Ouriques, J.F.S., Cartaxo, E.G., Machado, P.D.L., On the influence of model structure and test case profile on the prioritization of test cases in the context of model-based testing, in: *2013 27th Brazilian Symposium on Software Engineering*, pp. 119–128, 2013.

112. Morozov, A., Ding, K., Chen, T., Janschek, K., Test suite prioritization for efficient regression testing of model-based automotive software, in: *2017 International Conference on Software Analysis, Testing and Evolution (SATE)*, pp. 20–29, 2017.

113. Nejad, F.M., Akbari, R., Dejam, M.M., Using memetic algorithms for test case prioritization in model based software testing, in: *1st Conference on Swarm Intelligence and Evolutionary Computation, CSIEC 2016-Proceedings*, pp. 142–147, 2016.

114. Sharma, S. and Singh, A., Model-based test case prioritization using ACO: A review, in: *2016 4th International Conference on Parallel, Distributed and Grid Computing, PDGC 2016*, 2016.

115. Bhuyan, P., Ray, A., Das, M., Test scenario prioritization using UML use case and activity diagram, in: *Advances in Intelligent Systems and Computing*, vol. 556, pp. 499–512, 2017.

116. Parashar, P., Kalia, A., Bhatia, R., How time-fault ratio helps in test case prioritization for regression testing. *Int. J. Softw. Eng. (IJSE)*, 5, 2, 25–35, 2012.

117. Walcott, K.R., Lou Soffa, M., Kapfhammer, G.M., Roos, R.S., Timeaware test suite prioritization, in: *Proceedings of the 2006 International Symposium on Software Testing and Analysis-ISSTA '06*, p. 1, 2006.

118. Alspaugh, S., Walcott, K.R., Belanich, M., Kapfhammer, G.M., Soffa, M.L., Efficient time-aware prioritization with knapsack solvers. *Proc.-1st ACM Int. Work. Empir. Assess. Softw. Eng. Lang. Technol. WEASELTech 2007, Held with 22nd IEEE/ACM Int. Conf. Autom. Softw. Eng., ASE 2007*, pp. 13–18, 2007.

119. Zhang, L., Hou, S., Guo, C., Xie, T., Mei, H., Time-aware test-case prioritization using integer linear programming. *Proc. Eighteenth Int. Symp. Softw. Test. Anal.-ISSTA '09*, pp. 401–419, 2009.

120. You, D., Chen, Z., Xu, B., Luo, B., Zhang, C., An empirical study on the effectiveness of time-aware test case prioritization techniques. *Proc. 2011 ACM Symp. Appl. Comput.*, pp. 1451–1456, 2011.

121. Srivastava, P.R., Model for optimizing software testing period using non homogenous poisson process based on cumulative test case prioritization,

in: *IEEE Region 10 Annual International Conference, Proceedings/TENCON*, pp. 1–6, 2008.

122. Hou, S.S., Zhang, L., Xie, T., Sun, J.S., Quota-constrained test-case prioritization for regression testing of service-centric systems. *IEEE Int. Conf. Softw. Maintenance, ICSM*, pp. 257–266, 2008.

123. Kim, J. and Porter, A., A history-based test prioritization technique for regression testing in resource constrained environments, in: *Proceedings of the 24th International Conference on Software Engineering*, pp. 119–129, 2002.

124. Cho, Y., Kim, J., Lee, E., History-based test case prioritization for failure information, in: *Proceedings-Asia-Pacific Software Engineering Conference, APSEC*, 2017.

125. Park, H., Ryu, H., Baik, J., Historical value-based approach for cost-cognizant test case prioritization to improve the effectiveness of regression testing, in: *Proceedings-The 2nd IEEE International Conference on Secure System Integration and Reliability Improvement, SSIRI 2008*, pp. 39–46, 2008.

126. Huang, Y.C., Huang, C.Y., Chang, J.R., Chen, T.Y., Design and analysis of cost-cognizant test case prioritization using genetic algorithm with test history, in: *Proceedings-International Computer Software and Applications Conference*, pp. 413–418, 2010.

127. Huang, Y.C., Peng, K.L., Huang, C.Y., A history-based cost-cognizant test case prioritization technique in regression testing. *J. Syst. Softw.* Elsevier Inc., 85, 3, 626–637, 2012.

128. Carlson, R., Do, H., Denton, A., A clustering approach to improving test case prioritization: An industrial case study, in: *IEEE International Conference on Software Maintenance, ICSM*, pp. 382–391, 2011.

129. Czerwonka, J., Das, R., Nagappan, N., Tarvo, A., Teterev, A., CRANE: Failure prediction, change analysis and test prioritization in practice-experiences from windows, in: *Proceedings-4th IEEE International Conference on Software Testing, Verification, and Validation, ICST 2011*, pp. 357–366, 2011.

130. Fazlalizadeh, Y., Khalilian, A., Azgomi, M.A., Parsa, S., Incorporating historical test case performance data and resource constraints into test case prioritization, in: *Lecture Notes in Computer Science (including subseries Lecture Notes in Artificial Intelligence and Lecture Notes in Bioinformatics)*, pp. 43–57, p. 5668, 2009.

131. Khalilian, A., Azgomi, M.A., Fazlalizadeh, Y., An improved method for test case prioritization by incorporating historical test case data. *Sci. Comput. Program.*, 78, 1, 93–116, 2012.

132. Gupta, A., Mishra, N., Tripathi, A., Vardhan, M., Kushwaha, D.S., An improved history-based test prioritization technique using code coverage, in: *Lecture Notes in Electrical Engineering*, 2015.

133. Noguchi, T., Washizaki, H., Fukazawa, Y., Sato, A., Ota, K., History-based test case prioritization for black box testing using ant colony optimization.

2015 IEEE 8th Int. Conf. Softw. Testing, Verif. Validation, ICST 2015-Proc., pp. 2–3, 2015.

134. Qu, B., Nie, C., Xu, B., Zhang, X., Test case prioritization for black box testing, in: *31st Annual International Computer Software and Applications Conference-Vol. 1-(COMPSAC 2007)*, pp. 465–474, 2007.

135. Fazlalizadeh, Y., Khalilian, A., Azgomi, M.A., Parsa, S., Prioritizing test cases for resource constraint environments using historical test case performance data, in: *Proceedings-2009 2nd IEEE International Conference on Computer Science and Information Technology, ICCSIT 2009*, pp. 190–195, 2009.

136. Wang, X. and Zeng, H., History-based dynamic test case prioritization for requirement properties in regression testing, in: *Proceedings of the International Workshop on Continuous Software Evolution and Delivery-CSED '16*, pp. 41–47, 2016.

137. Kim, J., Jeong, H., Lee, E., Failure history data-based test case prioritization for effective regression test, in: *Proceedings of the Symposium on Applied Computing-SAC '17*, pp. 1409–1415, 2017.

138. Ulewicz, S. and Vogel-Heuser, B., Industrially applicable system regression test prioritization in production automation. *IEEE Trans. Autom. Sci. Eng.*, 15, 4, 1839–1851, Oct. 2018.

139. Stallbaum, H. and Pohl, K., An automated technique for risk-based test case generation and prioritization. *Autom. Softw. Test*, vol. 67, 2008.

140. Huang, P., Ma, X., Shen, D., Zhou, Y., Performance regression testing target prioritization via performance risk analysis. *Proc. 36th Int. Conf. Softw. Eng.-ICSE 2014*, pp. 60–71, 2014.

141. Kasurinen, J., Taipale, O., Smolander, K., Test case selection and prioritization. *Proc. 2010 ACM-IEEE Int. Symp. Empir. Softw. Eng. Meas.-ESEM '10*, p. 1, 2010.

142. Hettiarachchi, C., Do, H., Choi, B., Risk-based test case prioritization using a fuzzy expert system. *Inf. Softw. Technol.*, 69, 1–15, 2016.

143. Wang, Y., Zhu, Z., Yang, B., Guo, F., Yu, H., Using reliability risk analysis to prioritize test cases. *J. Syst. Softw.*, 139, 14–31, May 2018.

144. Li, Q. and Boehm, B., Improving scenario testing process by adding value-based prioritization: An industrial case study. *Proc. 2013 Int. Conf. Softw. Syst. Process-ICSSP 2013*, p. 78, 2013.

145. Kim, S. and Baik, J., An effective fault aware test case prioritization by incorporating a fault localization technique. *Proc. 2010 ACM-IEEE Int. Symp. Empir. Softw. Eng. Meas.-ESEM '10*, p. 1, 2010.

146. Gonzales-Sanchez, A., Piel, E., Gross, H.G., Van Gemund, A.J.C., Prioritizing tests for software fault localization, in: *Proceedings-International Conference on Quality Software*, 2010.

147. Gonzalez-Sanchez, A., Abreu, R., Gross, H.G., Van Gemund, A.J.C., Prioritizing tests for fault localization through ambiguity group reduction, in: *2011 26th IEEE/ACM International Conference on Automated Software Engineering, ASE 2011, Proceedings*, pp. 83–92, 2011.

148. Gonzales-Sanchez, A. *et al.*, Prioritizing tests for software fault diagnosis. *Softw. Pract. Exp.*, 41, 10, 1105–1129, 2011.

149. Jiang, B., Zhang, Z., Chan, W.K., Tse, T.H., Chen, T.Y., How well does test case prioritization integrate with statistical fault localization? *Inf. Softw. Technol.*, 54, 7, 739–758, 2012.

150. Jiang, B., Zhang, Z., Tse, T.H., Chen, T.Y., How well do test case prioritization techniques support statistical fault localization, in: *2009 33rd Annual IEEE International Computer Software and Applications Conference*, vol. 1, pp. 99–106, 2009.

151. Yoo, S., Harman, M., Clark, D., Fault localization prioritization. *ACM Trans. Softw. Eng. Methodol.*, 22, 3, 1, 2013.

152. Yoo, S., Harman, M., Clark, D., Fault localization prioritization: Comparing information-theoretic and coverage-based approaches. *ACM Trans. Softw. Eng. Methodol. (TOSEM)*, 22, 3, 1–29, 2013.

153. Jones, J., Harrold, M.J., Stasko, J., Visualization of test information to assist fault localization. *Proc. 24th Int. Conf. Softw. Eng.*, pp. 467–477, 2002.

154. Jiang, B. and Chan, W.K., On the integration of test adequacy, test case prioritization, and statistical fault localization, in: *Proceedings-International Conference on Quality Software*, pp. 377–384, 2010.

155. Laali, M., Liu, H., Hamilton, M., Spichkova, M., Schmidt, H.W., Test case prioritization using online fault detection information, in: *Lecture Notes in Computer Science (including subseries Lecture Notes in Artificial Intelligence and Lecture Notes in Bioinformatics)*, 2016.

156. Ouriques, J.F.S., Cartaxo, E.G., Machado, P.D.L., Neto, F.G.O., Coutinho, A.E.V.B., On the use of fault abstractions for assessing system test case prioritization techniques, in: *Proceedings of the 1st Brazilian Symposium on Systematic and Automated Software Testing-SAST*, pp. 1–10, 2016.

157. Zhang, X.Y., Towey, D., Chen, T.Y., Zheng, Z., Cai, K.Y., A random and coverage-based approach for fault localization prioritization, in: *Proceedings of the 28th Chinese Control and Decision Conference, CCDC 2016*, pp. 3354–3361, 2016.

158. Nayak, S. and Tripathi, S., Effectiveness of prioritization of test cases based on faults, pp. 657–662, 2016.

159. Fu, W., Yu, H., Fan, G., Ji, X., Test case prioritization approach to improving the effectiveness of fault localization, in: *2016 International Conference on Software Analysis, Testing and Evolution (SATE)*, pp. 60–65, 2016.

160. Wang, S., Nam, J., Tan, L., QTEP: quality-aware test case prioritization, in: *Proceedings of the 2017 11th Joint Meeting on Foundations of Software Engineering-ESEC/FSE 2017*, pp. 523–534, 2017.

161. Farooq, F. and Nadeem, A., A fault based approach to test case prioritization, in: *2017 International Conference on Frontiers of Information Technology (FIT)*, pp. 52–57, 2017.

162. Singh, Y., Kaur, A., Suri, B., Test case prioritization using ant colony optimization. *ACM SIGSOFT Softw. Eng. Notes*, 35, 4, 1, 2010.

163. Suri, B. and Singhal, S., Understanding the effect of time-constraint bounded novel technique for regression test selection and prioritization. *Int. J. Syst. Assur. Eng. Manage.*, 6, 1, 71–77, 2015.

164. Singhal, S., Gupta, S., Suri, B., Panda, S., Multi-deterministic prioritization of regression test suite compared: ACO and BCO, in: *Advances in Intelligent Systems and Computing*, vol. 452, pp. 187–194, 2016.

165. Kamna Solanki, K., Yudhvir Singh, Y., Sandeep Dalal, S., Srivastava, P.R., Test case prioritization: An approach based on modified ant colony optimization, in: *Emerging Research in Computing, Information, Communication and Applications*, pp. 213–223, Springer Singapore, Singapore, 2016.

166. Gao, D., Guo, X., Zhao, L., Test case prioritization for regression testing based on ant colony optimization. *Proc. IEEE Int. Conf. Softw. Eng. Serv. Sci. ICSESS*, November 2015, 91118007, pp. 275–279, 2015.

167. Ahmad, S.F., Singh, D.K., Suman, P., Prioritization for regression testing using ant colony optimization based on test factors, in: *Advances in Intelligent Systems and Computing*, vol. 624, pp. 1353–1360, 2018.

168. Panwar, D., Tomar, P., Harsh, H., Siddique, M.H., Improved meta-heuristic technique for test case prioritization, in: *Advances in Intelligent Systems and Computing*, vol. 583, pp. 647–664, 2018.

169. Lu, C. and Zhong, J., *An Efficient Ant Colony System for Coverage Based Test Case Prioritization*, pp. 91–92, 2018.

170. Bian, Y., Li, Z., Zhao, R., Gong, D., Epistasis based ACO for regression test case prioritization. *IEEE Trans. Emerg. Top. Comput. Intell.*, 1, 3, 213–223, Jun. 2017.

171. Tyagi, M. and Malhotra, S., Test case prioritization using multi objective particle swarm optimizer. *2014 Int. Conf. Signal Propag. Comput. Technol. ICSPCT 2014*, pp. 390–395, 2014.

172. Joseph, A.K., Radhamani, G., Kallimani, V., Improving test efficiency through multiple criteria coverage based test case prioritization using modified heuristic algorithm. *2016 3rd Int. Conf. Comput. Inf. Sci. ICCOINS 2016-Proc.*, pp. 430–435, 2016.

173. Rauf, A. and Alsalem, A., II, Intelligent web application systems testing through value based test case prioritization. *Prog. Syst. Eng.*, 1089, 765–768, 2015.

174. Yoo, S., Harman, M., Tonella, P., Susi, A., Clustering Test Cases to Achieve Effective and Scalable Prioritisation Incorporating Expert Knowledge. *Proc. ISSTA*, pp. 201–212, 2009.

175. Klindee, P. and Prompoon, N., Test cases prioritization for software regression testing using analytic hierarchy process. *12th Int. Jt. Conf. Comput. Sci. Softw. Eng.*, pp. 168–173, 2015.

176. Epitropakis, M.G., Yoo, S., Harman, M., Burke, E.K., Empirical evaluation of pareto efficient multi-objective regression test case prioritisation, in: *Proceedings of the 2015 International Symposium on Software Testing and Analysis-ISSTA 2015*, pp. 234–245, 2015.

177. Bian, Y., Kirbas, S., Harman, M., Jia, Y., Li, Z., Regression test case prioritisation for guava, in: *Lecture Notes in Computer Science (including subseries Lecture Notes in Artificial Intelligence and Lecture Notes in Bioinformatics)*, 2015.

178. Shin, S.Y., Nejati, S., Sabetzadeh, M., Briand, L.C., Zimmer, F., Test case prioritization for acceptance testing of cyber physical systems: A multi-objective search-based approach, in: *Proceedings of the 27th ACM SIGSOFT International Symposium on Software Testing and Analysis-ISSTA 2018*, pp. 49–60, 2018.

179. Arrieta, A., Wang, S., Markiegi, U., Sagardui, G., Etxeberria, L., Employing multi-objective search to enhance reactive test case generation and prioritization for testing industrial cyber-physical systems. *IEEE Trans. Industr. Inform.*, 14, 3, 1055–1066, Mar. 2018.

180. Marchetto, A., Islam, M.M., Asghar, W., Susi, A., Scanniello, G., A multi-objective technique to prioritize test cases. *IEEE Trans. Softw. Eng.*, 42, 10, 918–940, Oct. 2016.

181. Wang, S., Ali, S., Yue, T., Bakkeli, Ø., Liaaen, M., Enhancing test case prioritization in an industrial setting with resource awareness and multi-objective search, in: *Proceedings of the 38th International Conference on Software Engineering Companion-ICSE '16*, pp. 182–191, 2016.

182. Ray, M. and Mohapatra, D.P., Multi-objective test prioritization via a genetic algorithm. *Innov. Syst. Softw. Eng.*, 10, 4, 261–270, 2014.

183. Tulasiraman, M., Vivekanandan, N., Kalimuthu, V., Multi-objective test case prioritization using improved pareto-optimal clonal selection algorithm. *3D Res.*, 9, 3, 32, Sep. 2018.

184. Wang, S., Buchmann, D., Ali, S., Liaaen, M., Multi-objective test prioritization in software product line testing : An industrial case study. *SPLC '14 Proc. 18th Int. Softw. Prod. Line Conf.*, pp. 32–41, 2014.

185. Conrad, A. P., Roos, R. S., Kapfhammer, G. M., Empirically studying the role of selection operators duringsearch-based test suite prioritization, in: *Proceedings of the 12th Annual Conference on Genetic and Evolutionary Computation*, pp. 1373–1380, 2010, July.

186. Sabharwal, S., Sibal, R., Sharma, C., Prioritization of test case scenarios derived from activity diagram using genetic algorithm, in: *2010 International Conference on Computer and Communication Technology, ICCCT-2010*, pp. 481–485, 2010.

187. Ferrer, J., Kruse, P., Chicano, F., Alba, E., Evolutionary algorithm for prioritized pairwise test data generation. *Proc. Fourteenth Int. Conf. Genet. Evol. Comput. Conf.*, pp. 1213–1220, 2012.

188. Catal, C., On the application of genetic algorithms for test case prioritization, in. *Proc. 2nd Int. Workshop Evidential Assess. Software Technol. - EAST '12*, p. 9, 2012.

189. Yuan, F., Bian, Y., Li, Z., Zhao, R., Epistatic genetic algorithm for test case prioritization, in: *Lecture Notes in Computer Science (including subseries Lecture Notes in Artificial Intelligence and Lecture Notes in Bioinformatics)*, 2015.

190. Mishra, D.B., Panda, N., Mishra, R., Acharya, A.A., Total fault exposing potential based test case prioritization using genetic algorithm. *Int. J. Inf. Technol.*, 11, 4, 633–637, 2019.

191. Mishra, D.B., Mishra, R., Acharya, A.A., Das, K.N., Test case optimization and prioritization based on multi-objective genetic algorithm, in: *Advances in Intelligent Systems and Computing*, vol. 741, pp. 371–381, 2019.

192. Di Nucci, D., Panichella, A., Zaidman, A., De Lucia, A., A test case prioritization genetic algorithm guided by the hypervolume indicator. *IEEE Trans. Softw. Eng.*, 46, 6, 674–696, 2018.

193. Yadav, D.K. and Dutta, S., Regression test case prioritization technique using genetic algorithm, in: *Advances in Intelligent Systems and Computing*, vol. 509, pp. 133–140, 2017.

194. Jiang, B. and Chan, W.K., Bypassing code coverage approximation limitations via effective input-based randomized test case prioritization, in: *Proceedings-International Computer Software and Applications Conference*, pp. 190–199, 2013.

195. Jiang, B. and Chan, W.K., Input-based adaptive randomized test case prioritization: A local beam search approach. *J. Syst. Softw.*, 105, 91–106, 2015.

196. Conrad, A.P., Roos, R.S., Kapfhammer, G.M., Empirically studying the role of selection operators duringsearch-based test suite prioritization. *Proc. 12th Annu. Conf. Genet. Evol. Comput. - GECCO '10*, p. 1373, 2010.

197. Maia, C.L.B., do Carmo, R.A.F., de Freitas, F.G., de Campos, G.A.L., de Souza, J.T., Automated test case prioritization with peactive GRASP. *Adv. Softw. Eng.*, 2010, 1–18, 2010.

198. Simons, C. and Paraiso, E.C., Regression test cases prioritization using failure pursuit sampling, in: *Proceedings of the 2010 10th International Conference on Intelligent Systems Design and Applications, ISDA '10*, pp. 923–928, 2010.

199. Zhao, X., Wang, Z., Fan, X., Wang, Z., A clustering–bayesian network based approach for test case prioritization. *2015 IEEE 39th Annu. Comput. Softw. Appl. Conf. (COMPSAC)*, vol. 3, pp. 542–547, 2015.

200. Sherriff, M., Lake, M., Williams, L., Prioritization of regression tests using singular value decomposition with empirical change records, in: *Proceedings-International Symposium on Software Reliability Engineering, ISSRE*, pp. 81–90, 2007.

201. Harikarthik, S.K., Palanisamy, V., Ramanathan, P., Optimal test suite selection in regression testing with testcase prioritization using modified Ann and Whale optimization algorithm. *Cluster Comput.*, 22, 5, 11425–11434, 2019.

202. Zhang, C. and Alipour, M.A., Using test case reduction and prioritization to improve symbolic execution. *Proc. 2014 Int. Symp. Software Test. Anal.*, pp. 160–170, 2014.

203. Hasan, M.A., Rahman, M.A., Siddik, M.S., Test case prioritization based on dissimilarity clustering using historical data analysis, in: *Communications in Computer and Information Science*, vol. 750, pp. 269–281, 2017.

204. Xiao, L., Miao, H., Zhuang, W., Chen, S., An empirical study on clustering approach combining fault prediction for test case prioritization, in: *Proceedings-16th IEEE/ACIS International Conference on Computer and Information Science, ICIS 2017*, pp. 815–820, 2017.

205. Xiao, L., Miao, H., Zhuang, W., Chen, S., Applying assemble clustering algorithm and fault prediction to test case prioritization, in: *Proceedings-2016 International Conference on Software Analysis, Testing and Evolution, SATE 2016*, 2016.

206. Ramya, P., Sindhura, V., Sagar, P.V., Clustering based prioritization of test cases, in: *2018 Second International Conference on Inventive Communication and Computational Technologies (ICICCT)*, pp. 1181–1185, 2018.

207. Williams, Z.D. and Kapfhammer, G.M., Using synthetic test suites to empirically compare search-based and greedy prioritizers. *Proc. 12th Annu. Conf. Genet. Evol. Comput. (GECCO '10)*, pp. 2119–2120, 2010.

208. Li, S., Bian, N., Chen, Z., You, D., He, Y., A simulation study on some search algorithms for regression test case prioritization. *2010 10th Int. Conf. on Qual. Softw. (QSIC)*, pp. 72–81, 2010.

209. Gupta, D. and Gupta, V., Test suite prioritization using nature inspired meta-heuristic algorithms, in: *Advances in Intelligent Systems and Computing*, vol. 557, pp. 216–226, 2017.

210. Ozturk, M.M., Adapting code maintainability to bat-inspired test case prioritization, in: *2017 IEEE International Conference on INnovations in Intelligent SysTems and Applications (INISTA)*, pp. 67–72, 2017.

211. Mirarab, S. and Tahvildari, L., A prioritization approach for software test cases based on Bayesian networks, in: *Fundamental Approaches to Software Engineering*, vol. 4422, pp. 276–290, Springer, Berlin Heidelberg, 2007.

212. Mirarab, S. and Tahvildari, L., An empirical study on Bayesian network-based approach for test case prioritization, in: *2008 International Conference on Software Testing, Verification, and Validation*, pp. 278–287, 2008.

213. Ufuktepe, E. and Tuglular, T., Automation architecture for Bayesian network based test case prioritization and execution, in: *Proceedings-International Computer Software and Applications Conference*, vol. 2, pp. 52–57, 2016.

214. Islam, M.M., Marchetto, A., Susi, A., Scanniello, G., MOTCP: A tool for the prioritization of test cases based on a sorting genetic algorithm and latent semantic indexing, in: *IEEE International Conference on Software Maintenance, ICSM*, pp. 654–657, 2012.

215. Bryce, R.C. and Memon, A.M., Test suite prioritization by interaction coverage. *Work. Domain Specif. Approaches to Softw. Test Autom. Conjunction with 6th ESEC/FSE Jt. Meet.-DOSTA '07*, pp. 1–7, 2007.

216. Wang, X., Dynamic test case prioritization based on multi-objective, in: *Software Engineering, Artificial Intelligence, Networking and Parallel/Distributed Computing*, pp. 0–5, 2014.

217. Islam, M.M., Marchetto, A., Susi, A., Scanniello, G., A multi-objective technique to prioritize test cases based on latent semantic indexing, in: *Proceedings*

of the European Conference on Software Maintenance and Reengineering, CSMR, pp. 21–30, 2012.

218. Marijan, D., Multi-perspective regression test prioritization for time-constrained environments, in: *Proceedings-2015 IEEE International Conference on Software Quality, Reliability and Security, QRS 2015*, pp. 157–162, 2015.

219. Li, Z., Bian, Y., Zhao, R., Cheng, J., A fine-grained parallel multi-objective test case prioritization on GPU, in: *Lecture Notes in Computer Science (including subseries Lecture Notes in Artificial Intelligence and Lecture Notes in Bioinformatics)*, vol. 8084, pp. 111–125, 2013.

220. Azizi, M. and Do, H., Graphite: A greedy graph-based technique for regression test case prioritization, in: *2018 IEEE International Symposium on Software Reliability Engineering Workshops (ISSREW)*, pp. 245–251, 2018.

221. Strandberg, P.E., Sundmark, D., Afzal, W., Ostrand, T.J., Weyuker, E.J., Experience report: Automated system level regression test prioritization using multiple factors, in: *Proceedings-International Symposium on Software Reliability Engineering, ISSRE*, pp. 12–23, 2016.

222. Abid, R. and Nadeem, A., A novel approach to multiple criteria based test case prioritization. *Proc.-2017 13th Int. Conf. Emerg. Technol. ICET 2017*, January 2018, pp. 1–6, Dec. 2018.

223. Pradhan, D., Wang, S., Ali, S., Yue, T., Liaaen, M., REMAP: Using rule mining and multi-objective search for dynamic test case prioritization, in: *2018 IEEE 11th International Conference on Software Testing, Verification and Validation (ICST)*, pp. 46–57, 2018.

224. Kerani, M. and Sharmila, Novel technique for the test case prioritization in regression testing, in: *Advances in Computing and Data Sciences*, pp. 362–371, 2018.

225. Mei, L., Chan, W.K., Tse, T.H., Merkel, R.G., Tag-based techniques for black-box test case prioritization for service testing, in: *Proceedings-International Conference on Quality Software*, pp. 21–30, 2009.

226. Mei, L., Chan, W.K., Tse, T.H., Merkel, R.G., XML-manipulating test case prioritization for XML-manipulating services. *J. Syst. Softw.*, 84, 4, 603–619, 2011.

227. Mei, L. *et al.*, A subsumption hierarchy of test case prioritization for composite service. *IEEE Trans. Serv. Comput.*, 8, 5, 658–673, 2015.

228. Zhai, K., Jiang, B., Chan, W. K., Prioritizing test cases for regression testing of location-based services: Metrics, techniques, and case study. *IEEE Trans. Serv. Comput.*, 7, 1, 54–67, 2012.

229. Zhai, K., Jiang, B., Chan, W.K., Tse, T.H., Taking advantage of service selection: A study on the testing of location-based web services through test case prioritization, in: *IEEE International Conference on Web Services (ICWS)*, pp. 211–218, 2010.

230. Kwon, J., Ko, I., Rothermel, G., Prioritizing browser environments for web application test execution, in: *2018 IEEE/ACM 40th International Conference on Software Engineering (ICSE)*, pp. 468–479, 2018.

231. Sampath, S., Bryce, R.C., Viswanath, G., Kandimalla, V., Koru, A.G., Prioritizing user-session-based test cases for web applications testing, in: *Proceedings of the 1st International Conference on Software Testing, Verification and Validation, ICST 2008*, pp. 141–150, 2008.

232. Nurmuradov, D., Bryce, R., Piparia, S., Bryant, B., Clustering and combinatorial methods for test suite prioritization of GUI and web applications, in: *Advances in Intelligent Systems and Computing*, vol. 738, pp. 459–466, 2018.

233. Wang, H., Xing, J., Yang, Q., Han, D., Zhang, X., Modification Impact analysis based test case prioritization for regression testing of service-oriented workflow applications. *2015 IEEE 39th Annu. Comput. Softw. Appl. Conf*, pp. 288–297, 2015.

234. Raj, G., Singh, D., Tyagi, I., *Test case optimization and prioritization of web service using bacteriologic algorithm*, pp. 731–744, Springer, Singapore, 2018.

235. Azizi, M. and Do, H., A collaborative filtering recommender system for test case prioritization in web applications, in: *Proceedings of the 33rd Annual ACM Symposium on Applied Computing-SAC '18*, pp. 1560–1567, 2018.

236. Yang, C.-Z., Luo, Y.-F., Chien, Y.-J., Wen, H.-L., Learning to prioritize GUI test cases for Android laboratory programs, in: *Proceedings of the International Conference on Artificial Intelligence and Robotics and the International Conference on Automation, Control and Robotics Engineering-ICAIR-CACRE '16*, pp. 1–5, 2016.

237. Chen, L., Wang, Z., Xu, L., Lu, H., Xu, B., Test case prioritization for web service regression testing, in: *Proceedings-5th IEEE International Symposium on Service-Oriented System Engineering, SOSE 2010*, pp. 173–178, 2010.

238. Garg, D. and Datta, A., Parallel execution of prioritized test cases for regression testing of web applications. *Proc. Thirty-Sixth Australas. Comput. Sci. Conf.*, vol. 135, pp. 61–68, 2013.

239. Panigrahi, C.R. and Mall, R., Model-based regression test case prioritization, in: *Information Systems, Technology and Management, Proceedings*, 2010.

240. Vedpal, Chauhan, N., Kumar, H., A hierarchical test case prioritization technique for object oriented software. *Proc. 2014 Int. Conf. Contemp. Comput. Informatics, IC3I 2014*, pp. 249–254, 2014.

241. Kundu, D., Sarma, M., Samanta, D., Mall, R., System testing for object-oriented systems with test case prioritization. *Softw. Test. Verif. Reliab.*, 19, 4, 297–333, 2009.

242. Chen, J. *et al.*, Test case prioritization for object-oriented software: An adaptive random sequence approach based on clustering. *J. Syst. Softw.*, 135, 107–125, Jan. 2018.

243. Chen, J. *et al.*, An adaptive sequence approach for OOS test case prioritization, in: *Proceedings-2016 IEEE 27th International Symposium on Software Reliability Engineering Workshops, ISSREW 2016*, 2016.

244. Vedpal, and Chauhan, N., A multi-factored cost-and code coverage-based test case prioritization technique for object-oriented software, in: *Advances in Intelligent Systems and Computing*, vol. 731, pp. 27–36, 2019.

245. Singh, A., Bhatia, R.K., Singhrova, A., Object oriented coupling based test case prioritization. *Int. J. Comput. Sci. Eng.*, 6, 9, 747–754, Sep. 2018.

246. Noor, T.B. and Hemmati, H., A similarity-based approach for test case prioritization using historical failure data. *2015 IEEE 26th Int. Symp. Softw. Reliab. Eng. (ISSRE)*, pp. 58–68, 2015.

247. Wu, K., Fang, C., Chen, Z., Zhao, Z., Test case prioritization incorporating ordered sequence of program elements, in: *2012 7th International Workshop on Automation of Software Test, AST 2012-Proceedings*, pp. 124–130, 2012.

248. Al-Hajjaji, M., Scalable sampling and prioritization for product-line testing. *Software Engineering & Management*, pp. 12–15, 2015.

249. Ledru, Y., Petrenko, A., Boroday, S., Mandran, N., Prioritizing test cases with string distances. *Automat. Softw. Eng.*, 19, 1, 65–95, 2012.

250. Fang, C., Chen, Z., Wu, K., Zhao, Z., Similarity-based test case prioritization using ordered sequences of program entities. *Softw. Qual. J.*, 22, 2, 335–361, 2014.

251. Maheswari, R.U. and JeyaMala, D., A novel approach for test case prioritization. *2013 IEEE Int. Conf. Comput. Intell. Comput. Res.*, pp. 1–5, 2013.

252. Miranda, B., Cruciani, E., Verdecchia, R., Bertolino, A., FAST approaches to scalable similarity-based test case prioritization, in: *Proceedings of the 40th International Conference on Software Engineering*, 2018.

253. Flemström, D., Potena, P., Sundmark, D., Afzal, W., Bohlin, M., Similarity-based prioritization of test case automation. *Softw. Qual. J.*, 26, 4, 1421–1449, Dec. 2018.

254. Huang, R., Zhou, Y., Zong, W., Towey, D., Chen, J., An empirical comparison of similarity measures for abstract test case prioritization, in: *Proceedings-International Computer Software and Applications Conference*, vol. 1, pp. 3–12, 2017.

255. Haghighatkhah, A., Mäntylä, M., Oivo, M., Kuvaja, P., *Test Case Prioritization Using Test Similarities*, pp. 243–259, Springer, Cham, 2018.

256. Magalhães, C., Andrade, J., Perrusi, L., Mota, A., Evaluating an automatic text-based test case selection using a non-instrumented code coverage analysis. *Proc. 2nd Braz. Symp. Syst. Autom. Software Test.-SAST*, pp. 1–9, 2017.

257. Yang, Y., Huang, X., Hao, X., Liu, Z., Chen, Z., An industrial study of natural language processing based test case prioritization, in: *Proceedings-10th IEEE International Conference on Software Testing, Verification and Validation, ICST 2017*, pp. 548–549, 2017.

258. Thomas, S.W., Hemmati, H., Hassan, A.E., Blostein, D., Static test case prioritization using topic models. *Empir. Softw. Eng.*, 19, 1, 182–212, 2014.

259. Qu, X., Cohen, M.B., Woolf, K.M., Combinatorial interaction regression testing: A study of test case generation and prioritization, in: *IEEE International Conference on Software Maintenance, ICSM*, pp. 255–264, 2007.

260. Qu, X., Cohen, M.B., Rothermel, G., Configuration-aware regression testing: An empirical study of sampling and prioritization. *ISSTA '08 Proc. 2008 Int. Symp. Softw. Test. Anal.*, 2008.

261. Qu, X., Configuration aware prioritization techniques in regression testing, in: *2009 31st International Conference on Software Engineering-Companion Volume, ICSE 2009*, pp. 375–378, 2009.

262. Srikanth, H., Cohen, M.B., Qu, X., Reducing field failures in system configurable software: Cost-based prioritization, in: *Proceedings-International Symposium Software Reliability Engineering, ISSRE*, pp. 61–70, 2009.

263. Salecker, E., Reicherdt, R., Glesner, S., Calculating prioritized interaction test sets with constraints using binary decision diagrams, in: *Proceedings-4th IEEE International Conference on Software Testing, Verification, and Validation Workshops, ICSTW 2011*, pp. 278–285, 2011.

264. Kruse, P.M. and Schieferdecker, I.K., Comparison of approaches to prioritized test generation for combinatorial interaction testing, in: *Federated Conference on Computer Science and Information Systems-FedCSIS 2012 Proceedings*, Wroclaw, Poland, September 9-12, 2012, pp. 1323–1330, 2012.

265. Huang, R., Chen, J., Li, Z., Wang, R., Lu, Y., Adaptive random prioritization for interaction test suites, in: *SAC*, pp. 1058–1063, 2014.

266. Wu, H., Nie, C., Kuo, F.C., Test suite prioritization by switching cost, in: *Proceedings-IEEE 7th International Conference on Software Testing, Verification and Validation Workshops, ICSTW 2014*, pp. 133–142, 2014.

267. Chen, X., Gu, Q., Wang, X., Li, A., Chen, D., A hybrid approach to build prioritized pairwise interaction test suites, in: *Proceedings-2009 International Conference on Computational Intelligence and Software Engineering, CISE 2009*, 2009.

268. Huang, R., Chen, J., Towey, D., Chan, A.T.S., Lu, Y., Aggregate-strength interaction test suite prioritization. *J. Syst. Softw.*, 99, 36–51, 2015.

269. Huang, R., Zhou, Y., Chen, T.Y., Towey, D., Chen, J., Zong, W., Prioritizing random combinatorial test suites, in: *Proceedings of the Symposium on Applied Computing-SAC '17*, pp. 1183–1189, 2017.

270. Huang, R., Zhang, Q., Chen, T.Y., Hamlyn-Harris, J., Towey, D., Chen, J., An empirical comparison of fixed-strength and mixed-strength for interaction coverage based prioritization. *IEEE Access*, 6, 68350–68372, 2018.

271. Huang, R. *et al.*, On the selection of strength for fixed-strength interaction coverage based prioritization. *Proc.-Int. Comput. Softw. Appl. Conf*, vol. 1, pp. 310–315, 2018.

272. Huang, R., Zong, W., Chen, J., Towey, D., Zhou, Y., Chen, D., Prioritizing interaction test suites using repeated base choice coverage, in: *2016 IEEE 40th Annual Computer Software and Applications Conference (COMPSAC)*, pp. 174–184, 2016.

273. Bryce, R.C. and Colbourn, C.J., Prioritized interaction testing for pair-wise coverage with seeding and constraints. *Inf. Softw. Technol.*, 48, 10, 960–970, 2006.

274. Gao, J. and Zhu, J., Prioritized test generation strategy for pair-wise testing, in: *2009 15th IEEE Pacific Rim International Symposium on Dependable Computing, PRDC 2009*, pp. 99–102, 2009.

275. Marijan, D. and Liaaen, M., Test prioritization with optimally balanced configuration coverage, in: *Proceedings of IEEE International Symposium on High Assurance Systems Engineering*, pp. 100–103, 2017.

276. Satish, P., Nikhil, P., Rangarajan, K., A test prioritization algorithm that cares for "don't care" Values and higher order combinatorial coverage. *ACM SIGSOFT Softw. Eng. Notes*, 42, 4, 1–9, Jan. 2018.

277. Aggarwal, M. and Sabharwal, S., Combinatorial test set prioritization using data flow techniques. *Arab. J. Sci. Eng.*, 43, 2, 483–497, Feb. 2018.

278. Nakornburi, S. and Suwannasart, T., Constrained pairwise test case generation approach based on statistical user profile. *Int. Multi Conference Eng. Comput. Sci.*, vol. 1, pp. 445–448, 2016.

279. Henard, C., Papadakis, M., Harman, M., Jia, Y., Le Traon, Y., Comparing white-box and black-box test prioritization, in: *Proceedings of the 38th International Conference on Software Engineering-ICSE '16*, pp. 523–534, 2016.

280. Sujata, and Purohit, G.N., Classification model for test case prioritization techniques, in: *Proceeding-IEEE International Conference on Computing, Communication and Automation, ICCCA 2017*, January 2017, pp. 919–924, 2017.

281. Lachmann, R., Nieke, M., Seidl, C., Schaefer, I., Schulze, S., System-level test case prioritization using machine learning, in: *Proceedings-2016 15th IEEE International Conference on Machine Learning and Applications, ICMLA 2016*, 2017.

282. Busjaeger, B. and Xie, T., Learning for test prioritization: An industrial case study, in: *Proceedings of the 2016 24th ACM SIGSOFT International Symposium on Foundations of Software Engineering-FSE 2016*, pp. 975–980, 2016.

283. Muzammal, M., *Test-Suite Prioritisation by Application Navigation Tree Mining*, pp. 205–210.

284. Bin Noor, T. and Hemmati, H., Studying test case failure prediction for test case prioritization, in: *Proceedings of the 13th International Conference on Predictive Models and Data Analytics in Software Engineering-PROMISE*, pp. 2–11, 2017.

285. Palma, F., Abdou, T., Bener, A., Maidens, J., Liu, S., An improvement to test case failure prediction in the context of test case prioritization, in: *Proceedings of the 14th International Conference on Predictive Models and Data Analytics in Software Engineering-PROMISE '18*, pp. 80–89, 2018.

286. Yu, Y.T., Ng, S.P., Chan, E.Y.K., Generating, selecting and prioritizing test cases from specifications with tool support, in: *Proceedings-International Conference on Quality Software*, January 2003, pp. 83–90, 2003.

287. Chen, J. *et al.*, Optimizing test prioritization via test distribution analysis, in: *Proceedings of the 2018 26th ACM Joint Meeting on European Software Engineering Conference and Symposium on the Foundations of Software Engineering-ESEC/FSE 2018*, pp. 656–667, 2018.

288. Jiang, B., Zhang, Z., Chan, W.K., Tse, T.H., Adaptive random test case prioritization, in: *ASE2009-24th IEEE/ACM International Conference on Automated Software Engineering*, pp. 233–244, 2009.

289. Hao, D., Zhao, X., Zhang, L., Adaptive test-case prioritization guided by output inspection, in: *Proceedings-International Computer Software and Applications Conference*, pp. 169–179, 2013.

290. Pei, H., Yin, B., Xie, M., Dynamic random testing strategy for test case optimization in cloud environment, in: *2018 IEEE International Symposium on Software Reliability Engineering Workshops (ISSREW)*, pp. 148–149, 2018.

291. Mariani, L., Riganelli, O., Santoro, M., Ali, M., Sarca, V., Ali, M., G-RankTest: Regression testing of controller applications. *2012 7th Int. Work. Autom. Softw. Test, AST 2012-Proc.*, pp. 131–137, 2012.

292. Ding, J. and Zhang, X.-Y., Comparison analysis of two test case prioritization approaches with the core idea of adaptive, in: *2017 29th Chinese Control And Decision Conference (CCDC)*, pp. 1723–1730, 2017.

293. Zhang, X., Xie, X., Chen, T.Y., Test case prioritization using adaptive random sequence with category-partition-based distance, in: *Proceedings-2016 IEEE International Conference on Software Quality, Reliability and Security, QRS 2016*, pp. 374–385, 2016.

294. Spieker, H., Gotlieb, A., Marijan, D., Mossige, M., Reinforcement learning for automatic test case prioritization and selection in continuous integration, in: *Proceedings of the 26th ACM SIGSOFT International Symposium on Software Testing and Analysis-ISSTA 2017*, pp. 12–22, 2017.

295. Liang, J., Elbaum, S., Rothermel, G., Redefining prioritization: Continuous prioritization for continuous integration, in: *Proceedings of the 40th International Conference on Software Engineering*, 2018.

296. Haghighatkhah, A., Mäntylä, M., Oivo, M., Kuvaja, P., Test prioritization in continuous integration environments. *J. Syst. Softw.*, 146, 80–98, Dec. 2018.

297. Marijan, D., Gotlieb, A., Sen, S., Test case prioritization for continuous regression testing: An industrial case study, in: *IEEE International Conference on Software Maintenance, ICSM*, pp. 540–543, 2013.

298. Ensan, A., Bagheri, E., Asadi, M., Gasevic, D., Biletskiy, Y., Goal-oriented test case selection and prioritization for product line feature models, in: *Proceedings-2011 8th International Conference on Information Technology: New Generations, ITNG 2011*, pp. 291–298, 2010.

299. Sanchez, A.B., Segura, S., Ruiz-Cortes, A., A comparison of test case prioritization criteria for software product lines, in: *2014 IEEE Seventh International Conference on Software Testing, Verification and Validation*, pp. 41–50, 2014.

300. Lachmann, R., Lity, S., Lischke, S., Beddig, S., Schulze, S., Schaefer, I., Delta-oriented test case prioritization for integration testing of software product lines. *Proc. 19th Int. Conf. Softw. Prod. Line-SPLC '15*, pp. 81–90, 2015.
301. Lachmann, R., Lity, S., Al-Hajjaji, M., Fürchtegott, F., Schaefer, I., Fine-grained test case prioritization for integration testing of delta-oriented software product lines, in: *Proceedings of the 7th International Workshop on Feature-Oriented Software Development-FOSD 2016*, pp. 1–10, 2016.
302. Saraswat, P. and Singhal, A., *A Hybrid Approach for Test Case Prioritization and Optimization Using Meta-Heuristics Techniques*, pp. 1–6.
303. Silva, D., Rabelo, R., Campanha, M., Neto, P.S., Oliveira, P.A., Britto, R., A hybrid approach for test case prioritization and selection, in: *2016 IEEE Congress on Evolutionary Computation (CEC)*, pp. 4508–4515, 2016.
304. Tahvili, S., Afzal, W., Saadatmand, M., Bohlin, M., Sundmark, D., Larsson, S., Towards earlier fault detection by value-driven prioritization of test cases using fuzzy TOPSIS, in: *Advances in Intelligent Systems and Computing*, vol. 448, pp. 745–759, Springer, Cham, 2016.
305. Ozawa, M., Dohi, T., Okamura, H., How do software metrics affect test case prioritization?, in: *2018 IEEE 42nd Annual Computer Software and Applications Conference (COMPSAC)*, pp. 245–250, 2018.
306. Reider, M., Magnus, S., Krause, J., Feature-based testing by using model synthesis, test generation and parameterizable test prioritization, in: *2018 IEEE International Conference on Software Testing, Verification and Validation Workshops (ICSTW)*, pp. 130–137, 2018.
307. Nejad Dobuneh, M.R., Jawawi, D.N.A., Ghazali, M., Malakooti, M.V., Development test case prioritization technique in regression testing based on hybrid criteria. *2014 8th Malaysian Softw. Eng. Conf. MySEC 2014*, pp. 301–305, 2014.
308. Huang, R., Zong, W., Towey, D., Zhou, Y., Chen, J., An empirical examination of abstract test case prioritization techniques. *Proceedings-2017 IEEE/ACM 39th International Conference on Software Engineering Companion, ICSE-C 2017*, pp. 141–143, 2017.
309. Nayak, S., Kumar, C., Tripathi, S., Enhancing efficiency of the test case prioritization technique by improving the rate of fault detection. *Arab. J. Sci. Eng.*, 42, 8, 3307–3323, Aug. 2017.
310. Luo, Q., Moran, K., Zhang, L., Poshyvanyk, D., How do static and dynamic test case prioritization techniques perform on modern software systems? An extensive study on GitHub projects. *IEEE Trans. Softw. Eng.*, 45, 11, 1054–1080, 2018.
311. Luo, Q., Moran, K., Poshyvanyk, D., Di Penta, M., Assessing test case prioritization on real faults and mutants. *2018 IEEE Int. Conf. Softw. Maint. Evol.*, pp. 240–251, Sep. 2018.
312. Paterson, D., Kapfhammer, G.M., Fraser, G., McMinn, P., Using controlled numbers of real faults and mutants to empirically evaluate coverage-based

test case prioritization, in: *Proceedings of the 13th International Workshop on Automation of Software Test-AST '18*, pp. 57–63, 2018.

313. Lima, L., Iyoda, J., Sampaio, A., Aranha, E., Test case prioritization based on data reuse an experimental study. *2009 3rd Int. Symp. Empir. Softw. Eng. Meas.*, pp. 279–290, 2009.

314. Do, H., Elbaum, S., Rothermel, G., Supporting controlled experimentation with testing techniques: An infrastructure and its potential impact. *Empir. Softw. Eng.*, 2005.

315. Utting, M. and Legeard, B., *Practical Model-Based Testing: A Tools Approach*, Elsevier, 2010.

316. Belli, F., Eminov, M., Gokce, N., A comparative soft-computing approach and case studies. *32nd Annu. Ger. Conf. Adv. Artif. Intell. (KI'09)*, pp. 425–432, 2009.

317. Han, X., Zeng, H., Gao, H., A heuristic model-based test prioritization method for regression testing, in: *Proceedings-2012 International Symposium on Computer, Consumer and Control, IS3C 2012*, pp. 886–889, p. 61073050, 2012.

318. Belli, F., Eminov, M., Gokce, N., Prioritizing coverage-oriented testing process-an adaptive-learning-based approach and case study. *31st Annu. Int. Comput. Softw. Appl. Conf.-Vol. 2-(COMPSAC 2007)*, pp. 197–203, 2007.

319. Sapna, P.G. and Mohanty, H., Prioritization of scenarios based on UML activity diagrams. *2009 First Int. Conf. Comput. Intell. Commun. Syst. Networks*, pp. 271–276, 2009.

320. Hao, D., Zhang, L., Mei, H., Zhou, J., Zhang, L., *Prioritizing JUnit Test Cases in Absence of Coverage Information*, 2009.

A Systematic Review of the Tools and Techniques in Distributed Agile Software Development

Dipti Jadhav*, Jyoti Kundale, Sumedha Bhagwat and Jyoti Joshi

Department of Information Technology, Dr. D Y Patil's Deemed to be University, Nerul, Navi Mumbai, India

Abstract

A software project is the entire methodology of development, from gathering requirements to testing and support, concluded by execution procedures, in a specific time frame to produce the desired software product. Agile is an iterative project management and software development methodology that enables teams to deliver value to customers efficiently with minimal setbacks. In agile software development, project planning is very vital. The lack of in person communication and the incapability to share paper index cards among all meeting participants have a significant impact on project planning in distributed environments. This chapter discusses the benefits of Distributed Agile Software Development and the various distributed agile planning tools that are available to resolve these concerns. These tools differ in terms of features, operations, usage and pricing. This chapter aims at providing deeper insights into the most contemporary agile planning tools used by distributed agile professionals. The agile tools studied and compared are both open source as well as proprietary tools. We also provide a brief description of 17 distributed agile tools such as Jira, nTask, ActiveCollab, Monday.com, ProofHub, GitLab etc. This chapter also provides a complete study of these tools in terms of features and pricing.

Keywords: Distributed Agile Software Development, pair programming, tools, techniques, Jira, nTask, distributed programming, distributed project management

Corresponding author: dipti.jadhav@rait.ac.in

Susheela Hooda, Vandana Mohindru Sood, Yashwant Singh, Sandeep Dalal and Manu Sood (eds.) *Agile Software Development: Trends, Challenges and Applications*, (161–186) © 2023 Scrivener Publishing LLC

8.1   Introduction

Agile Software Development (ASD) largely defines how software is developed worldwide. A survey conducted in 2005, in US and Europe revealed that 14% of companies were already using agile practices and nearly 50% of the companies were ready to embrace the agile methodology for software development. Agile Development is a time bound software development methodology which is iterative, incremental right from the inception of the project [1].

8.1.1   Why Agile?

The different process models focus on the Software Development Life Cycle (SDLC) which begins by requirements elicitation and documenting the whole requirements. In middle of 1990's many developers found this step in SDLC as time consuming because the requirements and business environment kept changing during the software development. The customers of the software were also unable to define their requirements completely.

The four principles underlying the agile methodology are [2]:

1. Individuals members and interactions are preferred over processes and tools
2. Working software is preferred over comprehensive documentation
3. Customer collaboration more important than contract negotiation
4. Responding to change instead of following a plan

8.1.2   Distributed Agile Software Development (DASD)

ASD methods for co-located teams facilitated face to face collaboration, rapid releases of the working software, delivering value to the business, timely changes and improved rates for fixing the software. The benefits of ASD were extended to large scale software projects, where the team members are in distributed locations. This use of ASD in Distributed Software Development led to several benefits such as follow-the-sun development, increased productivity, reduced costs as work was shifted to lower cost countries and access to a broad pool of talent across the globe. In spite of the benefits the application of agile methods in distributed environment is very challenging due to the variance between agility and distribution. It is very difficult to apply the agile principles in distributed environment [3].

8.1.3   Challenges of DASD

Along with the benefits of DASD, there are certain challenges faced by the distributed agile team. The challenges discussed below leads to incompatibility between agile approach and distributed environment.

8.1.3.1   Documentation

The agile teams normally have the tendency to downplay the documentation. It is greatly based on the study that a large part of documentation work is usually wasted. So in this distributed scenario, team members may overlook certain particulars in the project which can affect the quality of the project.

8.1.3.2   Pair Programming

Agile practice features pair programming. In pair programming two members of the team work on the same set of code. In DASD it is difficult to support this feature unless some comparable practice is available.

8.1.3.3   Different Working Hours

In DASD, the team members are present in different time zones. Aligning the working hours of such members is a challenging task, as it affects clarity of work.

8.1.3.4   Training on Agile Practices

The new team members need to be trained for agile practices. Distributed environment and cultural differences makes training difficult.

8.1.3.5   Distribution of Work

The distribution of work should not be as per the geographical location. This will lead to overspecialization in a particular component. The challenge is that it will become tedious to complete the use case in the given iteration. Thus it is important to distribute the work more closely across the geographical boundary. It helps to reduce the gaps in terms of functionality. The solution to this challenge is to divide the distributed teams by modules/packages which are loosely coupled [4].

8.2   Literature Review

The authors in [4] presented the challenges as well as advantages of the DASD. The authors also provide a summary of various techniques which can be used by the distributed agile software development team.

The requirements for distributed agile planning and the overview of existing agile planning tools are provided by Miller, A. [5]. The authors also evaluated various tools such as WiKi, Web Based Form Application, Card Based Planning System etc., based on tool requirements.

Smits, H. [6] presented a systematic understanding of distributed agile software programming. The authors provide an insight into various questions such as need for DASD, risks and the mitigation strategies due to the adoption of DASD and which agile techniques can be adopted for DASD.

The effectiveness of Agile Practices in Global Software Development is presented in [7]. The authors present the advantages as well as challenges of distributed agile practices. The supporting tools as well as practices suitable for DASD is also discussed in [7].

Claudio De Meo and *et al.* [8] proposed a DADE architecture based on the emerging Liquid Multi-Device Software paradigm.

Mohammad Abdur Razzak and *et al.* [9] presented how knowledge sharing techniques and strategies can be utilized by the developers in DASD. The authors also discuss various challenges faced by the DASD team members during knowledge sharing in distributed agile projects.

This chapter aims at understanding the various contemporary techniques used in distributed agile software development. We also provide deeper insight in various contemporary tools used by the DASD teams today in the software industry. This chapter covers 17 popular distributed agile tools in terms of features and pricing.

8.3   Techniques for DASD

The effectiveness of DASD largely depends upon communication. The dispersed locations puts additional burden on communication. In order to overcome this burden, the DASD team members have to adopt new techniques and tools.

In this section we discuss new practices that should be adopted by the team members to ensure the effectiveness of DASD.

8.3.1   Effective Communication

The DASD team members have to use various means such as video conferencing, web cameras, and virtual meeting platforms to communicate with remote team members. The team members can face issues due to non-overlapping working hours. These issues can be solved using e-mail communications [4].

8.3.2   Face Visits or Contact Visits

Trust, rapport can be build amongst the DASD team members by having few contact visits in initial iterations. Contact meetings between the DASD team members in last iterations helps in improved release and shipping decisions of the final product [5].

8.3.3   Team Distribution

The time zone differences can lead to severe black outs, which can in turn affect the communication between the DASD team members. If the time zone difference is just 3-4 hours, meetings can be set in afternoon or evening hours. If the time zone difference is large, then there should be a team representative who will work with the off-shore team and attend the meetings [4]. Nested SCRUM which involves multi-level reporting and multiple daily SCRUM meetings is an effective technique for DASD [6].

8.3.4   Distribution of Work

The work should not be distributed as per the geographical location. If the work distribution is as per the location, it will be reflected in the architecture. A particular location will be overspecialized in a particular component or skill. The DASD team should consciously distribute work in terms of completing the use cases. The tasks related to a particular user story should be spread across all the locations. Thus all the team members in DASD team would build up the knowledge [5].

8.3.5   Documentation

Documentation is an important factor to maintain close collaboration among the DASD team members. Use Case diagrams and other relevant documents should be stored in globally accessible locations or backlogs.

This avoids misunderstanding and improves collaboration amongst the team members [5].

8.4   Tools for DASD

The DASD environment utilizes various tools and platforms to improve communication in a distributed environment. It is very important to provide a shared experience to all the team members, and the tools listed below helps to minimize the virtual distance among the team members. These Software Configuration Tools (SCM) helps the DASD team members to work at the same speed.

The various contemporary tools used for Distributed Agile Software Development are as listed below:

8.4.1   Monday.com

monday.com

This project management tool is helpful for handling complex project. It has a remarkable capacity as a Scrum tool to deliver on project tasks. Using monday one can create roadmap and visualize the roadmap that will be shared among all the users. Monday.com provides easily accessible interface. The main advantage is that it is available in English, Dutch, French language. Visual layout is same as Kanban board style. The drawback of this tool is by adding number of user charges is more and subtask of division is difficult to handle [10]. The Figure 8.1 represents dashboard of monday.com.

Figure 8.1 https://monday.com/ [10].

8.4.1.1   Features

It is more flexible for integration of existing tools in runtime environment to do work faster and efficient. All team members can collaborate in one shared space. There is provision for synchronizing the colored timeline with the calendar. It gives location based map view. Team can work together flawlessly anytime anywhere.

8.4.1.2   Pricing

The basic plan is $39 per month for 5 users. The cost is up to $799 for 100 user. Pro plan is $16 per month.

8.4.2   nTask

It is new to the market but popularly used by companies and project manager due to its robust feature and friendly support. It gives three views that are list, grid and window. It makes use of Microsoft spreadsheet to manage of task, meeting and project [11, 21]. The Figure 8.2 depicts nTask agile tool.

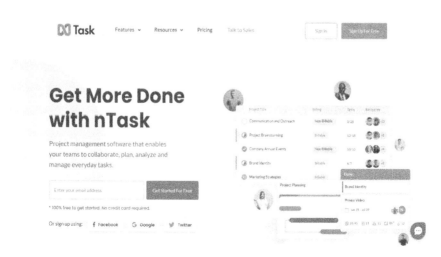

Figure 8.2 nTask [11, 21].

8.4.2.1   Features

nTask creates systematic project planning where developer will able to set start and end date for any task based on dependencies and to-do lists. It is also useful for assigning the task to multiple users and collaborate them in real time. It also keeps the track of all the current ongoing activity. Tasks are separated based on category and labeled them for better understanding. It makes use of Gantt chart to schedule and track the performance of the overall project. nTask issue management system is useful for tracking, fixing bug based on priority. To assure that everyone should be informed of issue improvements, the bug tracker allows both remarks and documents.

8.4.2.2   Pricing

According to pricing nTask is free for individual. Using Basic plan we can use timelines and track issue. We can arrange meeting with unlimited task and workspaces. Team member capacity is up to 5 members. In the premium plan which gets for $3, where we have all features of basic plan along with team members can perform bulk action and get custom filter with 5GB storage. The business plan is having pricing $8 per month. Additional premium filter can give 10GB storage and perform risk management task. In enterprise customizable plan gives dedicated cloud and dedicated account manager along with business plan.

8.4.3   Jira

Jira is derived from the Japanese word "Gojira," which signifies "Godzilla." Jira is a well-known and well-proven tool that is utilized by numerous enterprises throughout the world. It is customized tool and highly widespread which is used as per the customer requirement. It is much more user friendly and suitable for small as well as large scale project. By making use of Scrum broad it gives clear picture of task carried out in every

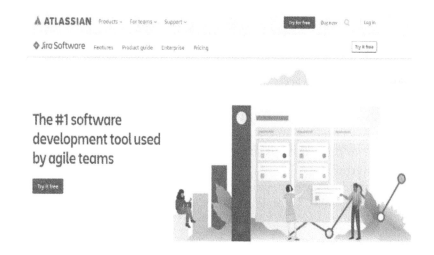

Figure 8.3 Jira [12].

sprint. With the help of flowchart, velocity chart progress of the task can be seen properly. JQL (JeeraQurey Language) is used to process queries. While working remotely, the software provides a variety of personalization choices to make you feel as if you're sitting at your desk. It also uses Kanban board to improve the efficiency. Jira helps to plan, track, release, report project progress easily, so whenever any new member join, for him it is easy to understand. The biggest disadvantage is of Jira is its complex nature to use it. Developer with high skill only learns easily. The current version of Jira is 6 [12]. The Figure 8.3 represents active frontend of Jira tool.

8.4.3.1   Pricing

It has free plan with signup using Gmail id for 7 days. The standard and premium plan is for $7 for 11–100 and $10 per month up to 10 users starting price respectively.

8.4.3.2   Version Control

In Jira search field, where we can update related to different version used till now. Through Jira it is easy to find out what defects were there and how to overcome those defects in future.

8.4.3.3   *Key Features*

Jira is a bug-tracking program that is primarily used to track, categorize, and prioritize problems, new features, and enhancements for specific software versions. [Project is split into problems, which might include a variety of activities such as bug fixes, new features, improvements, and documentation. It also provides centralized approach where drag and drop interface is given. Project timeline is easily understood so that the delivery of project can be done in time. There is scope for keeping backlog management and sprint management.

As per popularity, it is popularly used in manual testing. It can be used with software as well as mobile app.

8.4.4   ActiveCollab

This is a robust management tool that aids in everything from job juggling to time monitoring and bill generation. It is alternative to Jira which is based on cloud approach. It makes use of KANBAN boards so task can move. It is type of project management software which gives control over the work [13]. The Figure 8.4 shows ActiveCollab dashboard.

8.4.4.1   *Pricing*

There are two plans that annual and monthly billing.

	FREE	PLUS	PRO
ANNUAL	Smaller project, personal use, limited to 3 people	3 seats, smaller teams, $7.5	Lager team, $6.25 most popular used for business purpose
MONTH	Same as Annual	Limited to 3 seats $9	$7 per person/month

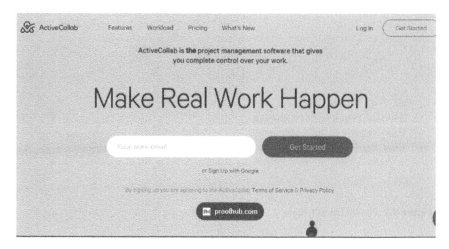

Figure 8.4 ActiveCollab [13].

8.4.4.2   *Features*

Work management is done by dividing whole project into subtask. With the help of team collaboration tab different user can chat, share file, they can specify their roles, give real time notifications. An embedded clock in ActiveCollab could be started on a project or a job. Users can be invoiced using the time records that have been uploaded. Trying to keep track of vacation days and sick days in spreadsheets can be difficult, especially when they must be synced with deadlines and responsibilities. Activecollab provides transparent communication between customer and user.

8.4.5   Pivotal Tracker

Pivotal Tracker is a popular agile tool that can be used in distributed environment. It provides the developers with a platform for real time collaboration with combined, prioritized backlog provided in Figure 8.5 [14].

8.4.5.1   *Features*

It provides workspaces for multiple projects. In this case we can report features, provide analytical representations of various trends in the project, represent cumulative flow and showcase cycle time report. It also provides file sharing, task management and options to create correct labels. It also helps the developers with linking of stories and automatic planning which is based on velocity.

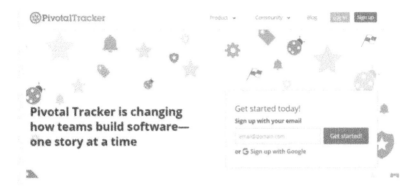

Figure 8.5 PivotalTracker [14].

8.4.5.2   Pricing

Pivotal Tracker is free for collaborators ranging from 1-5. The start up plan is $10 per month for 6-10 collaborators. The standard plan is $6.50 per collaborator per month for more than 10 collaborators.

8.4.6   Clarizen

Clarizen supports agile as well as hybrid methodologies. It helps the agile teams with streamlined workflows and portfolio management. This feature helps the team members to align the projects in terms of the business objectives [15]. The Figure 8.6 shows Clarizen agile tool dashboard.

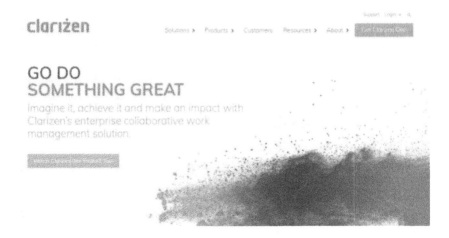

Figure 8.6 Clarizen [15].

8.4.6.1 *Software Features*

Clarizen provides workflow automation, task management and planning tools. It also provides with dashboard facility which helps the distributed agile teams to become more aligned and collaborated. Project planning is easy with project timelines feature. It also helps the agile team to run scenarios. The real time insights feature helps to keep track of available resources, schedules and tasks. It also helps the agile developers to integrate with other enterprise tools.

Pricing of the product can be identified from the enterprise website.

8.4.7 Axosoft

Axosoft is a scrum management software shown in Figure 8.7. It provides Axosoft graph features that help the distributed agile team to visualize each step of the project and view the progress also. It helps for collaboration of document creation [16].

8.4.7.1 *Software Features*

It provides features such as estimation of time, stacks ranking, burndown charts, daily scrum mode, backlog management, Kanban boards, negative feedback management, status tracking and management of workflow.

8.4.7.2 *Pricing*

Axosoft can be purchased at $126 per month.

Agile Project Management Software
Scrum, bug tracking, help desk and wiki software for dev teams

Figure 8.7 AxoSoft [16].

8.4.8 MeisterTask

The main characteristic of this software is that it accommodates various kinds of workflows. It provides flexible project boards, which helps the distributed agile team members to easily adapt to your team's workflow. It also helps agile team members to integrate with other tools. MeisterTask has a smart automation technique which leads to efficient and consistent work shown in Figure 8.8 [17].

8.4.8.1 Software Features

It provides management of backlogs. It also provides various avenues to check the progress of the project. It also helps to generate reports based on Gantt charts. It assists in management of requests and resources, status tracking, team management, workflow management, Kanban boards and milestone tracking.

8.4.8.2 Pricing

MieisterTask provides a basic plan as a free agile tool. The pro plan is at $4.19 per month and business plan is given at the rate of $10.39 per month. The team needs to contact the enterprise website for custom enterprise plan.

8.4.9 GitLab

GitLab is a prominent agile software development tool and a cloud-based DevOps platform. GitLab supports Agile teams from planning to

Figure 8.8 MeisterTask [17].

Figure 8.9 GitLab [18].

deployment phases. It manages more than a single project in the same system. GitLab is scalable i.e. manages multiple Agile Teams. It adds new functionality according to the need of methodology. This means it can adapt to new features [18]. The Figure 8.9 shows active dashboard of GitLab.

8.4.9.1   Features

Start with an issue that captures a single feature that provides users with business value.

1. A user story is frequently broken down into various tasks. To further identify those particular activities, you can build a task list within an issue's description in GitLab.
2. Everything is in one convenient place. Without jumping between products, you can keep track of concerns and share progress. Follow your issues from backlog to completion from a single interface.
3. Track groupings of issues that share a theme across projects and milestones with epics to manage your project portfolio more efficiently and with less work.
4. With GitLab milestones, you can keep track of problems and merge requests that were produced to fulfill a larger goal over a set period of time.
5. A timeline can be used to display the start and/or due dates.
6. Individual issues can be created and assigned to labels, allowing you to filter issue lists by a single or several labels.

7. Work is tracked·in real-time, and hazards are mitigated as they arise. Burndown charts let teams visualize the work scoped in a current sprint as it progresses.
8. Assign weight attributes to issues to indicate estimated effort and indicate estimated effort.
9. Conversational contributions are available across GitLab in problems, epics, merge requests, commits, and more.
10. Align your team's concerns with subsequent merge requests to provide total traceability from the start of the issue to the finish of the process.

8.4.9.2   Pricing

As GitLab provides a DevOps platform, the following is the list of getting DevOps platform [19]:

ANNUAL	Forever features for individual users $0	Enhance team productivity and coordination Price: USD 228	Organization-wide security, compliance, and planning Price: USD 1188
MONTH	Same as Annual	$19 per user/month	$99 per user/month

8.4.10   Productboard

Productboard is a product management solution that helps teams get the right goods to market more quickly. Productboard, which is based on the Product Excellence architecture, serves as a dedicated system of record for product managers, ensuring that everyone is on the same page on which features to build next [20]. The Figure 8.10 shows view of Productboard.

8.4.10.1   Features

1. Productboard helps agile product teams confidently select what to build next.

Figure 8.10 ProductBoard [20].

2. Being agile involves being adaptive. It entails progressing beyond the tools of the waterfall period. Authority persons like directors, executives have been loaded with stagnant excel data and previously created data for far too long. This tool is adaptable and collective as their agile procedures.
3. Gather user feedback and research in one place to make feature priority and design decisions.
4. Productboard can aid with the recording of product ideas as well as the establishment of explicit criteria for data-driven priority decisions
5. Share your plans with coworkers across the company so that everyone is aware of the product's direction and understands the difficult trade-offs that went into your prioritizing selections.
6. Productboard is a tool that helps you organize customer feedback and product ideas that are distributed across multiple systems. Pricing [21]:

Individual Plan	Team Plan	Business Plan
$59 per month user for 5 contributors	$119 per user per month for 20 contributors	$119 per user per month for 50 contributors

8.4.11   ZohoSprints

The next piece of software on our list is Zoho Sprints, which bills itself as a planning and monitoring solution for agile teams. Zoho Sprints is designed to help teams plan and track projects in an agile manner, making it ideal for everyone who wants to take efforts in iterative manner [22]. The Figure 8.11 represents ZohoSprint dynamic tool view.

8.4.11.1   Features

Zoho sprints divide the work into three steps:

A. Create project and invite users:

 1. He starts a 'Marketing' project in which he will oversee all marketing, promotion, and event-related tasks.
 2. He then invites all of his marketing team members to join his initiative. Because they are the leaders, a few are assigned the managerial job.
 3. He establishes the project's estimation type, which aids the team in determining the estimation points for the project's work items.

B. Build your backlog and start your sprint

 1. In the Backlog, he and his team scribble down all of the project's requirements. (Things like writing articles,

Figure 8.11 ZohoSprints [22].

tweeting, promoting events, holding workshops, and so forth.)

2. In the project, he creates important sprints. (All materials connected to tweets, Facebook contests, community building articles, and forums are included in the Social Media Sprint.) The blog sprint keeps track of all upcoming articles to be written, for example.
3. He distributes sprint owners to the managers (leads).
4. The task items are prioritized and moved from the backlog to the sprint.
5. The sprint can now be started by John or the sprint owner.
6. John is also capable of working with epics. More on epics can be found here.

C. Work around your world:

1. As the sprint starts, the sprint team moves the work items across the statuses on the board.
2. Once all the items in the sprint are moved to the 'Closed' status, the team completes the sprint successfully. A part of the project is ready for delivery.

8.4.11.2   Pricing

Rs. 350 per user per month
For 50 users price is Rs.17500/month billed annually [23].

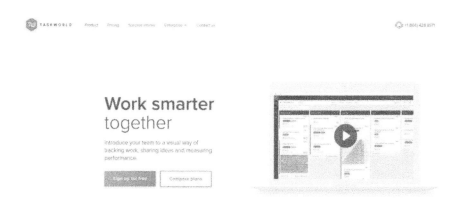

Figure 8.12 TaskWorld [24].

8.4.12   Taskworld

Taskworld helps the agile teams to keep the path of various tasks involved in the agile project. It is a platform for project management, team collaboration, visual task management, project planning, remote work tracking [24]. The Figure 8.12 depicts Taskworld dashboard.

8.4.12.1   Features

1. Users can link tasks to various project locations, which allows them to update multiple projects at once instead of creating numerous copies of a single job and updating them one by one.
2. Users can utilize task points to organize tasks based on difficulty, thus making it easier to manage and balance their daily workloads.
3. Users can see project analytics to see a list of planned, finished, and overdue tasks, as well as burndown and burnup charts that highlight the project scope and completed tasks.
4. Users can send messages straight to one another, individually or in groups, using the built-in chat feature, which also allows them to attach and exchange files.
5. Users can receive notifications and updates through email and can even reply to messages, and create tasks directly from within their inbox.

8.4.12.2   Pricing

$0 for free for five users
$11 per user per month for unlimited users [25]

8.4.13   CoSchedule

This project management tool furnishes a common platform to arrange all marketing wants at one place. The platform consists of substansialy huge agile marketing products It helps Teams to stay focused and thus resulting in ontime delivery of projects [26]. The Figure 8.13 represents CoSchedule agile tool.

8.4.13.1   Features

1. Gantt charts or timeline panorama for user progress reports is available in tool
2. Tool provides Workflow management
3. Team management facility is available in this tool

Figure 8.13 CoSchedule [26].

4. The app assists Scrum a lot.
5. Coschedule provides Kanban board
6. Status searching options are available in Coschedule

8.4.13.2   Pricing

The cost for basic features set of blog calendar is $19 every month every users. And Marketing calendar cost is $39 every month for every user.

8.4.14   Nostromo

It is new tool in industry and is competing in industry with its own set of comprehensive features like job management, report creation and analysis of diff sets. It has very outstanding user interface experience with advanced functionality [27]. The Figure 8.14 represents NOSTROMO interface.

8.4.14.1   Features

1. Nostromo uses interface to plan tasks around using drag and drop
2. Nostromo can organize your job fast and smoothly.
3. It gives fast overview of hours logged across your organization
4. Handles our estimate and actual hours on project separately.
5. It can Group your jobs in columns as per their progress of project by using Nostromo's Plan board for the planning phase and Work board while implementing the project

Figure 8.14 Nostromo [27].

6. It helps you to keep track of project performance using monthly reports.
7. It has design module which helps in design collaboration
8. It allows you to plan your mock-ups and designs in folders and connect them to relevant tasks
9. Nostromo can handle your to do task within your projects.
10. Nostromo allows Nostromo's Plan board for the planning phase and Work board while implementing

8.4.14.2   Pricing

Free option is available and advances are at $5 per month per user.

8.4.15   Todo.vu

Todo.vu is a cloud-rested influential tool that provides common platform for managing task, records and client communication. It is a user-convivial project and client management application. It has institutive interface. todo.vu's properties like labeling customers allow users to sort tasks smartly. This application task bookmarking feature helps users to mark follow-up items effectively. Moreover this application allows users to snooze jobs, flag jobs and follow jobs directly to help users arrange job as per its importance [28].

8.4.15.1   Features

1. Todo.vu provides completely integrated time tracking and billing resulting to less number of errors, best quality of reports and effectiveness in use of application and in project execution.
2. Todo.vu supports email integration, allowing both users and clients to email tasks directly into todo.vu.
3. Todo.vu provides user access controls which allow users to identify exactly what information clients and team members can see and accesses.
4. Application provides users a cloud-based application; todo.vu allows users the flexibility to access jobs as per their comfort on the multiple devices like desktop and mobile.
5. This application consists of features like custom labels, providing users with a effective way to differentiate, filter and arrange jobs easily on interface.

8.4.15.2   Pricing

It has free plan with signup using Gmail id at $0 cost for freelancers for single user with1Gb file storage. Business Plan costs $9 each user for each month for Team advances features plus time billing. (Max at $99 each month)

8.4.16   VersionOne

This tool is a robust management tool that helps us to work in multiple teams which are simultaneously working on many different projects. VersionOne offers the facility to create and trace issues, stories, defects. Defects from project can be entered and traced. The tool has fraternization and notifications pop facility can be used and team members can subscribe to various notifications facility. Voting feature can also be used through this tool. VersionOne tool can be integrated into our SDLC process and has become a part of life for doing things [29].

8.4.16.1   Pricing

The free version of this application is available. It can be used as a trial to know the tool before spending any money on the subscription.

The subscription price starts at $29.0 per month

8.4.16.2   Features

1. Inventory maintenance is available in VersionOne tool
2. VersionOne tool provides Notifications facility.
3. Planning for sprints and releases both can be done in this tool
4. Bug tracking facility is also available
5. Storyboards to express ideas and messages is possible in this tool
6. Collaboration is also possible in this tool

8.4.17   ProofHub

ProofHub is tool which consists of set of features that team need to complete the project and all features are agile in itself. It facilitates teams to work in collaboration hassle free. ProofHub acts like one shelter of multiple project and multiple teams working in parallel. This is possible because of one work management system facility provided in this. This tool can do planning for jobs, schedule and work [30].

8.4.17.1   Features

1. Chats and messages in ProofHub allow you to share ideas quickly and keep everyone of project in the loop.
2. Managers can get clear picture of everything through gang charts and reports to make decisions faster.
3. User interface is user friendly .Teams don't have any learning curve to go through. They can start using tool from day 1.
4. Team member can get auto reminder of jobs messages and notification.
5. Team member are hidden from irrelevant information which results in effective working of teams.

8.4.17.2   *Pricing*

Proof Hub provides flexible cost as per team size and required features. Free trail is available to get experience of tool for 5 users its 45 $ per month billed annually. For 10 users it is 90$ per month billed annually. For 50 users it is 135$ per month billed annually.

8.5   Conclusion

Distributed Agile Software Development is definitely helping the software industry to reach globally and make best use of the global talent. The agile principles and practices needs to be adapted in terms of the global scenario. The geographically dispersed locations throws a lot of challenges as well as advantages. The success of the agile team in distributed environment largely depends on the tools and techniques used by the team. In the current situation there are many agile project planning tools available. The distributed agile teams should consciously adopt the tools and techniques discussed here to tap the potential of agile principles in distributed environment.

References

1. Dybå, T. and Dingsøyr, T., What do we know about agile software development? *IEEE Softw.*, 26, 6–9, 2009.
2. Hoda, R., Salleh, N., Grundy, J., The rise and evolution of agile software development. *IEEE Softw.*, 35, 1–1, 2018.
3. Ghani, I., Lim, A., Hassnain, M., Ghani, I., Babar, M., II, Challenges in distributed agile software development environment: A systematic literature review. *KSII Trans. Internet Inf. Syst.*, 13, 4555–4571, 2019.
4. Shrivastava, S. and Date, H., Distributed agile software development: A review. *J. Comput. Sci. Eng.*, 1, 1, 10–17, 2010.
5. Miller, A., Distributed agile development at microsoft patterns and practices. *J. Comput. Sci. Eng.*, 1, 1, 10–17, 2010, (retrieved on March 9, 2010). http://www.pnpguidance.net/Post/DistributedAgile 16 Development Microsoft Patterns Practices.
6. Smits, H., Implementing scrum in a distributed software development organization. *Agile*, IEEE, pp. 371–375, 2007.
7. Jain, R. and Suman, U., Effectiveness of agile practices in global software development. *Int. J. Grid Distrib. Comput.*, 9, 10, 231–248, 2016.

8. De Meo, C., Siena, N., Riccardi, L., Nocera, F., Parchitelli, A., Mongiello, M., Di Sciascio, E., Mäkitalo, N., LiquiDADE: A liquid-based distributed agile and adaptive development environment (DADE) multi-device tool, in: *Proceedings of the 1st ACM SIGSOFT International Workshop on Ensemble-Based Software Engineering (EnSEmble 2018)*, NY, USA, ACM, New York, pp. 9–12.
9. Razzak, A. and Touhid, B., *Knowledge Management in Distributed Agile Software Development Projects*, vol. 469, pp. 107–131.
10. https://monday.com/
11. ntaskmanager.com
12. https://www.atlassian.com/software/jira
13. https://activecollab.com
14. https://www.pivotaltracker.com
15. https://www.clarizen.com
16. https://www.axosoft.com
17. https://www.meistertask.com
18. https://about.gitlab.com/solutions/agile-delivery
19. https://about.gitlab.com/pricing
20. https://www.productboard.com/agile-product-management-tool
21. https://www.ntaskmanager.com/blog/best-kanban-tools/
22. https://help.zoho.com/portal/en/kb/sprints/get-started/articles/getting-started-zoho-sprints
23. https://www.zoho.com/sprints/pricing.html
24. https://www.getapp.com/project-management-planning-software/a/taskworld
25. https://taskworld.com/pricing
26. https://coschedule.com
27. https://nostromo.io
28. https://todo.vu
29. www.collab.net/products/versionone
30. www.proofhub.com

Distributed Agile Software Development (DASD) Process

Samli[1], Monisha Gupta[1]*, Abhishek Sharma[1], Susheela Hooda[2] and Jaswinder Singh Bhatia[1]

[1]Department of Computer Science, Chandigarh University, Gharuan, Mohali, Punjab, India
[2]Chitkara University Institute of Engineering and Technology, Chitkara University, Rajpura, Punjab, India

Abstract

Agile software development is a novel strategy that employs agile approaches to create a flexible architecture that can adapt to changing needs and resulting in a repetitive-gradual design of the agile software development process. In this chapter, the notion of agile software development, its benefits, objectives, factors which influences agile software development and its function has been discussed. Thereafter, we will discuss the distributed agile development teams, their benefits and common practices done by agile teams. With the whole software development process, scrum meetings play an important role in the whole development cycle. It helps developers to organize the whole process efficiently and as a result reduces the overall time. Therefore, the whole scrum process has also been discussed. Today, more than ever before and often without noticing us, technology touches every part of our lives. It defines the current trend and rules of future development and principles in the making of complex software, with the subject of an improvement of the agile software development process by using new practices and attainment into the system as they develop.

Keywords: Agile software development, scrum master, success factors, distributed software development, scrum

*Corresponding author: monishagupta2705@gmail.com

Susheela Hooda, Vandana Mohindru Sood, Yashwant Singh, Sandeep Dalal and Manu Sood (eds.)
Agile Software Development: Trends, Challenges and Applications, (187–204) © 2023 Scrivener Publishing LLC

9.1   Introduction

Agile is a working technique that emphasizes efficiency and speed. Agile is a term that may be used to describe a variety of things. Individuals can be agile practitioners, teams can be agile, and organizations can call themselves agile [1]. Alternatively, you may use agile methodology in your processes or have adopted agile as a style of working.

But, in this case, we're talking about agile software development. Agile software development entails taking a step-by-step approach to development, with each step serving as a mini-project. The project is divided into sprints, each with its own set of objectives. The program is handed over to the client at the end of each sprint, who provides comments. Agile, in essence, reduces the rigidity associated with the waterfall process. Even after the contract is signed, there is greater flexibility and freedom to adjust the project's scope [2]. Agile development, unlike waterfall development, does not wait for one component of the process to finish before moving on to the next. Iterative software development is used in agile software development.

Design, development, testing, and other particular phases all have overlaps or improvements. Each step entails the creation of a new feature or the enhancement of an existing one. The client receives continuous product delivery across various sprints and testing environments [4].

It is based on the 12 principles outlined in the Agile Software Development Manifesto. Following the twelve software development principles allows teams to concentrate more on determining the best course of action throughout the process [4–6]:

1. The greatest objective is to delight customers with timely and consistent delivery.
2. Changes are always acceptable in software development.
3. Reduce the delivery time cycle by a few weeks/months and release functioning software.
4. On the project, developers and businesspeople should collaborate.
5. By creating the necessary environment, you can trust people to get the task done.
6. The most efficient approach of transmitting information is through face-to-face dialogue.
7. The functional software should be used to track project progress.

8. Agile development is all about long-term planning. Every member of the group should be able to work at their own speed.

9. Maintain a constant focus on technical quality and design competence.

10. Keep the project as simple as possible.

11. Encourage teams to self-organize in order to get the greatest design and architectural solutions.

12. At frequent intervals, teams should reflect on how they might improve and become more efficient

This chapter is divided into 5 sections. Section 9.1 explains the agile software development and its principles. Section 9.2 discusses the distributed software development (DSD) process and its factors. Section 9.3 discusses the challenges which are faced by agile distributed team and some common practices for agile team. Section 9.4 explains scrum global software development and its benefits in DSD. Section 9.5 discusses various tools and techniques for Agile Distributed Software Development (ADSD) and section 9.6 contains conclusion.

9.2   Distributed Software Development

Business has become more reliant on software. To succeed, you must use software to get an advantage over your competition. Many companies have begun building software remotely in order to save money and get access to qualified personnel. Furthermore, substantial expenditures have permitted a shift from local to global markets, resulting in new forms of rivalry and collaboration [7, 8].

As a result, multicultural software development and internationally distributed software has evolved. To attain greater profitability, productivity, quality, and cheaper costs, an increasing number of companies are spreading their software development process globally [9]. Software development may be distributed in four distinct ways. The geographical location of a project, as well as its control and ownership structure, can dictate its distribution [10, 11]. The control structure may be divided into two categories: outsourcing and in-sourcing. Outsourcing implies that the firm buys software from a third party, while in-sourcing indicates that the organization offers services internally through internal initiatives [12, 13].

9.2.1   Factors Influencing Agile Distributed Software Development

Team effectiveness, team management, motivation, and customer satisfaction are the four most important elements influencing their productivity. The most commonly cited cause for failing agile projects is a lack of agile team management assistance.

1. Distributed Development Factors: Software project teams have become more globalized, resulting in cost savings, improvement in the quality and productivity rate. In the areas of communication, cultural problems, and knowledge management, this presents extra challenges and hazards.

2. Poor Communication: Software development necessitates a considerable quantity of formal communication across key channels. The GSD's complicated infrastructure and large people network, which varies over time, result in a reduction in communication frequency and quality, which has a direct impact on production. This danger might be caused by a lack of network infrastructure or a lack of a collaborative workplace atmosphere. Inadequate network infrastructure: The use of numerous means of communication is another strategy that helps to mitigate the impact of this danger. Teleconference, net meeting, webcam, SMS, video conference, net meeting, Internet relay chat are some of the communication methods that may be employed. For dispersed session meetings, videoconferencing (preferable) or teleconferencing can be employed. Insufficient office infrastructure: office infrastructure should be able to enable dispersed agile development. The co-located team working in a single room is a frequent technique that fosters effective communication. Dedicated scrum meeting rooms with the necessary infrastructure also aid in communication. A virtual conference room can be used as a specialized scrum meeting room in specific cases.

3. Cultural Difference: When projects are spread, a variety of cultural issues develop, including language obstacles, differences in work cultures, and cultural prejudice. These issues might wreak havoc on the project's implementation. The manager of the project should make an effort to achieve

social integration by implementing techniques that help to mitigate the impact of cultural differences. Untransmitted information and misinterpretations are the result of language obstacles [21]. This issue was identified by all three organizations (ABC, DEF, and XYZ) as one that needed to be taken seriously. Differences in team behavior, perceptions of authority and hierarchy, planning, timeliness, and corporate culture may all contribute to work culture differences [10, 11]. During the project launch, the project manager might organize for cultural diversity training [12].

4. Time zone difference: Select distant locations in the same or nearby time zones. This will allow remote teams to have a greater number of overlapping hours, facilitating collaboration. Organization ABC also indicated that they want development centers with the same time difference as its clients (for example, for a US client, a close shore center such as Brazil is recommended).

5. A large number of widely dispersed sites: The project's administration becomes increasingly challenging as the number of locations grows. Because project stakeholders are dispersed across numerous sites and time zones, communication and collaboration among team members may be limited. This problem can be solved by following the procedures listed below: Limit the number of players on each squad. A properly integrated team may be limited to only a few locations. Distributing a project across many sites is one option.

6. Due to geographical distance: Among the team members, there is usually a lack of trust and collective awareness. This may be mitigated by bringing the team together, especially during critical times. The project manager can take a number of actions: Arrange for a team meeting during the first sprints and at the conclusion of the project. Face-to-face interactions are the only way to create trust and a common identity faster. Sending ambassadors to different locations helps the company communicate more effectively. The product owner, project manager, and developers may all communicate with each other across the scattered sites. This aids in the team's understanding of both the business and technical aspects of the project. This aids in the formation of group cohesiveness and trust. In addition to daily scrum

and sprint planning sessions, extra meetings promote trust and teamwork.

7. Lack of use of knowledge management: This is an issue that many enterprises are dealing with. They lack a well-developed and current knowledge base, or if they have, it is in its development phase. The project manager's, developers', scrum masters', and product owners' experiences with the project, as well as the methodologies employed, risks encountered, and mitigation measures implemented, should all be documented. When working on their project, new team members might benefit from the knowledge of their predecessors. ABC is currently working on knowledge management, although they do have case studies of some really successful initiatives available on their website as published papers.

8. Distribution of work: One of the issues with the team's job distribution is that it is not done according to location. The architecture will begin to reflect the team's geographical dispersion, according to Conway's Law. Different parts of the country will become overly specialized in specific components. Much of conventional understanding about onshore/offshore borders is based on people's activities. As a result, analysis and design are carried out onshore, building is carried out offshore, and acceptance testing is carried out onshore. This is clearly compatible with the waterfall concept. On the contrary, things become better when the offshore team is in charge of as many operations as feasible. When we collaborate with others, we are able to accomplish more.

9.3   Distributed Agile Software Development Team

There are some challenges which are faced by Agile Distributed Teams and are mentioned in below points:

1. Along with the previously mentioned advantages, combining agile and distributed development introduces a slew of additional obstacles. Despite the fact that there are business reasons for dispersing a team, communication is hindered, resulting in team dysfunction. Agile teams rely heavily on

one-on-one communication, both inside the team and with customers [13, 14]. As a result, when it comes to compatibility difficulties, these two trends, dispersed development and agile methodology, meet challenges.

2. Documentation: Minimal documentation is the utmost goal because in documentation some of the portion gets wasted and this is a preference of agile teams. When teams are scattered, some aspects about the project may be missed, and comprehension decreases as a result. For distant team members, the material on the narrative cards may be insufficient due to a lack of deep dialogue.

3. Pair programming: Same code is processed in this programming by two teams and this is a common element of agile approaches [15, 16]. With distributed teams, this technique is impossible. Teams in this situation will have to find an alternative option.

4. Different working hours: Another significant difficulty confronts teams that span many time zones. There are occasions when one of the team members is available while the other member is unavailable. Such teams' working hours must be synchronized in order to improve clarity and prevent rework.

5. Training on Agile Practices: When the remote team members are new, the impact of communication gaps is felt more acutely. They must be educated on agile approaches such as test-driven development. When teams are co-located, training is simple to deliver. Alternatives to the training offered

DISTRIBUTED AGILE TEAMS

Figure 9.1 Distributed agile teams.

to team members must be found by distributed teams. The problem is made much more challenging by the team members' cultural differences [17, 18].

6. Distribution of work: As demonstrated in Figure 9.1, work should not be distributed based on geography, which is a huge issue. As a result, the infrastructure will tend to represent the geographic dispersion of the team (Conway's law). Different parts of the country will become highly specialized in a certain field [19, 20].

9.3.1   Distributed Agile Development/Teams

The term "distributed development" refers to the process of designing, producing, and testing software products with dispersed teams located all over the world. Here, remote teams from all around the world collaborate on a variety of projects [21, 22].

Distributed teams, on the other hand, are professionals who operate from two or more geographical locations. The team has their own physical area and collaborates to create a high-quality product and operate the process efficiently [23, 24].

There are some benefits of Distributed Agile Development:

1. Product Quality Enhancement:
   In a distributed agile environment, agile teams focus solely on producing high quality, reliable products by breaking the project down into tiny sprints. Agile teams may producehigh-performing and engaging solutions by continuously developing and testing each iteration.

2. Access to Global Talent:
   The pool of brilliant experts from all around the world has resulted in distributed agile development. Expert developers from all around the world collaborate to create a solid product.

3. Cost-Effective:
   Developers' rates and wages differ depending on their geographical locations. For example, the typical hourly wage of developers in the United States is $30, whereas it is $20 in America and $25 in Europe. To grow your product development, you might recruit a knowledgeable and competentindividual.

4. Predefined Delivery Time:
   Remote teams in an agile distributed environment have pre-determined sprints, product features, and functions, and are allowed to conduct beta testing prior to the product launch. It enables them to enhance product quality and increase the worth of their company.
5. Transparent Involvement of the Client:
   End-users or clients can communicate with developers and offer suggestions and comments throughout the development of software. From sprint planning through review meetings to testing, they play an important role in selecting features and functionality. Everything is under their control, from top to bottom.
6. Improved Productivity:
   When working in a dispersed agile setting, there is always a lower risk of losing qualified and competent employees. In distributed agile contexts, remote team members frequently perform better, take fewer sick days, and complete tasks faster.

9.3.1.1 Some Common Practices for Agile Teams are Specified as Below

The agile methodology, which is built on an iterative framework, is centered on the interaction of self-organizing teams of persons with the cross-disciplinary skill sets required to develop tested, functional software. Best practices regarding how to encourage a group of individuals to work together more efficiently and successfully are also necessary [25]. Even the best engineers and testers need to work on their interpersonal skills in order to give value items to their customers.

a) Collaborate with the customer
The customer is happy when their expectations and requirements are met, and their wants and needs are realized. Apart from mindreading, software developers have invented a variety of approaches for determining and providing what the customer desires.

b) Work together daily
Organizational science scholars identified six factors of collaboration quality:

- Communication
- Coordination
- Balance of team member contributions
- Mutual support
- Effort
- Cohesion

c) Build projects around motivated individuals

Pushing through a lengthy development cycle and completing the work properly takes a lot of motivation. Agile teams are enthused about their job, dedicated to the team's objective, and helpful to one another. When colleagues trust and respect one another, agile teams build a fast-paced and predictable work rhythm. It's not easy to establish an atmosphere conducive to this. An Agile floor layout facilitates team collaboration, encourages spontaneous thinking, and keeps the team's activities on track. Individual workplaces can be used by team members for quiet time.

d) Form self-organizing teams

Self-organizing Teams decide how they will carry out the task and who will be in charge of what. They split the job into tasks that can be accomplished each day and into increments that can be finished within each iteration. Management does not assign duties or keep an eye on them. The team has been tasked with making the best judgments possible. To make this arrangement work, each team member must have faith in their job and be willing to persevere through the most tough and unpleasant obstacles. Teams as a whole share ownership and accountability for problems, moving beyond particular positions to find solutions.

9.4   Scrum in Global Software Development (GSD)

Global software development (GSD), in a remote context, software development needs effective management methods. According to a number of studies, the benefits indicated are not realized in real time, and GSD has problems owing to geographical, temporal, and cultural distances. In internationally distributed teams, teamwork and communication between and across teams and team members are critical. Several communication platforms are used by globally scattered teams to communicate. During the administration of GSD projects, however, various obstacles arise, including variances in language used by remote teams, socialist-cultural concerns, diverse backgrounds, and communication and coordination issues.

However, the absence of meetings in distant teams impedes "tameness," trust, and information exchange informally. Goals and practices are not discussed widely amongst and across teams due to a lack of face-to-face encounters. Due to the sense of time, communication methods, and hierarchy, cultural distance is another issue for GSD. Misunderstandings occur when persons from different backgrounds communicate, reducing project success rates.

Various approaches to overcoming these challenges have been mentioned in the literature, including meeting face-to-face to learn about the customs and traditions of other culturally diverse teams. Because the teams are physically divided, time zone differences are also a concern. When compared to sites with a smaller time difference, sites placed far apart with a large time difference have considerable communication challenges. Due to different time zones, feedback from other sites may be delayed. Ambiguities cannot be appropriately addressed with asynchronous communication technologies. Misinterpretations might also be caused by tools [21]. Some jobs in GSD take more work and time than they do in collocated teams [20]. When compared to collocated teams, the performance of remote teams gradually declines. GSD initiatives have been reported to fail not owing to a lack of capability, but due to a lack of awareness of the implications, difficulties, and restrictions associated with dispersed labor. Some of these issues have been considered to be solved by using agile principles. Agile strategies are used in highly unpredictable projects to ensure a successful end.

The focus of agile software development is on a wide interaction between developers and clients. It's also worth noting that numerous project managers working on internationally scattered projects are seriously considering using agile approaches. All agile approaches that may be used to manage GSD projects. The many agile approaches that are utilized in enterprises assist in maximizing profit. It is necessary to change agile techniques in order to overcome challenges caused by physical separation. Several new versions of agile techniques have been produced, each of which is tailored to maximize advantage in distributed projects. We look at the issues and practices of GSD when it comes to project management in this thesis. Because of its widespread use in industry, we will focus on SCRUM. SCRUM is an incremental software development and project management approach. According to several studies, SCRUM may be used effectively by worldwide development teams. SCRUM focuses on project management tasks that occur on a daily basis. It focuses on job prioritisation based on business scope, modifying the usefulness of deliverables, and generating income early. On the other hand, there are a number of dangers linked with using SCRUM in GSD.

A framework has been created to aid researchers in comprehending the numerous risks associated with using SCRUM in GSD. The necessity for training for remote teams to use SCRUM methods is also mentioned. Using SCRUM to encourage and ensure excellent communication yields positive results. SCRUM is mostly used to keep track of projects by making it simple to update documentation. Organizations are shifting their focus away from paperwork and toward continually enhancing team performance.

9.4.1   Aim and Objectives of Scrum Practices in GSD

- To determine the management problems that arise in internationally spread projects.
- To look into how SCRUM is used in GSD projects.
- To look into the advantages and disadvantages that GSD firms encounter while applying SCRUM approaches to handle management issues in GSD.

9.4.2   Background

The basic premise of this strategy is that the creation of a system is dependent on a number of unknowns, including technical, insecure, and incomplete needs, time-bound infrastructure, resources, and other technologies to build. SCRUM allows for such compliance in the development process, resulting in a solution that is delivered to the client efficiently and ahead of schedule, the entire scrum process is depicted in Figure 9.2.

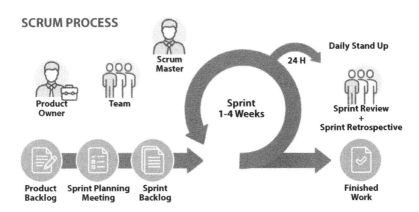

Figure 9.2 Depiction of scrum process.

9.4.3   Scrum Practices in GSD

GSD Scrum Practices Scrum is an incremental project management system that is iterative, time-boxed, and built on a simple "inspect and adapt" paradigm. The physical collocation of development team members is a significant cause for Scrum's success. However, there are examples of Scrum techniques being used successfully in GSD in the literature. According to recent research, Scrum principles boost communication, trust, motivation, and quality in GSD. Some reports also indicate that certain Scrum methods might help to alleviate some of the known GSD issues. Scrum procedures such as daily scrum, sprint planning, scrum of scrums, and retrospective sessions, for example, involve one team to create the report, members in cooperation, hidden problems, establish trust, help visualize and boost team spirit. Also, sprint planning is said to promote "teamness" by allowing for shared view of project activity.

9.5   Tools and Techniques for Agile Distributed Development

Various communication challenges must be addressed in order to construct an efficient remote agile team. Many dispersed teams fail because they act as though they are based in the same location and do not adequately address the additional communication challenges they face. Many of the most pressing communication issues necessitate the team's commitment to improve as well as the use of extra practices and tools. The strategies listed below can assist in overcoming the issues that agile distributed software development methodologies might cause.

1. Improve Communication: The key to successful remote cooperation is improved communication. Cost saving is done by using conference phones and it minimizes the 14 sites setup cost. Impromptu meetings may easily bring the entire staff together. If accessible, video conferencing is preferable than voice conferencing. It is vital to change the way team members engage with one another. Communication is informal in most collocated teams (verbal). Instead, formal nonverbal communication should be employed. In the instance of GSD, this strategy is advantageous since it addresses the issue of non-overlapping working hours. Communication can be included as an explicit component

as another team member's responsibilities. This might be accomplished by designating a representative for a remote sub team to assist in the recovery of lost hallway communication. It's also possible that meeting formats will need to be altered. Stand-up meetings may be too long since only issues that affect the entire team are covered. After the meeting, more concerns may be explored. Non-participating team members are allowed to depart and return to their work. Visits to Contact: Project teams can meet on collocation for the first little iteration to interact in person. This helps members of the team to build trust, and be familiar to one another. This is beneficial since many crucial decisions are made at the start of a project [2, 3].

2. Team Distribution: When the crew is absent throughout the day, significant time zone differences cause communication breakdowns. A three to four hour time zone distribution is possible with the full crew sharing. The team has to take advantage of overlapping meeting times. This individual will act as the team's backbone and attend daily stand-up meetings. He must have active talks and discussions in the team room before giving the outcomes to the offshore team. Exhaustion and burnout are common side effects of this work. In a recent publication, Hubert Smiths suggested a different approach to synchronized office hours. He suggests using layered scrum, which includes several daily scrum sessions and multilayer reporting.

3. Focus on Team coaching: Distributed teams have greater hurdles and need more help for agile team's fundamental practices. Because important practices appear to be too difficult, many scattered teams quit them. Many of the key Extreme Programming development techniques reinforce one another, thus it's necessary to modify or replace a practice with something equal rather than just discarding it. Pair programming, for example, may be supplemented, and narrative cards could need all of the knowledge gleaned during dialogues.

4. Distribution of work: According to Conway's Law, distributed teams should conceive rather than provide functionality to components, and describe their job in terms of satisfying user stories. Breaking down user stories into tasks and allocating assignments based on those tasks on location and/or

skill types is not a good idea. This would create knowledge silos over time, providing the team with new duties that only one or two individuals could fulfil.

5. Documentation: Keeping relevant documentation on hand can help the DSD team collaborate more effectively while employing agile methods. For example, putting user stories in globally accessible backlogs with use case diagrams can assist eliminate misunderstandings and promote team communication. Various technologies, such as issue trackers (such as Jira) and project management software (such as Scrum Works), aid in preserving documentation and transparency. Tool selection: Various tools for both official and informal communication and project assistance have been offered. Similarly, plans and schematics must be exchanged throughout different places. The choice to spread a team must be accompanied by a commitment to supply the team with the tools it requires to maximize communication, as well as an understanding that it will take some time for them to optimize around them. The main function of these tools may be classified as follows: Emails and instant messengers are examples of communication tools. Repositories and version control tools are two types of software configuration management technologies. Bug and issue tracking databases: these keep track of the bugs that have been discovered. Technical references and commonly asked questions can be found in knowledge centers. Collaborative development environments: in distributed agile projects, offering project management and repository tools, is suggested as an essential solution. Wikis, according to Fowler, are one of the best methods to store common information since they are easy to use, straightforward to set up.

9.6   Conclusion

Distributed Agile Software Development (DASD) is a new software developing methodology that blends the concepts of ASD and DSD. This chapter enlightens the concept of distributed agile software development, its benefits and challenges which are faced by agile software team during the software development process. This chapter also discusses the various tools and techniques which have been currently used for agile development. Scrum has also been discussed in details in this chapter.

References

1. Sutherland, J. and Schwaber, K., *The Scrum Papers: Nuts, Bolts, and Origin of an Agile Process*, http://scrumtraininginstitute.com/home/streamdownload/ scrumpapers, Last accessed 25 March 2009.
2. Jimeenez, M., Piattini, M., Vizcaino, A., Review article challenges and improvements in distributed software development: A systematic review. Hindawi Publishing Corporation, *Adv. Softw. Eng.*, 2009, Article ID 710971.
3. Carmel, E. and Agarwal, R., Tactical approaches for alleviating distance in global software development. *IEEE Softw.*, 18, 2, 22–29, Mar./Apr. 2001.
4. Jimeenez, M., Piattini, M., Vizcaino, A., Review article challenges and improvements in distributed software development: A systematic review. Hindawi Publishing Corporation, *Adv. Softw. Eng.*, 2009, Article ID 710971.
5. Park, S. and Maurer, F., The role of blogging in generating a software product vision, in: *Proc. of the ICSE Workshop on Cooperative and Human Aspects on Software Engineering*, IEEE Chase, Washington, DC, pp. 74–77, 2009.
6. Giuffrida, R. and Dittrich, Y., Empirical studies on the use of social software in global software development–A systematic mapping study. *Inf. Softw. Technol.*, 55, 7, 1143–1164, 2013. http://dx.doi.org/10.1016/j. infsof.2013.01.004.
7. Grammel, L., Treude, C., Storey, M.-A., Mashup environments in software engineering, in: *Proc. of the 1st Workshop on Web 2.0 for Software Engineering, Web2SE, '10*, NY, ACM, New York, pp. 24–25.
8. Siakas, K., Kermizidis, R., Kontos, K., Using social media in business as a tool for open innovations. *Business-Related Scientific Research Conference (ABSRC 2014)*, Milan, Italy, December, 2014.
9. Abbattista, F., Calefato, F., Gendarmi, D., Lanubile, F., Incorporating social software into distributed agile development environments. *2008 23Rd IEEE/ACM International Conference on Automated Software Engineering–Workshops*, 2008, http://dx.doi.org/10.1109/asew.2008.4686310.
10. Sutherland, J., Distributed teams: How to mitigate a significant business risk of the coronavirus. Retrieved May 13, 2020, from https://www.scruminc. com/distributed-teams-how-to-mitigate-a-significant-business-risk-of-the-coronavirus/.
11. Prikladnicki, R., Damian, D., Audy, J.L.N., Patterns of evolution in the practice of distributed software development: Quantitative results from a systematic review, in: *12th International Conference on Evaluation and Assessment in Software Engineering (EASE)*, June 2008.

12. Ramesh, B., Cao, L., Mohan, K., Xu, P., Can distributed software development be agile? *Commun. ACM*, 49, 10, 41–46, 2006.

13. Razavi, A.M. and Ahmad, R., Agile development in large and distributed environments: A systematic literature review on organizational, managerial and cultural aspects, in: *2014 8th. Malaysian Software Engineering Conference (MySEC)*, IEEE, September 2014.

14. Ghani, I., Lim, A., Hasnain, M., Ghani, I., Babar, M., II, Challenges in distributed agile software development environment: A systematic literature review. *KSII Trans. Internet Inf. Syst.*, 13, 4555–4571, 2019.

15. Paasivaara, M., Durasiewicz, S., Lassenius, C., Using scrum in distributed agile development: A multiple case study. *IEEE International Conference on Global Software Engineering*, pp. 195–204, 2000.

17. Shrivastava, S.V. and Rathod, U., Risks in distributed agile development: A review. *Procedia-Social Behav. Sci.*, 133, 417–424, 2014.

18. Mohindru, V. and Singh, Y., Node authentication algorithm for securing static wireless sensor networks from node clone attack. *Int. J. Inf. Comput. Secur.*, 10, 2-3, 129–148, 2018.

19. Miller, A., Distributed agile development at Microsoft patterns and practices, October 2020. http://www.pnpguidance.net/Post/DistributedAgile16 Development Microsoft Patterns Practices.

20. Smits, H. and Pshigoda, G., Implementing scrum in a distributed software development organization, in: *Agile 2007 (AGILE 2007)*, IEEE, pp. 371–375, August 2007.

21. Sutherland, J., Viktorov, A., Blount, J., Puntikov, N., Distributed scrum: Agile project management with outsourced development teams. *2007 40th Annual Hawaii International Conference on System Sciences (HICSS'07)*, Waikoloa, HI, pp. 274a–274a, 2007.

22. Mohindru, V. and Singh, Y., Performance analysis of message authentication algorithms in wireless sensor networks, in: *2017 4th International Conference on Signal Processing, Computing and Control (ISPCC)*, IEEE, pp. 468–472, September 2017.

23. Hossain, E., Babar, M.A., Paik, H.Y., Verner, J., Risk identification and mitigation processes for using scrum in global software development: A conceptual framework, in: *2009 16th Asia-Pacific Software Engineering Conference*, IEEE, pp. 457–464, December 2009.

24. Mohindru, V., Bhatt, R., Singh, Y., Reauthentication scheme for mobile wireless sensor networks. *Sustain. Comput. Inform. Syst.*, 23, 158–166, 2019.

25. Mohindru, V., Vashishth, S., Bathija, D., Internet of things (IoT) for healthcare systems: A comprehensive survey, in: *Recent Innovations in Computing. Lecture Notes in Electrical Engineering*, vol. 832, P.K. Singh, Y. Singh, M.H. Kolekar, A.K. Kar, P.J.S. Gonçalves, (Eds.), Springer, Singapore, 2022, https://doi.org/10.1007/978-981-16-8248-3_18.

Task Allocation in Agile-Based Distributed Project Development Environment

Madan Singh[1,2]*, Naresh Chauhan[2] and Rashmi Popli[2]

[1]CSE - AIML Department, ABES Engineering College, Ghaziabad, India
[2]Department of Computer Engineering, J. C. Bose University of Science &
Technology, YMCA, Faridabad, India

Abstract

Software development (ASD) has become one of the most important ways of developing software in the 21st century. Neighboring large multinationals have turned to ASDs in search of a larger market and cheaper cuts for fascinating decentralized software development (DASD). Activities can be set up in a hazardous zone environment, and defining incorrect activities can result in customers being driven away from the project at the expense of team members. And other project failures, a big deal. Many researchers have worked over the past decades on various allocation mechanisms in a distributed environment. These task allocation mechanisms, as they are manual in nature, cause many problems. These set of problems can be reduced, if an automated or semi – automated mechanism is applied for task allocation and other activities like – backlog prioritization and regression testing. In this chapter, a unsupervised learning based model has been presented for assisting in project development activities like – task allocation and backlog prioritization.

Keywords: Traditional Software Development (TSD), Agile Software Development (ASD), Distributed Agile Software Development (DASD), Task Allocation (TA)

*Corresponding author: madan.phdce@gmail.com

Susheela Hooda, Vandana Mohindru Sood, Yashwant Singh, Sandeep Dalal and Manu Sood (eds.)
Agile Software Development: Trends, Challenges and Applications, (205–220) © 2023 Scrivener
Publishing LLC

10.1   Introduction

10.1.1   Traditional Software Development

The first part of software development, "designing and editing", is designed for teaching methods. This means that the development process that programmers use to write code when programs at any level are not working on scheduling and scheduling [1]. This software development process is well suited for efficient operation. However, as your performance level increases, these methods take longer to resolve than the code, making them less effective and efficient. As part of the project expands, the design process for software development and all the necessary components, configuration, development and implementation documentation is identified. The absolute requirement is the strongest and most understood possible. Figure 10.1 shows the various steps adopted during the SDLC.

This approach creates a work plan that provides robust tools and design principles that are appropriate for the entire project [2]. All requirements are recorded in full at the beginning of the project and recorded in good customer communication. This document is submitted to the planning team for planning purposes. The team members take into account the total time, cost and effort to complete the project and consider the highest performance. These reports are sent to the implementation team after the protocol preparation and final debate with the client, and sent to the implementation team responsible for planning and implementation. After its implementation, the task is sent to the input cell and tested with the test team. Customers are delivered service soon. Therefore, it was found that the clients were discussing the project assembly at the end of the project without any interaction with the design and implementation team. Each team will perform different tasks for each team. There is no communication between the teams and it is not a hard paper to guide each team to the

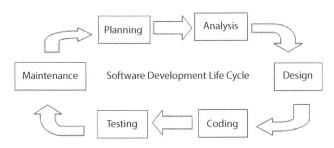

Figure 10.1 Steps followed during SDLC.

next step [3]. This process is called software development (SDLC). These follow the traditional SDLC software development process. The SDLC series follows a series of linear models or classic cascade models developed by WW Royce in 1970. Different SDLC models have been studied. During the design and analysis process, the SDLC program is performed first, followed by a document called Software Requirements Specification (SRS), which contains all the details and one description. This code reviewer is provided to correct any errors found during operation. Upon completion of the work, the repair process continues until the end of the service life [4]. Traditional and flexible type software is used in software development processes. These processes follow a set of programs in the same way by performing set tasks on top of the program settings. When adopting the liquidity model at the block-chain level, other models follow the same robust and important life cycle process.

10.1.2   Agile Software Development (ASD)

Agile software developers use "agile" as part of their business authority. The goal is to increase organizational change in programs and new opportunities. ASD compatibility and after the concept of power supply, there is a software development technology system based on regression and embedded development. After the first part of software development, creating a template and encoding and executing other models, is performed [5]. This first generation was called software development. The idea of this development process is to write code without planning or design ahead of time. Defects will be corrected later. It is not a structured, training or planning process. This software development is suitable for small, simple tasks. However, these functions present a problem of performance and forecasting. The warning system for high performance and performance is displayed. These methods are called hard-loading. They follow technological changes, or warnings. This development process first summarizes the needs of the customers and then works on high-end building, design, development and implementation. This design process requires proper planning and documentation. The process-based process, like the traditional process taken by software developers, is robust and knows all the requirements for the future [6].

These plans are organized in the usual way and not in the form of competition of a single program. This software is also used to gradually create different software. Customers are contacted at the beginning of the inspection process and at the end of the product delivery. Therefore, customers are no longer part of these processes. The main steps and plans based on this plan are summary requirements, design, and implementation and team testing, system installation, testing and maintenance [7]. In this way, these models follow a well-defined developmental process that is fully documented. They are easy to use and easy to understand. This is ideal for projects where the requirements are clear and uncomplicated. These models have a high number of projects that customers reject because of the complexity and flexibility of their requirements. In a difficult world of software development, where customer needs and ideas change daily, this traditional approach leads to job failure due to poor customer communication and lack of time.

Agile Software Development (ASD) is a software development process based on constant expansion and development. Emphasize. Customers can respond to new system changes at the level of service development. Flexible programs, two releases in addition, one-time development, and ongoing customer communication are the hallmarks of ASD [8]. An agile model emphasizes that an agile must be complex. Good communication between team members is an important part of the problem of different types of autism. Migration is an important process in an active environment. Earnings can range from one to four weeks. This transmission circuit is called a sprint [9]. The TSA continues to use a variety of communication methods. These tools are used for information communication and feedback. All the teams responsible for the development of intelligent software must have followed the famous philosophy of "Agile Manifesto" [10]. ASD is a file-based system for software development based on promoting growth and balance. It's the difference with change. This increases ductility. Thus, the growth-centric market area is likely to respond to rapid changes and changes. Customers can accept new system changes even after the project development process has been completed. The main characteristics of ASD are consistent fashion, frequent and gradual release, short growth time and ongoing communication with customers. The agile type suggests that one agile should be the same. Good communication between team members is an important part of the problem of different types of autism. The agile approach breaks down work into as few steps and as few plans as possible. Frequent and timely delivery is a critical process in a fast-paced environment. Earnings vary from one week to four weeks. This release cycle is called a sprint. At each level, the designers, testers and Sprint-master work together on the initial design, assembly needs, testing, design and architecture, code, and testing [11]. This relationship can include change and team development, thus reducing the risk of job failure and product rejection. ASD follows three principles that include part of the pre-project planning, construction and final approval. These events are in the organizational structure of the project. Define project objectives and objectives, select project implementation plans, meet needs, build team, create environment, evaluate project and monitor progress. The most important function of a construction system is to provide interested and interested people with, at the end of each run, delivering the requirements of software, analysis, design, quality control, analysis and continuous printing. The main tasks are also called end games; the main tasks are system analysis, document preparation, system expansion and training [12].

ASD is a file-based system for software development based on incremental frequency and frequency. It offers a variety of variations. As a result, local organizations will lie with a quick reaction to exchange change, for example. The customer may accept new changes in the system at least the completion of the development process. Making changes, to remove time continues, time to the customer's facility is a traditional facial faculty of the problem that works working. In the environment, the development work is performed by membership members [13]. The agile type suggests that one agile is the same. Good communication between team members is key to the TSA side. In a dynamic environment, social media marketing is an important process. Achieve flexible process management as well as development and delivery in stages in a short period of time. Remove inherited software development and support quick response to import request. This means moving Agile Quality programs. It is a software development process that seeks to grow the business community through a fast-paced development process. This is not trivial, but busy and fast in a busy work environment. That way, the law will not be cold before ordering [14, 15].

ASD was released in 2001. In line with this statement, the work and business and safety and planning of each individual, intensive documentation programs will be conducted, and contract negotiations will include collaborations and changes in customer planning. As the statement shows, taking people and talking to them costs more than one process and equipment [16, 17]. Relationships and communication with customers are more important than contract negotiations. Customers are an important part of the whole development process and should be satisfying. Customers can request a change at any time and will not follow the planned schedule. After some time, the product will be delivered to the customer. ASD focuses on customer satisfaction that can increase customer acceptance and success in this process after this process. Simple, practical, cost-effective, customer-centric, collaboration, scalability, agile development for innovative and innovative solutions, continuous improvement of design quality and deployment of first delivery within a week. With ASD, you do not need a large design. This saves a lot of paper, time, effort and energy.

Agile performance is known as agile design. Team members welcome last minute changes, including a short release schedule, daily meetings for everyone, including clients, and other months. It's over. This is done with a team of volunteers involved in the development, maintenance of the best technology and optimization and the constant use of design/motivation methods. ASD is a developmental program. Various ASD systems include crystal systems, powerful software development, task-based development, intermediate programming, and Scrum [18, 19]. Table 10.1 depicts about different Agile approaches and their working mechanisms along with roles assigned to team members.

Table 10.1 Different agile approaches and their working mechanisms.

S. no.	Name of methodology	Year	Developed by	Working mechanism and roles of team members
1	Dynamic Software Development Method	1997	Stapleton	It contains Five Phases – Feasibility Study, Business Study, Functional Model Iteration, Design and Build Iteration, Implementation It has following roles – Developer, Senior Developer, Technical Coordinator, Ambassador User, Advisor User, Visionary, Executive Sponsor
2	Extreme Programming	1999	Beck	It contains Five Phase – Exploration, Planning, Iterations to release, Product ionizing, Maintenance, Death It has following roles – Programmer, Customer, Tester, Tracker, Coach, Consultant, Manager

(*Continued*)

Table 10.1 Different agile approaches and their working mechanisms. (*Continued*)

S. no.	Name of methodology	Year	Developed by	Working mechanism and roles of team members
3	Rational Unified Process	2000	Kruchten	It contains Four Phases – Inception, Elaboration, Construction, Transition It has following roles – Business Process Analyst, Business Designer, Business Model Reviewer, Course Developer, Tool smith and additional thirty roles
4	Crystal Methodologies	2002	Cockburn	It Contains a number of different methodologies to select most suited methodology for each individual project It has three main crystal methodologies – Crystal Clear, Crystal Orange, Crystal Orange Web
6	Scrum	2002	Schwaber & Beedle	It contains three phases – Pre - Game, Development, Post – Game It has following roles – Scrum Master, Product Owner, Scrum Team, Customer, User, Management

10.1.3   Distributed Software Development

Distributed agile software distribution (DASD) is a software development environment for software vendors and development teams that are unpopular and often used locally, state, nationally and continentally. Communication, team building, learning and learning, fast delivery of results, all ASD standards can be challenging when using DASD. As a result, your relationship with the client works well, requests are easy to collect, and it can be difficult to send code regularly to shared memory. DASD is the source of many organizations around the world doing the same thing. IT staff and equipment may vary [20, 21]. There are also differences in ethnicity, language, political and legal. Despite all these differences, teams can work efficiently and in a timely manner if they work in a distributed environment. DASD is in demand today due to the high demand for sophisticated software, lack of skilled professionals, and low market share such as low production and low wages. In joint development, the team participates in common software. Large area openings, different time zones and different DASD cultures cause communication problems that do not affect the operation. All OSD actors should be on the same page, but avoiding actors at the airport can be a problem. This situation is called Agile Distributed Software (DASD). Thanks to better service, global access, more sales and faster shipping, they are growing faster. This can be explained by the fact that rural and remote services achieve the same goals. This means that a network of teams will be created to achieve the desired goals. We will refund this product to you. Speakers or team members may participate in the DASD. In this example, development teams are in countries around the world. The main characteristics of non-distributed distribution are property, territory, diversity, society and culture, language and diversity, politics and language. The information is used by the server Portal as one of the communication channels. Connect the computer through an advanced network. There are two types of server types: distribution systems and different distribution systems. Each port has the same hardware, configuration and operating system as an individual distribution system, as well as different distributed systems, each computer having an operating system and machine configuration. The equipment is distributed or distributed in a distributed area. Agile distributed software development follows the nature of the distributed environment. General software development can include a number of companies with different geographic areas of distribution as well as a group of intelligent people. Major distribution software distribution efforts include various development sites known as Agile Distributed Software (DASD) [22, 23]. One or two server development services can be configured to generate value for software customers from the hosting company. Divided states can include local and corporate relationships, such as coastal crime, crime, crime, and breach of promise. Here Multisite Development is an independent system that works in systems across different sectors of the industry. Distributed development is the development of different vendors operating in different locations. Outsourcing is a service that helps another person or business. It is not always available for sharing. Water crime is a common occurrence in villages far away from the consumer. The sea must trade with the nearest economic city. Global Software Development (GSD) is the elimination of software development programs, often across continental levels. The key to sustainable development is communication regardless of distance. DASD's vision is to empower employees, expand into new markets and reduce costs.

10.1.4   Motivation and Goal

The computer and the client may or may not be in the same place and in the same environment. While the benefits of distributed agile software development include saving money, development time involves not only better quality, but also a larger environment that fits everything in terms of reliability. In the distribution area, teams visit each other to make donations at different locations. DASD enables volunteers to leave development sites as members. In this case, the same problem will be solved for better communication. Other issues are language barriers, cultural barriers, channel size, and time zone limits. However, time zones also perform some important functions for local key auditors. Electrical distribution (PLR) is a major problem in some parts of the region. The main task of a team leader is to ensure communication between members [24]. Choose a guide where any possible links can be found. The domain management department then goes to the domain management page and contacts can be assigned to the principal and the client. This leader establishes a communication channel and is responsible for the success of the team. Other conditions in the environment are not ideal for use, so it is not possible to work on them based on experience, performance, comfort and goals. In this case, you need to change some job forecasts to solve the problem of job description in the distribution environment. While choosing the most important thing in a beautiful place, backlight control should be well controlled because it will help you get the job done faster and move your product faster. In the place of fulfillment, members in different places share at different times. For example, these groups will complete one task at a time. B. Completion of a process or project is delayed due to logical time due to delay. This issue has not been properly addressed. In this case, you will face the same problem. Other issues are language barriers, cultural barriers, channel size, and time zone limits. However, the research team is working temporarily in the local time zone.

10.2   Task Allocation

10.2.1   Traditional Task Allocation Methods

Events are an important part of any job. He often came to criticize her in a divided environment. In general, there are three ways to distribute the service. The media system allows you to offer any service to a developer who performs it on a daily basis, based on your preferences, your energy level, and more [25, 26]. This process increases flexibility by reducing exposure to limited resources. Record visits on certain days and pick up the same group activity as soon as possible, as do all the members responsible for the activity and related activities. This approach has weaknesses such as inability to promote team members, aggregation, and failure of self-employment. When everyone looked at him, he looked like a ruler. As each story unfolds, the developer, many developers, are responsible for maintaining the historical context. Moreover, it is the least variable. The logic of responsibility is destructive. The most important advantage of this system is that each developer has a responsibility to complete the history of at least one employee and to understand the role of public law. This method is also useful for groups that do not cooperate or do not want to work together. This process is unique due to the fact that it does not always work or spreads over many time zones. It can also fit in with the variation that starts with the insult and uses it on its own. This approach also has setbacks: lack of good intentions to share and lack of daily interaction. If there is a restricted report, the manufacturer may restrict it and will not be able to pay for sick leave, vacation, production accidents, etc. It works on one story and the number of stories can be up to two. or three stories at a time. The advantage of this method is that it increases the level of performance. Another important advantage of this method is that it avoids the hassle of repeating too many stories [27–29]. To achieve this, teams working together more closely with the FCC have experienced problems for unprecedented losses. This method can reduce the total, but it can still reduce half of the whole story. This system provides a lot of information that can cause us problems. This approach also has some of the potential risks of reporting further.

10.2.2   Need of Machine Learning in Task Allocation

Machine learning can be defined as an application that produces and produces the results of a computer system. According to Tom Mitchell, "computer programming" teaches computer programming based on experience, programs and processes, and progress. "You have to learn when you don't have human skills. People can define their abilities and change their solutions over time or fix them in certain situations. The system does not control certain classifications. Learn machine and machine. You also know that the car is not doing well. By promoting a controlled machine, the required number of production and operation of the production machine is sent using the available input. It can be used to predict the future and gain insight. Good education is essential for guided learning. Other examples of guided learning include regression, resolution trees, random forests, and vector support machines (SVMs) [30–32]. This process predicts intentional change through independent change. In controlled learning, work is inherited and maintained as a vector of morality. These functional vectors are transmitted by machine learning algorithms. This algorithm generates predictions based on the training process as well as the test set task. Create predictions based on possible predictions. Machine learning is a normal learning experience with no required jobs. The device has an input that has no output where it goes. No external training required. It is used to find examples. Pool is one of the curriculum that does not take care of where one model is associated. As the machine learns to start, it inspires to receive unique feedback and rewards. The purpose of this device is to maximize these costs. Training for the machine can be done by immediate or indirect experience in the form of feedback. When designing a learning curriculum, select and demonstrate relevant learning experience and business objectives before selecting objective algorithms. Memory plays an important role in the initial training process. In fact, the dataset is a model of these records that can be used for learning and testing algorithms [33–35]. If the model is taken or tested as a false record, it may be a false prediction and lose its purpose entirely due to prophecy and machine learning. In order to represent the correct data set in the form of learning immediately, you need to follow the data processing process. These techniques are very useful when modifying representative data for educational and experimental purposes. These processes include data collection, data collection, reorganization, training and testing.

10.3   Machine Learning-Based Task Allocation Model

With the emphasis on improvement in project development in a distributed environment, a machine learning based task allocation model has been proposed. The proposed model prepares the relevant task sets on the arrival of a new project. The processed task set list is passed to different

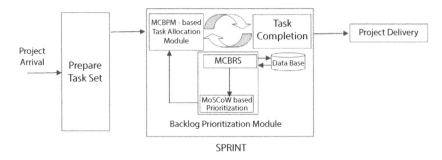

Figure 10.2 Machine learning-based task allocation model.

"Sprint" cycles as shown in the Figure 10.2. In each and every sprint the task sets are passed through unsupervised - learning based MCBPM model [12, 28, 29]. The model applies clustering of common task set and allocates these tasks to most relevant developer, which is finalized based on a number of parameters. The allotted tasks are made complete by the MBPM based task allocation model. The backlogs generated in each sprint are processed by MCBRS model with the help of MoSCoW based backlog prioritized list. In this way, all available backlogs are processed in different sprint cycles. In this way, machine learning based mechanisms are applied to accomplish task allocation and backlog prioritization process. These products are further passed to regression testing mechanism for removal of bugs and errors. The final product is further passed for delivery to the customer. In this way, the complete process of project development takes place with the help of machine learning based support mechanisms. The advantages of following the model is that manual interference can be reduced in task allocation and backlog prioritization, which will result in reduction of project development time and end product delivery time. Along with this, it will also help in reduction in project failures caused due to inappropriate task allocations.

10.4   Conclusion

For large software companies, distributed clusters are a costly option for creating state-of-the-art services. However, it is very important to separate it internally because there are many things that project managers should consider before assigning a team member. Task allocation in distributed environment remains to be the need of the hour due to a number of factors which work in favor of distributed Agile environment. Machine learning mechanisms add more flavor to existing men made mechanisms and provide an automated support to task allocation. Machine learning based methods have proven to be helpful in faster allocations and timely delivery of the end product to the end user. Further, machine learning based mechanisms at its lowest level can be applied to each and every activity of project management so that the processes of software project management become more useful and they may help in faster, hassle-free delivery of the finished product.

References

1. Singh, M., Chauhan, N., Popli, R., A framework for transitioning of traditional software development method to distributed agile software development. *2019 International Conference on Issues and Challenges in Intelligent Computing Techniques (ICICT)*, pp. 1–4, 2019.

2. Shen, M., Tzeng, G.-H., Liu, D.-R., Multi-criteria task assignment in workflow management systems, in: *Proc. 36th Annu. Hawaii Int. Conf. Syst. Sci.*, pp. 1–9, Jan. 2003.

3. Singh, M., Chauhan, N., Popli, R., A review on quantitative task allocation in agile software development. *Proceedings of International Conference on Sustainable Computing in Science, Technology and Management (SUSCOM)*, Amity University Rajasthan, Jaipur-India, pp. 268–273, Available at SSRN: https://ssrn.com/abstract=3351645.

4. Duggan, J., Byrne, J., Lyons, G.J., A task allocation optimizer for software construction. *IEEE Softw.*, 21, 76–82, 2004.

5. Mak, D.K.M. and Kruchten, P.B., Task coordination in an Agile distributed software development environment, in: *Proc. Can. Conf. Elect. Computer Eng.*, pp. 606–611, May 2006.

6. Lamersdorf, A., Münch, J., Rombach, D., A decision model for supporting task allocation processes in global software development, in: *Proc. 10th Int. Conf. Product-Focused Software Process Improvement (PROFES)*, Oulu, Finland, pp. 332–346, Jun. 2009.

7. Singh, M., Chauhan, N., Popli, R., A technique for transitioning of plan driven software development method to distributed agile software development. *Proceedings of International Conference on Innovative Computing and Communications (ICICC-2020)*, Delhi University, India, 2020, Available at SSRN: https://papers.ssrn.com/sol3/papers.cfm?abstract_id=3595294.

8. Lin, J., Context-aware task allocation for distributed agile team, in: *Proc. 28th IEEE/ACM Int. Conf. Autom. Softw. Eng. (ASE)*, pp. 758–761, Nov. 2013.

9. Singh, M., Chauhan, N., Popli, R., Machine learning based backlog prioritization techniques in distributed agile software development. *Int. J. Adv. Sci. Technol.*, 29, 6, 8699–8704.

10. Filho, M.S., Pinheiro, P.R., Albuqueruqe, A.B., Applying verbal decision analysis in distributed software development: Rank ordering the influencing factors in task allocation. *11th Iberian Conference on Information Systems and Technologies (CISTI)*, 2016.

11. Singh, M., Chauhan, N., Popli, R., Implementation of machine learning based task allocation in distributed agile software development. *Int. J. Grid Distrib. Comput.*, 13, 2, 454–461 2020.

12. Singh, M., Chauhan, N., Popli, R., Framework for machine learning based task allocation in DASD environment. *2021 Fourth International Conference on Computational Intelligence and Communication Technologies (CCICT)*, pp. 29–34, 2021.

13. Singh, M., Chauhan, N., Popli, R., Survey on test case reduction and prioritization in agile software development. *3rd International Conference on Frontiers of Science & Technology (ICFST–2021)*, organized on August 13-14, 2021.

14. Coulouris, G., Dollimore, J., Kindberg, T., *Distributed Systems: Concepts and Design*, 5th edition, 4/E, Pearson Education Ltd., London, 2017.

15. Singh, M., Chauhan, N., Popli, R., Task allocation in distributed agile software development environment using unsupervised learning. *J. Eng. Res.*, 1–15, 2022.

16. Bokhari, S.H., A shortest tree algorithm for optimal assignments across space and time in a distributed processor system. *IEEE Trans. Softw. Eng.*, 7, 6, 583–589, 1981.

17. Lamersdorf, A., Münch, J., Rombach, D., Towards a multi-criteria development distribution model: An analysis of existing task distribution approaches. *IEEE International Conference on Global Software Engineering, ICGSE*, pp. 109–118, 2008.

18. Lamersdorf, A., Münch, J., Rombach, D., A survey on the state of the practice in distributed software development: Criteria for task allocation. *Proceedings of the Fourth IEEE International Conference on Global Software Engineering, ICGSE*, pp. 41–50, 2009.

19. Lamersdorf, A. and Münch, J., TAMRI: A tool for supporting task distribution in global software development projects. *International Workshop on Tool Support Development and Management in Distributed Software Projects, Proceedings of the Fourth International Conference on Global Software Engineering*, pp. 322–327, 2009.

20. Lamersdorf, A. and Münch, J., A multi-criteria distribution model for global software development projects. *J. Braz. Comput. Soc.*, 16, 2, 97–115, 2010.

21. Larichev, O.I. and Moshkovich, H.M., *Verbal Decision Analysis for Unstructured Problems*, Kluwer Academic Publishers, Boston, 1997.

22. Bokhari, S.H., *Assignment Problems in Parallel and Distributed Computing. The Kluwer International Series in Engineering and Computer Science*, 32, Springer, Science & Business Media, Switzerland, 1987.

23. Filho, M.S., Pinheiro, P.R., Albuquerque, A.B., Task allocation approaches in distributed agile software development: A quasi systematic review. *4th Computer Science On-line Conference, Proceedings of the 4th Computer Science On-line Conference (CSOC2015), Software Engineering in Intelligent Systems*, vol. 3, pp. 243–252, 2015.

24. Filho, M.S., Pinheiro, P.R., Albuquerque, A.B., Task allocation in distributed software development aided by verbal decision analysis. *5th Computer Science On-line Conference 2016 (CSOC2016), Proceedings of the 5th Computer Science On-line Conference*, pp. 127–137, 2016.

25. Filho, M.S., Pinheiro, P.R., Albuquerque, A.B., Applying verbal decision analysis to task allocation in distributed development of software. *28th Int. Conf. on Software Engineering and Knowledge Engineering (SEKE2016)*, pp. 402–407, 2016.

26. Filho, M.S., Pinheiro, P.R., Albuquerque, A.B., Task assignment to distributed teams aided by a hybrid methodology of verbal decision analysis. *IET Softw.* Wiley Online Library, 11, 5, 245–255, 2017.

27. Hole, S. and Moe, N.B., A case study of coordination in distributed Agile software development, in: *Communications in Computer and Information Science, Software Process Improvement, Part 5*, pp. 189–200, 2008.

28. Mohindru, V., Singh, Y., Bhatt, R., Securing wireless sensor networks from node clone attack: A lightweight message authentication algorithm. *Int. J. Inf. Comput. Secur.*, 12, 2–3, 217–233, 2020.

29. Singh, M., Chauhan, N., Popli, R., Unsupervised learning based backlog prioritization in distributed agile software development. *J. Des. Eng.*, 2021, 8, 14160–14168, 2021.

30. Mohindru, V. and Singh, Y., Efficient approach for securing message communication in wireless sensor networks from node clone attack, *Ind. J. Sci. Tech.*, 9, 32, 1–7, 2016.

31. Singh, M., Maggo, C., Pokhra, K.R., Ram, S., Nagar, G., Gajrani, J., Jain, V., Cloud attack classification using supervised machine learning and deep neural network. *J. Des. Eng.*, 2021, 9, 3729–3737, 2021.

32. Mohindru, V., Singh, Y., Bhatt, R., Hybrid cryptography algorithm for securing wireless sensor networks from node clone attack. *Recent Adv. Electr. Electron. Eng.*, 13, 2, 251–259, 2020.

33. Filho, M.S., Pinheiro, P.R., Albuquerque, A.B., Verbal decision analysis applied to the prioritization of influencing factors in distributed software development, pp. 49–66, Springer International Publishing AG, New York, 2018.

34. Mohindru, V., Singh, Y., Bhatt, R., A review on lightweight node authentication algorithms in wireless sensor networks, in: *2018 Fifth International Conference on Parallel, Distributed and Grid Computing (PDGC)*, IEEE, pp. 517–521, December 2018.

35. Kotsiantis, S.B., Zaharakis, I., Pintelas, P., Supervised machine learning: A review of classification techniques, in: *Emerging Artificial Intelligence Applications in Computer Engineering*, vol. 160, pp. 3–24, 2007.

Software Quality Management by Agile Testing

Sharanpreet Kaur[1]*, Susheela Hooda[2] and Harsimrat Deo[1]

[1]PG, Department of Computer Sciences, Mata Gujri College, FGS, Punjab, India
[2]Chitkara University Engineering Institute of Technology,
Chitkara University, Rajpura, Punjab, India

Abstract

Software quality management is a critical segment of development process of a software for the quality engineers. It becomes even more tedious and complex task when the development shifts to usage of Agile tools and techniques. As the methodologies and issues managed in the Agile Software Development (ASD) framework are absolutely poles apart from conventional software development quality assurance architecture and testing phenomenal. In ASD a concentration on people is more focused than processes and methods. Moreover an ASD Test plan is energetic throughout the development process resulting in a high quality product through rigorous feedback and analysis. ASD test plans are written after every phase and release of software where load and performance testing is one of the key elements. The fourth quadrant of the Agile testing (load and performance testing) concentrates on the non-functional requirements such as performance, security and stability. Apache's open source testing tool – JMeter – has been used for quality improvement of open source software for Load testing. It is a java based application used to analyze the performance of software, application and web pages with feature of reliable IDE and Test Plan Recording. Moreover it is capable enough to manage with both Load and Performance Testing techniques for static and dynamic resources. This is made possible by simulating thousands of users to the target server or host software and responses in the form of statistics and graphical formats. The results generated in the chapter revealed that performance testing is efficiently performed by JMeter for quality enhancement over the open source software.

*Corresponding author: sharancgm@gmail.com

Susheela Hooda, Vandana Mohindru Sood, Yashwant Singh, Sandeep Dalal and Manu Sood (eds.)
Agile Software Development: Trends, Challenges and Applications, (221–234) © 2023 Scrivener
Publishing LLC

Keywords: Agile testing, JMeter, performance testing and load testing

11.1   Introduction

Agile testing is a software testing method that adheres to the agile software development concepts. Agile testing incorporates all members of the project team, with testers contributing their unique expertise. Testing is not a stand-alone step; it is woven throughout all phases of development, including requirements, design, coding, and test case generation. Throughout the Development Life Cycle [1], testing happens in parallel. Adding to it, by involving testers in the full Development Lifecycle alongside cross-functional team members, testers can contribute to the development of software that meets client needs and has better design and code. Testers in Agile projects [2] are in charge of the following daily tasks like: Assisting the developers with coding by providing clarifications on the system's desired behavior, Helping developers in the creation of efficient and effective unit tests and creating scripts for automation. In most Agile software development projects, a Continuous Integration (CI) system that allows CI of code and test components is utilized to ensure that these tasks are completed effectively and quickly. Numerous tools are available in the market for performing the Performance Testing like Selenium [3], Jira [4] and JMeter [5]. An Apache test tool – JMeter – has been used for analyzing and measuring the performance of applications and its services. JMeter is free software developed entirely in Java that can be used to test both web and FTP applications. It is used to test the performance, load, and functionality of web applications less complicated in nature. Apache JMeter [5] can also simulate a high load on a server by establishing numerous virtual users on the same web server at the same time. In agile projects, testers and developers can use a variety of technologies to manage testing sessions and write and submit defect reports.

11.2   A Brief Introduction to JMeter

Stefano Mazzocchi of the Apache Software Foundation was the first to write and implement JMeter. It was created specifically to evaluate Apache JServ's performance (currently known as Apache Tomcat project).

JMeter was revamped by Apache to improve the user interface and include more functionality and functional testing capabilities. It is an Apache test instrument for dissecting and estimating the exhibition of uses, programming administrations, and items. It's free programming grew totally in Java that can be utilized to test both web and FTP applications as long as the machine has a Java Virtual Machine introduced (JVM). It's utilized to test the exhibition, burden, and usefulness of web applications that are surprisingly straightforward. Apache JMeter can likewise recreate a high burden on a server by laying out various virtual clients on a similar web server simultaneously.

For JDBC database connections, web services, HTTP, TCP and OS-native processes, JMeter can be used as a unit-testing tool. JMeter can also be used as a monitor, albeit this is more commonly utilized for basic monitoring than complex monitoring. JMeter also has a Selenium interface, allowing it to run automation scripts alongside performance or load testing. Variable parameterization, assertions, per-thread cookies, configuration variables, and a number of reports are all supported by JMeter. Plug-in are the foundation of JMeter's architecture which are used to implement the majority of its capabilities. JMeter isn't a browser; it's a protocol analyzer. In particular, does not run Javascript present in HTML pages. It also doesn't produce HTML pages like a browser one can examine the answer as HTML and so on, but the timings aren't included in any samples, and only one sample from each thread is ever displayed at a time.

11.3   Review of Literature

Many examinations have been directed in the previous for execution and burden testing, we will discover these reviews individually. An examination was once directed on the importance of execution trying out of net functions and breaking down the bottleneck purposes [4]. This assessment elements the exhibition checking out in light of the heap test. Everybody desires the utility to be particularly quick, simultaneously, dependability of the utility moreover assumes a big part, to such an extent that client's success is the push for execution checking out of a given application. Execution checking out decides a couple of components of framework execution beneath the pre-characterized responsibility. Execution checking out is estimated when the commercial enterprise receives pinnacle by using its hits. One extra examination was once directed on number units to do execution trying out [6, 7]. Apache JMeter is a free java software execution checking out instrument.

It has a outstanding deal of modules to assist the trying out apparatuses. Execution checking out making use of JMeter is a form of checking out to determine the responsiveness, throughput, interoperability, dependability, and adaptability of a software below a given responsibility. In the existing serious world it has turn out to be simple to the associations to take a look at their internet utility [8]. Load checking out is the most frequent way of exposing a whole framework to a work stage transferring towards its cutoff points. Load checking out is completed to determine the way of behaving of the framework below everyday instances and pinnacle load conditions. The goal of burden trying out is to determine the most intense restriction of an application. One extra examination was once achieved on net administrations utilized usually in all components of public pastime [9]. For internet applications, execution trying out is obtaining vast consideration. This overview aspects first we dissect and discover the sorts, and strategies for execution trying out of the net and later we do some trying out interplay strategies. The evaluation used to be directed that the exhibition gadget used to be utilized to take a look at net applications. This equipment is utilized for execution, burden and stress trying out of internet purposes or websites [10].

One greater examination used to be directed on internet utility execution trying out which assumes a sizeable phase in giving Quality of administration [11]. This overview points the presentation checking out of net purposes utilizing a responsive primarily based gadget which helps in lowering the rate and builds the productiveness of execution testing.

An exhibition checking out shape for a rest-based internet utility used to be proposed [12]. This shape intends to supply programming analyzers an included cycle from scan configuration, check scripts, and check execution. One greater exploration used to be directed on ajax primarily based internet functions [13] which have received notoriety given that it brings the lavishness of work region applications. An exploration used to be led in regards to difficulties and encounters to understand a respectable reply for main execution checking out on net purposes [14, 15]. There was once every other evaluation led which depicted three open-source devices and appeared at their exhibition, ease of use and programming stipulations [16, 17]. Testing net functions is solely discovering errors [18, 19]. This evaluates elements specific execution checking out apparatuses and tried with JMeter to work on the presentation of web site or net application. There used to be any other exploration led which offers the examination of burden checking out gadgets [19]. In this listen on the main burden check apparatuses available on the lookout and their advantages had been talked about.

A assessment used to be led on execution testing thoughts and relative investigation of net functions [20, 21]. The most important goal of execution trying out is not to distinguish messes with on the other hand to wipe out execution bottlenecks.

Execution trying out and burden checking out are a component of the crucial sources to check net software execution [22, 23]. This evaluation featured the heap trial of internet functions with JMeter using burst meter in cloud-based load testing. One extra overview used to be directed in distinction with apparatuses [24, 25].

11.4   Performance Testing Using JMeter

When JMeter launches, we will see a blank test plan in the graphical user interface. Begin by configuring the many components that will influence how the load test will be simulated. In the test plan, the configuration element is used to set the default settings for HTTP requests. During testing, this is especially useful for sending several HTTP queries to the same server. We can add an HTTP cookie supervisor to the thread team if the internet server makes use of cookies. During the test, each thread (user) will access a page request represented by an HTTP request sampler. It is possible to add several requests, in which case each thread will handle all of them. We need to run the test plan to receive some results once it's been established. When the test is completed, the findings are displayed in a variety of listeners including graphs, views, tables, and reports. The performance testing findings will be in the form of:

1. Latency is that the time between once JMeter sends letter of invitation and once it receives an initial response in milliseconds.
2. Sample time is the amount of milliseconds it took the server to fully fulfill the request (response + latency).

11.5   Proposed Work

Software testing is an important aspect of the development process. There are a variety of software testing tools on the market right now. Some of them are only used for specialized tasks. In many types of testing, it is critical to make a list of requirements that assist us in selecting a tool performance. But below are the few benefits of JMeter as a performance testing tool.

1. It's a lightweight tool that's simple to set up.
2. A simple load of 50-100 users can be imposed or monitored with ease.
3. There are no licensing fees.
4. Adding plugins to generate appropriate reports is simple. Google can be used to look for plugins.
5. No infrastructure is required; it can be installed on a user's desktop and used to study.
6. When employed during unit testing, performance flaws can be found early in the process.

For the proposed work, the most commonly used search engine "Google" and "Yahoo" have been used for evaluation of performance. To simulate varied user loads and http requests, the JMeter testing tool is employed as per the process shown in Figure 11.1. The same machine generates all of the http requests. Different performance parameters, such as Sample Time (Turn around time), Latency, and Throughput, will be generated during the experiment and will be recorded and examined. For better results, the experiment is run in Non GUI mode, as recommended by the JMeter documentation.

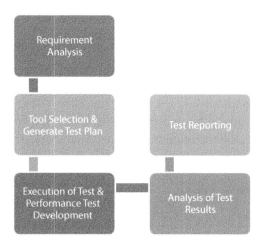

Figure 11.1 Performance testing process.

11.6   Results and Discussions

The performance parameters that were measured in this experiment are listed below.

1. Latency: The time it took the server to fully serve the request (response + latency) in milliseconds. Sample Time: The time it took the server to fully serve the request (response + latency) in milliseconds.
2. Requests per unit of time are used to calculate throughput. From the establishing of the first pattern to the give up of the final sample, the time is calculated. As the load on the server is anticipated to be represented, this consists of any pauses between samples.
   The formula is:

$$\text{Throughput} = (\text{number of requests})/(\text{number of requests}) (\text{total time})$$

3. The most critical parameter is throughput. It denotes the server's ability to handle a large amount of traffic. The more throughput there is, the better.
4. The deviation is a measure of how far something has deviated from the norm. The better the server performance, the higher the Throughput.
5. Latency is not automatically subtracted by time. The metric will be equal to the time it took to reconnect in the event of a connection problem.
6. When confronted with an error, such as Timeout, it should be equivalent to the connection timeout.
7. The deviation is a measure of how far something has deviated from the norm.

Parameters used in Google and Yahoo Test Plan are listed below in Table 11.1. The diagrammatic representation has been shown in Figure 11.2 and Figure 11.3. Google and Yahoo search engines have been used for the performance analysis and four different modes of listeners have been used to display the results in different ways.

Table 11.1 Parameters used for performance testing of Google and Yahoo.

Test plan	No. of threads	Ramp up period (in seconds)	Loop count	Http sampler request	Listener
GoogleTestPlan.jmx	10	1	1	http://www.google.com	View Result Tree Aggregate Report Aggregate Graph
YahooTestPlan.jmx	10	1	1	http://www.yahoo.com	View Result Tree Aggregate Report Aggregate Graph

View Result Tree for GoogleTestPlan.jmx

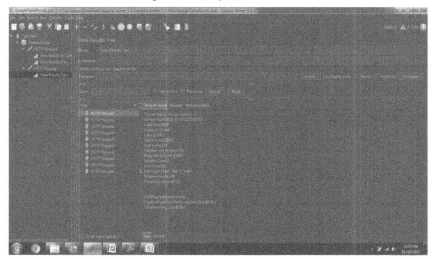

Figure 11.2 Listener-view result tree for Google Test Plan.

View Result Tree for YahooTestPlan.jmx

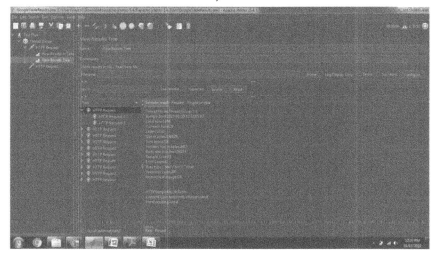

Figure 11.3 Listener-view result tree for Yahoo Test Plan.

Aggregate Report

The results for GoogleTestPlan and YahooTestPlan have been shown in Table 11.2 with a detailed results about the performance testing of Google and Yahoo search engine. Figure 11.4 and Figure 11.5 shows the result in the form of graphs.

Table 11.2 Aggregate report results for Google and Yahoo.

Label	Google HTTP request	Yahoo HTTP request
# Samples	10	10
Average	923	3487
Median	523	3619
90% Line	1115	4558
95% Line	1115	4558
99% Line	3528	5078
Min	494	1404
Max	3528	5078
Error %	0.00%	0.00%
Throughput	2.34577	1.7325
Received KB/sec	42.2	257.25
Sent KB/sec	0.27	0.4

Aggregate Graph for GoogleTestPlan.jmx

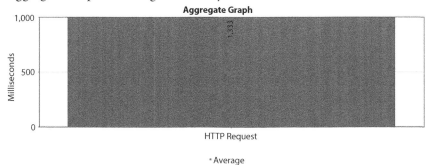

Figure 11.4 Listener-aggregate graph for Google Test Plan.

The experiment's findings reveal the following key points.

1. In the case of YahooTestPlan highest latency is obtained, whereas GoogleTestPlan has the lowest. A lower score indicates stronger network connectivity.

Aggregate Graph for YahooTestPlan.jmx

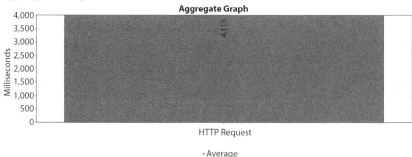

Figure 11.5 Listener-aggregate graph for Yahoo Test Plan.

2. GoogleTestPlan, has the value of high Throughput as compare to Yahoo which means the server's has the ability to handle a large amount of traffic. The more throughput there is, the better.
3. In case of GoogleTestPlan, the Average Sample Time is the shortest, indicating a faster response time for web requests and better website performance.
4. In the case of YahooTestPlan, the amount of bytes received is the highest. It indicates that the page is heavily loaded. The performance of a page can be improved by making it lighter in weight.

11.7   Conclusion

JMeter may be an extremely useful tool for evaluating how to modify your web application server setup in order to decrease bottlenecks and boost performance. JMeter may be used to generate new test plans for evaluating our servers' performance in various circumstances. Although the test we provided as an example does not accurately reflect a typical user's behavior, JMeter provides the ability to run a number of tests that you might find useful in our own setting. JMeter, for example, may be set up to simulate a user logging into our application, client-side caching, and URL rewriting to handle user sessions. Many other built-in samplers, listeners, and setup tools are available to assist you in creating our desired situation.

References

1. Prabaharan, S. and Bhuvaneswari, T., A survey on software development life cycle models. *Int. J. Comput. Sci. Mobile Comput.*, 2, 5, 262–267, 2013.
2. Alnoukari, M., Alzoabi, Z., Hanna, S., Applying adaptive software development (ASD) agile modeling on predictive data mining applications: ASD-DM methodology. *Proceedings-International Symposium on Information Technology 2008, ITSim*, vol. 2, pp. 1–6, 2008.
3. Selenium Tool, Accessed date-January 12, 2022, Available at https://www.selenium.dev/selenium-ide/.
4. Jira Tool, Accessed date-January 14, 2022, Available at https://www.atlassian.com/software/jira.
5. JMeter Tool, Accessed date-January 14, 2022, Available at https://jmeter.apache.org/download_jmeter.cgi.
6. Khan, R. and Amjad, M., Performance testing (load) of web applications based on test case management. *Perspect. Sci.*, 8, 355–357, 2016.
7. Erinle, B., *Performance Testing With JMeter 2.9*, Packt Publishing Ltd, 2013.
8. Arul, D.P. and Asokan, M., Load testing for query based e-commerce web applications with cloud performance testing tools. *IJCET*, 5, 10, 01–10, 2014.
9. Zhu, K., Fu, J., Li, Y., Research the performance testing and performance improvement strategy in web applications, in: *2010 2nd international Conference on Education Technology and Computer*, vol. 2, p. 328, IEEE, 2010.
10. Van, P.H.O. D.A. Phipps, S. Lin, U.S. Patent Application No. 14/730,692, 2016.
11. Rasal, Y.M. and Nagpure, S., Web application: Performance testing using the reactive based framework. *IJRCCT*, 4, 2, 114–118, 2015.
12. Kao, C.H., Lin, C.C., Chen, J.N., Performance testing framework for rest-based web applications, in: *2013 13th International Conference on Quality Software*, pp. 349–354, IEEE, 2013.
13. Dhote, M.R. and Sarate, G.G., Performance testing complexity analysis on Ajax-based web applications. *IEEE Softw.*, 30, 6, 70–74, 2012.
14. Kiran, S., Mohapatra, A., Swamy, R., Experiences in performance testing of web applications with unified authentication platform using JMeter. *2015 International Symposium on Technology Management and Emerging Technologies (ISTMET)*, pp. 74–78, IEEE, 2015.
15. Hussain, S., Wang, Z., Toure, I.K., Diop, A., *Web Service Testing Tools: A Comparative Study*, 2013, arXiv preprint arXiv:1306.4063.
16. Mohindru, V., Singh, Y., Bhatt, R., Hybrid cryptography algorithm for securing wireless sensor networks from node clone attack. *Recent Adv. Electr. Electron. Eng.*, 13, 2, 251–259, 2020.
17. Patil, S.S. and Joshi, S.D., Identification of performance improving factors for web application by performance testing. *Int. J. Emerg. Technol. Adv. Eng.*, 2, 8, 433–436, 2012.

18. Mohindru, V., Singh, Y., Bhatt, R., A review on lightweight node authentication algorithms in wireless sensor networks, in: *2018 Fifth International Conference on Parallel, Distributed and Grid Computing (PDGC)*, pp. 517–521, IEEE, December 2018.

19. Sharma, M., Vaishnavi, S., II, Sugandhi, S., Abhinandhan, S., A comparative study of load testing tools. *IJIRCCE*, 4, 2, 1906–1912, 2016.

20. Mohindru, V., Chitranshi, U., Bhatt, R., Singh, Y., Possibilities of block chain in Indian market and notably in advertising industry, in: *2019 5th International Conference on Signal Processing, Computing and Control (ISPCC)*, IEEE, pp. 84–89, October 2019.

21. Jha, N. and Popli, R., Comparative analysis of web applications using JMeter. *Int. J. Adv. Res. Comput. Sci.*, 8, 3, 2017.

22. Mohindru, V. and Garg, A., Security attacks in internet of things: A review, in: *The International Conference on Recent Innovations in Computing*, Springer, Singapore, pp. 679–693, March 2020.

23. Arslan, M., Qamar, U., Hassan, S., Ayub, S., Automatic performance analysis of cloud- based load testing of web-application & its comparison with traditional load testing, in: *2015 6th IEEE International Conference on Software Engineering and Service Science (ICSESS)*, pp. 140–144, IEEE, 2015.

24. Mohindru, V. and Singla, S., A review of anomaly detection techniques using computer vision, in: *The International Conference on Recent Innovations in Computing*, pp. 669–677, Springer, Singapore, March 2020.

25. Bhardwaj, S. and Sharma, A.K., Performance testing tools: A comparative analysis. *Int. J. Eng. Technol. Manage. Appl. Sci.*, 3, 4, 2015.

A Deep Drive into Software Development Agile Methodologies for Software Quality Assurance

Mitali Chugh[1]* and Neeraj Chugh[2]

[1]*Cybernetics Cluster, School of Computer Science, University of Petroleum and Energy Studies (UPES), Bidholi, Dehradun, India*
[2]*Systemics Cluster, School of Computer Science, University of Petroleum and Energy Studies (UPES), Bidholi, Dehradun, India*

Abstract,

Agile software development has enhanced software quality assurance from merely considering it as fulfilling the needs of clients, verification, and validation. Agile development innovatively unlocks the novel horizons in software quality assurance. Agility in software development is a step ahead of the conventional development method that aims to meet the clients' changing requirements until the product deployment. This chapter systematically analyses software development agile methodologies from the viewpoint of software quality assurance and presents a technique to understand similarities in diverse agile processes. The understanding of the agile software development methodology is presented from the different perspectives as theoretical, scientific, and contextual.

Even though software development projects that incorporate agile methodologies have extended the margins that cannot be overlooked in the context of product relevance or timely delivery, few are following this innovative methodology of software development because of not having a clear understanding of core agile methodologies. Therefore, this chapter comprehensively defines agile methodologies and reveals the role of agile methodologies over the traditional approaches in the perspective of software quality assurance.

Corresponding author: mchugh@ddn.upes.ac.in

Susheela Hooda, Vandana Mohindru Sood, Yashwant Singh, Sandeep Dalal and Manu Sood (eds.)
Agile Software Development: Trends, Challenges and Applications, (235–256) © 2023 Scrivener Publishing LLC

Next, a technique is presented that will expose agile methods *viz.* scrum, crystal methodology, lean development, Kanban, extreme programming, etc. using a new approach and discuss the adoption apprehensions of agile methodologies. The idea of the proposed technique is to explore each state of art agile methodology focusing on core values and practices and present to incorporate an additional layer in agile projects for quality assurance. The intent is to utilize the expert's knowledge for software process improvement, resulting in better product quality.

The subsequent sections of the chapter will cover the issues and controversies in agile software development that are the grey areas to agile methodology related to innovative thinking, cost of projects developed using agile methodologies, etc. The chapter finally concludes with a discussion on the challenges in agile software development.

Keywords: Agile methodologies, software development, software quality assurance, quality factors

12.1   Introduction

In software development, the quality assurance activities form the backbone of the process and improve the product quality. In traditional development, a dedicated team is responsible for quality assurance, however, with the advent of agile development, the process of quality assurance has changed from merely meeting customer requirements, validation, and verification. An aspect of agile strategy [1] exposes that agile software development manages to cope with the fluctuating customer requirements till the product release.

In this chapter, the authors have emphasized the significance of software Quality Assurance in diverse agile methodologies. In agile development, the focus is to improve the product quality, however, there is a necessity to enhance process quality in agile development that targets to get an organized and standardized product. The literature that discusses the diverse agile methodologies has unquestionably reformed the approach of software development though there is a need for a further comprehensive evaluation to compare the standardized and actual agile development approach. Although the application of agile methodologies in software development projects has gained margins that cannot be overlooked for product relevance (an outcome of embracing requirements unsteadiness) and fast delivery (an outcome of iterative enhancement), few are not following this innovative way of software development because of the dearth of understanding of the basic conceptions of agile methodologies. Therefore, this chapter aims to present the holistic view of agile methodology in the software development life cycle (SDLC) and systematically describes agile methodologies specifically emphasizing the aspect of software quality assurance. In addition, we find the key independent and dependent quality factors of each agile method that can lead to software success or failure. We recommend incorporating Quality Assurance as a supplementary layer in agile projects to better understand and evaluate the agile methodologies to the evaluation framework presented by Dubielewicz *et al.* [2] to accomplish quality in the development process, which improves product quality.

12.2 Background Work

This section will begin with an overview of quality and an understanding of agile in software development followed by a perspective on software quality assurance.

Software quality has long been the subject of discussion. The quality perceptions introduced by Deming [3] as adherence to customer needs and aptness for customer usage are employed in software products. Fournier has specified that "quality very often signifies different things to different people in the context of a software system" [4]. The concept of quality is hard to define and quantify as a software product is not physically visible and hence has been described from different perspectives. To define software quality:

1. "The degree to which a system, component, or process meets specified requirements."
2. "The degree to which a system, component, or process meets customer or user needs or expectations." (IEEE)

Quality legend Philip B. Crosby defined software quality in terms of user requirements: "Quality means conformance to requirements" [5] while Joseph M. Juran presents a different notion of software quality:

1. The product features that are in conformance with the user requirements and offer product satisfaction are referred to as quality.
2. Quality includes the removal of insufficiencies [6]. The definitions given by Crosby and Juran have a contextual preconception to production industries. Thus now we present some of the views of software engineers for software quality.

The researchers have viewed software quality as Meyer [7] describes software quality conferring to reformed quality factors as defined by McCall [8]. Pressman, in conformance with the view of Crosby, defined software quality as "conformance to explicitly state functional requirements, explicitly documented development standards, and implicit characteristics that are expected of all professionally developed software" [9].

In literature, agility is universally mentioned as readiness to motion and quality is an intrinsic part of agile project management. The word "agile" when discussed from a functional perspective brings with it inferences of flexibility, quickness, promptness for tasks, dexterousness in tasks, and adaptability [10]. According to Beck who has considered the scientific perspective, agile methodologies are a low-risk, lightweight, a foreseeable, efficient, flexible, technical, and great approach to software development [11]. According to the agile perspective, some practitioners define quality as under.

McBreen describes quality assurance in agile as the software development which can react to amendments as the client needs it to adapt. It is inferred as the regular deployment of tested, functional and client-approved software for each iteration of development is a significant trait of quality assurance in agile development [12]. Ambler [13] presents quality in agile development to be an outcome of effective collaborative work, iterative development accomplished through different practices *viz*. modeling, test-driven development, refactoring, and active communication. The quality in software development is challenging to explain however if it is present it is identified. In the opinion of Garvin's quality perspective, developers have adopted agile methodologies and appreciated enriched software products in terms of quality but then again could experience it challenging to describe quality in the agile world. In the literature, the studies have covered the quality of agile development in different scenarios. Rindell *et al.* [14] empirically validate the usage and influence of software security engineering activities in agile software development, as accomplished by software developers, and conclude security practices considered to have an utmost effect were preemptive and took place in the initial phases of software development. Jain *et al.* [15] investigated the inter-relationships and inter-dependencies among the well-known quality factors, thus outlining the quality factors of high driving power and dependence power, operational indirectly to the success of agile development process.

In the same line, to add to a comprehensive overview of the quality in agile software development, Software Quality Assurance (SQA) is defined as "a planned and systematic approach to the evaluation of the quality of and adherence to software product standards, processes, and procedures" [16]. SQA is the key to successful IT projects. There are 14 factors that affect the quality of software in the phases of software development as recommended by the SQA group.

12.2.1   Factors of Quality Assurance in Agility

Several methodologies consider multiple but not all quality factors. Though blends of practices are used to confirm the essential quality factors however these factors are difficult to define because these are non-functional attributes of the system.

1. Correctness: The capability of a system to perform as per predefined specifications. Various agile methodologies are based on high customer involvement thus correctness in requirements and the behavior of the developing system is also accomplished.

2. Robustness: Appropriate performance of a system under the scenarios that are not mentioned in the specification. This is paired with correctness. Robustness is confirmed by practicing development standards.

3. Extendibility is the easily adaptable system to new specifications. Practically, the agile methodologies practice OOP designs to attain it.

4. Reusability: Software comprising components that are used to build various applications. OO designs are grounded on the principle of reusability.

5. Compatibility: Software comprising of components that can effortlessly associate with other components. It is also be attained by using an OO (Object Oriented) design.

6. Efficiency: The system's ability to put limited loads on hardware resources, such as memory, processor time, etc.

7. Portability: The easiness of software installation on different hardware and software platforms. The portability in agile is increased through distributed computing and web service design.

8. Timeliness: Delivering the software before or when it is required by the client. Incremental development and small iterations are used to accomplish timeliness.

9. Integrity: The protection of the program and data of software against unauthorized access. Low coupling amongst

design iterations supports to attainment integrity of the data and system.

10. Verification and validation: Ease of testing the system. Interface testing, regression testing, and unit testing are generally performed to confirm validation and verification.

11. Ease of use: The easiness of people from diverse backgrounds to learn and use the software. Active customer participation enhances the requirement specification of the system, therefore, growing in the system's ease of use while interface design. It is certainly realized through methodologies such as Scrum, XP, etc.

12. Maintainability: The ease of altering the features of the software for defect correction or fulfilling fresh requirements. Crystal methodologies and feature-driven development play an imperative role in maintainability.

13. Performance: Optimum resource utilization, lesser time to response and failure, and recovery time describe the system performance. OO designs, Sprint, code ownerships support to enhance performance in nearly every prevailing agile methodology.

14. Cost-effectiveness: The system's ability to be finished in a specified budget. The iterative and incremental aspect supports attaining it by providing the ordered needs in iterations.

Various researchers have explored these factors in the agile context and infer that software quality is enhanced by using agile methodologies [17–20].

12.3 Understanding Agile Software Methodologies

Agile methods are based on an iterative enhancement that follows iterations having activities that extend requirement analysis, design, test, and implementation [21]. At the end of each iteration, there is an iteration release that incorporates all software and is an evolving subsection of the final system. The small iterations are beneficial as feedback from the preceding iteration(s) can refine the subsequent iteration(s). The client specifies the needs for the following release based on the observations of developing software instead of speculation at the project inception [22]. To fill the iteration length scope is chosen and the iteration length is not varied to fit in scope, in spite scope can be reduced to suit the length of the iteration.

In traditional methods of software development, iterations vary from 3-6 months however in agile it is 1-4 weeks that lowers complexity and risk, improves productivity, enhances success rates, and delivers better feedback [23]. The commonalities in agile methods include the importance of people performing different roles in the process that are considered empirical by all the agile methods. Agile comprises various methods, including Agile Unified Process (AUP), Adaptive Software Development (ASD), Dynamic System Development Methodology (DSDM), EXtreme Programming (XP), Feature Driven Development (FDD), Crystal Methods, Lean Software Development (LSD), Kanban and Scrum.

12.3.1   Need for Agile Software Methodology Framework

There are salient similarities among agile methodologies practices as they are built on the four agile values and twelve principles. It is fascinating to observe that the agile methodology developers themselves put no more emphasis on methodology precincts and employ other methodology practices as and when they are suitable for a given scenario. A comprehensive examination of agile methodologies shows that agile practices take into consideration similar concerns using diverse real-life models. In LD software development is viewed in the context of manufacturing, Scrum views it in the perspective of control engineering and extreme programming contemplates it as a social activity. Tables 12.1 to 12.7 summarize the proposed evaluation framework to address commonalities of diverse agile methodologies. Another potential area of concern for agile methods is the capability to survive with the deficits of the software product. The introduced framework addresses these potential areas in agile software development.

12.4   Agile Methodology Evaluation Framework

12.4.1   Extreme Programming (XP)

Extreme Programming (XP) is used when the client requirements change frequently and software is small to medium size as it is a lightweight methodology [11]. Beck [11] in the second version of XP included constraints of lightweight, adaption to rapidly changing requirements, and scalable team size. The five phases of extreme Programming are Exploration, Planning, and Iteration to release, Productionizing, Maintenance, and death. At the initiation of software, the development client presents the stories that describe the functionality of the software (Exploration) which

Table 12.1 Evaluation framework for Extreme Programming (XP).

Extreme Programming	
Focus	Software development-technical perspective
Scope	A maximum of 10 developers in a chamber. Expandable to a larger team.
Technique	Pair programming, system metaphor, refactoring, continuous integration, test-driven development
Process	Step 1: User stories writing. Step 2: Estimation of efforts, story prioritization. Step 3: Coding and testing (unit and integration). Step 4: Small release. Step 5: Revised release. Step 6: Last release (Abrahamsson *et al.*, 2002)
Outputs	**Working system**
Factors of QA	Quality Activities
Correctness	User stories, Customer feedback, Unit tests
Robustness	Standard OO design practices
Efficiency	Simple, has Pair programming and coding standard
Portability	Design practices employed are OO and generic
Compatibility	Inherent in OO systems
Reusability	Design practices employed are OO and generic
Extendibility	Simple design
Integrity	Design practices employed are OO and generic
Verifiability and validation	Unit testing, Continuous integration.
Timeliness	Iterative incremental development (IID).
Ease of use	On-site customer and design simplicity
Cost-effectiveness	Development is iterative, quick delivery
Maintainability	Iterative development

takes 1-2 weeks for coding and testing. Coders provide approximations for the stories (planning) and finally, the client decides to prioritize the stories considering their cost and value. XP follows iterative enhancement and in the span of two weeks, each of the developers provides working stories to the client. Next, the client decides on another two weeks' work. In the productionizing additional testing is done, maintenance phase copes with the rapidly changing requirements of a client and focuses on the implementation of quality assurance activities. In the death phase product is completely delivered. The software develops in functionality incrementally, steered by the client. Few recent studies in XP include Sohaib [24], Sadath [25]. Table 12.1 presents the use of the evaluation framework to XP.

12.4.2   Scrum

Scrum is a widely used agile methodology along with XP that focuses on "defined and repeatable processes only work for tackling defined and repeatable problems with defined and repeatable people in defined and repeatable environments" [26] that is not possible. Scrum has three phases: pre-game phase, development phase, and post-game phase. To resolve the issues of demarcated and recurrent processes, a project is divided into sprints that run for 30 days. The functionality of the software to be delivered is decided when the sprint starts and the team is left to deliver it. Table 12.2 shows the evaluation framework to Scrum, application. Recent studies in the field of Scrum include Cláudia [27], Maciel [28]. Table 12.2 shows use of the evaluation framework to Scrum.

12.4.3   Lean Development

Lean development was introduced by Bob Charette in the 1980s and lures on the realization that lean manufacturing extended in the locomotive industry. Although other agile methodologies alter the process of development however in lean is grounded on lean thinking that originated in Toyota Automotive manufacturing company [29]. It is grounded on mending difficulties in design and documentation. Recent studies in LD include Zorzetti [30] Alahyari [31]. Table 12.3 presents the use of the evaluation framework to LD.

Table 12.2 Evaluation framework for Scrum.

Scrum	
Focus	Development process management
Scope	Size of a team with less than 10 members, however expandable to bigger teams
Technique	Sprint, scrum backlogging
Process	Step1: Planning, product backlog & design Step 2: Sprint backlog, sprint. Step 3: System testing, integration, documentation, and release
Outputs	Working Product
Factors of QA	**Scrum quality activities**
Correctness	Manageable user stories, Backlog grooming
Timeliness	IID
Robustness	Design practices employed are OO and generic
Efficiency	coding standard, Pair programming
Reusability	Design practices employed are OO and generic
Compatibility	Inherent in OO systems
Integrity	Design practices employed are OO and generic
Portability	Design practices employed are OO and generic
Extendibility	Continuous improvement
Verifiability and validation	Repeating events, milestones, and meetings
Cost effectiveness	Iterative development, rapid delivery
Ease of use	Lightweight process framework
Maintainability	Iterative development

Table 12.3 Evaluation framework for Lean Development (LD).

Lean Development (LD)	
Focus	Project and change management
Scope	No specific size for the teams
Technique	Lean manufacturing techniques
Process	No pre-defined processes
Outputs	Delivers knowledge for project management
Factors of QA	LD Quality Activities
Correctness	Meet customer requirements
Robustness	Generic OO design practices
Reusability	Case dependent
Extendibility	Continuous improvement
Compatibility	This might conflict with removing waste
Efficiency	Lessen inventory
Integrity	Dependent on scenario
Timeliness	IID, Maximize flow, Do it right the first time
Portability	Design practices employed are OO and generic
Verifiability and validation	Do it correctly in the initial phase
Cost-effectiveness	Iterative development, rapid delivery
Ease of use	Collaborate with providers
Maintainability	Iterative development

12.4.4   Crystal Methodology

Crystal Methodology is a methods family, as Cockburn considers that not any "one-size-fits-all" for processes of development. The methods in the family are specified with different colors based on rising opaqueness, Crystal clear being most agile tailed by Crystal Yellow, Crystal Orange, and Crystal Red. There are simply two outright rubrics for the Crystal methodologies. First, each incremental cycle is a maximum of four months. Second, the methodology is self-adapting i.e. after each delivery reflection workshops are conducted. At present, only Crystal Clear and Crystal Orange exist. Table 12.4 shows the application of the evaluation framework to crystal methodology.

Table 12.4 Evaluation framework for crystal methodology.

Crystal methodology	
Focus	Addresses the variance of Environment and specific features of the project
Scope	Three to eight people in a room, but scalable to large teams
Technique	Incremental delivery, automated testing, direct user involvement, and methodology tuning retrospectives
Process	1. Incremental cycles not exceeding four months. 2. Reflection workshops held after every delivery for self-adapting methodology
Outputs	Software deliverable or major decisions reached
Factors of QA	**Crystal quality activities**
Correctness	Two user reviews per release, methodology-tuning retrospective, printing whiteboards
Robustness	Self-adapting/Tuning methodology
Extendibility	Continuous improvement, Versioning system
Reusability	Common object model
Compatibility	Frequent team adjustments, coding reversal, and reconstruction as and when required

(Continued)

Table 12.4 Evaluation framework for crystal methodology. (*Continued*)

Factors of QA	Crystal quality activities
Efficiency	Group of suggested procedures, a fundamental group of roles, products, practices, and representations
Portability	Generic design practices
Timeliness	Iterative incremental development (IID) maximum 4 weeks
Integrity	Common object model
Verifiability and validation	Automated regression testing of functionality, Interface Testing, reflection workshops
Ease of use	GUI Designs, User manuals
Maintainability	iterative development or incremental delivery
Cost effectiveness	Iterative development, quick delivery

12.4.5   Kanban Methodology

The basic elements of any Kanban software development process include Visualize Work, Limit Work in Process, Focus on Flow, and Continuous Improvement. It involves real-time communication of ability and complete clarity of tasks. Work elements are denoted in a visual format on a Kanban board, letting team members comprehend the status of all elements of work at any time. Kanban offers several surplus advantages to task planning and output for variable size teams that include planning flexibility, Shortened time cycles, continuous delivery, etc. Recent studies using Kanban methodology include Weflen [32], Hofmann [33]. Table 12.5 shows the application of the evaluation framework to Kanban.

12.4.6   Feature Driven Development (FDD) Methodology

The feature-driven development methodology is a football-driven development, extremely iterative and collaborative agile development method that emphasizes on:

- Providing recurrent, perceptible, functional results (around every 2 weeks)
- Modeling and design-driven on domain

Table 12.5 Evaluation framework for Kanban.

Kanban	
Focus	Visualization, flow and limiting work in progress
Scope	No team size limitation
Technique	Continuous delivery, continuous improvement, shortened WIP
Process	Phase 1: Visualize the current workflow Phase 2. Apply Work-in-progress limits Phase 3. Policies incorporated are explicit. Phase 4. Manage and measure flow Phase 5. Enhance iteratively with data.
Outputs	Working system
Factors of QA	**Kanban quality activities**
Correctness	"Pull System" for systematic workflow
Robustness	
Extendibility	Continuous improvement (kaizen)
Reusability	Standard design practices
Compatibility	Intrinsic OO system
Efficiency	Continuous delivery of features, products, or services
Portability	Generic OO design
Timeliness	Measures Cycle Time, Limits WIP for individual items
Integrity	Generic design practices
Verifiability and validation	Alterations were done to a stage of the project, permitting for reiterations and continuous improvement
Ease of use	Less process and overhead, Changes can be made at any time -> more flexible
Maintainability	non-disruptive evolutionary change management system
Cost-effectiveness	Continuous delivery of features, products, or services

- Constructing quality for each phase
- Generating precise and significant development/status with marginal overhead and interruption for developer

FDD has five distinct stages: Develop an overall model, Build a features list, Plan by Feature, Design by Feature, and Build by feature [34] and as a significant aspect it covers domain modeling and software configuration management (SCM) that enhances the performance of the system. The defect prevention strategy in FDD is inspection. The domain model is considered more significant when compared to documentation and source code. The source code is quite important, however, the model is more significant, and it is an added visual method of collaborating system info to more than simply coders. Table 12.6 shows the application of the evaluation framework to FDD.

Table 12.6 Evaluation framework for Feature Driven Development (FDD).

Feature Driven Development (FDD)	
Focus	Adequate practices to confirm scalability and repeatability along with innovation
Scope	No specific team size
Technique	Domain-driven modeling and design, Delivering frequent, tangible, and working results, Software configuration management
Process	Phase 1: Develop a whole prototype. Phase 2: Prepare a features list. Phase 3: Feature-based planning. Phase 4: Feature-based design. Phase 5: Feature-based development.
Outputs	
Factors of QA	FDD quality activities
Correctness	Domain walkthrough, Design inspection, Code inspection

(*Continued*)

Table 12.6 Evaluation framework for Feature Driven Development (FDD). (*Continued*)

Factors of QA	FDD quality activities
Robustness	Domain object modeling
Extendibility	UML models are used extensively
Reusability	Model –centric
Compatibility	Highly-specified development practices
Efficiency	Design/Build by feature
Portability	Generic design practices
Timeliness	Two-week features
Integrity	Development are architectural shape, UML models used all through
Verifiability and validation	six markers for a specific feature: design, design inspection, domain walkthrough, code, code inspection, and promote-to-build
Ease of use	Entry and exit criteria defined specifically for all the five sub process
Maintainability	iterative development or incremental delivery
Cost-effectiveness	Incremental iterative process driven by feature sets

12.4.7   Dynamic System Development Method (DSDM)

DSDM is a dynamic methodology that was developed to support Rapid Application Development (RAD) methodology to software development. It is an incremental and iterative method that stresses the uninterrupted participation of the client. DSDM is built on learning, speculation, and collaboration phases [35, 36] and is usually chosen for huge and intricate systems. The planning and initiation are done in the speculation phase followed by the collaboration phase that has different component-based methodologies for coordination. In the concluding stage quality review and assurance is completed and software is released [37, 38]. Table 12.7 shows the application of the evaluation framework to DSDM.

Table 12.7 Evaluation framework for DSDM.

DSDM methodology	
Focus	Iterative step by step approach for addressing current user needs
Scope	Seven members (+/-2)
Technique	Prototyping, time boxing, workshops, MoSCow, modeling
Process	Phase 1. Pre-project. Phase 2. Feasibility study. Phase 3. Business study. Phase 4. Functional model iteration. Phase 5. Design and build iteration. Phase 6. Implementation. Phase 7. Post project.
Outputs	Working system
Factors of QA	**DSDM quality activities**
Correctness	User feedback
Robustness	Generic OO design
Extendibility	Prototyping, modeling
Reusability	Generic OO design
Compatibility	Generic OO design
Efficiency	Reversible changes
Portability	Generic OO design
Timeliness	Time boxing
Integrity	Extensive testing and validation
Verifiability and validation	Testing, configuration management
Ease of use	All changes are reversible
Maintainability	iterative development or incremental delivery
Cost-effectiveness	Incremental iterative process driven by feature sets

Several significant concepts of agile methodologies are presented in this chapter. To summarize the evaluation framework is designed to divulge the similarities among the discussed agile methodologies. The elements used here were selected to tell the similarities and evaluate quality factors relative to the conforming agile methodologies that apply the factors. Each factor has some practices associated with it that we consider will increase software quality assurance in agile development.

The significance of illuminating these similarities is to provide direction to the developers who are lost in the jungle of agile methodologies and speculate which methodology is to be selected. The selection of agile methodology may not directly contribute project success and improve the quality of the software product however if a wrong methodology is selected it may fail the project.

12.5   Agile Software Development – Issues and Challenges

In this section, the grey areas of agile methodologies are discussed as under:

1. To address the area of innovative thinking in agile development in the context of quality assurance and a higher level of process maturity.
2. To estimate the cost of projects that follows the agile methodology in the development that is iterative.
3. As agile processes start to come into areas as patterns, and software reuse, the software process gets loaded and if this is not inspected by agile followers we may have a condition in the forthcoming phase a different software development evolution surfaces to sustain the legacy of agility.

12.6   Conclusion

This chapter presents a description of prevalent agile methodologies. The goal of the chapter was to provide a comprehensive overview of agile approaches, including a detailed definition of agility, agile quality assurance, and its dimensions. To enhance concepts/basics of agile practices, an evaluation framework was proposed. The viewpoint of this evaluation framework is to dig deep in the domain of agile development and present the central concepts, philosophies, and practices of the methodology for comparing similar activities amongst agile processes. The goal of this type of analysis is to provide a method for balancing the two extreme ends of holding onto one methodology or practicing many of the agile methodologies together. The advantage of using this evaluation framework is to get in-depth knowledge of all the analyzed agile methodologies. This evaluation framework should facilitate for preparation and implementation of agile methodologies from a general viewpoint and assist to implement factors of quality insurance to develop an improved quality of software. All agile methodologies contemplate the development of software as an empirical process that needs small "inspect and adapt" opinion rounds during the project.

References

1. Beedle M., Bennekum A. van, Cockburn A., Cunningham W., Fowler M., Highsmith J., *et al.* Manifesto for Agile Software Development. 2001.
2. Dubielewicz, I., Hnatkowska, B., Huzar, Z., Tuzinkiewicz, L., *Quality Assurance in Agile Software Development*, US Rome Air Development Center Reports, 2001.
3. Deming, E., Deming, A., Bakken, J.F., Co, F.M., Drucker, P.F., *William Edwards Deming (1900–1993), no. from 1946*, Cambridge, United Kingdom, 1982.
4. Fournier, R., *Practical Guide to Structured System Development and Maintenance*, Prentice-Hall, Englewood Cliffs, NJ, 1991.
5. Crosby, P.B., *Quality is Free*, McGraw-Hill, New York, 1979.
6. Juran, J.M. and Godfrey, B.A., *Juran's Quality Handbook*, McGrawHill, New York, 1998.
7. Meyer, B., *Object-Oriented Software Construction*, Prentice Hall, New Jersey, United States, 2000.
8. McCall, J., Richards, P., Walters, G., *Factors in Software Quality NTIS AD-A049-014, 015, 055*, Rome Air Development Center, Rome, 1977.
9. Pressman, R.S., *Software Engineering Practitioner's Approach*, McGraw-Hill, New York, 2010.
10. Abrahamsson, A.P. and Ronkainen, J., *Agile Software Development Methods: Review and Analysis*, vol. 478, VTT Publication, Espoo, Finland, 2002.
11. Beck, K., Embracing change with extreme programming. *Computer*, 32, 10, 70–77, 1999.
12. McBreen, P. and Consulting, M., *Quality Assurance and Testing in Agile Projects*, McBreen Consulting, Cavan, Ireland, 2003, http://www.mcbreen.ab.ca/talks/CAMUG.pdf (accessed Feb. 16, 2022).

13. S.W. Ambler, Scaling agile software development through lean governance, *Proceedings of the 2009 ICSE Workshop on Software Development Governance*, Washington, DC, USA, 1–2, 2009.

14. Rindell, K., Ruohonen, J., Holvitie, J., Hyrynsalmi, S., Leppänen, V., Security in agile software development: A practitioner survey, *Inf Softw Technol.*, 131, 2021, 106488, ISSN 0950-5849, https://doi.org/10.1016/j.infsof.2020.106488.

15. Jain, P., Sharma, A., & Ahuja, L., A customized quality model for software quality assurance in agile environment. *International Journal of Information Technology and Web Engineering (IJITWE)*, 14, 3, 64-77, 2019.

16. Kitchenham, B. and Pfleeger, S.L., Software quality: The elusive target. *IEEE Softw.*, 13, 1, 12–21, 1996.

17. Subih, M.A., Malik, B.H., Mazhar, I., Yousaf, A., Sabir, M.U., Comparison of agile method and scrum method with software quality affecting factor. *Int. J. Adv. Comput. Sci. Appl.*, 10, 5, 531–535, 2019.

18. Rossi, B., Kalenda, M., Hyna, P., Rossi, B., Scaling agile in large organizations: Practices, challenges, and success factors. *J. Softw. Evol. Process*, 30, 10, 1–25, 2018.

19. Wadood, K., Shahzad, M.K., Iqbal, M., Employability assessment of Agile methods for software quality: An empirical case study, in: *European Conference on Software Process Improvement*, pp. 598–614, 2020.

20. Fischbach, J., Mendez, D., Vogelsang, A., What makes agile test artifacts useful? An activity-based quality model from a practitioners perspective, in: *ACM/IEEE International Symposium on Empirical Software Engineering and Measurement (ESEM) (ESEM '20)*, p. 10, 2020.

21. Basil, V.R. and Turner, A.J., Iterative enhancement: A practical technique for software development. *IEEE Trans. Softw. Eng.*, SE-I, 4, 390–396, 1975.

22. Boehm, B., A spiral model for software development and enhancement computer. *Computer*, 21, 5, 61–72, 1988.

23. Larman, C., *Agile and Iterative Development: A Manager's Guide*, Addison Wesley, Boston, 2004.

24. Sohaib, O., Solanki, H., Dhaliwa, N., Hussain, W., Integrating design thinking into extreme programming. *J. Ambient Intell. Humaniz. Comput.*, 10, 6, 2485–2492, 2019.

25. Sadath, L., Karim, K., Gill, P.S., Extreme programming implementation in academia for software engineering sustainability, in: *2018 Advances in Science and Engineering Technology International Conferences (ASET)*, pp. 1–6, 2018.

26. Fowler, M., The agile manifesto: Where it came from and where it may go. Martin Fowler article, 2002. http://martinfowler.com/articles/agileStory.html.

27. Cláudia, A., Mira, M., Pereira, R., Gonçalves, M., Using agile methodologies for adopting COBIT. *Inf. Syst.*, 101, 101496, 2021.

28. Maciel, C.P.C., DeSouza, E.F., Falbo, R.D.A., Felizardo, K.R., Vijaykumar, N.L., Knowledge management diagnostics in software development

organizations: A systematic literature review, in: *Proceedings of 17th Brazilian Symposium on Software Quality-SBQS*, p. 1410150, 2018.

29. Poppendeick, T. and Poppendeick, M., *Lean Software Development: An Agile Toolkit*, Addison Wesley, Boston, US, 2003.

30. Zorzetti, M., Signoretti, I., Salerno, L., Marczak, S., Bastos, R., Improving agile software development using user-centered design and lean startup. *Inf. Softw. Technol.*, 141, 106718, 2022.

31. Alahyari, H., Gorschek, T., Berntsson, R., An exploratory study of waste in software development organizations using agile or lean approaches: A multiple case study at 14 organizations. *Inf. Softw. Technol.*, 105, 78–94, 2019.

32. Weflen, E., Mackenzie, C.A., Rivero, I.V., An influence diagram approach to automating lead time estimation in agile Kanban project management. *Expert Syst. Appl.*, 187, 115866, 2022.

33. Hofmann, C., Lauber, S., Haefner, B., Lanza, G., Development of an agile development method based on Kanban for distributed part-time teams and an introduction framework. Costing models for capacity optimization in industry between used capacity operational efficiency. *Proc. Manuf.*, 23, 45–50, 2018.

34. Palmer, S.R. and Fesling, J.M., *A Practical Guide to Feature Driven Development*, Prentice Hall, Upper Saddle River, 2002.

35. Highsmith, J.A., *Adaptive Software Development, a Collaborative Approach to Managing Complex Systems*, Dorset House Publishing, New York, NY, 2000.

36. Mohindru, V. and Singla, S., A review of anomaly detection techniques using computer vision, in: *The International Conference on Recent Innovations in Computing*, pp. 669–677, Springer, Singapore, March 2020.

37. Mohindru, V., Chitranshi, U., Bhatt, R., Singh, Y., Possibilities of block chain in Indian market and notably in advertising industry, in: *2019 5th International Conference on Signal Processing, Computing and Control (ISPCC)*, pp. 84–89, IEEE, October 2019.

38. Rai, V. *et al.*, Cloud computing in healthcare industries: Opportunities and challenges, in: *Recent Innovations in Computing. Lecture Notes in Electrical Engineering*, P.K. Singh, Y. Singh, J.K. Chhabra, Z. Illés, C. Verma, (Eds.), vol. 855, Springer, Singapore, 2022, https://doi.org/10.1007/978-981-16-8892-8_53.

Factors and Techniques for Software Quality Assurance in Agile Software Development

Gagandeep Kaur*, Inderpreet Kaur, Shilpi Harnal and Swati Malik

Chitkara University Institute of Engineering and Technology
Chitkara University, Punjab, India

Abstract

Technology advances faster than ever in the current era, requiring global software companies to work in an environment of fast-paced change. In today's booming software industry, there are changing demands daily. To meet these gradually demanding requirements, many organizations are seeking new software development methodologies. Software development has been significantly changed by agile practices. The umbrella term Agile refers to the ability to make changes quickly and swiftly.

Quality Assurance refers to a systematic process that ensures the excellence of products and services. It should be involved throughout the entire agile process, in line with the new agile paradigm. In agile, every step is analyzed to minimize the number of activities at any given time. Agile software development quality assurance provides a firm grasp of the key concepts, trends, and technologies.

This chapter provides a detailed introduction to agile software development, addresses their importance in the information technology sector, and presents a comprehensive overview of the factors and techniques followed by challenges and limitations of agile technology. The overview of this research can serve as an important resource for the software industry to improve development processes as well as for researchers interested in exploring the topic further.

Keywords: Agile methodologies, agile quality assurance, software development, software quality

**Corresponding author*: gaganmalhotra1791@gmail.com

Susheela Hooda, Vandana Mohindru Sood, Yashwant Singh, Sandeep Dalal and Manu Sood (eds.)
Agile Software Development: Trends, Challenges and Applications, (257–272) © 2023 Scrivener
Publishing LLC

13.1   Introduction

Software project development is a collaborative effort in which the project's completion is contingent on a variety of events and conditions. In conventional development, the client received the finished product when development was completed, and testing revealed whether the final product satisfied or dissatisfied the consumer [1, 2].

On the other hand, the agile methodology is iterative and flexible, unlike the traditional model, which is more predictable and phased in its approach [3]. The agile approach is a software development philosophy that strives to provide better value to customers by reducing development cycles and incorporating frequent updates as shown in Fig. 13.1. Agile development's greatest benefit is that it enables teams to offer more value quicker, with better quality and predictability, and higher flexibility to adjust to change with a lot of customer's involvement [4]. It divides the product into small increasing constructs. Iterations of these constructs are provided to end-users. Each iteration lasts up to three weeks.

Software quality assurance begins with the planning stage where, it is necessary to verify the entire product and begin resource planning. As software progresses through the development process and begins to implement various software functionalities, all these features are documented and disseminated [5]. As a result, this must be accepted to pass this step of Quality Assurance. User experience is a requirement that must be updated

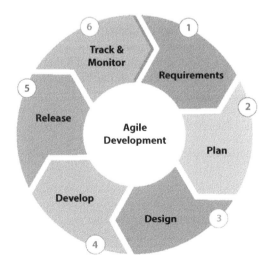

Fig. 13.1 Agile process.

and enhanced regularly; otherwise, the user will abandon the current program in favor of a superior solution. The user experience should be fluid and constantly improved, with faults being identified and fixed with an agile approach. The software development process is all about continuous improvement [6]. Furthermore, prevention is always preferable to treatment. Thus, it is preferable to start a quality improvement strategy for the entire software development process.

Customer involvement in software quality assurance is continuous and ongoing through regular meetings, in accordance with agile development. The agile technique comprises four agile manifesto and twelve principles [7]. The Agile technique solves the challenges associated with conventional development. Teams can self-organize and manage individual tasks using agile techniques [8]. Employees can cooperate, develop, and increase product quality and efficiency as a result of this. Although several attempts have been made in the past to address the difficulties encountered by software teams, all of their problems can be resolved if the stakeholders are engaged, consumers' interests are considered, and software quality is maintained [9]. There may be divergent views among the software team about issues such as software project success, delivery time, as well as failure and risk factors resulting from varying duties and quality standards.

13.1.1   Values of the Agile Manifesto

The Agile Manifesto [10] consists of 4 fundamental ideas and 12 principles that govern and support the process of Agile software development.

Individuals and Interactions vs. Tools and Processes: The Agile Manifesto's first value is the importance of individuals and interactions over procedures and tools. Humans seem to be valued more than procedures or tools because they are the ones who respond to business demands and drive development.

Useful Software vs. Extensive Documentation: Historically, a significant amount of time was spent documenting the product in preparation for development and eventual delivery. Documentation is an important aspect of Agile, but working software is even more important. Documentation is not removed by Agile; it is simplified to the extent that the developer is provided with all the information needed to accomplish the task without becoming bogged down in details. Agile records requirements using user stories and these stories are sufficient to allow developers to work on new projects.

Collaboration with Customers Rather Than Contract Negotiation: The customer negotiates the product requirements in detail via Waterfall-style development methodologies before any work begins. In other words, the customer was involved only in the beginning and end of the development, not in the middle. Developers will be able to meet customer demand much more easily this way.

Adapting to Change by Sticking to a Plan: Previously, change was seen as an expense in project development, thus it was avoided. Changes, according to Agile, always improve a project by bringing new value. Because Agile iterations are short, priorities can vary and new features can be added from one iteration to the next.

13.1.2   The Twelve Agile Manifesto Principles

The 12 principles serve as a set of guiding principles for the approaches that build up "The Agile Methodology." They aim to define a work environment where modification is welcomed, and the client is the center of attention [11].

One of the signatories, Alistair Cockburn has expressed the main Agile Manifesto aims to bring development in line with business demands. For agile development the 12 included principles are:

1. Customer satisfaction achieved by early and frequent product delivery: Clients are receiving functioning software at frequent intervals despite waiting for a long gap of time between every release.
2. Change needs as they arise during the development process: When a requirement or request for feature changes arises, there are no delays.
3. Workable project delivery frequently: This idea is supported by Scrum, which is a team-based software development method ensuring delivery of working software regularly through software sprints or iterations.
4. Throughout the project, developers and business stakeholders collaborate: Better choices are made when the business and technical teams are on the same page.
5. Motivate, support, and trust the members involved: Teams that are happy are more likely to perform well.
6. Allow for face-to-face interactions: Direct team members interactions are more effective.
7. The delivery of working software to the customer is the most important indicator of progress: Providing functional

software to the client is the most crucial aspect in assessing progress.

8. Support for a consistent development pace: Teams define a repeatable and controllable pace with which they can generate a working release for the product, and then use agile techniques to rerelease it with each iteration.

9. Attention to technical design and detail improves agility: A team with the right talents and a prominent design can keep up with the pace to update the product for every release to react to change.

10. Simplicity: Only make necessary updates as required to fulfil the work at hand.

11. Self-organizing teams support great architectures, requirements, and designs: Teams with competent and motivated members are likely to produce quality goods, as long as they are capable of making decisions, taking responsibility, communicating regularly, and exchanging ideas.

12. Reflections on how to be more effective regularly: Team members may improve their self-awareness, procedures, and acquire new skills and approaches to be more effective.

13.1.3   Agile for Software Quality Assurance

Quality is crucial when it comes to software development. Quality Assurance (QA) is a systematic procedure that ensures the highest level of product and service quality.

Most have shifted from traditional waterfall approaches to agile methods in some fashion. "When and where do we start testing in the development life cycle?" is the fundamental question. QA must be involved as early as possible in Agile projects, so that issues can be foreseen, test cases developed and executed, and any gaps in requirements identified [12]. Because QA engineers are only working for a brief, rapid amount of time, the project is separated into iterative stages, which boosts their attention. QA personnel must concentrate on the task at hand. Testing is postponed until the conclusion of the project as waterfall approaches since fixing problems is costly [13]. The agile methodology strives to include quality assurance (QA) at every stage of the project's life cycle to discover problems as early as feasible. It improves communication and transparency within each sprint.

Increased transparency is one of the numerous advantages of sprints. When working in sprints, you should have daily meetings. Motive of these sessions is to make the sprint run more smoothly and to improve team communication. It is anticipated that you will communicate any difficulties or possible concerns so that everyone is aware of them and can help solve them [14]. This improves not just individual transparency (where people are in their projects), but also team openness. Project leaders were brought up to speed on essential project information by holding daily status meetings [15]. With each new feature added, QA engineers test and retest the product to ensure that the new features were implemented correctly and to identify any issues that may have arisen [16]. By allowing testers to provide input as soon as the functionality is introduced, early and often testing saves time and money.

The chapter is organized in the following sections. Section 13.2 gives overview of use of agile methodology in literature while Section 13.3 focuses on agile factors in Software quality assurance. Section 13.4 highlights the techniques used by agile methodology followed by challenges & limitations of agile methodology in Section 13.4. Conclusion and future scope of the chapter are listed in Section 13.5.

13.2　Literature Review

The project team's excitement and other resources have an impact on the software development process. When project development technology and the business environment change, one of the most critical challenges with software development occurs [5]. In Brazil and the United Kingdom, agile projects in government and commercial sectors were investigated [6] included five sociological (such as team members' experience, subject competence, and specialism) and five project-related (team size, project estimation, product delivery, and so on) aspects.

By selecting the 1996 papers, of which 36 were empirical research, Tore Dyba marks a significant divergence from typical methods to agile software development. These four categories of research were introductory and adoption, human and social variables, perception of agile techniques, and comparative studies [8]. Harnsen discussed a variety of issues, including culture, stability, temporal changes, technology, and stability, among others [10].

During a review of four projects, Mahanti [12] identified six essential criteria in the agile approach. The author talked about the office climate, team mentality, and documentation mentality, among other things. Various drivers and impediments to agile implementation were identified as having a substantial impact on agile approaches [13].

13.3   Agile Factors in Quality Assurance

Agile development mainly has success and failure factors that impact the overall process of software development. These factors could be technical or non-technical. Technical factors include quality of requirement, technical dependency, non-functional requirements etc. Non-technical factors which impact the process are communication, hardware dependency, domain and customer communication etc. [17].

13.3.1   Success Factors

The essential areas where good results will enable the firm and managers to achieve their objectives are known as success factors. The five key areas of agile success factors are organizational, people, process, project, and technology [17, 18]. To tackle the issues of the waterfall technique, agile principles were proposed in the early 1990s. The term "agile" refers to a person's ability to move fast and easily. Table 13.1 shows the measure, success factor and subfactor of success factors.

13.3.2   Failure Factors

According to the survey [19], 44 per cent of respondents believe that the failure of agile projects is primarily due to insufficient training and lack of expertise with agile practice. Agile is founded on the reality of what you're doing and how you're doing it [20]. As a result, when teams are poor and unable to use basic agile methods, they get into difficulty. Furthermore, training agile methodologies and providing sufficient coaching for their application becomes an expensive approach [21]. Table 13.2 shows the failure factors with measures and subfactors of failure factors.

13.4   Quality Assurance Techniques

Quality can be defined as the set of factors that determine how well an entity can meet the needs of its customers. QA (Quality Assurance) is an efficient approach to ensuring high-quality products, services which is applicable for the entire process. An important goal of quality assurance (QA) is to prevent errors and defects in products and services that are delivered to customers. To ensure software's integrity and reliability, software quality assurance (SQA) is used [22]. Research in this area has led to several significant approaches to verify software quality control.

Table 13.1 Success factors.

Measure	Success factor	Subfactors of success factor
Organizational	Workplace Culture	Support from executive management
		Cooperation among team members
People	Customer communication	Managing business demands and constraints
		Collaborator's politics
	Team Proficiency	Efficient project managerial skills
		Good communication and feedback
		Smart skills for handling complex problems
Process	Process of project management	Minimal change in requirements
		Simpleton process for project
		Regular status update
	Process of Defining Project	Time management
		Risk analysis and management
		Estimation of resources required
	Active Testing	Active review of project
Project	Lucid objectives and goals	Type of Project
		Nature of Project
		Lucid requirements and specification
	Pragmatic budget	Division of team
		Size of team
Technology	Selection of Agile Method	Configuration of necessary tools and technologies
	Utilization of Advanced Technologies	Skills required for using advanced technologies

Table 13.2 Failure factor.

Measure	Failure factor	Subfactors of failure factor
Organizational	Workplace Culture	Management commitment is not defined
		Organizational culture is conventional
		Political situation in an organization
		Organizational scalability difficulty Underprovided logistical arrangements
People	Customer communication	Project managers are not challenging and competent
		Customer connections are strained
	Team Proficiency	Set of required abilities is lacking
		No teamwork is encouraged
		Naysayers, whether individuals or in groups, resist change
Process	Process of project management	Frequent change in requirements
		Complex process for project development
		Irregular status update
		Lack of Resources
	Process of Defining Project	Poor Time management
		Poor Risk analysis and management
		The project's requirements and scope are unclear
	Delayed Testing	Delay in reviewing and testing of project

(Continued)

Table 13.2 Failure factor. (*Continued*)

Measure	Failure factor	Subfactors of Failure factor
Project	Vague objectives and goals	Type of Project is not clear
		Nature of Project is not well defined
		Vague requirements and specification
	Pragmatic budget	Uneven Division of team
		Inappropriate size of team
Technology	Selection of Agile Method	Inappropriate usage of agile methodologies
	Utilization of Advanced Technologies	The tools and technology employed are ineffective

In the context of agile, some practitioners define quality assurance as follows: Following McBreen [23], agile quality assurance involves developing software that can respond to change by client's requirement. In Ambler's perspective [24], agile quality is achieved through practices such as effective collaboration, incremental development, iterative development, as well as test-driven development, modelling, and effective communication methods. According to Khan's view [25], testing and quality are interconnected since testing is intended to detect flaws before a product is delivered, providing the developer with an opportunity to verify the quality of the product through bug fixing.

Change is the only constant is a very familiar phrase, and the same holds for the software industry. Using an Agile methodology, a project can be broken up into phases for more effective management. The Agile life cycle starts with gathering requirements and ends with the delivery of a software product based on customer feedback [26]. In traditional heavyweight development models such as the waterfall model, quality assurance techniques are based on inspections and reviews done at the end, whereas in agile development, quality assurance techniques are based on routine activities performed by teams [27, 28].

Techniques of Software Quality Assurance can be categorized as, static and dynamic as shown in Fig. 13.2. The requirements and nature of the project determine the technique's aims and organization, and selection

Fig. 13.2 Categorization of quality assurance techniques.

is based on very diverse criteria depending on the methodology utilized. Both static and dynamic strategies are used in the waterfall model. Agile methods, on the other hand, primarily employ dynamic strategies. The techniques applied in software quality assurance in the case of agile are stated below.

- Refactoring
  Code refactoring is a disciplined method of changing the internal structure of existing code without changing the behavior externally [29, 30]. It is a process that improves software's design, structure, or implementation while maintaining its functionality.

- Continuous Integration
  Agile projects can be considered to be built on the pillar of Continuous Integration. It is a technique in which code is integrated continuously, instead of once or twice [31, 32]. Continuous integration decreases the time people spend finding bugs and resolving them.

- Acceptance Testing
  An acceptance test refers to the practice of testing a new feature, function, or system against predefined criteria for acceptance. A Waterfall method includes acceptance testing, but an agile method conducts it earlier and more frequently; it is not performed only once [33, 34].

- Pair Programming
  It is a crucial technique that involves two programmers' drivers and observers working at the same workstation at

the same time. The driver is in charge of writing code, while the observer or navigator is in charge of reviewing each line as it is typed in [35, 36]. Therefore, it is a useful strategy for producing higher-quality code more quickly.

- System Metaphor
  The agile community has adopted the System Metaphor as a core component in software development which provides insight into the key structure of how the problem is viewed and solved [37, 38]. The utmost benefit of this architecture is that it streamlines the process of discussing the system with customers, stakeholders, and users in a non-technical format. By facilitating communication between team members and users, this practice will aid the team in architecture evaluation.

- Frequent Customer Feedback
  A key characteristic of agile methods is the ability to gather customer feedback. As a result of getting frequent customer feedback throughout the project, agile teams can incorporate the majority of new changes into subsequent iterations of the product. Quality is about meeting the demands of customers [39, 40].

13.5   Challenges and Limitations of Agile Technology

Though agile technology has proven to be very effective in various sectors there are some limitations to its use and it's critical to be aware of these limitations as listed below:

- Inadequate resource planning: It's impossible to predict project costs, time, and resources from the start of Agile projects because teams don't know what the final product will look like until they're halfway through.
- The Output that is fragmented: The incremental delivery of products may help get products to market faster, but it also has major drawbacks. Teams working on separate components in different cycles often produce a fragmented result instead of a coherent result.
- There is no end: Because Agile involves very little planning at the start, it's simple to become side-tracked by delivering

new, unanticipated capabilities. Moreover, since this "finished result" is never clearly understood, projects never have
an ending.

- Measurement is difficult: Measuring success is tough since
  Agile operates in chunks, which demands looking back over
  numerous cycles.
- Maintaining a high level of collaboration can be difficult.

Most IT firms will face challenges because they are used to traditional
project management practices. IT leaders who can foresee these issues and
know how to address or avoid them can make the move go more smoothly.

- Financial clashes
- Resistance to agile change due to a lack of preparation
- Legacy HR procedures
- When it comes to agile rollouts, take a waterfall strategy
- Burnout due to agility
- Obstacles of a structural nature
- Frenzy for agility
- There is a lack of clarity in regards to positions
- Pursuit of agility for the sake of agility

13.6   Conclusion and Future Scope

Agile refers to more than just using a specific strategy or framework on
a single project. Agile methods are built on iterative software development. Each iteration culminates in the creation of a working module. Agile
approaches are well-suited to changing contexts due to new practices and
concepts that allow a team to build a product in a short period of time.

Before embarking on an Agile path, you must have a solid rationale. You
should avoid it if you simply wish to follow the crowd. "Why do you desire it?"
try to figure out. You will feel a lot more at ease to begin your Agile journey
after answering this question. Whether you commit to a specific technique or
begin by applying some Agile concepts, you will face day-to-day operational
challenges, and you may still question "why Agile doesn't work." As a result,
having the support of your company's management and experienced team
members, who can help mitigate any problems or challenges, is critical.

Most research in agile quality assurance focuses on testing. However, in
order to boost quality, standardize and organize development processes in
agile projects, we need quality experts with deep knowledge of quality issues.

References

1. Dhir, S., Kumar, D., Singh, V.B., Success and failure factors that impact on project implementation using agile software development methodology, in: *Software Engineering*, pp. 647–654, Springer, Singapore, 2019.

2. Jyoti, and Hooda, S., A systematic review and comparative study of existing testing techniques for aspect-oriented software systems. *Int. Res. J. Eng. Technol.*, 4, 05, 879–888, 2017.

3. Conboy, K., Coyle, S., Wang, X., Pikkarainen, M., People over process: Key people challenges in agile development. *IEEE Softw.*, 99, 47–57, 2010.

4. Kaisti, M., Mujunen, T., Mäkilä, T., Rantala, V., Lehtonen, T., Agile principles in the embedded system development, in: *International Conference on Agile Software Development*, pp. 16–31, Springer, Cham, May 2014.

5. Williams, L.A. and Cockburn, A., Guest editors' introduction: Agile software development: It's about feedback and change. *IEEE Comput.*, 36, 6, 39–43, 2003.

6. Harnal, S., Sharma, G., Malik, S., Kaur, G., Khurana, S., Kaur, P., ... & Bagga, D., Bibliometric mapping of trends, applications and challenges of artificial intelligence in Smart Cities. *EAI Endorsed Transactions on Scalable Information Systems*, 9, 4, e8–e8, 2022.

7. Huisman, M. and Iivari, J., Deployment of systems development methodologies: Perceptual congruence between IS managers and systems developers. *Inf. Manag.*, 43, 1, 29–49, 2006.

8. Dybå, T., & Dingsøyr, T., Empirical studies of agile software development: A systematic review. *Inf. Softw. Technol.*, 50, 9-10, 833–859, 2008.

9. Misra, S.C., Kumar, V., Kumar, U., Identifying some important success factors in adopting agile software development practices. *J. Syst. Softw.*, 82, 11, 1869–1890, 2009.

10. Harnsen, F., van den Brand, M., Hillergerberg, J., Mehnet, N.A., Agile methods for offshore information systems development. *First Information Systems Workshop on Global Sourcing: Knowledge and Innovation*, 2007.

11. Williams, L., What agile teams think of agile principles. *Commun. ACM*, 55, 4, 71–76, 2012.

12. Mahanti, A., Challenges in enterprise adoption of agile methods-A survey. *J. Comput. Inf. Technol.*, 14, 3, 197–206, 2006.

13. Asnawi, A.L., Gravell, A.M., Wills, G.B., An empirical study: Understanding factors and barriers for implementing agile methods in Malaysia, in: *5th International Doctoral Symposium on Empirical Software Engineering*, pp. 192–207, October 2010.

14. Mnkandla, E. and Dwolatzky, B., Defining agile software quality assurance, in: *2006 International Conference on Software Engineering Advances (ICSEA'06)*, pp. 36–36, IEEE, October 2006.

15. Arcos-Medina, G. and Mauricio, D., Aspects of software quality applied to the process of agile software development: A systematic literature review. *Int. J. Assur. Eng. Manag.*, 10, 5, 867–897, 2019.

16. Sagheer, M., Zafar, T., Sirshar, M., A framework for software quality assurance using agile methodology. *Int. J. Sci. Technol. Res.*, 4, 2, 44–50, 2015.

17. Hamdani, M. and Butt, W.H., Success and failure factors in agile development, in: *2017 International Conference on Computational Science and Computational Intelligence (CSCI)*, pp. 981–986, IEEE, December 2017.

18. Tsoy, M. and Staples, D.S., What are the critical success factors for agile analytics projects? *Inf. Syst. Manag.*, 38, 4, 324–341, 2021.

19. Tanner, M. and Willingh, U.V., *Factors Leading to the Success and Failure of Agile Projects Implemented in Traditionally Waterfall Environments*, 2014.

20. Lin, L. Z., & Hsu, T. H., The qualitative and quantitative models for performance measurement systems: The agile service development. *Qual. Quant*, 42, 4, 445–476, 2008.

21. Tam, C., da Costa Moura, E.J., Oliveira, T., Varajão, J., The factors influencing the success of on-going agile software development projects. *Int. J. Proj. Manag.*, 38, 3, 165–176, 2020.

22. Lee, M.C., Software quality factors and software quality metrics to enhance software quality assurance. *Br. J. Appl. Sci.*, 4, 21, 3069–3095, 2014.

23. Alsaqaf, W., Daneva, M., Wieringa, R., Quality requirements in large-scale distributed agile projects–A systematic literature review, in: *International working conference on requirements engineering: foundation for software quality*, 219-234, Springer, Cham, 2017 February.

24. Ambler, S., Quality in an agile world. *SQP*, 7, 4, 34, 2005.

25. Kharb, L., Proposed CEM (Cost Estimation Metrics): Estimation of cost of quality in software testing. *Int. J. Comput. Sci. Inf. Technol. Res.*, 6, 2, 10–14, 2015.

26. Abdalhamid, S., Mohammed, A.O., Mishra, A., Agile and quality: A systematic mapping study, in: *2019 International Conference of Computer Science and Renewable Energies (ICCSRE)*, pp. 1–7, IEEE, July 2019.

27. Jain, P., Ahuja, L., Sharma, A., The current state of the research in agile quality development, in: *2016 3rd International Conference on Computing for Sustainable Global Development (INDIACom)*, pp. 1177–1179, IEEE, March 2016.

28. Sinha, A. and Das, P., Agile methodology vs. traditional waterfall SDLC: A case study on quality assurance process in software industry, in: *2021 5th International Conference on Electronics, Materials Engineering & Nano-Technology (IEMENTech)*, pp. 1–4, IEEE, September 2021.

29. Vassallo, C., Palomba, F., Gall, H.C., Continuous refactoring in CI: A preliminary study on the perceived advantages and barriers, in: *2018 IEEE International Conference on Software Maintenance and Evolution (ICSME)*, pp. 564–568, IEEE, September 2018.

30. Mohindru, V. and Singh, Y., Node authentication algorithm for securing static wireless sensor networks from node clone attack. *Int. J. Inf. Comput. Secur.*, 10, 2–3, 129–148, 2018.

31. Ali, S., Hafeez, Y., Hussain, S., Yang, S., Enhanced regression testing technique for agile software development and continuous integration strategies. *Softw. Qual J.*, 28, 2, 397–423, 2020.

32. Mohindru, V. and Singh, Y., Performance analysis of message authentication algorithms in wireless sensor networks, in: *2017 4th International Conference on Signal Processing, Computing and Control (ISPCC)*, pp. 468–472, IEEE, September 2017.

33. Karapantelakis, A., Estimating costs for adopting and using model-based testing in agile SCRUM teams, in: *2021 IEEE International Conference on Software Testing, Verification and Validation Workshops (ICSTW)*, pp. 199–204, IEEE, April 2021.

34. Mohindru, V., Bhatt, R., Singh, Y., Reauthentication scheme for mobile wireless sensor networks. *Sustain. Comput. Inform. Syst.*, 23, 158–166, 2019.

35. Misra, S., Pair programming: An empirical investigation in an agile software development environment, in: *International Conference on Lean and Agile Software Development*, pp. 195–199, Springer, Cham, January 2021.

36. Mohindru, V., Singh, Y., Bhatt, R., Securing wireless sensor networks from node clone attack: A lightweight message authentication algorithm. *Int. J. Inf. Comput. Secur.*, 12, 2–3, 217–233, 2020.

37. Subih, M.A., Malik, B.H., Mazhar, I., Yousaf, A., Sabir, M.U., Wakeel, T., Nawaz, H., Comparison of agile method and scrum method with software quality affecting factors. *Int. J. Adv. Comput. Sci. Appl.*, 10, 5, 531–535, 2019.

38. Mohindru, V., Singh, Y., Bhatt, R., Hybrid cryptography algorithm for securing wireless sensor networks from node clone attack. *Recent Adv. Electr. Electron. Eng.*, 13, 2, 251–259, 2020.

39. Bai, X., Li, M., Pei, D., Li, S., Ye, D., Continuous delivery of personalized assessment and feedback in agile software engineering projects, in: *Proceedings of the 40th International Conference on Software Engineering: Software Engineering Education and Training*, pp. 58–67, May 2018.

40. Mohindru, V., Singh, Y., Bhatt, R., A review on lightweight node authentication algorithms in wireless sensor networks, in: *2018 Fifth International Conference on Parallel, Distributed and Grid Computing (PDGC)*, pp. 517–521, IEEE, December 2018.

Classification of Risk Factors in Distributed Agile Software Development Based on User Story

Esha Khanna*, Rashmi Popli and Naresh Chauhan

Department of Computer Engineering J. C. Bose University of Science and Technology, YMCA, Faridabad, Haryana, India

Abstract

Distributed Agile Software Development (DASD) is the most frequently used software development life cycle model in the software industry. DASD is a blend of Distributed Software Development (DSD) and Agile Software Development (ASD). Although DASD integrates the speed and cost benefits of ASD and DSD, however, it brings along various risk factors that arise due to the contrary working principles of ASD and DSD. These associated risks must be addressed and resolved in time for the success of the project. This chapter presents the importance of software risk management in DASD. The chapter reviews the existing literature and presents risk factors associated with DASD. The chapter further presents the current challenges in the existing literature and proposes a novel user story based DASD risk classification technique. This technique will help the practitioners to tag the risks associated with the type of user story. The work presents the scope of improvement in DASD risk management that will help both practitioners and researchers.

Keywords: Risk management, distributed agile software development, agile software developments, distributed software development

*Corresponding author: eshakhanna30@gmail.com

Susheela Hooda, Vandana Mohindru Sood, Yashwant Singh, Sandeep Dalal and Manu Sood (eds.)
Agile Software Development: Trends, Challenges and Applications, (273–290) © 2023 Scrivener Publishing LLC

14.1   Introduction

Risk management is one of the ten activities that directly affect the cost and quality of the software [1]. Risks negatively impact the success of the project by influencing the goals and objectives by exceeding time and cost and thereby reducing the overall quality [2]. Risk management is a procedure of identifying, analyzing and controlling risks [3]. The goal of risk management is to forecast any upcoming uncertainty that may hinder the completion project objectives. This aids the management to take timely decisions to mitigate such uncertain situations.

Distributed Agile Software Development (DASD) is a new software developing methodology that blends the concepts of ASD and DSD. Although DASD combines the merits of ASD and DSD, it brings along various risk factors that must be managed on time to meet the project deadlines [4]. These risks emerge due to the difference in the working principles of ASD and DSD [5]. In the literature many risks associated with DASD are identified. Further, DASD risks are classified into various categories including Software Development Life cycle, Project Management, Communication, Technology Based Risks, External Stakeholder and Group Awareness [6]. During the literature review, it has been observed that risks identified in DASD have not been associated with the type of user stories. This chapter aims to identify various risk factors associated with different types of user story in the DASD environment. The goals of the chapter are as follows.

- To present the importance of Risk Management in DASD.
- To carry out a literature review and present the risk factors associated with DASD.
- To propose a novel classification technique to segregate DASD risks according to type of user story.

The chapter is arranged as follows. Section 14.2 explains the significance of risk management. Section 14.3 reviews the existing literature and presents the various risk factors associated with DASD. Section 14.4 proposes user story based classification of risk factors. Section 14.5 presents future scope and Section 14.6 concludes.

14.2   Software Risk Management

Software risk management is a process of finding and dealing with risks during the early phases of SDLC which in turn prevents software

Figure 14.1 Steps in risk management.

disasters [3]. Early identification and management of risks ensures the quality of product and helps to complete the software in limited time and cost. Two pillars of risk management are risk assessment (estimation) and risk control [3]. Risk estimation is the process of identifying the risk, analyzing its impact and prioritizing them [7]. Figure 14.1 represents the steps involved in risk management. Process of managing risks in software projects are explained as follows.

14.2.1   Risk Assessment

Software risk management begins by assessing the upcoming risks. It is the process of recognizing the risk, analyzing its impact on the project and prioritizing the risk based on criticality [7]. Steps performed in risk assessment are as follows.

Step 1. Risk Identification
Risk identification is the task of determining risks that may impact the success of the software [8]. Early identification of upcoming future risks reduces its impact and cost. In order to anticipate the risks, risk managers must understand the goals and objectives of the project. Risk managers then forecast the expected risks, their cause and sources and record them in a risk

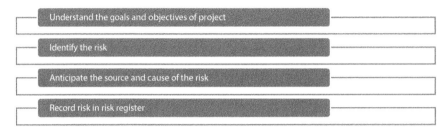

Figure 14.2 Steps in risk identification.

register. Risk register acts as a database and is used in all the steps of risk management. Process of risk identification is depicted in Figure 14.2.

Step 2. Risk Analysis
After identification, the risks are analyzed to assess its consequences on the project. Risks are analyzed in two ways i.e. qualitative and quantitative risk analysis. In the qualitative risk analysis, the risk value is calculated by multiplying the impact of the risk with its probability of occurrence. The risks are then represented in the risk assessment matrix in graphical form which is then used to prioritize the risks (Figure 14.3).

Using this matrix, the risks are prioritized as low, moderate, medium and extreme. Quantitative risk analysis is more data oriented. It assesses the risks

Likelihood of occurrence						
C		Rare	unlikely	Possible	Likely	Sure
o	Catastrophic					
n						
s	Major					
e						
q	Moderate					
u						
e	Minor					
n						
c	Negligible					
e						
s						

Figure 14.3 Risk assessment matrix using qualitative risk analysis.

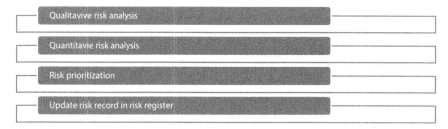

Figure 14.4 Steps in risk analysis.

in terms of cost overruns, project delays and assigns a numeric value to each risk. For example, Risk A has 20% probability of delaying X number of days and increase in cost by Y. While quantitative risk analysis gives more accurate results, qualitative analysis is faster and easier to implement. Further, the results of qualitative analysis are easily interpreted by all the stakeholders. Once the risks are assessed, they are then prioritized based on their criticality. The financial value and priority of the risks are updated in the risk register. Process of risk analysis is presented in Figure 14.4.

Step 3. Risk Management and Control
Once the risks are identified and analyzed, the risk managers respond to them by using appropriate risk management techniques. These includes risk mitigation, risk avoidance, risk transfer and risk acceptance (Figure 14.5).

Step 4. Monitor the Risk
The last and most important step in risk management is to track the mitigation plan and monitor the risk. Process of risk monitoring is depicted

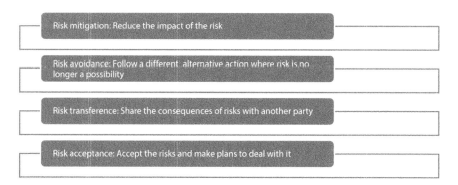

Figure 14.5 Risk management and control.

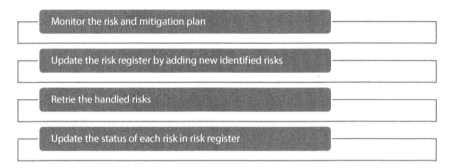

Figure 14.6 Risk monitoring.

in Figure 14.6. During the progress of the project, new risks may emerge and they are added to the risk register. The risks that have been handled are retired from the risk register. In this phase each risk is monitored again for any changes and its status is updated.

14.3   Literature Review

14.3.1   Review

A systematic review on risk management in DASD has been carried out to find the gaps in the existing literature. The review has been carried out in accordance to the guidelines of Kitchenham [9]. IEEE Explore, Wiley, ACM, Springer and Science Direct databases were explored. Some of the important studies are summarized in this section.

Eva Maria Schon, *et al.* [10], focused on the challenges associated with risk management in geographically distributed agile teams. A novel risk management tool for a scaled agile environment was designed. But the work was based on a single case study. Further there was biased data collection as claimed by the authors.

In one of the works by Esteki, *et al.* [11], used PRINCE 2 methodology to develop a risk management framework for DAD environment. Further, the work identified various risk factors associated with DAD and classified them into five categories.

Wan Suzila Wan Husin and Arzi Azmi [12] proposed an enhanced framework of risk management for a Telecommunication Company. The work identified communication as a major risk factor in DASD.

In the work by Suprka Shrivastava and Urvashi Rathod [13], a goal-based (time/cost/quality) risk management approach for DASD was presented. The study presented the most important risk factors for DAD considering time goal, cost goal or quality goal.

Odzaly, *et al.* [14] used software agents and proposed a semi-automated risk management framework for agile development. Software agents were used for risk identification, assessment and monitoring. Interaction between four software agents, i.e. manager agent, identify agent, assess agent and monitor agent were described.

In another work [15] a risk management framework for DASD was proposed by presenting the risks, their causes and mitigation strategies. Further, identified risks were ranked according to their impact and criticality. Software engineering practices, Communication for collaboration, Team organization and management, Third-party management and communication and infrastructure tools were identified as major risk areas. The purposive sampling technique was used to get responses from experienced practitioners working on DAD projects.

A. Elbanna, and S. Sarker [16] presented the risk factors which led to the lack of success of agile-based projects. Reported risks included development and deployment risks & Project Management risks.

Suprika V. Shrivastava, and Urvashi Rathod [6] identified 45 DASD associated risk factors and further they were categorized into 5 categories i.e. SDLC risks, Group awareness risks, External Stakeholder collaboration risks, Technology setup risks, and Project Management Risks.

Navid Vajdi, and Raja Manzan Abbass [17] presented 10 risk categories and their mitigation techniques in DASD. The risk categories were further elaborated into subcategories.

Khanna *et al.* [5] presented a novel Artificial Intelligence based framework for managing risks in Distributed Agile Software Development.

14.3.2   Risk Factors in Distributed Agile Software Development

During the literature review various risk factors affecting the success of DASD projects were identified [10–30]. These risk factors arise due to the difference in the working principles of ASD and DSD. In DSD, team members work together from different geographical location while ASD focuses on interaction and direct collaboration with customers. Risk factors identified during the review are further classified into different categories, i.e., Software Development Life Cycle-Based Risks, Project Management-Based Risks, Communication-Based Risks, Technology-Based Risks, External Stakeholder, and Group Awareness.

1. Software Development Life Cycle based Risks – Risks in this category includes requirement elicitation based risks, objective statement based risks, design risks, coding risks, testing risks and release and deployment risks. These risks are presented in Table 14.1.

2. Project Management Based Risks – Software project management is a process of planning, implementing, monitoring, and controlling a software project [31–33]. In the DASD environment various risk factors related to project management arises due to the contradicting properties of DSD and ASD. These risk factors related to this category are presented in Table 14.2.

3. Communication – Communication is the crucial factor that is responsible for successful risk management [12]. In the work by Wan Suzila Wan Husin, and Arzi Azmi [12] communication was identified as a major risk factor. Risk factors related to communication are presented in Table 14.3.

4. Technology-Based Risks – Risks in this category include Lack of training, inadequate tool selection, and improper utilization of tools. Technology based risks are presented in Table 14.4.

5. External Stakeholder – Risk factors in this group include inappropriate user story estimates by different vendors, poor coordination among multiple vendors and outsourcing of modules and dependency on the third party (Table 14.5).

6. Group Awareness – These risk factors related to this category are presented in Table 14.6.

Table 14.1 Risk category: Software development life cycle.

Risk category	Risk subcategories	Risk factors
Software Development Life Cycle	Requirement Elicitation	Unclear Requirements in Multiple Development Sites
		Conflicts in Requirement due to Multiple Product Owners
		Inadequate Requirement Prioritization
		Frequent Requirements Changes
		Implicit Requirements
		Inadequate Communication With End Users About Requirements
	Objective Statement	Unclear Objective
		Ambiguity In Objective Meaning Due To Cultural Differences
		Inadequate Meetings With End-Users
	Design	Flexible Designs Due To Changing Requirements
		Conflicts In Design
		Design Inconsistency
	Coding	Inadequate Pair Programming
		Lack Of Coordination
	Testing	Unavailability Of Requirements Documents For Testing

(*Continued*)

Table 14.1 Risk category: Software development life cycle. (*Continued*)

Risk category	Risk subcategories	Risk factors
		Unavailability Of Real Testing Data
		Inadequacy In Transfer Of Large Testing Data
		Different Testing Tools
		Code Integration
	Release and Deployment	Inadequate Sprint Releases
		Integration And Deployment
		Difference In Agile Practices And Principles

Table 14.2 Risk category: Project management.

Risk category	Risk factors
Project Management	Exceeded Project Time (Lower Initial Velocity)
	Exceeded Project Cost (Difficulty To Execute Fixed Price Products)
	Infinite Sprints
	Infeasible Project
	Larger Team Sizes
	Reorganization Of Teams In Every Sprint (Task Distribution)
	Insufficient Knowledge At Certain Sites.
	Higher Interdependency among Teams
	Reorganization of team in each sprint
	Increment In Team Size
	Non availability Of Business Analyst
	Different Team Capability in multiple sites
	The Emergence Of Excessive Competition Between Teams Or Scrum Masters

Table 14.3 Risk category: Communication.

Risk category	Risk factors
Communication	Lack Of Communication Among Team Members
	Limited Communication Between Client And Team
	Poor Communication Skills
	Use Of Different Languages (Language Barriers)
	Delayed Feedbacks
	Misinterpretation Of Message
	Difference In Terminology
	Inadequate Documentation
	Poor Coordination
	No Face To Face Meetings
	Lack Of Trust Among Different Teams

Table 14.4 Risk category: Technology-based.

Risk category	Risk factors
Technology Based	Lack Of Training
	Inadequate Tool Selection
	Inadequate Communication
	Improper Utilization Of Tools

Table 14.5 Risk category: External stakeholder.

Risk category	Risk factors
External Stakeholder based	Unapproachable Product Owners
	Lack of Coordination Between Multiple Vendors
	Inefficient User Story Estimates By Multiple Vendors
	Code Integration Risks With Multiple Vendors
	Dependency On Third Party

Table 14.6 Risk category: Group awareness.

Risk category	Risk factors
Group Awareness based risks	Poor Communication Between Team And Client
	Poor Communication Between Team Members
	Under Investment On Travel By The Management
	Lack Of Documentation
	Lack Of Face To Face Communication
	Lack of Collaboration Between Different Sites
	Improper Coordination among the Scrum Masters And Product Owners
	Insufficient Trust among Offshore Teams and client
	Insufficient Trust among Offshore and onshore Teams
	Insufficient Collaboration Between QA Members and developers
	Unproductive Scrum Of Scrum Meetings
	Improper Coordination among Multiple Teams
	Inappropriate usage of Agile Approach in Large Organizations
	Delayed Decision Making
	Uncommon Language

14.3.3   Current Challenges

During the literature review, it has been observed that risks identified in DASD have not been associated to the type of user stories. In agile environment, user requirements are classified into user stories. User stories are the smallest unit of execution in agile development that describes software features from user perspective. The task of agile team is to complete a set of user story that in turn leads to incremental release of project. User stories are classified as functional, technical, infrastructural, refactoring, spikes and bug fixing [34].

14.4   User Story-Based Classification of Risk Factors in Distributed Agile Software Development

14.4.1   User Stories

User stories are smallest work unit in agile framework that leads to incremental development. They describe the software features from user's perspective [35]. A user story follows the role-feature-benefit pattern and follows the syntax- As a [role/type of user], I want [an action], so that [benefit] [35, 36].

User stories put the customer at the center of conversation. For development team, user stories provides user focused framework for daily work. User stories provide the context of what and why they are creating by customer's perspective, which in turn helps them to understand the business model.

User Stories are combined to form Epics and collection of epics that drive towards a common goal is called Initiatives. Each user story is completed within shorter period of time and therefore gives the sense of small win to the development team which in turn gives the sense of momentum to user. Some of the benefits of user stories are

- Team focus on user requirements
- Customer/user is continuously involved
- Collaboration tool between customer/End user and Development team
- Creates momentum for user and developer

A product backlog consists of pending (uncompleted) user stories. User stories are independent of each other and are freely moved around the product backlog. It must be negotiable, estimable, testable, and valuable to customer. A user story should be small and must be completed in few days. Each user story has an effort and acceptance criteria that marks the completion of that story. The 3 C's of user story are card, conversation and confirmation. A product backlog consists of user stories, non user stories and spikes. User Stories are further classified as functional, technical, infrastructural (product infrastructure and team infrastructure), refactoring, spikes and bug fixing [34].

14.4.2   Classification of Risk Factors on the Basis of User Story

DASD risks arise due to different working principles of ASD and DSD. The chapter aims to map the DASD risk factors according to the type of user story.

Table 14.7 User story-based classification of risk factors.

S. no.	Type of user story	Associated risk categories
1	Functional	Project Management, Communication
2	Technical	Coding, Release and deployment, communication, Technology based
3	Quality Assurance (QA)	Design, Testing, Communication
4	UX-User Experience	Requirement Elicitation, Objective statement, Design, Communication
5	Architectural	Design, Communication, Group Awareness
6	End to End testing	Testing, Communication
7	Spikes/RND	Technology Based, External Stakeholder based

User stories are classified as Technical, Quality Assurance (QA), UX-User Experience, Architectural, End to End testing and Spikes/RND [34, 35, 37]. The work used the list of DASD risk factors from previous studies [10–30, 38], and asked the industry practitioners playing different roles in DASD projects to map them according to the type of user story on the basis of survey questionnaire [39, 40]. The analysis of survey responses resulted the novel classification of DASD risk factors based on the type of user story (Table 14.7).

14.5 Future Scope

Risk management is one of the 10 important tasks in software development life cycle that reduces the probability of project failure. Timely risk management aids to successful project completion within time and cost constraints. Bohem defined risk management as "a discipline that aims to identify, address and eliminate risk items before they turn out to be a threat to a successful software project or become the main sources of software rework" [3]. It has been observed that industrial risk management practices are manual and are not up to the mark of satisfaction [5]. Risk management is the first activity to be eliminated when project exceeds its budgets. This lack of importance of risk management by project managers hinders the success of the project [12].

DASD is a new approach of developing the software which blends the principles of ASD and DSD. In DASD environment, many risk factors arise due to the contradictory nature of ASD and DSD principles. In the existing literature, several DASD related risks have been reported. These risks are further classified into several categories like communication risks, project management risks, external stakeholder risks, and Software Development Life Cycle risks. It has been observed that these risks are not classified according to user stories of agile. Further, identified risks have not been mapped to software development tools. Mapping the risks to software development tools will enhance the efficiency of the risk management process.

14.6 Conclusion

Risk management is one of the crucial activities that are performed in each agile sprint to increase the efficiency of the software. Timely Identification and management of risks reduces the probability of project failure. This chapter presents the importance of risk management practices in DASD. The chapter reviews the existing literature and enlists the risk factors associated to DASD. These risk factors are segregated in different categories i.e. software development life cycle, project management, communication, technology based risks, external stakeholder, and group awareness. The chapter presents the current challenges in the literature and proposes a novel DASD risk classification technique based on user story. The work further discusses the shortcomings of risk management practices in DASD and presents the scope of improvement. The work concludes that practicing proper risk management in software development is one of the crucial factors for its success.

References

1. PMI, *A Guide to the Project Management Body of Knowledge (PMBOK Guide)*, 4th Edition, Project Management Institute, Newtown Square, 2008.
2. Keshlaf, A.A. and Hashim, K., A model and prototype tool to manage software risks. *Proceedings of the First Asia-Pacific Conference on Quality Software, APAQS '00*, IEEE Computer Society, pp. 297–305, 2000.
3. Boehm, B.W., Software risk management: Principles and practices. *IEEE Softw.*, 8, 1, 32–41, 1991.

4. Supriya, V. and Shrivastava, H.D., A framework for risk management in globally distributed agile software development. *Intersci. Manag. Rev.*, 2, 1, 32–41, 2010.

5. Khanna, E., Popli, R., Chauhan, N., Artificial intelligence based risk management framework for distributed agile software development. *8th International Conference on Signal Processing and Integrated Networks (SPIN)*, pp. 657–660, 2021.

6. Suprika, V.S. and Urvashi, R., Categorization of risk factors for distributed agile projects. *Inf. Softw. Technol.* Elsevier, 58, 1–15, 2014.

7. Mauro, E., Best practice and common practice in risk assessment. *Petroleum and Chemical Industry Conference Europe (PCIC EUROPE)*, pp. 1–11, 2019.

8. Kasap, D. and Kaymak, M., Risk identification step of the project risk management. *Portland International Conference on Management of Engineering & Technology*, 2007.

9. Kitchenham, B. and Charters, S., *Guidelines for Performing Systematic Literature Reviews in Software Engineering*, Technical Report EBSE, School of Computer Science and Mathematics, Keele University and Durham University Joint Report, 2007.

10. Eva, M.S., Dirk, R., Christian, J., Improving risk management in a scaled agile environment. *International Conference on Agile Software Development XP, Agile Process in Software Engineering and Extreme Programming*, Springer, pp. 132–141, 2020.

11. Mohammad, E. *et al.*, A risk management framework for distributed scrum using PRINCE2 methodology. *Bull. Electr. Eng. Inform.*, 9, 3, 1299–1310, 2020.

12. Wan, S., Wan, H., Arzi, A., Risk management framework for distributed software team-a case study of telecommunication company. *Proc. Comput. Sci. Sci. Direct*, 161, 178–186, 2019.

13. Suprka, S. and Urvashi, R., Risk management approach for distributed agile developments projects. *Australas. J. Inf. Syst.*, 23, 1–30, 2019.

14. Odzaly, E., Greer, D., Stewart, D., Agile risk management using software agents. *J. Ambient Intell. Humaniz. Comput.*, Springer, 9, 823–841, 2018.

15. Suprika, V.S. and Urvashi, R., A risk management framework for distributed agile projects. *Inf. Softw. Technol.*, Elsevier, 85, 1–15, 2017.

16. Elbanna, A. and Sarker, S., Risks of agile software development: Learning from adopters. *IEEE Softw.*, 33, 5, 72–79, 2016.

17. Navid, V. and Raja, M.A., *Distributed Software Development Agile Risk Management Framework: A Systematic Literature Review*, M. Tech Thesis, Dept of CSE, Chalmers University of Technology, University of Gothenbung, Sweden, 2014.

18. Keshlaf, A.A. and Riddle, S., Risk management for web and distributed software development projects. *Fifth International Conference on Internet Monitoring and Protection (ICIMP)*, IEEE, 2010.

19. Lamersdorf, A., Jurgen, M., Alicia, F.V.T., Carlos, R.S., A risk-driven model for work allocation in global software development projects. *Proceedings of the 6th IEEE International Conference on Global Software Engineering, ICGSE11*, vol. 8, IEEE Computer Society, pp. 15–18, 2011.

20. Nguyen, T.H.D., Bram, A., Hassan, A.E., Does geographical distance effect distributed development teams: How aggregation bias in software artifacts causes contradictory findings. *27th International Symposium on Software Reliability Engineering (ISSRE)*, IEEE, 2016.

21. Yasser, C. *et al.*, Software project management tools in global software development: A systematic mapping study. *SpringerPlus*, article no. 2006, 2016.

22. Nurdiani, I., Jabangwe, R., Šmite, D., Damian, D., Risk identification and risk mitigation instruments for global software development: Systematic review and survey results. *Global Software Engineering Workshop (ICGSEW)*, IEEE, 2011.

23. Nordio, M., Christian, H.E., Meyer, B., Tschmannen, J., Ghezzi, C., Nitto, E.D., How do distribution and time zones affect software development? A case study on communication. *Global Software Engineering*, 2011.

24. Bosnić, I., Ciccozzit, F., Čavrak, I., Mirandola, R., Orlić, M., Multi-dimensional assessment of risks in a distributed software development course. *3rd International Workshop on Collaborative Teaching of Globally Distributed Software Development (CTGDSD)*, IEEE, 2013.

25. Honório, F.J., Ivaldir, R.R., Hermano, P.M., Silva, D.S.M., Elicitation of communication inherent risks in distributed software development. *IEEE Seventh International Conference on Global Software Engineering Workshops (ICGSEW)*, 2013.

26. Mudumba, V. and Lee, O.D., A new perspective on GDSD risk management: Agile risk management. *5th IEEE International Conference on Global Software Engineering (ICGSE), Int. J. Comput. Sci.*, 2008.

27. Wattanapokasin, W. and Wanchai, R., Cross-cultural risk assessment model. *International Conference on Signal Processing Systems*, IEEE, 2009.

28. Reed, A. and Knight, L., Project risk differences between virtual and collocated teams. *J. Comput. Inf. Syst.*, 51, 1, 19–30, 2010.

29. Betz, S., Hickl, S., Oberweis, A., Risk management in global software development process planning. *Proceedings of the 37th EUROMICRO Conference on Software Engineering and Advanced Applications, SEAA11*, IEEE Computer Society, pp. 357–361, 2011.

30. Jurgen, M., Risk management in global software development projects: Challenges, solutions, and experience. *Global Software Engineering Workshop (ICGSEW)*, IEEE, 2011.

31. Khan, Q. and Ghayyur, S., Software risks and mitigation in global software development. *J. Theor. Appl. Inf. Technol.*, 58–69, 2010.

32. Mohindru, V., Chitranshi, U., Bhatt, R., Singh, Y., Possibilities of block chain in Indian market and notably in advertising industry, in: *2019 5th International*

Conference on Signal Processing, Computing and Control (ISPCC), IEEE, pp. 84–89, October 2019.

33. Abufardeh, S. and Magel, K., The impact of global software cultural and linguistic aspects on global software development process (GSD): Issues and challenges. *4th International Conference on New Trends in Information Science and Service Science (NISS)*, 2010.

34. Mohindru, V. and Garg, A., Security attacks in internet of things: A review, in: *The International Conference on Recent Innovations in Computing*, Springer, Singapore, pp. 679–693, March 2020.

35. Pressman, R.S., *Software Engineering: A Practitioner's Approach*, McGraw-Hill Higher Education, New York, 2010.

36. Mohindru, V. and Singla, S., A review of anomaly detection techniques using computer vision, in: *The International Conference on Recent Innovations in Computing*, Springer, Singapore, pp. 669–677, March 2020.

37. Amna, A.R. and Poels, G., Systematic literature mapping of user story research. *IEEE Access*, 10, 51723–51746, 2022.

38. Mohindru, V., Vashishth, S., Bathija, D., Internet of Things (IoT) for healthcare systems: A comprehensive survey, in: *Recent Innovations in Computing. Lecture Notes in Electrical Engineering*, vol. 832, P.K. Singh, Y. Singh, M.H. Kolekar, A.K. Kar, P.J.S. Gonçalves, (Eds.), Springer, Singapore, 2022, https://doi.org/10.1007/978-981-16-8248-3_18.

39. Dalpiaz, F. and Brinkkemper, S., Agile requirements engineering with user stories. *26th International Requirements Engineering Conference (RE)*, IEEE, 2018.

40. Rai, V. *et al.*, Cloud computing in healthcare industries: Opportunities and challenges, in: *Recent Innovations in Computing. Lecture Notes in Electrical Engineering*, vol. 855, P.K. Singh, Y. Singh, J.K. Chhabra, Z. Illés, C. Verma, (Eds.), Springer, Singapore, 2022, https://doi.org/10.1007/978-981-16-8892-8_53.

Software Effort Estimation with Machine Learning – A Systematic Literature Review

Ritu[1,2]* and Pankaj Bhambri[2]

*Department of Computer Science & Engineering, APEX Institute of Technology,
Chandigarh University, Mohali, Punjab, India*
[2]Guru Nanak Dev Engineering College, Ludhiana, Punjab, India

Abstract

In 1959 the concept of machine learning techniques and algorithm was introduced by Artur Samuel, an IBmer from the United States who made a name for himself in the fields of computer gaming and artificial intelligence.

The influence of literature reviews which is done systematically (SLRs), which are the preferred techniques and methods for aggregating effort, is examined in this study. We conducted a systematic literature review using the conventional procedure, which included a manual search of nine periodicals and a few conference proceedings. Eight of the twenty studies that were relevant focused on latest trends in research instead of technique evaluation. Seven LRs dealt with the estimation of effort. The SLR's quality was best suited with only those in which fields are qualitatively checked not quantitatively. SLRs currently cover a large number of topics, but not all of them. Systematic literature reviews appear to be the most popular among researchers from Asia and Europe, particularly those at the Simula Laboratory.

Keywords: Software effort estimation, machine learning, software engineering, software development life cycle (SDLC), software process, software development

Corresponding author: ratheeritu@yahoo.in

Susheela Hooda, Vandana Mohindru Sood, Yashwant Singh, Sandeep Dalal and Manu Sood (eds.)
Agile Software Development: Trends, Challenges and Applications, (291–308) © 2023 Scrivener
Publishing LLC

15.1   Introduction

Since the 1960s, the Software Engineering field has grown and gained tremendous expertise [1]. There has been observed a lot of criticism of research in software engineering throughout the years because it claims much more than it examines [2]. A number of studies have tried to define research in software engineering, but none have succeeded in providing a comprehensive picture [3, 4]. SEE estimates the time it will take to execute and implement tasks based on data-driven approach that is often partial, unclear, or noisy. Researchers and practitioners have occasionally addressed problems and challenges with SEE. However, the building of formal SEE models is the focus of much of the research [5]. The advantages and disadvantages of the models developed by researchers are well known. The huge amount of literature available on the subject made it difficult for the scholar to investigate and choose the best path for their investigation.

Manual or automated review of the literature is possible. Despite the fact that the manual review gives information on the literature, it is never without bias because researchers tend to favor higher cited studies [6]. A powerful approach for extracting unforeseen pattern and trends from a large collection of texts is provided by natural language processing. Unlike manual tagging, which takes time and needs knowledge of the topics, texts and procedure based analysis [7–9] is a fully automated process. It takes a corpus, finds patterns, and gives the vocabulary semantic meaning. Topic modelling can employ both clustering and topic analysis techniques. However, as Evangelopoulos *et al.* [10–17] point out, a document is assigned to a combination of themes in topic analysis, in clustering; however, each document must join exactly one cluster.

The goal of this research is to assess the present state of research trends and patterns, with a focus on articles that provide systematic approaches. Review of the literature in the field of software engineering and particularly in effort estimation. In Sections 15.2 and 15.3, we outline our technique and report our findings. Furthermore, we respond to our four primary research questions in Section 15.4. In addition to this Conclusion and future scope explained in Section 15.5 and Section 15.6 respectively.

15.2   Method

This research was carried out as a thorough literature evaluation based on Kitchenham's original instructions [18]. The review's purpose in this situation is to evaluate systematic literature reviews. The stages involved in conducting a literature review which is more systematic are outlined below.

15.2.1   Questionnaires for Research

The following are the research questions that this article addresses:

RQ1. How much has there been in terms of SLR activity since 2010?
RQ2. What are the current research topics?
RQ3. Who's winning and who's ahead in SLR research?

Starting our quest for RQ1 at the beginning of 2010 was probably a decent decision. We discovered that the term "systematic literature review" was not often used during the period of literature reviews published in 2004. Prior to 2004, there were, however, examples of meta-analysis studies and thorough literature study. Despite the fact that a number of scholars have undertaken systematic literature research in the previous few decades. However, when compared to other methods and patterns, ours is more efficient and systematic.

We looked at the amount of SLRs published each year, as well as the journals and conferences where they appeared, to answer RQ1. We evaluated the study's scope in terms of RQ2, whether it looked at research pattern and trends or tackled a research related to technology and algorithm and software engineering problem. We examined every researcher, the institution to which they were connected, and the nation detail in which the organization is located in accordance with RQ3.

15.2.2   Search Process

Since 2010, the main target has been a manual search of specific conference proceedings and journal papers [19–28] was the primary goal. Table 15.1 lists the periodicals and conferences that were chosen. The articles are chosen because they are pure source of empirical research or literature, and they had previously been utilized as origin for other SLR relevant to software engineering, particularly in effort management (e.g. [10, 36]). We read and researched each journal and conference proceedings, and we established a tabular format for collecting each author's findings [30–45], which is depicted and elaborated in tabular format in Table 15.2.

Table 15.1 Journals and proceedings from conferences that have been selected.

Source	Acronym
Information And and Software Technology	IST
International Journal of Intelligent Systems and Applications	IJISA
The Journal of Systems and Software	JSS
International Conference on Electrical, Electronics, and Optimization	
Techniques	EEOT
International Conference on Computer Science and Information	
Technology	CSIT
Computers and Electrical Engineering	CEE
Current Drug Metabolism	CDM
Computer Science Review	CSR
IEEE Symposium on High Performance Computer Architecture	HPCA

Table 15.2 Excluded articles details.

Number of articles	Remarks
242	Inadequate and duplicate literature

15.2.3   Criteria for Inclusion and Removal

The following themes were covered in peer-reviewed articles published between January 1, 2010 and January 1, 2021.

- Systematic literature reviews (SLRs) are literature study with explanation of research questions, techniques for searching data, extraction and presentation of data.
- Meta-analysis (MA).

Note that we included publications in which the literature study was merely one component of the article as well as papers in which the literature review was the article's primary goal. Articles on the following subjects were not embraced:

- Inadequate analysis of the literature (There were no clearly specified research topics, no clearly defined search procedure, and no clearly defined data extraction process.)
- Reports that have been reproduced from the same study.

15.2.4   Data Gathering

The following information was taken from each study:

- The source that is journal or conference as well as the reference.
- Study Type (SLR, Meta-Analysis MA); Study Scope (SLR, Meta-Analysis MA); Research trends and question related to specific technology evaluation; Main topic area.
- The thorough details for the author(s), institution details, and the nation in which they are located.
- The key research questions and their results are summarized in this report.
- Identify a research subject or problem.
- Evaluation of quality.
- Whether or not the study included any practitioner-based recommendations.
- In the SLR, how many primary studies were used?

15.2.5   Analyzing Data

The information was arranged in a table to show:

- The annual number of literature published and their source (relating to RQ1).
- The number of studies in each key topic, such as research pattern or technological issues (concerning RQ2).
- The topics and scope of the SLRs' research (addressing RQ2).
- The affiliations and institutions of the authors (addressing RQ3).
- Whether or not the study included any practitioner-based recommendations.
- In the SLR, how many primary studies were used?

Here it is generally mentioned that few researchers extracted the data and rest other double-checked it. The approach of using extractor and checker does not conform to the medical criteria outlined in Kitchenham's guidelines [22, 43–50], but it is one that we have found to be effective in practice [2, 29]. All of the authors of this paper were active in the data extraction and verifying duties, which Kitchenham coordinated. The allocation was not random; instead, it was based on the individual researchers' time availability. In case of agreement, we spoke about it until we negotiated a deal.

15.3   Result

This section outlines the study's findings.

15.3.1   Findings

The results of the search procedure are shown in Table 15.3. Despite the fact that this search yielded 19 articles, one of them [19] is a condensed version of another [18]. As a result, we discovered 18 unique studies. Furthermore, we discovered two more peer-reviewed studies: one by contacting scholars about their ongoing projects [1] and the other by scanning the research laboratory sites like Simula [14]. Other studies that

Table 15.3 The finding of each author.

Author	Finding
Sumeet Kaur Sehra	In this study, twelve core research areas and sixty research trends was identified, with the detected research trends semantically matched to core research area [43]. Based on a corpus of 1178 papers, this analysis summarized research trends in SEE. The patterns and trends discovered in this study can aid in the identification of future research areas [43].
Przemysław Pospieszny	The goal of this paper was to bridge the gap between current research findings and organizational implementations by offering effective and practical machine learning deployment and maintenance methodologies based on research findings and industry best practices [44].

(Continued)

Table 15.3 The finding of each author. (*Continued*)

Author	Finding
Usharani K.	This survey report drew on fifteen journal articles from a variety of publications [45]. All of the studies were about software work estimation algorithmic approaches and prediction algorithms [45]. This paper highlighted those notions and discussed how to evaluate them, as well as what areas they might be improved in. It also discusses what data preprocessing approaches are effective in improving the accuracy of the methods for software effort estimation [45].
Ahmed BaniMustafa	This research recommended accomplishing this prediction using three machine learning techniques: Nave Bayes, Logistic Regression, and Random Forests [46], which were applied to preprocessed COCOMO NASA benchmark data covering 93 projects [46]. Classification Accuracy, Precision, Recall, and AUC were used to evaluate the produced models, which were tested using five folds cross validation [46]. The estimation results were then compared to COCOMO estimation [46].
Muhammad Ilyas Azeem	Long Method, Functional Decomposition, God Class, and Spaghetti Code have all been thoroughly considered in the literature, according to the findings [47]. Support Vector Machines and Decision Trees are the most commonly used machine learning approaches for detecting code smells [47].
Neelamdhab Padhy	The suggested research could be crucial in next-generation computation systems, particularly for software reusability, survivability, dependability, ageing prediction and stability, and software excellence assurance [48].
Natalie Stephenson	The goal of this survey was to learn about the current state of machine learning approaches especially in the field of drug discovery in both academic and industry contexts, as well as to discuss their potential future applications [49]. This survey [49] discussed several intriguing themes for machine learning techniques in drug discovery sectors.

(Continued)

Table 15.3 The finding of each author. (*Continued*)

Author	Finding
P. Suresh Kumar	Different Artificial Neural Networks (ANN) utilized for effort estimation were reviewed in this study [50]. It has been found that using ANN to forecast software effort is more exact and accurate than using traditional approaches such as Function point, Use-case methods, and COCOMO, for example [50].

were excluded after applying the criteria of elimination and inclusion are listed in Table 15.4. The data extracted from each study related to authors' details is shown in Table 15.5. Additionally, we find out the details of the top 10 researchers, top 10 publications who dominates in the field of systematic literature review especially in the field of effort estimation using machine learning. And it is being represented in Figures 15.1 and 15.2 respectively. Furthermore, a graphical representation of number of publication years wise since 2010 to till Jan 2021 is displayed and described in Figure 15.3.

Table 15.4 Author affiliation details.

ID	Author	Institution	Country
ID1	Sumeet Kaur Sehra	Guru Nanak Dev Engineering College	India
ID2	Pichai Jodpimai	Chulalongkorn University	Thailand
ID3	Ekrem Kocaguneli	West Virginia University	USA
	Tim Menzies	West Virginia University	USA
ID4	Jianfeng Wen	Sun Yat-sen University	China

(Continued)

Table 15.4 Author affiliation details. (*Continued*)

ID	Author	Institution	Country
ID5	Ricardo Britto	Blekinge Institute of Technology	Sweden
ID6	Ali Idri	Mohammed V University	Morocco
ID7	Mohamed Hosni	École de Technologies Supérieure	Canada
ID8	Shashank Mouli Satapathy	VIT University	India
ID9	Przemysław Pospieszny	Institute of Information Systems and Digital Economy	Poland
ID10	P. Suresh Kumar	Veer Surendra Sai University of Technology	India

Figure 15.1 Year wise publication details.

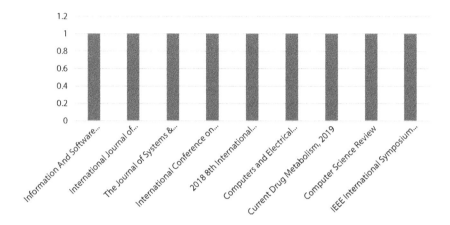

Figure 15.2 Top 10 publications.

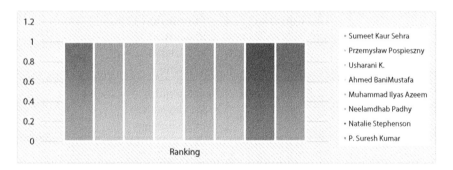

Figure 15.3 Top 10 authors.

15.4 Discussion

We will discuss the answers to our research questions in this part.

In terms of where SLRs are published, IEEE published four studies, the journal of system and software three, and Information and software technology two. As a result, it looked that IST's efforts to foster the release of SLRs had failed [6]. However, a subsequent search of IST papers revealed seven more SLRs, whilst identical searches of TSE publications yielded no results. Although the magazine released a literature analysis in the field of education [25], we were initially shocked that ACM Computer Surveys contain only few relevant software studies related to software engineering. However, the lack of software SLRs in ACM Computer Surveys could be due to the journal's publication lag, as it only publishes four issues each year.

15.4.1   What Kinds of Research are Being Conducted?

Eight of the papers were on research patterns rather than focusing on individual research questions in terms of their subject matter. The SLRs address the following topics in software engineering:

- Seven relating to the estimation of software work.
- A total of three articles about software engineering experiments related to research trends.
- There are three articles about test methods.
- Approximately 30% and stable [31].
- Researchers are addressing specific research topics in the area of effort estimation.
- What is the current level of software project, and how is it changing with time?
- Is it true that models based on regression are more accurate than models based on analogy?
- Not if you work for a small business that specializes in specialty applications [21].
- Do researchers consistently and appropriately use effort estimation terms?
- When is it appropriate to rely on expert opinion estimates?
- The following topics were explored in the testing studies.
- Whether or not testing is preferable than inspections.

15.4.2   Who is the Research Leader in SLR?

Many of the projects have involved Asian and European researchers, with the Simula Research Laboratory in Norway being involved in ten of them. Two of the researchers that contributed to more than two SLRs, Przemysaw Pospieszny and Natalie Stephenson, have long been involved in research. Authors from North America were only present in two of the investigations. Many of the extensive effort estimating studies that I have authored or co-authored have been published in peer-reviewed journals. Many researches were based on a database of over seventy papers on effort estimation, as well as a database of over one hundred software experiments, which allowed scholars to look on a number of specific software experimentation research patterns and trends.

Table 15.5 Sources looked up for the years 2010 to 2021 (including articles up until January 2021).

Year	2010	2011	2012	2013	2014	2015	2016	2017	2018	2019	2020	2021
IST(T)	25	24	13	14	14	20	14	19	12	13	16	20
IST(R)	4	4	4	4	-	-	4	4	4	4	4	4
IST(S)	6	6	6	6	6	6	4	4	6	6	6	6
ISS(T)	2	3	3	-	3	3	3	4	4	5	3	2
ISS(R)	3	4	6	5	4	4	6	5	4	3	3	2
ISS(S)	1	2	1	2	1	2	2	1	2	1	2	1
IJESA(T)	25	24	13	14	14	20	14	19	12	13	16	20
IJESA(R)	4	4	4	4	-	-	4	4	4	4	4	4
IJESA(S)	6	6	6	6	6	6	4	4	6	6	6	6
CSIT(T)	25	24	13	14	14	20	14	19	12	13	16	20
CSIT(R)	4	4	-	-	4	6	4	4	4	4	4	4
CSIT(S)	6	6	6	6	6	6	4	4	6	6	6	6
CEE(T)	25	24	-	-	-	-	-	-	-	-	20	19
CEE(R)	12	12	-	-	-	-	-	-	-	-	10	10

(Continued)

Table 15.5 Sources looked up for the years 2010 to 2021 (including articles up until January 2021). (*Continued*)

Year	2010	2011	2012	2013	2014	2015	2016	2017	2018	2019	2020	2021
CEE(S)	13	12		-	-	-	-	-	-	-	10	9
CDM(T)	10	9	9	8	9	9	9	9	10	9	9	9
CDM(R)	4	5	6	4	4	4	4	4	4	4	4	4
CDM(S)	6	4	3	4	3	5	4	5	3	2	2	2
CSR(T)	25	24	14	16	19	18	20	20	20	20	20	20
CSR(R)	8	9	9	9	9	9	9	9	9	9	9	9
CSR(S)	5	6	7	8	9	4	5		6	5	5	5
HPCA(T)	3	3	3	2	3	2	2	3	3	2	3	2
HPCA(R)	2	2	2	2	-	-	-	-	-	-	2	1
HPCA(S)	2	1	1	1	1	-	-	-	-	-	-	-
Total	178	154	145	121	122	101	100	98	97	95	76	56
Total(R)	53	13	14	29	27	30	33	33	30	33	31	31
Total(S)	18	14	14	10	10	18	11	10	14	14	15	15

15.4.3   The Study's Limitations

In numerous areas, the methodologies followed in this study differed from the recommendations given in Kitchen ham's instructions [22].

Instead of using an automatic search, the researchers conducted a manual search of a small number of publications and conference proceedings. This was in line with other academics' habits of focusing on research trends rather than software technology evaluation.

- The potential studies were chosen by a single researcher, however another researcher double-checked the papers that were included and excluded.
- According to Brereton *et al.* [2] A single researcher extracted the data, which was then double-checked and cross verified by another researcher.

As a result of the first point, we may have neglected some relevant studies, resulting in an underestimation of the study's scope. Articles in national journals and conference proceedings, in particular, will have been overlooked. We have also missed papers presented at specific conferences devoted to software engineering fields, in which main focus was to discuss issues related to research in form of questions. As a result, our findings should be limited to SLR published in prominent ISE journals, as well as important general and specific software engineering conferences. For instances, we emphasize in literature which is organized, rather than excluding any relevant studies. The final point implies that some of the information we gathered may be incorrect. However, because there were few primary studies in this tertiary study and the data gathered from the selected publications was very objective, we do not hope much data extraction problems.

15.5   Conclusion

The following are the crucial outcome of the study in response to our work: We examined the performance of the studies in term of accuracy that include a total of 45 selected studies in which 27 belongs to ensemble approach and 18 lie in the solo zone, which are further examined using MMRE and PRED among multiple techniques in software effort estimation. Tables 15.3 and 15.5 highlight the summarized study to answer this question. In the scientific literature, we discovered that both kind of approach solo as well as ensemble and have been used for computation of effort. However, we discovered that machine learning ensemble approach outperform other methods in terms of producing accuracy. The main reason for ensemble technique's superior performance is that, unlike the technique, which are employed and performed individually it employs a suitable set of ensemble rules and techniques to calculate effort estimation.

15.6 Future Scope

The outcome of the research provides various avenues for future and further research. The effect of numerous factors like cost and effort concerned to the accuracy of the various models related to effort estimation will be an interesting research direction. Predicting the number of man-hours required to accomplish a project using agile software environment is somewhat dependent on the development team's ability to be consistent for budget and on time. The research may now be carried out to enquire related to the accuracy of effort in multiple software development approach using individual and ensemble or hybrid techniques. Another notable advancement is a better understanding and investigation of how to improve effort estimates in ensemble-based models by combining algorithmic, nonalgorithmic.

References

1. Zelkowitz, M.V., Yeh, R.T., Hamlet, R.G., Gannon, J.D., Basili, V.R., Software engineering practices in the US and Japan. *Computer*, 17, 6, 57–70, 1984.
2. Glass, R.L., Vessey, I., Ramesh, V., Research in software engineering: An analysis of the literature. *Inf. Softw. Technol.*, 44, 8, 491–506, 2002.
3. Jorgensen, M., Boehm, B., Rifkin, S., Software development effort estimation: Formal models or expert judgment? *IEEE Softw.*, 26, 2, 14–19, 2009.
4. Shaw, M., What makes good research in software engineering? *Int. J. Softw. Tools Technol. Trans.*, 4, 1, 1–7, 2002.
5. Trendowicz, A., Münch, J., Jeffery, R., *Software Engineering Techniques*, pp. 232–245, Springer, Czech Republic, 2008.
6. Yalcinkaya, M. and Singh, V., Patterns and trends in building information modelling (bim) research: A latent semantic analysis. *Autom. Constr.*, 59, 68–80, 2015.
7. Campbell, J.C., Hindle, A., Stroulia, E., *The Art and Science of Analysing Software Data*, pp. 139–159, Morgan Kaufmann, 2015.

8. Canini, K.R., Shi, L., Griffiths, T.L., Online inference of topics with latent Dirichlet allocation. *J. Mach. Learn. Res.*, 5, 65–72, 2009.

9. Saini, S., Kasliwal, B., Bhatia, S., Language identification using glda. *Int. J. Res. Eng. Technol.*, 2, 11, 42–45, 2013.

10. Evangelopoulos, N., Zhang, X., Prybutok, V.R., Latent semantic analysis: Five methodological recommendations. *Eur. J. Inf. Syst.*, 21, 1, 70–86, 2012.

11. Wester, S.D., Dumais, S.T., Furnas, G.W., Landauer, T.K., Harshman, R., Indexing by latent semantic analysis. *J. Am. Soc. Inf. Sci.*, 41, 6, 391–407, 1990.

12. Blei, D.M., Ng, A.Y., Jordan, M.I., Latent dirichlet allocation. *J. Mach. Learn. Res.*, 3, 993–1022, 2003.

13. Thomas, S.W., Mining software repositories using topic models, in: *33rd International Conference on Software Engineering*, Waikiki, USA, pp. 1138–1139, 2011.

14. Lukins, S.K., Kraft, N.A., Etzkorn, L.H., Source code retrieval for bug localization using latent Dirichlet allocation, in: *15th Working Conference on Reverse Engineering*, IEEE, Antwerp, Belgium, pp. 155–164, 2008.

15. Clark, B. and Zubrow, D., How good is the software: a review of defect prediction techniques. *Software Engineering Symposium*, Pittsburgh, Pennsylvania, 2001.

16. Tian, K., Revelle, M., Poshyvanyk, D., Using latent Dirichlet allocation for automatic categorization of software, in: *6th IEEE International Working Conference on Mining Software Repositories*, IEEE, Vancouver, Canada, pp. 163–166, 2009.

17. Fu, Y., Yan, M., Zhang, X., Xu, L., Yang, D., Kymer, J.D., Automated classification of software change messages by semi-supervised latent Dirichlet allocation. *Inf. Softw. Technol.*, 57, 369–377, 2015.

18. Banitaan, S. and Alenezi, M., Software evolution via topic modelling: An analytic study. *Int. J. Softw. Eng. Appl.*, 9, 5, 43–52, 2015.

19. Kitchenham, B.A., *Procedures for Undertaking Systematic Reviews*, Joint Technical Report, Computer Science Department, Keele University (TR/SE0401) and National ICT Australia Ltd., Papua New Guinea, (0400011T.1, 2004.

20. Kitchenham, B., Mendes, E., Travassos, G.H., A systematic review of cross company vs. within-company cost estimation studies. *Proceedings of EASE06, BSC*, pp. 89–98, 2006.

21. Kitchenham, B., Mendes, E., Travassos, G.H., A systematic review of cross- vs. within company cost estimation studies. *IEEE Trans. Softw. Eng.*, 33, 5, 316–329, 2007.

22. Kitchenham, B.A., *Procedures for Undertaking Systematic Reviews*, Joint Technical Report, Computer Science Department, Keele University (TR/SE0401) and National ICT Australia Ltd. (0400011T.1), Papua New Guinea, 2004.

23. Kitchenham, B.A., Dyba, T., Jorgensen, M., Evidence-based software engineering, in: *Proceedings of the 26th International Conference on Software Engineering, (ICSE'04)*, IEEE Computer Society, Washington DC, USA, pp. 273–281, 2004.

24. Kitchenham, B., Brereton, O.P., Budgen, D., Turner, M., Bailey, J., Linkman, S., *A Systematic Literature Review of Evidence-Based Software Engineering*, EBSE Technical Report, EBSE-2007-03, UK, 2007.

25. Ma, J. and Nickerson, J.V., Hands-on, simulated and remote laboratories: A comparative literature review. *ACM Surv.*, 38, 3, 1–24, 2006.

26. Mahmood, S., La, R., Kim, Y.S., A survey of component-based system quality assurance and assessment. *IET Softw.*, 1, 2, 57–66, 2005.

27. Mair, C. and Shepperd, M., The consistency of empirical comparisons of regression and analogy-based software project cost prediction. *International Symposium on Empirical Software Engineering*, pp. 509–518, 2005.

28. Mendes, E., A systematic review of web engineering research. *International Symposium on Empirical Software Engineering*, pp. 498–507, 2005.

29. Miller, J., Can results from software engineering experiments be safely combined?, in: *Proceedings 6th International Software Metrics Symposium*, IEEE Computer Press, pp. 152–158, 1999.

30. Miller, J., Applying meta-analytical procedures to software engineering experiments. *J. Syst. Softw.*, 54, 1, 29–39, 2000.

31. Molokken-Ostvold, K.J., Jorgensen, M., Tanilkan, S.S., Gallis, H., Lien, A.C., Hove, S.E., A survey on software estimation in the Norwegian industry. *Proceedings Software Metrics Symposium*, pp. 208–219, 2004.

32. Petersson, H., Thelin, T., Runeson, P., Wohlin, C., Capture–recapture in software inspections after 10 years research–theory, evaluation and application. *J. Syst. Softw.*, 72, 249–264, 2004.

33. Pickard, L.M., Kitchenham, B.A., Jones, P., Combining empirical results in software engineering. *Inf. Softw. Technol.*, 40, 14, 811–821, 1998.

34. Ramesh, V., Glass, R.L., Vessey, I., Research in computer science: An empirical study. *J. Syst. Softw.*, 70, 1–2, 165–176, 2004.

35. Runeson, P., Andersson, C., Thelin, T., Andrews, A., Berling, T., What do we know about defect detection methods? *IEEE Softw.*, 23, 3, 82–86, 2006.

36. Sjoberg, D.I.K., Hannay, J.E., Hansen, O., Kampenes, V.B., Karahasanovic, A., Liborg, N.K., Rekdal, A.C., A survey of controlled experiments in software engineering. *IEEE Trans. Softw. Eng.*, 31, 9, 733–753, 2005.

37. Tichy, W.F., Lukowicz, P., Prechelt, L., Heinz, E.A., Experimental evaluation in computer science: A quantitative study. *J. Syst. Softw.*, 28, 1, 9–18, 1995.

38. Torchiano, M. and Morisio, M., Overlooked aspects of COTS-based development. *IEEE Softw.*, 21, 2, 88–93, 2004.

39. Turner, M., Kitchenham, B., Budgen, D., Brereton, O.P., Lessons learnt undertaking a large-scale systematic literature review, in: *Proceedings of EASE'08 British Computer Society*, 2008.

40. Zannier, C., Melnik, G., Maurer, F., On the success of empirical studies in the international conference on software engineering. *ICSE06*, pp. 341–350, 2006.

41. Zelkowitz, M. and Wallace, D., Experimental validation in software engineering. *Inf. Softw. Technol.*, 39, 735–743, 1997.

42. Zelkowitz, M. and Wallace, D., Experimental models for validating computer technology. *IEEE Comput.*, 31, 5, 23–31, 1998.

43. Sehra, S.K., Brar, Y.S., Kaur, N., Sehra, S.S., Research patterns and trends in software effort estimation. *Inf. Softw. Technol.*, 91, 1–21, 2017.

44. Pospieszny, P., Czarnacka-Chrobot, B., Kobylinski, A., An effective approach for software project effort and duration estimation with machine learning algorithms. *J. Syst. Softw.*, 137, 184–196, 2018.

45. Usharani, K., Ananth, V.V., Velmurugan, D., A survey on software effort estimation. *Int. Conf. Electr. Electron. Optim. Tech. ICEEOT 2016*, pp. 505–509, 2016.

46. Banimustafa, A., Predicting software effort estimation using machine learning techniques. *2018 8th Int. Conf. Comput. Sci. Inf. Technol. CSIT 2018*, pp. 249–256, 2018.

47. Azeem, M., II, Palomba, F., Shi, L., Wang, Q., Machine learning techniques for code smell detection: A systematic literature review and meta-analysis. *Inf. Softw. Technol.*, 108, 4, 115–138, 2019.

48. Padhy, N., Singh, R.P., Satapathy, S.C., Software reusability metrics estimation: Algorithms, models and optimization techniques. *Comput. Electr. Eng.*, 69, 653–668, 2018.

49. Stephenson, N. *et al.*, Survey of machine learning techniques in drug discovery. *Curr. Drug Metab.*, 20, 3, 185–193, 2018.

50. Marco, R., Herman, N.S., Sakinah, S., Ahmad, S., Optimizing software effort estimation models based on metaheuristic methods: A proposed framework. *IJATCSE*, 8, 1, 294–304, 2019. Available Online at http://www.warse.org/IJATCSE/static/pdf/file/ijatcse5181.52019.pdf.

Improving the Quality of Open Source Software

Sharanpreet Kaur[1]* and Satwinder Singh[2]

[1]*Mata Gujri College, Fatehgarh Sahib Punjab, India*
[2]*Central University of Punjab, Bathinda, India*

Abstract

This study aims at development of generating metrics based code smells prediction to improve the software quality assurance by working at preventive maintenance level. In order to do so, Refactoring is the best solution for identification of smelly areas in the code to reveal the portions which demands patching. It not only increases the life of code but eventually increases the quality of software in long run, where versions of a software are launched one after the other. The empirical model development considered Deep learning based neural network technique for establishing the association between code smells and metrics in the source code of Eclipse which is a Java based application contributing efficiently on the open source platform. A statistical analysis was pre applied on the set of code smells and metrics for finding the connection between the both. Later on, Multi Layer Perceptron model development on four versions of Eclipse has been made. Subsequently Area Under Curve (ROC) has been generated for class & method level code smells. The value of ROC in predicting code smells pointed towards the fact that Neural Network Multi Layer Perceptron model perform fair to good in determining the presence of code smells based on software metrics in Eclipse. Therefore from the results obtained it is concluded that smelly classes are predicted efficiently by software metric based code smells prediction model. The present study will be beneficial to the software development community to locate the refactoring areas and providing resources for testing. The results of empirical study also guide the development community by providing information relative to code smells and its types. The aim of this study is to provide statistical proof of linkage between metrics and code smells. The software metric based prediction

**Corresponding author*: sharancgm@gmail.com

Susheela Hooda, Vandana Mohindru Sood, Yashwant Singh, Sandeep Dalal and Manu Sood (eds.)
Agile Software Development: Trends, Challenges and Applications, (309–324) © 2023 Scrivener Publishing LLC

model of code smells and its type's aids in development of prediction model based upon metrics values to improve the overall quality of software.

Keywords: Software quality maintenance, refactoring, code smells and deep learning

16.1   Introduction

Software maintenance is a complex process which has to be fulfilled in all the phases of software product. Software developers aims to launch the software which are easily maintainable in all the phases. As per Brown *et al.* [1], maintenance process devour over 90% cost from the entire software development. The maintenance process involves embracing new functionalities, updating of software and correcting. Hence maintenance process escorts towards improving the quality of product. The definition of software maintenance as given in the IEEE Standard for Software Maintenance is as follows: "*The totality of activities required to provide cost-effective support to a software system. Activities are performed during the pre-delivery stage as well as the post-delivery stage*" (IEEE Standard for Software Maintenance, 2006) [46].

According to this standard maintenance is of following four types.

    a. Adaptive Maintenance
       "The modification of a software product, performed after delivery, to keep a software product usable in a changed or changing environment."

    b. Corrective Maintenance
       "The reactive modification of a software product performed after delivery to correct discovered problems."

    c. Perfective Maintenance
       "The modification of a software product after delivery to detect and correct latent faults in the software product before they are manifested as failures."

    d. Preventive Maintenance
       "The modification of a software product after delivery to detect and correct latent faults in the software product before they become operational faults."

Apart from these studies some other studies like Khomh *et al.* [2], Zhao *et al.* [3], Luo *et al.* [4] and Yamashita and Moonen [5] have been found in the literature which improves software maintenance activities especially preventive maintenance. Maintenance is often linked with software metrics like Saraiva *et al.* [6] proposed a thorough examination of software maintenance considering multiple metrics. One such way of performing maintenance is by applying code re-constructing in the form of Refactoring. Its prime idea is to progress the understanding, performance and maintainability of code alike to preventive maintenance. While performing refactoring the program functionality remain the same as before. It is also possible that while performing refactoring complex changes can be made to code. It leads to addition of removal of specific code modules. Like, Counsell and Hassoun [7] described the refactoring of java based open source systems, while the re-engineering components are - Renaming and Moving methods. Refactoring is the process of identification of smelly areas of code known as "Code Smells". Code smell, an indication of deprived layout and programming option, emerged as a noteworthy influence on software maintainability. Bad smells are introduced into the code as a result of little understanding and inappropriate acquaintance of programming in the software developers for solving an exact problem. More than twenty types of code smells are recognized by the research community for performing refactoring. Similarly, software metrics, which determine various parameters of software code, have been found to be effective in predicting code smells in a software system via the development of various code smells prediction models. More specifically, the prediction of faults via metrics or potential flaws in software systems via code smells aids in software maintainability. Software code smells prediction is an important field in the research of software maintenance. It contributes to the field of software maintenance and improves the software through assisting in preventive maintenance. A lot of researchers are working development of prediction model for locating the areas of code where refactoring is demanded. Deep learning based neural network technique has been used in the current study for locating the flaws in the Eclipse software by firstly developing the statistical analysis and later on ROC curve for accuracy prediction of model. The empirical model generated an excellent perceptiveness in case of class level code smells and a fair accuracy while predicting the method level code smells. Thereby improving the quality of software if flaws will be identified at earlier stage of software development. Now we will discuss the literature review in the next sections related to code smells detection strategies followed by the researchers in the past.

16.2   Literature Review

Fowler *et al.* [8] wrote book on refactoring, with identifiable flaws in the code are described where refactoring could be possibly applied. At the same time the term "Code Smells" came into existence. Code smells help the software developers in identifying areas in source code for performing refactoring. However removal of code smells from code demands refactoring which engross both time and cost. More than 20 code smells were pioneered by Fowler *et al.* [8] on Refactoring. Numerous studies have been found in the literature to identify the association among the metrics and code smells. A large set of studies for code smell detection and refactoring based upon metrics value have been found in the systematic literature review. The studies have been arranged according to different types of approaches for identification of smelly area which are to be refactored in the coming parts of this section. Few milestones were provided by the researchers in the discipline of systematic literature review on refactoring and code smell detection like Dallal [9], Misbhauddin and Alshayeb [10], Zhang *et al.* [11], Mens and Tourwe [12] and Singh and Kaur [13]. The approaches use for the sake of performing refactoring and locating code smells are provided with a little description of each strategy.

a. Manual Detection Approach

This detection technique was performed manually for revealing code smells. Prominent research was made in this approach which involved contributions from Allen and Garlan [14], Travassos *et al.* [15], Smith and William [16] and Ghannem *et al.* [17]. The flaw in the methodology was that it demanded both time and effort as it was a tedious job. Similarly excellent knowledge for each type of code smell was demanded.

b. Visualization Based Strategy

In visualization based detection, usage of tool was made which provided the output in a visualized manner or Domain specific language. A need was stipulated for understanding such detection strategy and DLS. Some of the work conducted using this approach include that of Baudry *et al.* [18], Langelier *et al.* [19], Dhambri *et al.* [20], Binkley *et al.* [21], Bouhours *et al.* [22], Moha *et al.* [23] and Hosseini and Azgomi [24]. The drawback of this approach was that it required human intervention for the final selection of problems encountered and refactoring areas. It was complex to manage for large sized applications.

c. Semi Automatic Approach

Involvement of semi automatic tools was made for revealing code smells and application of refactoring. Some of the prominent studies that were conducted under this category are Noble [25], Feng *et al.* [26], Murphy-Hill *et al.* [27] and Kempf *et al.* [28].

d. Automatic Detection Methodology

Fully automatic detection tools has been considered along with frameworks and surveys in this type. The highest percentage of papers i.e. 28% have been found in systematic literature review process. Work had been done by Ekman and Schafer [29], Bansiya and Davis [30], Gueheneuc [31] and Borg and Kropp [32] which was remarkable in the field of refactoring and smells detection.

e. Empirical Studies

It involves the model generation based on empirical studies to perform the linkage between code smells and refactoring. Remarkable work have been found by Briand *et al.* [33], Mantyla *et al.* [34], Li and Shatnawi [35], Khomh and Gueheneuc [36] and Olbrich and Cruzes [37]. The empirical study can be visualization based, semi automatic or automatic in nature depending upon the requirement of work performed.

f. Metric Supported Detection

The metric based strategy makes use of metrics considering it an indicator of a n excellent internal quality and comparing it with the imperfections emerged out in the source code. Few studies that have been conducted in this category are: Singh and Kahlon [38, 39] and Fontana *et al.* [40].

16.3   Research Issues

As discussed earlier according to IEEE Standard for Software Maintenance 2006 Preventive Maintenance is defined as

"The modification of a software product after delivery to detect and correct latent faults in the software product before they become operational faults."

On the basis of above mentioned statement empirical study is to be carried out i.e. Preventive maintenance ensures the quality up gradation of software. From the vast literature survey, some serious issues came into limelight which are as follows:

a) Numerous efforts have been made in the field of software engineering in order to find relationship between code smells and metrics. But there has been no appreciable work that employs code smells to metrics with statistical analysis first and then applied deep learning technique which is needed to be explored further.

b) Some other issues which are highlighted by the literature survey; like, it has been observed that many authors have investigated on few code smells and limited metrics. In the present study more than fifteen metrics very carefully short-listed so that each and every aspect of object oriented programming should be covered.

c) Commonly used tools are made functional in various studies like Eclipse plug-in- jDeodorant (Christopoulou *et al.*, [41]), (Chatzigeorgiou and Manakos, [42]) and (Lakshmanan and Manikandan [43]) is most widely used which detects only four types of code smells. The use of iPlasma tool is made under the current study.

d) In addition, same datasets are used in the literature studies only the approach for uncovering code smells has been varied in the research methodologies. Therefore in the current study along with Eclipse source code is taken under consideration which is an industrial usage project.

On the basis of the above mentioned points, the work carried out in the study attempts to investigate the impact of code smells on metrics. The categorization of code smells is performed at two major aspects of code-Class Level and Method Level which is yet another benchmark of developing the prediction model. The data set for the experiment will be taken from object oriented open source software.

16.4   Research Method and Data Collection

In this section we have introduced a deep learning technique based on neural network approach for development of prediction model. The research methodology is based upon the field of deep learning which is an integrated field of machine learning associated with algorithms aroused by the arrangement and similarity of brain called artificial neural networks. Deep learning is a technique which is exactly replica of human brain and nervous system. It is a remarkable application in the field of Artificial Intelligence which is also a powerful tool support for data mining and prediction. Multi Layer Perceptron and Radial Function are the two methods/

functions available for generation of prediction model based on neural network. Under these two pre said methods - Feed forward and Feed backwards are two topologies of Neural Network. Supervised machine learning is the application of neural network based on machine learning used by researchers for prediction. Neural Network Multi Layer Perceptron (MLP) was applied for the development of prediction model. It was a feed forward neural network for data analysis which is a composite of multiple layers of nodes. It can have one or more hidden layers consisting of unseen nodes of network also called units. Every unit computed in hidden layer was a function of weighted sum of units at input layer. If the neural network contains more than one layer than successive layer was a weighted sum of units of the previous layer. The activation function connected the weighted sum of units in the previous layer to the next layer. Two activation functions were used under MLP. Under the study value for each neuron was calculated and then activation function was applied on each neurons. Hyperbolic Tangent Function and Softmax Activation Function were applied for Hidden Layer and Output Layer respectively.

a. Hidden Layer Activation Function (Hyperbolic tangent function)
The value of activation function lies between -1 to $+1$. The Hyperbolic tangent function in the hidden layers of Neural Network is given below:

$$\Phi(x) = \tanh(x) = (e^{-x} - e^{-x}) / (e^{-x} - e^{-x}) \qquad (16.1)$$

b. Output Layer Activation Function (Softmax activation function)
The range of softmax activation function varies from 0 to 1. The activation function for all hidden layers of neural network is as follows:

$$\Phi i = (exi) \Big/ \left(\sum j = 1 \text{ to c exj} \right) \qquad (16.2)$$

The accuracy of neural networks Prediction models is identified by Area under Curve (ROC). It is one of the methods to compare the accuracy of models and assistance examination of decision making. An ROC curve plots the relationship between sensitivity (y-axis) and 1- specificity (x-axis) is as follow:

   a) 0.90–1.00 implies that it is an excellent discrimination.
   b) 0.80–0.90 implies that it is a good discrimination.
   c) 0.70–0.80 implies that it is a fair discrimination.
   d) 0.60–0.70 implies that it is a poor discrimination.
   e) 0.50–0.60 implies that there is no discrimination.

For the proposed work, large sized open source project Eclipse IDE is finalized. Four versions of Eclipse: Eclipse 3.2, Eclipse 3.3, Eclipse 3.6 and Eclipse 3.7 were taken for analysis. In addition to this, Eclipse as an open source put in progressively on the way to research in open source platform, in terms which eventually helps in setting standards and construct the research replicable and inferable. Two type of categorization - Class Level and Method Level was performed on code smells with a set of eight smells. The class level smells include - Data Class, God Class, Schizophrenic Class and Refused Parent Bequest. Whereas the method level embrace - Brain Method, Feature Envy, Intensive Coupling and Extensive Coupling. This was done because the metrics considered for study were that of the class level. The allotment of total number of classes along with smelly and non smelly classes is given below in Table 16.1.

The results were obtained from iPlasma tool (Marinescu *et al.* [44]) at individual code smell and finally consolidated at Class level and Method level. Metrics collection is a difficult task as it requires a keen observation and thorough knowledge of each metric type. A total of seventeen metrics were selected which were classified into five basic groups. iPlasma tool (Marinescu *et al.* [44]) performed the analysis of the input source code and produced the metrics for each class. Results are provided in Table 16.2.

These will be considered as independent variables for the analysis. Appropriate reverse engineering code smell detection tool (code smell predictor) – iPlasma (Marinescu *et al.* [45]) was used which was able to detect the selected code smells.

Table 16.1 Smelly and non smelly classes in Eclipse.

Selected source code	Number of smelly classes	Number of non smelly classes	Total number of classes
Eclipse 3.2	1995	4925	6920
Eclipse 3.3	2399	5247	7646
Eclipse 3.6	2832	6188	9020
Eclipse 3.7	2856	6226	9082

Table 16.2 Selected metrics and quality attribute.

Quality factor	Concerned metrics
Coupling	ATFD, CBO, FDP, FANOUT, CC, CM
Complexity	WOC, WMC, AMW, NOA, LOCC
Inheritance	DIT, HIT, NOD
Encapsulation	NOAM, NOPA
Cohesion	TCC

16.5   Results and Discussion

Deep learning technique neural network cannot be applied until any statistical analysis between variables (code smells and metrics) has not been identified. Therefore, for detecting the relationship among metrics & code smells, Univariate Binary Regression Analysis was conducted. In the same way, Univariate Multinomial Regression Analysis was applied to examine the association between types of code smells and metrics. Two types of dependent variables are included in the study: Binary Variable and Categorical Variables. Binary Regression Analysis was performed on Eclipse versions between code smells and metrics. Multinomial Regression Analysis was applied to examine the association between types of code smells (class level and method level) and metrics. Area under Curve (ROC) is calculated in order to depict the accuracy of code smells prediction model based on metrics. The software metrics and code smells of four versions of Eclipse are considered as independent and dependent variables for Neural Network Multi Layer Perceptron respectively.

ATFD, CBO, FDP, FanOut, CC, CM, WOC, WMC, AMW, NOA, LOCC, NOAM, NOPA, HIT and DIT are selected for the development of Eclipse metric based code smell prediction model. The accuracy is measured with various parameters like Area under Curve (ROC), Precision, Recall and F-measure. Figure 16.1 represents the Area under ROC Curve for both class level and method level code smells. For all Eclipse versions an excellent perceptiveness is shown by class level code smells. The value of Area under Curve (ROC) lies between 0.874 and 0.958. The curves obtained for method level code smells are fair in their discrimination as the values were between the ranges of 0.50–0.74. Hence it is concluded that metric based code smells prediction model of Eclipse is effective in predicting the class level code smells. Table 16.3 represents the results obtained from Area under Curve (ROC) for Eclipse versions.

An excellent concern is observed from Area under Curve (ROC) for software metric based code smells prediction model for predicting class level code smells. Whereas a poor perceptiveness is revealed for method level code smells. Figure 16.1 represents the Area under Curve (ROC) for Eclipse versions. Like the lowest value for method level code smells is 0.579 for Eclipse 3.7. There is a slight variation of results of Eclipse

Table 16.3 Area under curve (ROC) for Eclipse.

Eclipse versions	Applied on	Categorization	Area under curve (ROC)
Eclipse 3.2	Eclipse 3.2	At Class	0.874
		At Method	0.607
	Eclipse 3.3	At Class	0.915
		At Method	0.580
	Eclipse 3.6	At Class	0.913
		At Method	0.585
	Eclipse 3.7	At Class	0.911
		At Method	0.579
Eclipse 3.3	Eclipse 3.3	At Class	0.933
		At Method	0.740
	Eclipse 3.6	At Class	0.900
		At Method	0.726
	Eclipse 3.7	At Class	0.912
		At Method	0.639
Eclipse 3.6	Eclipse 3.6	At Class	0.942
		At Method	0.649
	Eclipse 3.7	At Class	0.919
		At Method	0.937
Eclipse 3.7	Eclipse 3.7	At Class	0.958
		At Method	0.658

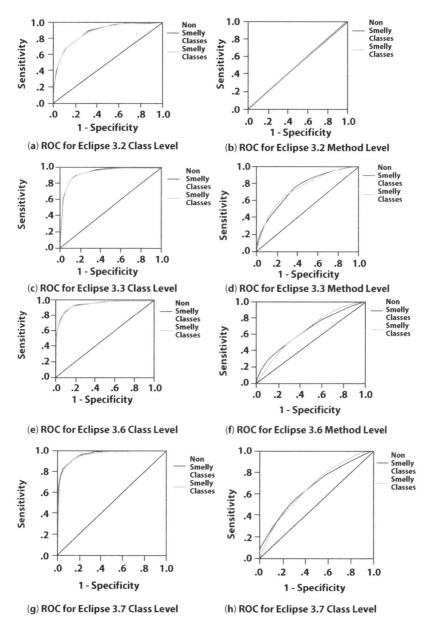

Figure 16.1 ROC curves for application of NN MLP model on four versions of Eclipse. (a, c, e, g) Application of model prediction on Eclipse Version 3.2, 3.3, 3.6, 3.7 at Class Level and (b, d, f, h) application of model prediction on Eclipse Version 3.2, 3.3, 3.6, 3.7 at Method Level.

versions for class level and method level smells. For Eclipse 3.3, Eclipse 3.6 and Eclipse 3.7 versions an excellent perceptiveness is disclosed by class level code smells model. The method level code smells have a range of value of Area under Curve (ROC) between 0.607and 0.740 which is an indication of fair discrimination. The value of ROC in case of predicting code smells pointed towards the fact that Neural Network Multi Layer Perceptron model perform fair to good in determining the presence of code smells based on software metrics. From the results obtained and discussed earlier it is concluded that smelly classes are predicted efficiently by software metric based code smells prediction model using Neural Network MLP.

All four versions of Eclipse predicted a good perceptiveness for both categories of code smells except Eclipse 3.2. These findings will not only help to predict smelly classes but also the categories of code smells The severity level information will guide the maintenance team to work on areas where probably more severe code smells occurrence is high.

16.6   Conclusion and Future Scope

The research work aimed at development of metrics based code smells prediction model based on Deep learning neural network technique. The average Area under Curve (ROC) for Eclipse (ROC) is greater than 0.90. Hence, based upon the results obtained from code smells prediction model development, it is clearly shown that a significance relation is found between code smells and metrics. The outcomes collected from the current empirical study aids software developers in locating refactoring areas and apply suitable refactoring technique. It leads to clear and understandable code. The approach could be used as a support for discovering additional association among code smells and metrics to aid the maintenance process. This aspect of the research will ensure optimal product performance for users, as the software will be expanded as appropriate. In future, the empirical study could be enlarged by considering a larger set of database along with the confirmed faults. In the same way a possibly changed set of code smells could be used with different code smells predictor. Furthermore, the bad smells can be dealt with on an individual level as well as according to the norms already established for their categorization, and the models' effectiveness can be evaluated. The selection of metrics other than metrics mentioned in study could help in generation of different results. Efforts will be made in the future to ensure the results of above mentioned problems with cross technology.

References

1. Brown, W.J., Malveau, R.C., McCormick III, H.W., Mowbray, T.J., *Anti patterns: Refactoring Software, Architectures and Projects in Crisis*, Wiley Publishers, 1998.

2. Khomh, F., Di Penta, M., Gueheneuc, Y., Antoniol, G., An exploratory study of the impact of anti patterns on class change and fault tendency, in: *Proceedings of 16th Working Conference on Reverse Engineering*, pp. 75–84, 2012.

3. Zhao, S., Bian, Y., Zhang, S.S., A review on refactoring sequential program to parallel code in multicore era. *IEEE International Conference on Intelligent Computing and Internet of Things*, 2015.

4. Luo, Y., Hoss, A., Carver, D.L., An ontological identification of relationships between anti-patterns and code smells. *IEEE Aerospace Conference*, 2010.

5. Yamashita, A. and Moonen, L., Do code smells reflect important maintainability aspects. *IEEE International Conference on Software Maintenance*, 2012.

6. de AG Saraiva, J., de França, M.S., Soares, S.C.B., Filho, F.J.C.L., de Souza, R.M.C.R., Classifying metrics for assessing object-oriented software maintainability: A family of metrics' catalogs. *J. Syst. Softw.*, 103, 85–101, 2015.

7. Counsell, S. and Hassoun, Y., Common refactorings, a dependency graph and some code smells: An empirical study of Java OSS. *IEEE International Symposium on Empirical Software Engineering*, pp. 288–296, 2006.

8. Fowler, M., Beck, M., Brant, K., Opdyke, J., William, R., *Refactoring-Improving the Design of Existing Code*, 1st Edition, Addison-Wesley, 1999.

9. Al Dallal, J., Identifying refactoring opportunities in object-oriented code: A systematic literature review. *Inf. Softw. Technol.*, 58, 231–249, 2015.

10. Misbhauddin, M. and Alshayeb, M., UML model refactoring: A systematic literature review. *Empir. Softw. Eng.*, 20, 206–251, 2015.

11. Zhang, M., Hall, T., Baddoo, N., Code bad smells: A review of current knowledge. *J. Softw. Maintenance Evolution: Res. Pract.*, 23, 3, 179–202, 2011.

12. Mens, T. and Tourwe, T., A survey of software refactoring. *IEEE Trans. Softw. Eng.*, 30, 2, 126–139, 2004.

13. Singh, S. and Kaur, S., A systematic literature review: Refactoring for disclosing code smells in object oriented softwares. *Ain Shams Eng. J. Elsevier*, 9, 4, 2129–2151, 2018.

14. Allen., R. and Garlan, D., A formal basis for architectural connection. *ACM Trans. Softw. Eng. Methodol.*, 6, 3, 213–249, 1997.

15. Travassos, G., Shull, F., Fredericks, M., Basil, R.V., Detecting defects in object-oriented designs: Using reading techniques to increase software quality. *Proceedings 14th Conference Object Oriented Programming, Systems, Languages, and Applications*, pp. 47–56, 1999.

16. Smith, C.U. and William, L.G., Software performance anti-patterns. *Proceedings of the 2nd International Workshop on Software and Performance*, pp. 127–136, 2000.
17. Ghannem, A., Boussaidi, G.E., Kessentini, M., On the use of design defect examples to detect model refactoring opportunities. *Softw. Qual. J.*, 24, 4, 947–965, 2015.
18. Baudry, B., Traon, Y.L., Sunye, G., Jezequel, J.M., Measuring and improving design patterns testability. *Proceedings of the IEEE International Software Metrics Symposium*, 2003.
19. Langelier, G., Sahraoui, H.A., Poulin, P., Visualization-based analysis of quality for large-scale software systems. *Proceedings of 20th IEEE/ACM International Conference on Automated Software Engineering*, pp. 214–223, 2005.
20. Dhambri, K., Shraoui, H., Poulin, P., Visual detection of design anomalies. *12th IEEE European Conference on Software Maintenance and Reengineering*, pp. 279–283, 2008.
21. Binkley, D., Harman, M., Gold, N., Mahdavi, K., Li, Z., Mahdavi, K., Wegener, J., Dependence anti patterns. *23rd IEEE/ACM International Conference on Automated Software Engineering Workshops*, 2008.
22. Bouhours, C., Leblanc, H., Percebois, C., Bad smells in design and design patterns. *J. Object Technol.*, 8, 3, 310, 2009.
23. Moha, N., Gueheneuc, Y., Duchien, L., Meur, A.L., DECOR: A method for the specification and detection of code and design smells. *IEEE Trans. Softw. Eng.*, 36, 1, 20–36, 2010.
24. Hosseini, S. and Azgomi, M.A., UML model refactoring with emphasis on behavior preservation. *2nd IFIP/IEEE International Symposium on Theoretical Aspects of Software Engineering*, pp. 125–128, 2008.
25. Noble, J., Classifying Relationship between object oriented design patterns. *Proceedings of IEEE Software Engineering Conference*, pp. 98–107, 1998.
26. Feng, T., Zhang, J., Wang, H., Wang, X., Software design improvement through anti-patterns identification. *Proceedings of the 20th IEEE International Conference on Software Maintenance*, 2004.
27. Murphy-Hill, E., Black, P.A., Dig, D., Parnin, C., Gathering refactoring data: A comparison of four methods. *Proceedings of the 2nd Workshop on Refactoring Tools*, 2008.
28. Kempf, M., Kleeb, R., Klenk, M., Sommerlad, P., Cross language refactoring for eclipse plug-ins. *Proceedings of 2nd Workshop on Refactoring Tools*, 2008.
29. Ekman, T., Schafer, M., Verbaere, M., Refactoring is not (yet) about transformation. *Proceedings of 2nd Workshop on Refactoring Tools*, 2008.
30. Bansiya, J. and Davis, C.G., A hierarchical model for object oriented design quality assessment. *IEEE Trans. Softw. Eng.*, 28, 1, 4–17, 2002.
31. Gueheneuc, Y., A systematic study of UML class diagram constituents for their abstract and precise recovery. *11th Asia-Pacific Conference on Software Engineering*, pp. 265–274, 2004.

32. Borg, R. and Kropp, M., Automated acceptance test refactoring. *Proceedings of the 4th Workshop on Refactoring Tools*, pp. 15–21, 2011.

33. Briand, L.C., Wust, J., Ikonomovski, S.V., Lounis, H., Investigating quality factors in object-oriented designs: An industrial case study. *Proceedings of the 21st International Conference on Software Engineering*, pp. 345–354, 1999.

34. Mantyla, M., *Bad Smells in Software-A Taxonomy and an Empirical Study*, PhD Thesis, Helsinki University of Technology, 2003.

35. Li., W. and Shatnawi, R., An empirical study of the bad smells and class error probability in the post-release object oriented system evolution. *J. Syst. Softw.*, 80, 1120–1128, 2007.

36. Khomh., F. and Gueheneuc, Y., Do design patterns impact software quality positively. *Proceedings of 12th IEEE Conference on Software Maintenance and Reengineering*, pp. 274–278, 2008.

37. Olbrich, S. and Cruzes, D.S., The evolution and impact of code sells: A case study of two open source systems. *3rd International Symposium on Empirical Software Engineering and Measurement*, pp. 390–400, 2009.

38. Singh, S. and Kahlon, K.S., Effectiveness of refactoring metrics model to identify smells and error prone classes in open source software. *ACM SigSoft Softw. Eng. Notes*, 36, 5, 1–11, 2011.

39. Singh, S. and Kahlon, K.S., Effectiveness of encapsulation and object oriented metrics to refactor code and identity error prone classes using bad smells. *ACM SigSoft Softw. Eng. Notes*, 37, 2, 1–10, 2012.

40. Fontana, F.A., Ferme, V., Marino, A., Walter, B., Martenka, P., Investigating the impact of code smells on system's quality: An empirical study on systems of different application domains. *IEEE International Conference on Software Maintenance*, 260–269, 2013.

41. Christopoulou, A., Giakoumakis, E.A., Zafeiris, V.E., Soukara, V., Automated refactoring to the strategy design pattern. *Inf. Softw. Technol.*, 54, 1202–1214, 2012.

42. Chatzigeorgiou, A. and Manakos, A., Investigating the evolution of bad smells in object-oriented code. *Proceedings of 7th IEEE International Conference on the Quality of Information and Communications Technology*, pp. 106–115, 2010.

43. Lakshmanan, M. and Manikandan, S., Multi-step automated refactoring for code smell. *Int. J. Res. Eng. Technol.*, 3, 3, 278–282, 2014.

44. Marinescu, C., Marinescu, R., Mihancea, P., Ratiu, D., Wettel, R., IPlasma: An integrated platform for quality assessment of object oriented design. *Proceedings of 21st International Conference on Software Maintenance Tools Section*, 2005.

45. Marinescu, R., Detection strategies: Metrics-based rules for detecting design flaws. *Proceedings of 20th International Conference Software Maintenance*, pp. 350–359, 2004.

46. 1219-1998 - IEEE Standard for Software Maintenance, https://ieeexplore. ieee.org/servlet/opac?punumber=5832, IEEE, 1998, ISBN: 978-0-7381-0533-8. INSPEC Accession Number: 6146511.

Artificial Intelligence Enables Agile Software Development Life Cycle

Sima Das[1]*, Ajay Kumar Balmiki[1] and Nimay Chandra Giri[2]

[1]Department of Computer Science and Engineering, Maulana Abul Kalam Azad University of Technology, West Bengal, India
[2]Department of Electronics and Communication Engineering, Centurion University of Technology and Management, Odisha, India

Abstract

An expert agile empowers the industry to react viably to inside and outside changes. Readiness starts and acknowledges changes to business processes, and simulated intelligence further empowers agility by giving opportune reports on the situation with a business to work with navigation. Artificial intelligence empowers entirely self-controlling encoding tests. The job of machine learning in programming testing is turning out to be increasingly more basic to the quality confirmation process. Additionally, differential testing looks at application renditions, group contrasts, and uses criticism to further develop its classification techniques. In the software development life cycle (SDLC), the highly intricate piece of creating fruitful software to a great extent depends on the underlying stages. This chapter will endeavor to plan and foster a specialist framework to help the product designer in the total programming advancement life cycle with various space experts like Telecom, Banking, Coordination, Medical services, Satellite, and a lot more information procurement. The particular objectives of this examination incorporate information obtaining explicit to the issues of utilizing numerous space specialists, plan and advancement of a model master framework for programming improvement, and approval of the agile technique.

Keywords: Artificial intelligence, agile software development, expert system, machine learning

**Corresponding author*: simadas@ieee.org

Susheela Hooda, Vandana Mohindru Sood, Yashwant Singh, Sandeep Dalal and Manu Sood (eds.) *Agile Software Development: Trends, Challenges and Applications*, (325–344) © 2023 Scrivener Publishing LLC

17.1   Introduction

Agile is the ability to create and respond to alternatives. It is a manner of coping with, and in the end, succeeding in unsure and turbulent surroundings. The authors of the Agile Manifesto selected "Agile" as the label for this complete idea because word represented the adaptiveness and reaction to exchange which became so crucial to their technique. It's truly approximately questioning through how you could apprehend what's happening inside the environment you're in these days, perceive what uncertainty you're facing, and parent out how you could adapt to that as you move alongside. An agile method is a confirmed approach for delivering software. However, in artificial intelligence (AI) [1–3] tasks, the development stack seems greater like a pyramid with a massive base assisting fewer user-visible outputs. Hence the standard Agile strategies fail in AI tasks. Research in data technological know-how needs huge data series and processing. Therefore, facts projects generally tend to awareness of studies and learning. However, there are specifically which could purpose problems with AI tries. First, there are some matters to preserve in thoughts concerning software improvement. Second, the developers presume that the answer design is efficient and will produce a properly coordinated and worthwhile final result. In AI tasks, the development stack seems greater like a pyramid. As a result, AI initiatives fail no longer because of a loss of era or AI expertise but rather because businesses pass over key processes, shorten statistics lifecycle operations, misalign commercial enterprise wishes and statistics talents, and others without problems addressed factors thru facts-centric techniques. Iterations in conventional agile strategies are time-boxed and install vertical pieces of capability throughout the whole era stack. If the answer is evolving as expected, it is going to be easier to song development. Today the product association adjusted numerous advancement procedures, plan devices, and space model devices. Be that as it may, the principal job and central consideration for progress or disappointment of the product are generally relied upon by the Area Specialists (Modelers, Business Experts, Plan Architects, and Stack Holders), in the current programming acknowledgment. Demonstrating and recreation innovation is broadly used in decision-making from both practice and hypothesis. The new advancement of direction, particularly decision-production for crisis occasion and online navigation, raise new test for demonstrating and reproduction. They require recreation to be adaptable, extensible, versatile, composable, and solid cooperation. Be that as it may, the greater part of the recreation situation is unbending and hard to change. In this chapter, another idea of Agile Model and Simulation (AgMS) is proposed to satisfy this necessity. The examination of lithe reproduction will give novel plans to complex framework study, open up a new worldview of recreation application, and advance the broad utilization of meta-manufactured framework.

17.2   Literature Survey

The upward thrust of Artificial intelligence (AI) has the potential to noticeably remodel the practice of mission control. Project management has a large socio-technical element with many uncertainties arising from variability in human elements, e.g. Customers' needs, developers' overall performance, and crew dynamics. AI can assist undertaking managers and group individuals with the aid of automating repetitive, high-extent obligations to enable project analytics for estimation and danger prediction, imparting actionable guidelines, and even making decisions. AI is doubtlessly a recreation changer for mission control in assisting to boost up productivity and growth venture success costs. In this chapter, we advocate a framework wherein AI technologies may be leveraged to provide support for handling agile initiatives, which have grown to be more and more famous in the industry [4].

The ethics guidelines recommend using the AI High-Level Expert Group (AI-HLEG) present a listing of seven key requirements that Human-centered, sincere AI structures need to meet. These guidelines are useful for the assessment of AI systems, however, can be complemented via implemented methods and tools for the development of sincere AI systems in practice. In this function chapter, we endorse a framework for translating the AI-HLEG ethics recommendations into the specific context within which an AI system operates. This method aligns nicely with a fixed of Agile principles commonly employed in software engineering [5].

Nowadays industries and agencies need to be flexible. Every cutting-edge company has one similar purpose on their timetable: to end up "greater Agile". These industries desire to acquire a bendy shape so that you can be able to live applicable and competitive. Some of the technology that makes the development of "agile manufacturing" viable are related to Artificial Intelligence and, specifically, Machine Learning. These methodologies are being applied within the layout segment of the R&D area of product improvement by way of using 3D printing as a device [6].

This chapter describes that with the advent of Artificial Intelligence (AI), Agile Government increasingly takes vicinity inside the context of so-known as Human-Agent Collectives (HAC). Such HAC is character-ized via the financial sample of micro-division of exertions which means a growing number of obligations being taken over through increasingly independent AI dealers. To efficiently group-up with AI the machine must be perceived as a colleague rather than as a device; organizational develop-ment is needed. This can be supported by way of Human-Factors Training. Based on adequate capabilities running with AI can assist governments to deal with the tensions of the Agile Government. But AI does also create new anxiety [7].

Machine getting to know strategies take verified operative in rec-ommender structures and different packages until now teams working towards setting up them deficiency some of the blessings that those in extra hooked up software disciplines today take with no consideration. The famous Agile technique advances tasks in a series of fast improve-ment cycles, with the next steps often knowledgeable with the aid of man-ufacturing experiments. Support for such workflow in system studying programs stays primitive. They require models to consume records from a time-ordered occasion history, and we awareness of facilitating creative characteristic engineering. They make it realistic for statistics scientists to use the equal version code in development and manufacturing deploy-ment and make it practical for them to collaborate on complex models. With the technique and structure defined here, our group can routinely cross from thoughts for brand new models to manufacturing-verified consequences inside weeks [8].

17.3   Proposed Work

The combination of the iterative and incremental processes is fabricated as an Agile SDLC model or this model is the mixture of these two pro-cesses. This model generally emphasizes and focuses on the customer's and user's demand, how to meet the demand which arrives from the customer and need to settle down as per guidelines and documentation. The agile method breaks the project into a small fragmented project. Some teams are present to take care of each stage of development and also every iteration works in numerous sectors such as shown in Figure 17.1.

i. Planning
This phase includes the pre-planning of the project. The planning for setup of the project, how to implement the project.

ii. Business analysis of various requirements

In this phase, we generally need to check the basic needs and requirements of the project just like time and resources. The documentation is done based on this information and after that, we need to check out if something more is missing or not.

iii. AI Solution and Experimentation

AI teams are focused on improvement and deployment, and your IT infrastructure is flexible and unbounded. AI that is facts-driven, manufacturing-oriented, and cloud-enabled, to be had each time, everywhere, and at any scale.

iv. Designing

This phase concludes the structure and blueprint of the project. In this phase, we draw the use case, flow chart of the project, UML diagram, and many more. After all these designs, now we have to look out how they will fit into the system.

v. Coding

After the designing phase, the coding phase starts, in this phase, the developer starts to develop the projects. This development is done under many circumstances though in the agile method we use the fragmentation method. We divide the project into small stages and within these stages, the developers perform their respective tasks.

vi. Unit testing

In this phase, the Quality Assurance teams only perform various testing and all permutations and combination of testing.

vii. Deployment

In the deployment phase, the teams used to deploy the project or product to the user or customer work environment.

viii. Feedback

This is the last phase, and in this phase, the management teams collect the feedback of the product or project, and after getting the feedback the team starts to works according to feedback if it needs.

If we use Agile with Artificial Intelligence then it will help to generate trust with the users and customers and we can also say that it will solve the trust issues in the project between the customer and teams. It helps to make visible the black box testing, and from outside we can see the performance of the project as well. This also intends better communication as well as better understanding related to projects. Various powerful tools

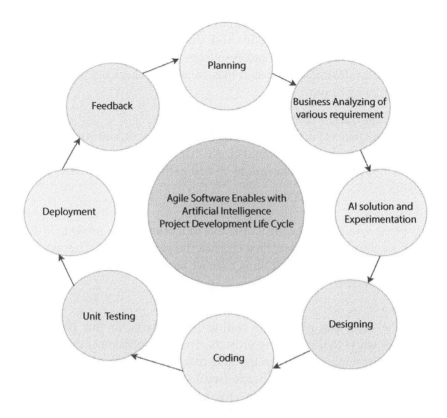

Figure 17.1 Artificial Intelligence enables Agile software development life cycle.

help the project to become better, reliable, and efficient if we used Artificial Intelligence mechanisms in the chapter.

Here are three essential elements for doing agile work for AI:

1. Build on Agile ideas, now not implementation frameworks.
2. Take a top-down and bottom-up method to AI records initiatives.
3. Include and adapt associated concepts along with lean startup and improvement operations.

The following benefits are executed from an agile method to AI development:

1. Manages the uncertainty involved in AI projects and mitigates the hazard that results.

2. Rather than spending the sources on unsuitable solutions, the researchers can also robotically validate and, if required, speedy disregard one inspiration in favor of another.

3. Delivery and marketplace entry instances are reduced.

17.3.1 Advantages and Limitations of Agile Software Development

In this section, we will discuss the advantages and limitations of Agile software development

a. Advantages of Agile software
   The advantages of Agile software are as follows

1. Costs are predictable
If we want to save the cost and estimation, we must go with the agile development technique. It gives us the idea and concept for cost-efficient model deployment and development. We only need a story timeline to analyze and predict the cost or budget of the project. It also gives us the effort to save the extra and irrelevant cost, there is no need for an extra project manager and middleman. Unit testing is also done here, while it saves time and resources with cost. The predicting of cost is only possible because in every frame of stage and steps there are checkpoints and this checkpoint helps to improve, upgrade and make certain changes that are directed by the user or customer, and these checkpoints help us to find or predict the cost as well.

2. Quality Improvisation
The guarantee of quality is provided by the agile model only. Testing and debugging is the main part and factor of quality, the more the testing the more improvisation of quality. So, to assure this the testing is done at every single phase of the sprint, and hence debugging is also done in every single phase of the sprint as well. With the help of debugging of code in every phase, the errors are corrected and this also makes the project more efficient. Just for the customer and user demand, we have the ease and ability to do some sort of certain changes and updates in every single phase of the stage or sprint.

3. Transparency
The most important feature is transparency and this is also done very easily. Users and project management heads and project management teams

are connected with the developer team and can watch every detail which is important to upgrade and improvise and the factors which are needed to cancel out or take off. They get all the updates and information about the very essential project. The project owner, development team, and deployment team also control and monitor the updates and details of the project regarding deployment.

4. Delivery in time

Generally iterative agile model helps the developer to deploy their project in time. They use the scrum method to execute the process, they assigned some time to complete the task. The project is divided into small parts and each is given to the development team, who execute it and test it. This technique helps to deliver the product at the correct time. Delivering the project at right time also attracts customers, and for businesses, the customer gives positive feedback because of positive feedback we get more customers in the market as well and also it gives benefit in costing and other issues if we deliver the project in time then we can save extra costing thus it makes the cost-efficient for the company as well.

    i.   Reduction of risk

        The overall project is scanned to predict or to find the risk, this job is performed by the scrum team. Not only this, the risk is managed and scanned by every single level in broad-spectrum and this starts with the beginning of the project. The error detection is done in each phase so this helps to minimize the risk and makes the project reliable and efficient. So, throughout the development cycle risk management is performed. That is why the main priority is to manage and analyze the risk and map the project's solution. After all, the important thing for a company is to deliver reliable and error-free work to the customer and user.

    ii. Satisfaction of customer or user

        Customer satisfaction is very important and the very first preference of the agile model is to deliver the best product as much as possible to satisfy the as its best. The important and main factor is to satisfy the customer no matter what the code is and what are its specification, if the product is great enough but it cannot able to satisfy the customer then it will be counted and considered as a failure or absurd. So, meeting the demand and criteria of the customers is important rather than the specification and feature of a project. The improvising of the project is performed concurrently as per the user and stakeholder so that it can fulfill all the criteria without any errors and issues. The feedback of the user or customer plays an important role here, according to the customer only the up-gradation and changes done in the project as per the feedback or suggestion.

iii. Productivity
One more important factor is performance, the performance of the team is essential for project implementation, project fabrication, project reliability, project scalability, completion of the project in time, project testing, mapping of the project, etc. It overall depends upon the performance what will be the outcome of the project how the project will look like. So, the team members and project management team have to focus on their respective implementation and delivery work. For better productivity, the programmers can work as per their need or how they want to do the work so as designer and coder rather than the following team manager or instructions because in the end, the meeting of demand of the product quality and criteria is important. So, for calculating and measuring the performance there are some specific tools like cycle time, lead time, real-time vs expected time, and many more.

iv. Possible changes can be done quickly on time
If changes are done very frequently then we need a flexible model, the model which can provide evolution and changes in every stage of development. The agile model is perfect for this factor, and hence we can do up-gradation, changes, and modification very easily in every stage therefore by performing and fabricating the required task we can meet the user or customer demand. We generally have the feature of adaptation and modification in every stage and these changes are done very quickly in every development stage.

b. Limitation of Agile software
   Limitation of Agile software as follows

1. Do not have proper resource planning
When we come to cost estimation or cost prediction, this method becomes challenging to predict the cost of the project at the very beginning or before the start. Not only cost there are also more factors like time, resources. Also, before starting the project team does not know or it is hard to calculate and predict the proper fact about their result or outcomes. In the end, within this Agile Model planning and prediction of cost, time, and resources before starting the project are the toughest work and hence this challenge becomes a serious issue overall in some of the places.

2. Non-integrated output
If we are using agile methodology for the project then we should keep in mind that this methodology or method has the feature of sprint and part-wise development, which means that at every stage they have a piece of code that they develop and fabricate separately. Now, the issue is that they do not fabricate the entire output as a whole, which means every stage have their output as respective to their codes, and then after they have to settle and merge with ones another output in every appropriate condition doing huge numbers of permutations and combinations as well.

3. Not appropriate for long-term projects
The Agile method or methodology is not suitable for long-term projects and it becomes more challenging and tough to implement the project. This happens because Agile methodology uses the differentiation or fragmentation method to implement and fabricate the project, this is very useful for small projects, but for the big project if we apply this method then the project will become more hectic, less reliable, less scalable, and it will lose all its root and can give huge numbers of errors. It also becomes more challenging to fragment such a big project and handle it without any issues. Management issues become bigger in the case of a big project in the Agile Method. So, before using the Agile method we have to go through the project very well, if everything is fine and if it looks like we can go for the Agile Methodology then we can use this method.

4. Not having proper documentation
There are documentation issues that occurred if we use Agile Methodology, generally, in Agile methodology, there are different levels of stages in which

codes are developed and within these stages, they have a particular amount of document which is necessary for their task only, so most of the project face error because each stage does not have the full details or appropriate amount of information related to the project. If all the teams do not have clear documentation, then confusion and hurdles might occur which can affect the project and makes it more challenging for the process to flow without any error as well.

5. Continuously changing and updating the project
In the Agile method we can do an update and changes in every stage, but if the user or customer do the update and changes numerous times then the developer might get confused and error may occur, not only this the developer can also lose track and the possibility is also there to miss out to feed important feature and specification in the project. Sometimes, developers might forget to add new and interesting features to the project due to this cycle of updates and changes. Normally if these cycles continue for a long period, then it might only make the project wider, and also it becomes more hectic for the developer team who are working in every fragment of stage and sprint as well.

c. Advantages and Limitations of Artificial Intelligence

i. Advantages of the Artificial Intelligence
Advantages of the artificial intelligence in this area are as follows

1. Risk analysis
In this modern and digital world, risks are increasing day by day. These risks are of many types so to handle this situation Artificial Intelligence has been introduced to us. If we are discussing the summary risk then the most dangerous risk is to detect the bomb, lots of humans have lost their lives by performing this activity. This was the main and vital limitation for humans and it has been taken up by Artificial Intelligence. Artificial Intelligence plays a major role in this sector and helps us to solve this issue. The Artificial Intelligence robot deal with this issue in the case of bomb-defusing and detection. Not only in the case of bomb detection there is also a risk in exploring the oceans and mines, in this case, the Artificial Intelligence robot is also a game-changer. When it comes to exploring a planet like Mars, Artificial Intelligence is also very helpful and overcomes the limitations of humans.

2. Error reduction

Error is something that which is needed to be taken care of and needs to manage in such a way that it will spread no effect in the project, program, or any other activity. In the case of humans, generally, huge mistakes come from them and this error sometimes becomes more critical and may be dangerous also sometimes, it can be in projects and programs. So, to neutralize the error and to make the system more efficient and error-free we use Artificial Intelligence. We use powerful algorithms, and that particular algorithm minimizes certain issues and errors. And this is done by summarizing previous data and information, and this data and information are injected within the system, with the help of an algorithm we can reduce the error. The errors which are going to occurred are identified early and the output which is going to be fabricated that output can also be predicted. For example, the Weather forecasting system.

3. All-time service

Generally, we all know it is impossible for a human to work all day long and cannot give full 24*7 service with dedicated concentration. So, to solve these functionality issues Artificial Intelligence is very beneficial to all of us. We can manage the system as well as workflow 24*7 with the help of Artificial Intelligence without any pause or break. And also, they do not take holidays and breaks just like humans. If we take the example of helpline centers then we can easily understand that there are Artificial Intelligence systems also working along with the human in the backend.

4. Application used in daily life

There are many applications that we used in our daily life non-stop. Some of these applications are Siri in Apple, ok google in Google, Cortana in windows, and many more. It helps us as a guide and provides us with the necessary information and also makes visible the path through which we can get the solution or answer to our queries. Just like if we want to find the location of some new place, if we want to give replies to text or mails, if we want to make a call to someone. All these tasks we can do with the help of Artificial Intelligence.

5. Faster in Decision making

Now let us discuss some important points and factors and one of the main important factors in decision making in the relevant and efficient time. In this field also Artificial Intelligence beats humans in almost every place. If we will compare humans and the machine for taking the decision faster and more appropriate then machines will be the winner because humans will interpret things with mind, emotion, and with other factors too but the machine will fabricate the things faster and more appropriate according to the algorithm, machine do not have emotions and all it only has algorithms which allow machines to work in a particular manner. Let us take the example of any games in machines like chess in windows, puzzle-solving, word guessing, and many more, if we will play these types of games against machines at a hard level then definitely, we will not win against the machine this is because in the backend there is Artificial Intelligence, and the machine will beat the human in a very short interval of time, this all depends on the working process which is followed by the provided algorithms.

6. Increase productivity and quality
Generally, in Artificial Intelligence productivity and quality is the main factor. In the machine or within the system the data and information are already installed according to that it takes the decision and performed the task. So, keeping that in mind a system and its algorithm were invented in such a way that it will fabricate the results which can meet user or customer demand. Though not only this it will also increase productivity and also Artificial Intelligence helps to improve the quality as well.

7. Helping out in repetitive jobs
In every office, school, college, university, and any other official place and sector which contain some repetitive job. And in daily life, there are also some repetitive jobs which we have to do like responding or sending the mail regularly and many more. So, with the help of Artificial Intelligence, we can perform this task automatically and very easily.

8. New Inventions in the digital world
This new world is becoming more digital, and every day new inventions take place. Artificial Intelligence is been used more rapidly. Artificial Intelligence provides better functionality, better production. Artificial Intelligence helps us to make things bigger and smarter. Previously there was lots of limitation and also there is the program and things which was impossible but thanks to Artificial Intelligence this has become easier and more possible to do. We can solve complex problems nowadays very easily just in a short interval of time. And also, prediction of problems can be done with the help of Artificial Intelligence. This prediction is used widely in healthcare systems, Weather forecasting systems (mostly for prediction), Agriculture, and many more.

ii. Limitation of Artificial Intelligence
Limitations of artificial intelligence in this area are as follows

1. Unemployment in the sector
Increasing digitalization and evolution in technology causing more unemployment these days. Industries are trying to replace humans with Artificial Intelligence robots. The employees who are minimum or less qualified are replaced by a robot because Artificial Intelligence robots are more capable to do work faster according to their algorithms. Artificial Intelligence does not need holidays and breaks, even they can work the entire day and night. Artificial Intelligence robots provide more accuracy and give more efficiency in a certain job than humans.

2. Emotionless robot
Generally, when it comes to working 24*7 without any breaks, in an efficient manner, productivity then Artificial Intelligence robot are the best way to execute the task, machines are better in performing and fabricating the tasks. But when it comes to connectivity to the teams, bonding, teamwork, and thinking out of the box for some projects and programs, thinking beyond the boundaries for benefit of the company, performing work differently and uniquely, and for many more reasons, the Artificial Intelligence fails in this case. Team management is very important for any project and program, in this case also Artificial Intelligence robot fails.

3. Increase in cost
When it comes to machines, there are many things like updates and setup which we need to do timely and regularly. And hence automatically this caring and upgradation make the price higher. The complex machine needs more maintenance and also it needs proper care and arrangement than the normal machines. Within the complex machine both software, as well as hardware, need servicing regularly, automatically this tends to increase the cost. If a machine performs another task or needs to meet the customer demand then also, we need to do some sort of changes, upgradation, and many more setups, ultimately this also cause an increase in cost related to service.

4. Fails to think out of the box
Normally humans can think uniquely and beyond the boundaries but machines and systems are unable to perform such tasks, machines will only perform the task as per the algorithms and programs which are embedded in the system. If there is a project and it has some specific arena then a

machine will work within that arena only or the way it is designed, it will work within that specific terms and conditions, within that project boundary only but if take the example of human then, in that case, humans will think wider and human will try to sort out the issue in an easy manner rather than taking the toughest path, humans creativity and thinking ability can give the possibilities of the easiest way to solve the problem.

5. Hard to find professionals

For the work of the project which is related to Artificial Intelligence, the extreme professional developer and employee are very difficult to find, and for the specific field and particular knowledge related to projects and works, it is more difficult to find that specific person. So, the implementation of some projects becomes difficult and after some time, the organizer of the project or the project manager has to pause the project for this small reason. So, this is why finding a professional is very important and also it is hard to get such professionals as well for Artificial Intelligence projects.

6. Dependent of humans towards technology

Modernization and evolution make our world more digital and advanced, and this is count as a benefit and advantage. But there is also some disadvantage that arrives when there is an advantage. Due to this high advancement in technology, humans are becoming more dependent on machines, robots, and new advanced technology as well. As a result, laziness and insincerity are also increasing towards work and duty. If this cycle continues in this manner no matter what our next generation will also become double lazy and dependent on machines and robots as well more than what we are today in this day. And this will harm our next generations only in terms of performance, health, and many more places. The most important point is unemployment, it will also tend to cause more unemployment in the future.

7. Less of ethics

The two most important and main features that are present in humans are morality and ethics, a human can easily persuade this feature and they also use it. But if we go for the machines, robots, and systems, it is impossible to feed these features in specific machines and robots. Machines and robots cannot work by following these features, though they only work according to the algorithms which have been embedded into the systems or according to the assigned program and work. Thus,

Artificial Intelligence completely fails in the sector of ethics and morality as well.

8. No Improvement in machines
Normally humans can update their knowledge. With the growing age the human brain also develops, and this improvement is only present in humans. In the case of machines, it is impossible to adapt this type of improvement. If humans gather experience, then their ability and capability of working will also increase, as experience plays a major role in development, but this is absent in Artificial Intelligence. Eventually, the Artificial Intelligence robots and machines do not have the capability also to compare within right and wrong, this feature is only present in human beings.

d. Application of Agile based Expert System
   Applications of Agile based Expert systems are as follows:

   a. Self-service kits to support autonomous teams [9]
   b. Mobile application development [10]
   c. Safety-critical systems [11]
   d. Animals wellness monitoring system [12]
   e. Scrum process [13]
   f. Computer vision [14]
   g. Agile Drone Flight [15]
   h. Cyber Security in agile manufacturing [16, 23]
   i. Sparse imaging method for frequency Agile synthetic aperture radar [17, 18]
   j. Blockchain-based framework [19, 20]
   k. Agile satellites scheduling [21, 22]
   l. Agile angle spoke wheel-based mobile robot [23, 24]
   m. Remote customer involvement [25, 26]
   n. Offshore Development Issues [27, 28]
   o. observation satellites [29, 30]

17.4   Conclusion

This chapter gives us the idea related to Agile methodology and the Agile model. For some places, the agile model is a game-changer and for some projects, it might not be appropriate as well. There are some benefits as well as limitations is also there in the Agile Model and hence in this chapter, it is briefly discussed after comparing each point and facts. And also, the places and applications where the Agile model is been used within the expert system. This chapter also contains the study of Artificial Intelligence, though we have also discussed the pros and cons of Artificial Intelligence briefly as well.

References

1. Das, S., Ghosh, L., Saha, S., *Analyzing Gaming Effects on Cognitive Load Using Artificial Intelligent Tools*, 2020.
2. Das, S. and Bhattacharya, A., *ECG Assess Heartbeat Rate, Classifying Using BPNN While Watching Movie and Send Movie Rating Through Telegram*, pp. 465–474, 2021.
3. Das, S., Das, J., Modak, S., Mazumdar, K., Internet of things and data mining for modern engineering and healthcare applications: Internet of things with machine learning-based smart cardiovascular disease classifier for healthcare in secure platform, Taylor & Francis, London, 2022.
4. Dam, H.K., Tran, T., Grundy, J., Ghose, A., Kamei, Y., Towards effective AI-powered agile project management. *IEEE/ACM 41st International Conference on Software Engineering: New Ideas and Emerging Results (ICSE-NIER)*, pp. 41–44, 2019.
5. Rudy, V.B., Stefan, L., Huib, A., Roland, B., Roelant, O., *An Agile Framework for Trustworthy AI*, 2020.
6. Ilieva, R.Y. and Nikolov, M.A., The impact of AI & ML in agile production. *2019 X National Conference with International Participation (ELECTRONICA)*, pp. 1–3, 2019.
7. Nicolas, D. and Wagner, D., *Agile Government and the Challenge of AI*, 2020.
8. Schleier-Smith, J., An architecture for agile machine learning in real-time applications, in: *Proceedings of the 21th ACM SIGKDD International Conference on Knowledge Discovery and Data Mining (KDD '15)*, NY, USA, Association for Computing Machinery, New York, pp. 2059–2068, 2015.
9. Poth, A., Kottke, M., Riel, A., Scaling agile on large enterprise level with self service kits to support autonomous teams. *15th Conference on Computer Science and Information Systems (FedCSIS)*, 2020, pp. 731–737, 2020.
10. Martinez, D., Ferre, X., Guerrero, G., Juristo, N., An agile-based integrated framework for mobile application development considering ilities. *IEEE Access*, 8, 72461–72470, 2020.
11. Kasauli, R., Knauss, E., Kanagwa, B., Nilsson, A., Calikli, G., Safety-critical systems and agile development: A mapping study. *44th Euromicro Conference on Software Engineering and Advanced Applications (SEAA)*, 2018, pp. 470–477, 2018.

12. van der Linden, D. and Zamansky, A., Agile with animals: Towards a development method. *2017 IEEE 25th International Requirements Engineering Conference Workshops (REW)*, pp. 423–426, 2017.

13. Gold, B. and Vassell, C., Using risk management to balance agile methods: A study of the Scrum process. *2015 2nd International Conference on Knowledge-Based Engineering and Innovation (KBEI)*, pp. 49–54, 2015.

14. Atakora, M. and Chenji, H., Agile neighbor discovery in MEMS-based free space optical networks: A computer vision approach. *J. Opt. Commun. Netw.*, 14, 4, 222–235, 2022.

15. Song, Y. and Scaramuzza, D., Policy search for model predictive control with application to agile drone flight. *IEEE Trans. Robot.*, 38, 2114–2130, 2022.

16. Arnarson, H., Kanafi, F.S., Kaarlela, T., Seldeslachts, U., Pieters, R., Evaluation of cyber security in agile manufacturing: Maturity of technologies and applications. *2022 IEEE/SICE International Symposium on System Integration (SII)*, pp. 784–789, 2022.

17. Zhou, K., Li, D., He, F., Quan, S., Su, Y., A sparse imaging method for frequency agile SAR. *IEEE Trans. Geosci. Remote Sens.*, 60, 1–16, 2022.

18. Farooq, M.S., Kalim, Z., Qureshi, J.N., Rasheed, S., Abid, A., A blockchain-based framework for distributed agile software development. *IEEE Access*, 10, 17977–17995, 2022.

19. Chatterjee, A. and Tharmarasa, R., Reward factor-based multiple agile satellites scheduling with energy and memory constraints, in: *IEEE Transactions on Aerospace and Electronic Systems*, vol. 58, no. 4, pp. 3090–3103, 2022.

20. Lee, K., Ryu, S., Kim, C., Seo, T., A compact and agile angled-spoke wheel-based mobile robot for uneven and granular terrains. *IEEE Robot. Autom. Lett.*, 7, 2, 1620–1626, 2022.

21. Alyahya, S., Bin-Hezam, R., Maddeh, M., Supporting remote customer involvement in distributed agile development: A coordination approach, in: *IEEE Transactions on Engineering Management*, 2021.

22. Mohindru, V., Chitranshi, U., Bhatt, R., Singh, Y., Possibilities of block chain in Indian market and notably in advertising industry, in: *2019 5th International Conference on Signal Processing, Computing and Control (ISPCC)*, IEEE, pp. 84–89, October 2019.

23. Raghavan, V.S., Kanoulas, D., Caldwell, D.G., Tsagarakis, N.G., Reconfigurable and agile legged-wheeled robot navigation in cluttered environments with movable obstacles. *IEEE Access*, 10, 2429–2445, 2022.

24. Mohindru, V. and Garg, A., Security attacks in internet of things: A review, in: *The International Conference on Recent Innovations in Computing*, Springer, Singapore, pp. 679–693, March 2020.

25. Tashtoush, Y.M. *et al.*, Agile approaches for cybersecurity systems, IoT and intelligent transportation. *IEEE Access*, 10, 1360–1375, 2022.

26. Mohindru, V. and Singla, S., A review of anomaly detection techniques using computer vision, in: *The International Conference on Recent Innovations in Computing*, Springer, Singapore, pp. 669–677, March 2020.

27. Kausar, M., Ishtiaq, M., Hussain, S., Distributed agile patterns-using agile practices to solve offshore development issues. *IEEE Access*, 10, 8840–8854, 2022.

28. Mohindru, V., Vashishth, S., Bathija, D., Internet of Things (IoT) for healthcare systems: A comprehensive survey, in: *Recent Innovations in Computing, Lecture Notes in Electrical Engineering*, vol. 832, P.K. Singh, Y. Singh, M.H. Kolekar, A.K. Kar, P.J.S. Gonçalves (Eds.), Springer, Singapore, 2022, https://doi.org/10.1007/978-981-16-8248-3_18.

29. Gu, Y., Han, C., Chen, Y., Xing, W.W., Mission replanning for multiple agile earth observation satellites based on cloud coverage forecasting. *IEEE J. Sel. Top. Appl. Earth Obs. Remote Sens.*, 15, 594–608, 2022.

30. Rai, V. *et al.*, Cloud computing in healthcare industries: Opportunities and challenges, in: *Recent Innovations in Computing, Lecture Notes in Electrical Engineering*, vol. 855, P.K. Singh, Y. Singh, J.K. Chhabra, Z. Illés, C. Verma (Eds.), Springer, Singapore, 2022, https://doi.org/10.1007/978-981-16-8892-8_53.

.

Machine Learning in ASD: An Intensive Study of Automated Disease Prediction System

Saindhab Chattaraj[1], Taniya Chakraborty[2], Chandan Koner[1] and Subir Gupta[1]*

[1]Department of CSE, Dr. B. C. Roy Engineering College, Durgapur, West Bengal, India
[2]Department of Basic Science and Humanities, Dr. B. C. Roy Engineering College, Durgapur, West Bengal, India

Abstract

Of late, due to drastic climate change and excessive pollution, people live in such an atmosphere where they have to combat continuously several deadly diseases. To get the proper treatment of such diseases, people must rely on appropriate diagnoses. There are a lot of signs or symptoms that bear the existence of a particular condition. Generally, almost all the people who suffer from viral infections, dengue, and COVID-19 get a common sign of high fever. Therefore, it is challenging for doctors to determine the exact disease with this particular symptom. Accordingly, a technically equipped medical system should be developed to get a more error-free diagnosis. In this context, a case study uses the Random Forest Algorithm to combine diagnostic prediction and technology, which will help medical practitioners detect diseases. Agile Software can be used here. One of the essential advantages of agile methodology is speed to market and risk reduction. This paper showcases a module developed with the help of Machine Learning. Here, Agile Software is designed to become very effective in detecting a particular disease more efficiently. In this specific system preventing errors and malfunctions has been proven to be 95% effective in the medical field.

---

*Corresponding author: subir2276@gmail.com

Susheela Hooda, Vandana Mohindru Sood, Yashwant Singh, Sandeep Dalal and Manu Sood (eds.) *Agile Software Development: Trends, Challenges and Applications*, (345–362) © 2023 Scrivener Publishing LLC

Keywords: ANN, ASD, disease detection, healthcare management, machine learning, random forest

18.1   Introduction

People in today's fast-paced world have to deal with many different illnesses. Today's fast-paced lifestyle and junk eating habits are responsible for many life-threatening conditions, such as cardiac arrests and other severe diseases. To stay up with the rest of the world, everyone, consciously or unconsciously, participates in the rat race of life. A range of lifestyle-related diseases, such as diabetes and high blood pressure, is causing enormous pain in people. On the other hand, a medical practitioner may be baffled when diagnosing a patient due to some common symptoms, such as fever or vomiting. As a result, a medical practitioner needed detailed information to do additional research. Specific facts must be relied on to discover and diagnose a particular illness correctly. Because of the vast amount of information that is easily accessible, data mining is one of the most essential and challenging academic topics in healthcare [1, 2]. At this point, many health apps are using data mining to solve the problem. Predictive analytics plays an increasingly important role in healthcare, from intrusion detection to pattern identification, from sickness diagnosis to patient access to more economical medical treatments and innovative procurement strategies. Improves the system's sensitivity and cognitive capabilities. Along with this, Machine learning (ML) employs AI (AI) to increase prediction accuracy [3].

Agile means the capacity to create and reciprocate to changes. It is a way of dealing with and ultimately pacifying any uncertain turbulent surroundings. It is a trustworthy system to identify the process to measure the components of the environment, leading to being complied and adapted with it. To figure out how to get the most out of an activity, you need to use principles to get the most out of all organizational operations. The Agile approach may be offered depending on the nature of a business process and if the prerequisites are satisfied. The frequentative method prescribed under the Agile Manifesto can be applied to measure the pace of AI development and implementation in big business houses. Although there are some primary issues at the time of execution of Agile to deliver value through AI, there are advantages worthy of taking time to adapt these methods. Let's know what happens when we merge Agile and Artificial Intelligence. Before reading the paper, familiarize yourself with agile software development (ASD). ASD is more inclusive than Scrum, Extreme

Programming, and FDD (FDD). Pair-programming, TDD, sign, scheduled events, and sprints are more demanding than ASD. ASD is an umbrella term for concepts and approaches based on the ASD Manifesto and its 12 guiding principles. When addressing software design in a particular manner, it is essential to adhere to specific ideas and values to determine the correct objectives.

Medical experts may utilize this case study's findings to help patients avoid certain diseases in the future. This strategy, which makes extensive use of data analysis, also enables the early detection of disease, reducing the possibility that the condition would be associated with danger. This essay aims to showcase a specific system that is user-friendly, inexpensive, and easily accessible to the general public. This model highlights the most significant components of AI and ML in healthcare that would be useful to all medical practitioners. The article has several levels, divided into sections to make it simpler to understand for a wide range of researchers from varied backgrounds [4, 5]. The first part, i.e., the introduction, initiates the topic and simultaneously gives a flavor to the entire chapter. Section 18.2 briefly summarizes ML. Section 18.3 presents an in-depth case study and a summary of the findings described in Section 18.4. The last part is the conclusion which comes out with specific novel proposals.

18.2   Overview of ML

ML is called computerized systems that can automatically grow machines, and humans using experience and data are called ML. Computer algorithms

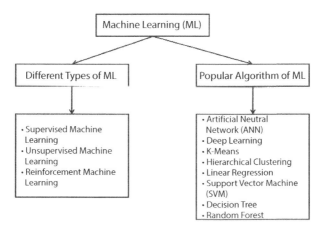

Figure 18.1 Machine learning (ML) steps.

learn from sample data. These are also called training data. They help make predictions or judgments without being specifically trained to do so. The classification of ML is shown in Figure 18.1. In a larger concept, ML can be categorized in two ways: Different types of ML and Popular algorithms of ML.

Furthermore, different types of ML may fall into three categories, namely,

1) Supervised Learning,
2) Unsupervised Learning, and
3) Reinforcement Learning.

On the other hand, the popular algorithm can be categorized in some order. The algorithms used in this particular chapter are ANN, Deep Learning, K-Means, Hierarchical Clustering, Linear Regression, SVM, Decision Tree, and Random Forest Algorithm [6–10].

18.2.1   Types of Machine Learning

18.2.1.1   *Supervised Machine Learning*

In Figure 18.2 there are two sets of data stores mentioned. One is known as the Labeled data store, and another is called the Labels data store. Several data are put indiscriminately in the Labeled data store, whereas some characters are predefined in the Labels data store. When different data from both the data stores will be channelized through Training, they will receive the defined data stored previously in the Labels store. Supervised

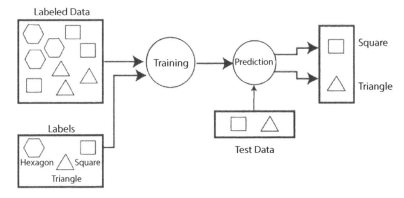

Figure 18.2 Supervised learning.

ML approaches include linear regression, Random Forest for classification, Support Vector Machines (SVM), and others for classification [11, 12].

Some popular supervised ML approaches are:

a) Naive Bayesian Model.
b) Random Forest Model.
c) Support Vector Machines.

Labeled data differentiates between supervised and unsupervised learning. The use of labeled datasets is the primary distinction between the two techniques. Unlike supervised learning, Unsupervised Learning does not use labeled input or output data [13, 14].

18.2.1.2   Unsupervised Machine Learning

Unsupervised learning employs systems to find patterns in unlabeled data sets. Unsupervised learning, in other words, enables automated pattern recognition. The Unsupervised Learning steps are shown in Figure 18.3. It's helpful when the output labels aren't known. Unsupervised learning algorithms include K-Means Clustering, PCA, and Hierarchical Clustering. As contrasted to supervised learning, unsupervised learning provides no correct answers or methods for correcting errors. Data may be learned and classified even without labels. It is simpler to organize data with more labels once it has been arranged. It aids in detecting patterns in data that other approaches cannot. This approach is used to extract generative characters and to investigate experimental possibilities [15, 16].

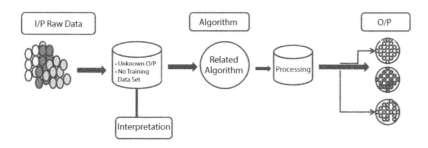

Unsupervised Learning

Figure 18.3 Unsupervised learning.

18.2.1.3   Reinforcement ML

A Continuum of Support Students can learn how to behave in a specific scenario by participating in activities and witnessing the outcomes. Positive (+) feedback is given to the representative for positive acts, while negative (-) feedback is provided for negative behavior. In this case, an ML method in which a mediator learns by trying things out and making decisions based on what it knows and has done before.

18.2.2   Popular ML Algorithm

18.2.2.1   Artificial Neural Network (ANN)

Neuronal networks are ML algorithms that replicate the behavior of human neurons. It functions like the human brain. Many coupled data processing and transmission units make up an ANN. They expect significant repercussions. An ANN seeks to mimic the network of neurons in the human brain so that a computer can learn and make decisions like a human. ANNs are organized brain cells that may be generated by programming traditional computers. ANN is a set of algorithms that compare a piece of data to human brain activity. The input can be modified to achieve the best results without affecting the output strategy. An ANN is a flexible, data-driven modeling tool that may be utilized for highly nonlinear, dynamic, and identification modeling. Their universal approximation and flexible structure enable them to recognize complex nonlinear processes. In Figure 18.4, the essential techniques and functionalities of an artificial neural network [17, 18].

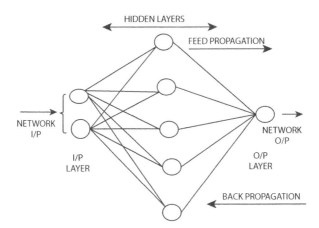

Figure 18.4 Artificial neural network (ANN) diagram.

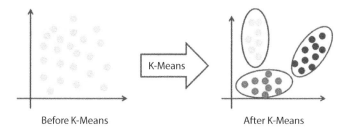

Figure 18.5 K-Means clustering

18.2.2.2   K-Means Clustering Algorithm

A K-means clustering approach for similar grouping components is shown in Figure 18.5. The letter K represents the group count. Each item is retained inside the group to which it belongs to create collections. Unsupervised learning techniques such as K-means clustering are well-known. These results show a link between unsupervised dimension reduction and unsupervised learning.

18.2.2.3   Hierarchical Clustering

HCA (hierarchical cluster analysis) is a method for organizing data into clusters. The endpoints are a collection of groups that are unique from one another yet have numerous commonalities. There are two forms of hierarchical clustering: divisive (top-down) and agglomerative (bottom-up) (bottom-up). AGNES stands for agglomerative clustering (Agglomerative Nesting). It's a bottom-up strategy. DIANA (Devise Analysis) is a top-down technique for hierarchical clustering division [19].

18.2.2.4   Linear Regression in Machine Learning

It merely adds more words. If the parameters are linear, you can exponent an independent variable to fit a curve. Nonlinear regression models, on the other hand, do not. Lagnidometric regression is a type of unsupervised machine learning. Rather than categorizing values, it anticipates them (e.g., cat, dog). Linear regression is an unsupervised procedure. It uses independent variables to control weight. Forecasting and analysis are common uses. Linear regression studies the predictor-result relationship. It may also assess the result variable's relative influence. The most basic regression type in ML is linear. Uncertainty is a regression predictor. The prediction error in this Example is -0.01. Tall parents, for example, tend to have shorter offspring. Parents are taller and slower than their children. The term "regression to the mean" (regression = return) described this observation [20–23].

18.2.2.5   Support Vector Machine (SVM)

It applies to both linear and nonlinear situations. It would be helpful to describe SVM. As a result, the technique constructs a classification line. The method is capable of classifying, predicting, and detecting outliers. As a result, the LSVM algorithm chooses a line that avoids the nearest samples. An SVM is a kernel. They aid in the avoidance of complicated calculations. The beauty of a seed is that it is capable of computation. Infinity of kernels SVM classifies nonlinear data. After establishing a category separator, the data is processed to create a hyperplane. ML with supervision is typically used for sorting. It locates an N-dimensional hyperplane that categorizes the data. The input determines the size of the hyperplane. The hyperplane is a two-input line [24, 25].

18.2.2.6   Decision Tree

A decision tree is made. It is a picture of an attribute test. Each leaf node represents a different class name (a decision taken after computing all the details). Uncertainty, resource costs, and utility can all come from a decision tree. It shows only one type of algorithm, a conditional algorithm, which it offers. It probability tree may be used to choose which approach to apply. You may use this method to do both regression and classification jobs. As it continues through the process, it creates a decision tree by subdividing the information into smaller subgroups. A decision tree is a graphical depiction of all possible outcomes of a decision. Each step or node of a classification decision tree is related to a feature requirement.

18.2.2.7   Random Forests

Random Forests (RF) are used in classification and regression ensemble learning. We learn to tackle problems as a group. For regression, a random forest is employed [26–29]. It manages hundreds of components with a subset of characteristics. Random forests are used to eliminate bias. When squared prejudice outweighs danger, bias correction is required. Unbiased decision trees construct a random forest. Diverse data training benefits Random Forests. It is also possible to have a random subset of characteristics [8]. RF is the class with the most trees. The mean forecast of the tree is obtained by regression. Stop overexerting yourself. It is used to seed the random generator in preparation for duplication. Assume the random component is not present. The bare minimum is leaf samples. For example, if Min divides, the leaves are thinnest near the base.

18.2.2.8   Agile Software Development (ASD)

ASD is more strict than Pair Programming, Test-Driven Development, Stand-Ups, Design Meetings, and Sprints methods. ASD is an umbrella term for a group of ideas and behaviors based on the 12 rules and the ASD Manifesto. When we take a particular approach to project management, it is always best to promote these principles and values and use them to figure out what is right in a given situation.

The Agile Manifesto includes four fundamental values:

1. It is applicable for individual and collaborative interactions over the process and tools.
2. It is working Software over understandable documentation.
3. User collaboration on contract accord.
4. It is very responsive to any change over the following plan.

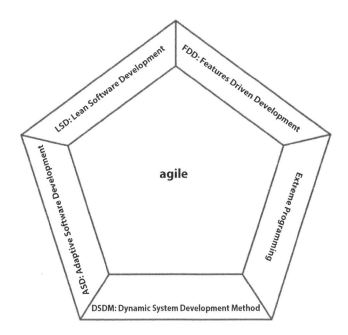

Figure 18.6 Agile menifesto.

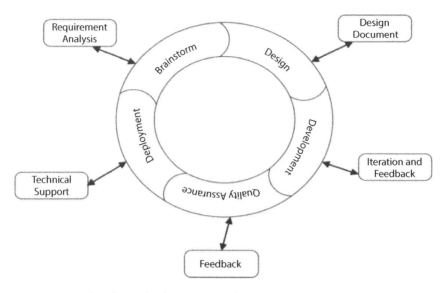

Figure 18.7 Agile software development procedure.

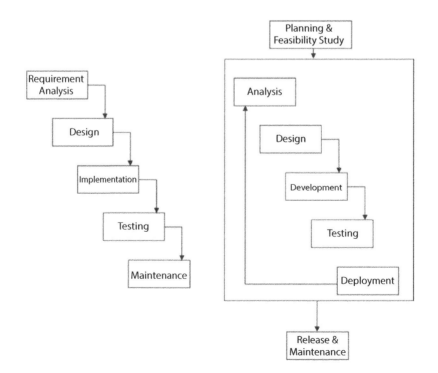

Figure 18.8 Waterfall model vs. Agile software development procedure.

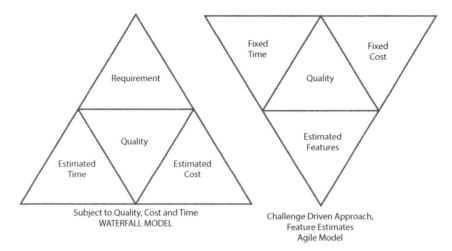

Figure 18.9 Waterfall model vs. Agile software development (ASD).

Agile Manifesto is a project management process that is used for software development. It is a collaborative field that serves the immediate demands and solutions evolving through the confluence of self–organizing and cross-functional teams and their customers.

There are two different models in the combined Figure 18.6 and Figure 18.7. The model on the left side is the waterfall model, and the right side is known as agile. The agile process is bi-directional in its application. In this process, we set a plan first, then we proceed toward executing that plan. This process has a bi-directional way of application. It is more effort-free than the traditional waterfall process, which is unidirectional in its application and thus is more error-prone. Figures 18.8 and 18.9 shows the difference between Waterfall model and ASD.

18.3 Case Study

18.3.1 Methodology

A component schematic is shown in Figure 18.9. Display a patient's point of view. A prediction algorithm scans a symptom database. After that, the predictor examines its sign database for symptoms that match (putting them into the appropriate field). Professionals may have misunderstood the patient's requests. A single signal can no longer detect problems.

The first thing we need to do is remove all the evidence. There was a random forest, and then there was a predictor. It uses Random Forest to group symptoms. The Random Forest classifier can tell if someone is sick

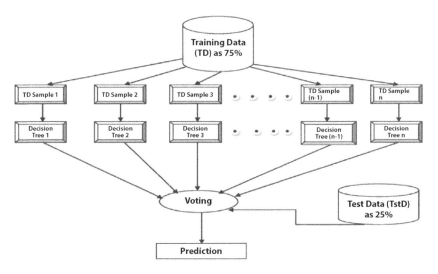

Figure 18.9 Methodology diagram.

and predict how long it will last. One hundred forty signs could treat 40 different diseases, so they were used. Symptoms and illnesses have been found. That means there are 40 diseases and 140 characters for each one. In each node, you'll see it. Compile the data from practice with two different datasets, namely the training and testing datasets. To do unsupervised learning, you need to use a graded training dataset. Using a random forest classifier, you can develop a prediction model. Use it to teach new things. Table 18.1 shows the sample dataset of the training model.

In Table 18.1, The example data set specified those 40 different diseases, each with its own set of 140 symptoms, beginning with the A_1 and ending with the A_{140}. Similarly, the disease prediction started with D_1 and ended with D_{40}. To collect information for this survey, we will use 40 different disorders, such as fungal infection, medication reactions, jaundice, hepatitis B, etc. Itching, skin rashes, and other symptoms are also present in this case. If the symptoms of a particular illness describe it, give it a value of one (1); otherwise, give it a matter of zero (0). For Example, because itching is a common symptom of D_{40} (Hepatitis B), we assign it the value one (1); however, blister (A_{140}) is set to the value zero (0), implying that blisters are not among the typical symptoms of D_{40}.

As a consequence, a "forest" is formed. Bagging aids in the investigation. A random forest is a composition of trees. It can help with regression and classification. As an example of ML, consider a Random Forest. They make use of hyperparameters. Random forests might be used instead of decision trees. Using the regressor to troubleshoot random forest regression,

Table 18.1 Sample dataset.

A$_1$	A$_2$	A$_2$	....	A140	Prediction
1	1	0	....	0	D$_1$
1	1	0	....	0	D$_2$
1	0	0	....	0	D$_3$
.	.	.	....	.	.
.	.	.	....	.	.
.	.	.	....	.	
1	0	0	....	.	D$_{40}$

A$_1$ = Itching; A$_2$ = Skin rash; A$_3$ = Blood_in_sputum; A$_{140}$ = Blister.
D$_1$ = Fungal infection; D$_2$ = Drug Reaction; D$_3$ = Jaundice; D$_{40}$ = Hepatitis B.

the model is indeterminate because of the random forest. It selects the best attribute from a random pool of features. Having multiple options is usually advantageous. A random sample of data is evaluated using this procedure. To boost randomness, assign arbitrary thresholds to each characteristic (like a typical decision tree does). Then there's a dataset that's based on real-world data. After collecting all symptoms, this classifier will be used to forecast the patient's illness. The first 140 nodes represent the symptoms. In a random forest, guided learning takes place. A "forest" of decision trees is built.

Bagging is a technique for increasing the quality of experiments. Random forest is a forecasting method that combines several decision trees. It can help with classification and regression in machine learning. To categorize data, ML use random forests. They make use of hyperparameters. Random forests might be used instead of decision trees. Using the regressor to troubleshoot random forest regression, the model is indeterminate because of the random forest. It selects the best attribute from a random pool of features. Having multiple options is usually advantageous. This function assesses a set of random qualities. To boost randomness, assign arbitrary thresholds to each characteristic (like a typical decision tree does).

18.3.2   Result Analysis

This study's graphical user interface discusses the symptoms and makes predictions about how they could manifest in the future. We'll show you

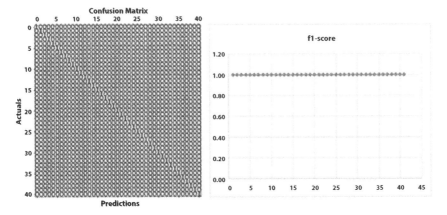

Figure 18.10 The confusion matrix and F1-score accuracy curve.

fifteen signs out of 140, beginning with A_1 and A_{140}. Before making a choice, the system module evaluates the states' output, the authentication, and the validity of the predicted outcome.

The system component that examines the state's output, verification, the correctness of the result, and the general acceptability of the system is known as results analysis. This system's outcomes component is divided into two teams. The first component is the system's technical or fundamental programming precision. The system's code or core software must be correct and genuine as the project's backbone. As a result, accuracy will be emphasized in this section. The labels or names it carries are Results and Final Result. Another algorithm will be used to validate the final tale. Without further ado, let's get started. Accuracy, F1 score, and mean square error were all assessed. According to the numbers: 14.89, 0.03, and 0.03, a lovely and standard score denotes the suggested system's programming. Figure 18.10 shows the F1-score accuracy curve and the confusion matrix, and Figure 18.11 shows the Graphical User Interface of the Automated Disease Predicting System. Finally, the conclusion demonstrates that the outcome was correct. The ultimate accuracy of this procedure is 95 percent which is satisfactory and near to the industry standard for originality and precision.

18.4   Conclusion

As long as the accuracy level is high, an authentic destiny fulfills the requirements of this research. The COVID scenario has clearly shown that the number of patients is sometimes a significant pressure on the doctors

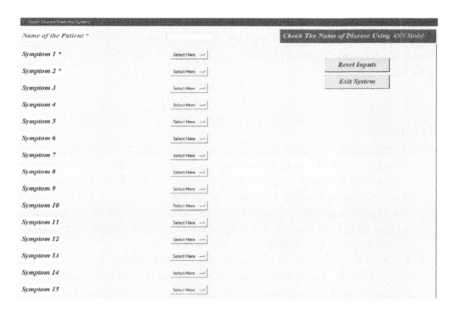

Figure 18.11 GUI of automated disease predicting system.

as the patient-doctor ratio is miserably poor. Our system can be tremendously helpful in an emergency when a patient requires an immediate decision. So, if ML has substantiation with medical science to provide a beneficiary system to the healthcare social group, we strongly propose implementing this idea. This automated disease prediction system using Machine Learning-based Random Forest Model is an excellent stepping stone toward an innovative and better health care service. One of the most critical and exciting areas of research is ML. We have conjoined medical science and ML so that the medical field can also bear the outgrowth of the Software's correctness, leading the entire process more perfect.

This system will function effectively and establish itself as an essential global tool and a very beneficial human helping hand. Overall, the proposed ML-based Random Forest Model auto diagnosis system mitigates errors and faults to a minimum level, with a success rate of around 90%. Therefore, we highly recommend an Automated Disease prediction system for a better healthcare service. It is a model that may provide a better approach using the higher model like the reinforcement learning concept, which might be a bridge to meet the challenge of the inadequate ratio of doctors and patients in this country.

This proposed model is highly recommended in the health care system for more error-free diagnosis. It is user-friendly and economical, and simultaneously it has been observed that Agile Software is more efficient than the waterfall model. Therefore, the proposed ML-based Random Forest Model auto diagnosis system can be used in every healthcare system in India.

References

1. Stokes, K. *et al.*, A machine learning model for supporting symptom-based referral and diagnosis of bronchitis and pneumonia in limited resource settings. *Biocybern. Biomed. Eng.*, 41, 4, 1288–1302, 2021.
2. Kondilis, E. *et al.*, The impact of the COVID-19 pandemic on refugees and asylum seekers in Greece: A retrospective analysis of national surveillance data from 2020. *EClinicalMedicine*, 37, 100958, 2021.
3. Kourou, K., Exarchos, K.P., Papaloukas, C., Sakaloglou, P., Exarchos, T., Fotiadis, D., II, Applied machine learning in cancer research: A systematic review for patient diagnosis, classification and prognosis. *Comput. Struct. Biotechnol. J.*, 19, 5546–5555, 2021.
4. Mandal, K., Rajkumar, M., Ezhumalai, P., Jayakumar, D., Yuvarani, R., Improved security using machine learning for IoT intrusion detection system. *Mater. Today Proc.*, Dec. 2020.
5. Bhadeshia, H.K.D.H., Physical metallurgy of steels, in: *Physical Metallurgy*, Fifth Edition, 2014.
6. Park, D.-C., Image classification using Naïve Bayes classifier. *Int. J. Comput. Sci. Electron. Eng.*, 4, 3, 135–139, 2016. [Online]. Available: http://www.vision.caltech.edu/html-files/archive.html.
7. Marques, G., Agarwal, D., de la Torre Díez, I., Automated medical diagnosis of COVID-19 through EfficientNet convolutional neural network. *Appl. Soft Comput. J.*, 96, 106691, 2020.
8. Gupta, S. *et al.*, Modelling the steel microstructure knowledge for *in-silico* recognition of phases using machine learning. *Mater. Chem. Phys.*, 252, 123286, Sep. 2020.
9. Mondal, B., Koner, C., Chakraborty, M., Gupta, S., Detection and investigation of DDoS attacks in network traffic using machine learning algorithms. *Int. J. Innov. Technol. Explor. Eng.*, 11, 6, 1–6, May 2022.
10. Mondal, B., Banerjee, A., Gupta, S., A review of SQLI detection strategies using machine learning. *Int. J. Health Sci.*, 9663–9676, May 2022.
11. Diao, X. *et al.*, EMCNet: Automated COVID-19 diagnosis from x-ray images using convolutional neural network and ensemble of machine learning classifiers. *Lancet Digit. Health*, 22, 100146, February 2021.
12. Gupta, S., Chan-vese segmentation of SEM ferrite-pearlite microstructure and prediction of grain boundary. *Int. J. Innov. Technol. Explor. Eng.*, 8, 10, 1495–1498, 2019.

13. Ning, B., Junwei, W., Feng, H., Spam message classification based on the Naïve Bayes classification algorithm. *IAENG Int. J. Comput. Sci.*, 46, 1, 2019.

14. Bashar, A., Latif, G., Ben Brahim, G., Mohammad, N., Alghazo, J., COVID-19 pneumonia detection using optimized deep learning techniques. *Diagnostics*, 11, 11, 1–18, 2021.

15. Wang, Y. *et al.*, Unsupervised machine learning for the discovery of latent disease clusters and patient subgroups using electronic health records. *J. Biomed. Inform.*, 102, 103364, May 2020.

16. Gupta, S., Sarkar, J., Banerjee, A., Bandyopadhyay, N.R., Ganguly, S., Grain boundary detection and phase segmentation of SEM ferrite–pearlite micro-structure using SLIC and skeletonization. *J. Inst. Eng. Ser. D*, 100, 2, 203–210, Oct. 2019.

17. Cheng, A., Guan, Q., Su, Y., Zhou, P., Zeng, Y., Integration of machine learning and blockchain technology in the healthcare field: A literature review and implications for cancer care. *Asia-Pac. J. Oncol. Nurs.*, 8, 6, 720–724, 2021.

18. Ahsan, M.M. *et al.*, Detecting SARS-CoV-2 from chest x-Ray using artificial intelligence. *IEEE Access*, 9, 35501–35513, 2021.

19. Horng, S.J. *et al.*, A novel intrusion detection system based on hierarchical clustering and support vector machines. *Expert Syst. Appl.*, 38, 1, 306–313, Jan. 2011.

20. Breiman, L., Bagging predictors. *Mach. Learn.*, 24, 2, 123–140, 1996.

21. Mohindru, V., Chitranshi, U., Bhatt, R., Singh, Y., Possibilities of block chain in Indian market and notably in advertising industry, in: *2019 5th International Conference on Signal Processing, Computing and Control (ISPCC)*, IEEE, pp. 84–89, October 2019.

22. Al-Azzam, N. and Shatnawi, I., Comparing supervised and semi-supervised machine learning models on diagnosing breast cancer. *Ann. Med. Surg.*, 62, 53–64, January 2021.

23. Mohindru, V. and Garg, A., Security attacks in internet of things: A review, in: *The International Conference on Recent Innovations in Computing*, Springer, Singapore, pp. 679–693, March 2020.

24. Kiziloz, H.E., Classifier ensemble methods in feature selection. *Neurocomputing*, 419, 97–107, 2021.

25. Mohindru, V. and Singla, S., A review of anomaly detection techniques using computer vision, in: *The International Conference on Recent Innovations in Computing*, Springer, Singapore, pp. 669–677, March 2020.

26. Ho, T.K., Random decision forests. *Proc. Int. Conf. Doc. Anal. Recognition, ICDAR*, vol. 1, pp. 278–282, 1995.

27. Mohindru, V., Vashishth, S., Bathija, D., Internet of Things (IoT) for health-care systems: A comprehensive survey, in: *Recent Innovations in Computing, Lecture Notes in Electrical Engineering*, vol. 832, P.K. Singh, Y. Singh, M.H. Kolekar, A.K. Kar, P.J.S. Gonçalves, (Eds.), Springer, Singapore, 2022, https://doi.org/10.1007/978-981-16-8248-3_18.

28. Gupta, S., Sarkar, J., Kundu, M., Bandyopadhyay, N.R., Ganguly, S., Automatic recognition of SEM microstructure and phases of steel using LBP and random decision forest operator. *Measurement*, 151, 107224, Feb. 2020.

29. Rai, V. *et al.*, Cloud computing in healthcare industries: Opportunities and challenges, in: *Recent Innovations in Computing, Lecture Notes in Electrical Engineering*, vol. 855, P.K. Singh, Y. Singh, J.K. Chhabra, Z. Illés, C. Verma, (Eds.), Springer, Singapore, 2022, https://doi.org/10.1007/978-981-16-8892-8_53.

Index

Acceptance criteria, 80
Acceptance testing, 267
Accuracy, 305
ActiveCollab, 170
Adaptive random testing-based
    prioritization, 124
Agile, 188–190, 192–195, 197,
    199–203, 257
Agile architecture trends in the digital
    world, 9–11
Agile benefits,
    coverage, 44
    feedback, 46
    flexibility, 45
    quality, 44
    risk, 44–45
    speed, 45
    transparency, 44
Agile development, 235
Agile IoT project for interoperability, 60–62
Agile IoT project for smart domains, 62–64
Agile manifesto, 208, 259
Agile practices, 41
Agile software development, 2–3, 23,
    24, 53, 162, 188, 189, 197, 201,
    203, 207, 328
    adaptive software development,
        56–57
    dynamic software development
        model, 57–58
    extreme programming, 55–56
    feature driven development, 58
    Kanban method, 59
    scrum methodology, 54–55

Artificial intelligence (AI), 24, 33, 34,
    326–327, 329, 335–341
Axosoft, 173

Brainstorming, 78
Brief introduction to jMeter, 222

Case study,
    methodology, 355–357
    result analysis, 357–358
Challenges faced in the digital
        world through agile software
        development, 13–14
Clarizen, 172
Code coverage-based prioritization,
    109
    call graph-based, 111
    path coverage-based, 110
    refactoring-based, 112
    slicing-based, 111
    statements coverage-based, 109
Combinatorial interaction testing-
        based prioritization, 123
Comparative studies, 125
CoSchedule, 180
Covid, 24, 27, 32–34
Critical factors,
    cultural, 46
    environment, 47
    process, 47
    project team, 46
    psychological, 46
    technology, 47
Crystal methodology, 246

Distributed agile software development (DASD), 162, 211
Distributed software development, 189, 199, 202, 203
Dynamic software development method, 210
Dynamic system development, 250

Empirical research, 293
Evaluation criterion for model-based prioritization, 128
Expert system, 340–341
Extreme programming (XP), 24, 25, 34, 210, 241

Fault localization-based prioritization, 115
Feature driven development, 247
Focus groups, 78

Generic guidelines to improve the agile transformation in digital world, 18
GitLab, 174
Global software development (GSD), 213

History-based prioritization, 114
Human agent collectives, 328
Human-human linkages, 23–29, 32–34
Hybrid approaches,

Inter-IoT framework for interoperability, 64–65
interoperability aspects, 65–67
Internet of Things (IOT), 24, 26, 33, 34, 39, 59–60

Jira, 168
JQL (JeeraQurey language), 169

Kanban, 170, 246
Kitchenham's guideline, 296

Lean development, 243
Literature review, 91–94

Machine learning, 214, 327
Machine learning techniques, 297
Machine learning-based, 124
MeisterTask, 174
Meta analysis (MA), 294
Model-based prioritization, 113
Monday.com, 166

Need matrix, 23, 29–32
Nostromo, 181
nTask, 167

Object-oriented testing-based prioritization, 122

Pair programming (PP), 23, 25, 28, 32, 34, 163, 267
Performance, 305
Performance testing using jMeter, 225
Pivotal tracker, 171
Prioritization for continuous integration (CI), 125
Productboard, 176
ProofHub, 184
Proposed methodology, 94–96
Prototyping, 79

Quality assurance, 257

Refactoring, 267
Regression testing, 81
Reported challenges – cause and potential solutions, 15–17
Requirements-based prioritization, 112
Research gaps, 136
Research issues, 313
Research method and data collection, 314
Resolution matrix, 23, 25, 32
Risk factor-based prioritization, 115

Risk factors in distributed agile software development, 279–284
Roleplay, 78

Scrum, 24–27, 32, 34, 42–43, 197–202, 243
Scrum master, 187, 192
Sectors,
    aerospace, 27, 28, 31, 34
    consultancy, 27, 29, 32, 34
    education, 27, 28, 30, 33
    military, 27, 28, 31, 34
    research, 28, 30
    software, 24, 25
Similarity-based prioritization, 122
Smart applications, 40
Soft computing techniques-based prioritization, 116
    (1+1) EA-based, 118
    analytical hierarchy process (AHP)-based, 117
    ant colony optimization (ACO)-based, 116
    based on multi-objective approaches, 121
    Bayesian network-based, 120
    clustering-based, 120
    genetic algorithm (GA)-based, 118
    local beam search (LBS)-based, 119
    non-dominated sorted genetic algorithm (NSGA)-based, 118
    pareto convergence genetic algorithm (PCGA)-based, 118
    particle swarms optimization, 117
Software development life cycle (SDLC), 23, 24, 34, 162, 206, 207, 328
Software effort estimation (SEE), 292

Software engineering, 301
Software product lines (SPL), 125
Software quality assurance, 236
Software risk assessment,
    risk analysis, 276
    risk identification, 275
    risk management and control, 277
    risk monitoring, 277
Software risk management, 274
Sprint, 216
Subject systems for prioritization, 126
Surveys and reviews on prioritization, 126
Systematic literature review (SLR), 293

Taskworld, 180
Team work development, 4–6
Test driven design (TDD), 23, 24, 34
Test driven development (TDD), 82
Time and cost-aware prioritization, 114
Todo.vu, 182
Traditional software development, 206
Types of requirements,
    functional requirements, 74–76
    non-functional requirements, 74–76

Use cases and scenarios, 78
User stories, 285
User story-based risk factors in DASD, 285–286

Version one, 183
Vulnerabilities, 40–41

Web-based prioritization, 121

Zohosprints, 178

Printed and bound by CPI Group (UK) Ltd, Croydon, CR0 4YY

27/10/2024

14580178-0002